D1231815

SINNERS
IN THE
HANDS OF AN
ANGRY GOD
AND OTHER WRITINGS

NELSON'S
ROYAL
CLASSICS

SINNERS
IN THE
HANDS OF AN
ANGRY GOD
AND OTHER WRITINGS

JONATHAN
EDWARDS

THOMAS NELSON PUBLISHERS
Nashville

Copyright © 2000 by Thomas Nelson, Inc.

Published in Nashville, Tennessee, by Thomas Nelson, Inc.

Library of Congress Cataloging-in-Publication Data

Edwards, Jonathan, 1703–1758.
   Sinners in the hands of an angry God and other writings / Jonathan Edwards.
     p.   cm.   (Nelson's royal classics series; 12)
     ISBN 0-7852-4523-5

Complete CIP information available on request

Printed in the United States of America
1 2 3 4 5 6 7 — 05 04 03 02 01 00

CONTENTS

PUBLISHER'S PREFACE ix

INTRODUCTION xi

TIMELINE xv

SINNERS IN THE HANDS OF AN ANGRY GOD 1

A DIVINE AND SUPERNATURAL LIGHT 19

GOD'S SOVEREIGNTY IN THE SALVATION OF MEN 39

AN ESSAY ON THE TRINITY 61

A FAREWELL SERMON 81

FREEDOM OF THE WILL 107

PUBLISHER'S PREFACE

Since the birth of the Christian church, thousands of writers have examined the teachings of the church and chronicled the experience of faith. Yet only a few of these works stand out as true classics—books that had and continue to have a significant impact on the church and the everyday lives of believers. They describe the core of our beliefs and capture the essence of our Christian experience. They remain an essential part of every Christian's library, and they continue to challenge the way we conceive our faith and our world.

Welcome to Nelson's Royal Classics—our commitment to preserving these treasures and presenting them to a new generation of believers. Every book contains an introduction that will detail the life and faith of the author and define why these works have such an important place in the history of our faith. As you read, you'll find that the timeless wisdom of the writers in this series is not only encouraging and enlightening but also very stimulating. These rich resources will strengthen your spiritual growth and show you ways to grow ever closer to God.

Each volume, such as Sheldon's *In His Steps,* Bunyan's *Pilgrim's Prog-*

ress, or St. Augustine's *Confessions,* is a treasure to be read and cherished. As a series, they become an heirloom library of invaluable worth. Read them now, and share them with others as a way to pass on the heart of Christianity.

INTRODUCTION

The spring day was glorious and bright, but inside his tiny room, a young man was struggling with an unrelenting darkness. Although he was only seventeen, he had recently graduated from Yale and was set to enter the master's program in theology later that year. Highly intelligent and devout since childhood, his faith and understanding of doctrine was secure . . . except for one belief: Jonathan Edwards could not accept the sovereignty of God.

"It used to appear like a horrible doctrine to me," he wrote. Struggling with one of Christianity's main tenets, he turned back to Scripture, and opened his Bible to 1 Timothy 1:17: "Now to the King eternal, immortal, invisible, to God who alone is wise, *be* honor and glory forever and ever."

The verse spoke to his heart, overwhelming him. He later wrote that he felt "a sense of the glory of the Divine Being . . . a new sense, quite different from anything" he had ever experienced. Renewed, Edwards plunged into his work, and found both his faith and his ministry expanding. Going on to complete a master's degree in divinity, Edwards spent a short time as a tutor at Yale before answering the call to be an associate pastor at his grandfather's church in Northhampton, Massachusetts.

This was not an unexpected path for Edwards, who was born October 5, 1703, in East Windsor, Connecticut. His parents taught him at home for the first thirteen years of his life, schooling him in Latin, Greek, Hebrew, the Scriptures and classic literature. His grandfather, Solomon Stoddard, was a well-known and highly respected pastor in Massachusetts, so no one was surprised that the young Jonathan seemed destined to follow in his footsteps. But few could have foreseen that the seventeen-year-old plagued with doubt would become one of America's foremost theologians, who would oversee one of the greatest revivals of the church the world has ever seen.

Edwards' sermons, which preached an adherence to Calvinism in the light of the growing sentiment of "man-centered" philosophies coming out of Europe at the time, were being published as early as 1731, when "God Glorified in Man's Dependence" was one of several sermons that taught, in lay terms, those ideas that characterized much of his life's theology; that human sin is the root of dissent against God, that sin deserved extreme punishment from God, that conversion meant a complete and total change in a believer's heart, mind, and actions, and that true Christianity meant living a life of beauty, love, holiness and truth, as well as growing in understanding of God and the Bible.

The centerpiece of this theology was the classic sermon, "Sinners in the Hands of an Angry God," preached at Enfield, Connecticut, in 1741. In it, Edwards reminded his congregation that "natural men are held in the hand of God, over the pit of hell; they have deserved the fiery pit, and are already sentenced to it; and God is dreadfully provoked, his anger is as great towards them as to those that are actually suffering the executions of the fierceness of his wrath in hell, and they have done nothing in the least to appease or abate that anger . . . all that preserves them every moment is the mere arbitrary will, and uncovenanted, unobliged forbearance of an incensed God." Thus, we are always at God's mercy, and any salvation from the pit is through His grace, and His son.

The revival that came to be known as the Great Awakening changed America forever, cementing Calvinism in the mindset of Christianity, and securing Edwards' place as the country's greatest theologian. But Edwards's unrelenting stances on salvation, sin, and conversion did not meet with everyone's approval. In 1750, following a disagreement with his home congregation over the rite of the communion, Edwards was asked to leave. He moved to Stockbridge, Massachusetts, and served as a missionary to the Native American settlement there, until 1757.

During those years, Edwards turned his mind and soul to his writing, producing some of his greatest works, including "A Careful and Strict Inquiry in the Modern Prevailing Notions of that Freedom of Will, Which is Supposed to Be Essential to Moral Agency, Virtue and Vice, Reward and Punishment, Praise and Blame"—an imposing title which came to be known simply as "Freedom of Will." In this Edwards speaks to the nature of our "will," that motivation within us that drives our actions. True conversion, then, means a complete change not only of behavior but of the motivations that are a part of our very being. The change must entail, as Edwards puts it, a new "sense of heart."

It was such works as this that carried Edwards' theological impact on Christianity beyond the Great Awakening. His views on ethics, philosophy, and theology continue to be a part of religion beliefs worldwide, and it is his voice that resounds the strongest concerning virtue, personal piety, complete renewal of the spirit, and a personal relationship with God.

JONATHAN EDWARDS, 1703–1758

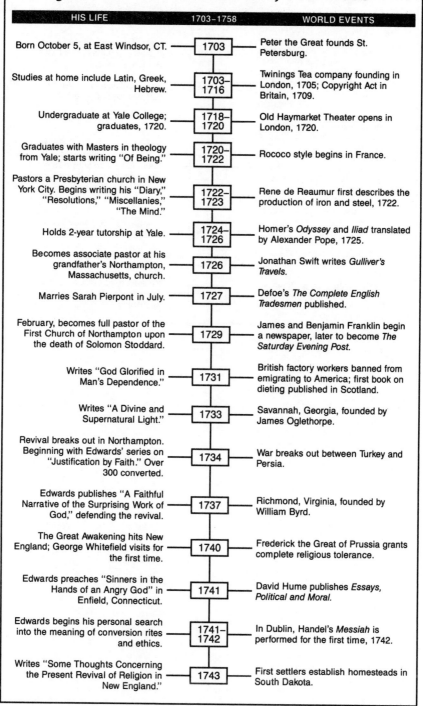

HIS LIFE	1703–1758	WORLD EVENTS
Born October 5, at East Windsor, CT.	1703	Peter the Great founds St. Petersburg.
Studies at home include Latin, Greek, Hebrew.	1703–1716	Twinings Tea company founding in London, 1705; Copyright Act in Britain, 1709.
Undergraduate at Yale College; graduates, 1720.	1718–1720	Old Haymarket Theater opens in London, 1720.
Graduates with Masters in theology from Yale; starts writing "Of Being."	1720–1722	Rococo style begins in France.
Pastors a Presbyterian church in New York City. Begins writing his "Diary," "Resolutions," "Miscellanies," "The Mind."	1722–1723	Rene de Reaumur first describes the production of iron and steel, 1722.
Holds 2-year tutorship at Yale.	1724–1726	Homer's *Odyssey* and *Iliad* translated by Alexander Pope, 1725.
Becomes associate pastor at his grandfather's Northampton, Massachusetts, church.	1726	Jonathan Swift writes *Gulliver's Travels*.
Marries Sarah Pierpont in July.	1727	Defoe's *The Complete English Tradesmen* published.
February, becomes full pastor of the First Church of Northampton upon the death of Solomon Stoddard.	1729	James and Benjamin Franklin begin a newspaper, later to become *The Saturday Evening Post*.
Writes "God Glorified in Man's Dependence."	1731	British factory workers banned from emigrating to America; first book on dieting published in Scotland.
Writes "A Divine and Supernatural Light."	1733	Savannah, Georgia, founded by James Oglethorpe.
Revival breaks out in Northampton. Beginning with Edwards' series on "Justification by Faith." Over 300 converted.	1734	War breaks out between Turkey and Persia.
Edwards publishes "A Faithful Narrative of the Surprising Work of God," defending the revival.	1737	Richmond, Virginia, founded by William Byrd.
The Great Awakening hits New England; George Whitefield visits for the first time.	1740	Frederick the Great of Prussia grants complete religious tolerance.
Edwards preaches "Sinners in the Hands of an Angry God" in Enfield, Connecticut.	1741	David Hume publishes *Essays, Political and Moral*.
Edwards begins his personal search into the meaning of conversion rites and ethics.	1741–1742	In Dublin, Handel's *Messiah* is performed for the first time, 1742.
Writes "Some Thoughts Concerning the Present Revival of Religion in New England."	1743	First settlers establish homesteads in South Dakota.

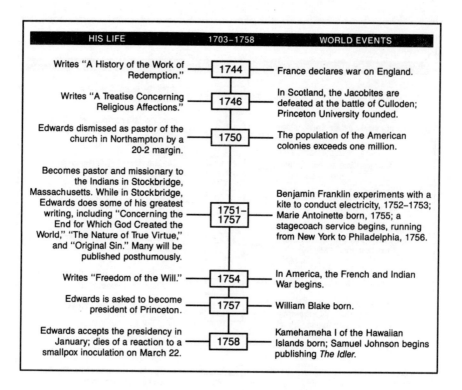

HIS LIFE	1703–1758	WORLD EVENTS
Writes "A History of the Work of Redemption."	1744	France declares war on England.
Writes "A Treatise Concerning Religious Affections."	1746	In Scotland, the Jacobites are defeated at the battle of Culloden; Princeton University founded.
Edwards dismissed as pastor of the church in Northampton by a 20-2 margin.	1750	The population of the American colonies exceeds one million.
Becomes pastor and missionary to the Indians in Stockbridge, Massachusetts. While in Stockbridge, Edwards does some of his greatest writing, including "Concerning the End for Which God Created the World," "The Nature of True Virtue," and "Original Sin." Many will be published posthumously.	1751–1757	Benjamin Franklin experiments with a kite to conduct electricity, 1752–1753; Marie Antoinette born, 1755; a stagecoach service begins, running from New York to Philadelphia, 1756.
Writes "Freedom of the Will."	1754	In America, the French and Indian War begins.
Edwards is asked to become president of Princeton.	1757	William Blake born.
Edwards accepts the presidency in January; dies of a reaction to a smallpox inoculation on March 22.	1758	Kamehameha I of the Hawaiian Islands born; Samuel Johnson begins publishing *The Idler*.

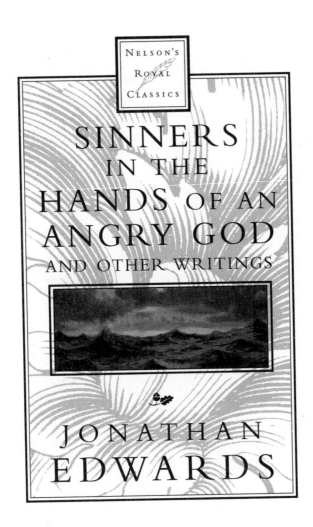

NELSON'S
ROYAL
CLASSICS

SINNERS
IN THE
HANDS OF AN
ANGRY GOD
AND OTHER WRITINGS

JONATHAN
EDWARDS

SINNERS
IN THE HANDS
OF AN ANGRY
GOD

SINNERS IN THE HANDS OF AN ANGRY GOD

Enfield, Connecticut, July 8, 1741

Their foot shall slide in due time.—Deuteronomy 32:35

In this verse is threatened the vengeance of God on the wicked unbelieving Israelites, who were God's visible people, and who lived under the means of grace; but who, notwithstanding all God's wonderful works towards them, remained (as vers 28.) void of counsel, having no understanding in them. Under all the cultivations of heaven, they brought forth bitter and poisonous fruit; as in the two verses next preceding the text.—The expression I have chosen for my text, their foot shall slide in due time, seems to imply the following things, relating to the punishment and destruction to which these wicked Israelites were exposed.

1. That they were always exposed to destruction; as one that stands or walks in slippery places is always exposed to fall. This is implied in the manner of their destruction coming upon them, being represented by their foot sliding. The same is expressed, Psalm 72:18. "Surely thou didst set them in slippery places; thou castedst them down into destruction."

2. It implies, that they were always exposed to sudden unexpected destruction. As he that walks in slippery places is every moment liable to fall, he cannot foresee one moment whether he shall stand or fall the next; and when he does fall, he falls at once without warning: Which is also expressed in Psalm 73:18,19. "Surely thou didst set them in slippery places; thou castedst them down into destruction: How are they brought into desolation as in a moment!"

3. Another thing implied is, that they are liable to fall of themselves, without being thrown down by the hand of another; as he that stands or walks on slippery ground needs nothing but his own weight to throw him down.

4. That the reason why they are not fallen already and do not fall now is only that God's appointed time is not come. For it is said, that when that due time, or appointed time comes, their foor shall slide. Then they shall be left to fall, as they are inclined by their own weight. God will not hold them up in these slippery places any longer, but will let them go; and then, at that very instant, they shall fall into destruction; as he that stands on such slippery declining ground, on the edge of a pit, he cannot stand alone, when he is let go he immediately falls and is lost.

The observation from the words that I would now insist upon is this.—"There is nothing that keeps wicked men at any one moment out of hell, but the mere pleasure of God."—By the mere pleasure of God, I mean his sovereign pleasure, his arbitrary will, restrained by no obligation, hindered by no manner of difficulty, any more than if nothing else but God's mere will had in the least degree, or in any respect whatsoever, any hand in the preservation of wicked men one moment.—The truth of this observation may appear by the following considerations.

1. There is no want of power in God to cast wicked men into hell at any moment. Men's hands cannot be strong when God rises up. The strongest have no power to resist him, nor can any deliver out of his hands.—He is not only able to cast wicked men into hell, but he can most easily do it. Sometimes an earthly prince meets with a great deal of difficulty to subdue a rebel, who has found means to fortify himself, and has made himself strong by the numbers of his followers. But it is not so with God. There is no fortress that is any defence from the power of God. Though hand join in hand, and vast multitudes of God's enemies combine and associate themselves, they are easily broken in pieces. They are as great heaps of light chaff before the whirlwind; or large quantities

of dry stubble before devouring flames. We find it easy to tread on and crush a worm that we see crawling on the earth; so it is easy for us to cut or singe a slender thread that any thing hangs by: thus easy is it for God, when he pleases, to cast his enemies down to hell. What are we, that we should think to stand before him, at whose rebuke the earth trembles, and before whom the rocks are thrown down?

2. They deserve to be cast into hell; so that divine justice never stands in the way, it makes no objection against God's using his power at any moment to destroy them. Yea, on the contrary, justice calls aloud for an infinite punishment of their sins. Divine justice says of the tree that brings forth such grapes of Sodom, "Cut it down, why cumbereth it the ground?" Luke 13:7. The sword of divine justice is every moment brandished over their heads, and it is nothing but the hand of arbitrary mercy, and God's mere will, that holds it back.

3. They are already under a sentence of condemnation to hell. They do not only justly deserve to be cast down thither, but the sentence of the law of God, that eternal and immutable rule of righteousness that God has fixed between him and mankind, is gone out against them, and stands against them; so that they are bound over already to hell. John 3:18. "He that believeth not is condemned already." So that every unconverted man properly belongs to hell; that is his place; from thence he is, John 8:23. "Ye are from beneath:" And thither he is bound; it is the place that justice, and God's word, and the sentence of his unchangeable law assign to him.

4. They are now the objects of that very same anger and wrath of God, that is expressed in the torments of hell. And the reason why they do not go down to hell at each moment, is not because God, in whose power they are, is not then very angry with them; as he is with many miserable creatures now tormented in hell, who there feel and bear the fierceness of his wrath. Yea, God is a great deal more angry with great numbers that are now on earth: yea, doubtless, with many that are now in this congregation, who it may be are at ease, than he is with many of those who are now in the flames of hell.

So that it is not because God is unmindful of their wickedness, and does not resent it, that he does not let loose his hand and cut them off. God is not altogether such an one as themselves, though they may imagine him to be so. The wrath of God burns against them, their damnation does not slumber; the pit is prepared, the fire is made ready, the furnace is now hot, ready to receive them; the flames do now rage

5

and glow. The glittering sword is whet, and held over them, and the pit hath opened its mouth under them.

5. The devil stands ready to fall upon them, and seize them as his own, at what moment God shall permit him. They belong to him; he has their souls in his possession, and under his dominion. The scripture represents them as his goods, Luke 11:12. The devils watch them; they are ever by them at their right hand; they stand waiting for them, like greedy hungry lions that see their prey, and expect to have it, but are for the present kept back. If God should withdraw his hand, by which they are restrained, they would in one moment fly upon their poor souls. The old serpent is gaping for them; hell opens its mouth wide to receive them; and if God should permit it, they would be hastily swallowed up and lost.

6. There are in the souls of wicked men those hellish principles reigning, that would presently kindle and flame out into hell fire, if it were not for God's restraints. There is laid in the very nature of carnal men, a foundation for the torments of hell. There are those corrupt principles, in reigning power in them, and in full possession of them, that are seeds of hell fire. These principles are active and powerful, exceeding violent in their nature, and if it were not for the restraining hand of God upon them, they would soon break out, they would flame out after the same manner as the same corruptions, the same enmity does in the hearts of damned souls, and would beget the same torments as they do in them. The souls of the wicked are in scripture compared to the troubled sea, Isa. 57:20. For the present, God restrains their wickedness by his mighty power, as he does the raging waves of the troubled sea, saying, "Hitherto shalt thou come, but no further;" but if God should withdraw that restraining power, it would soon carry all before it. Sin is the ruin and misery of the soul; it is destructive in its nature; and if God should leave it without restraint, there would need nothing else to make the soul perfectly miserable. The corruption of the heart of man is immoderate and boundless in its fury; and while wicked men live here, it is like fire pent up by God's restraints, whereas if it were let loose, it would set on fire the course of nature; and as the heart is now a sink of sin, so if sin was not restrained, it would immediately turn the soul into fiery oven, or a furnace of fire and brimstone.

7. It is no security to wicked men for one moment, that there are no visible means of death at hand. It is no security to a natural man, that he is now in health, and that he does not see which way he should now

immediately go out of the world by any accident, and that there is no visible danger in any respect in his circumstances. The manifold and continual experience of the world in all ages, shows this is no evidence, that a man is not on the very brink of eternity, and that the next step will not be into another world. The unseen, unthought-of ways and means of persons going suddenly out of the world are innumerable and inconceivable. Unconverted men walk over the pit of hell on a rotten covering, and there are innumerable places in this covering so weak that they will not bear their weight, and these places are not seen. The arrows of death fly unseen at noon-day; the sharpest sight cannot discern them. God has so many different unsearchable ways of taking wicked men out of the world and sending them to hell, that there is nothing to make it appear, that God had need to be at the expense of a miracle, or go out of the ordinary course of his providence, to destroy any wicked man, at any moment. All the means that there are of sinners going out of the world, are so in God's hands, and so universally and absolutely subject to his power and determination, that it does not depend at all the less on the mere will of God, whether sinners shall at any moment go to hell, than if means were never made use of, or at all concerned in the case.

8. Natural men's prudence and care to preserve their own lives, or the care of others to preserve them, do not secure them a moment. To this, divine providence and universal experience do also bear testimony. There is this clear evidence that men's own wisdom is no security to them from death; that if it were otherwise we should see some difference between the wise and politic men of the world, and others, with regard to their liableness to early and unexpected death: but how is it in fact? Eccles. 2:16. "How dieth the wise man? even as the fool."

9. All wicked men's pains and contrivance which they use to escape hell, while they continue to reject Christ, and so remain wicked men, do not secure them from hell one moment. Almost every natural man that hears of hell, flatters himself that he shall escape it; he depends upon himself for his own security; he flatters himself in what he has done, in what he is now doing, or what he intends to do. Every one lays out matters in his own mind how he shall avoid damnation, and flatters himself that he contrives well for himself, and that his schemes will not fail. They hear indeed that there are but few saved, and that the greater part of men that have died heretofore are gone to hell; but each one imagines that he lays out matters better for his own escape than others

7

have done. He does not intend to come to that place of torment; he says within himself, that he intends to take effectual care, and to order matters so for himself as not to fail.

But the foolish children of men miserably delude themselves in their own schemes, and in confidence in their own strength and wisdom; they trust to nothing but a shadow. The greater part of those who heretofore have lived under the same means of grace, and are now dead, are undoubtedly gone to hell; and it was not because they were not as wise as those who are now alive: it was not because they did not lay out matters as well for themselves to secure their own escape. If we could speak with them, and inquire of them, one by one, whether they expected, when alive, and when they used to hear about hell, ever to be the subjects of misery: we doubtless, should hear one and another reply, "No, I never intended to come here: I had laid out matters otherwise in my mind; I thought I should contrive well for myself—I thought my scheme good. I intended to take effectual care; but it came upon me unexpected; I did not look for it at that time, and in that manner; it came as a thief— Death outwitted me: God's wrath was too quick for me. Oh, my cursed foolishness! I was flattering myself, and pleasing myself with vain dreams of what I would do hereafter; and when I was saying, Peace and safety, then sudden destruction came upon me."

10. God has laid himself under no obligation, by any promise to keep any natural man out of hell one moment. God certainly has made no promises either of eternal life, or of any deliverance or preservation from eternal death, but what are contained in the covenant of grace, the promises that are given in Christ, in whom all the promises are yea and amen. But surely they have no interest in the promises of the covenant of grace who are not the children of the covenant, who do not believe in any of the promises, and have no interest in the Mediator of the covenant.

So that, whatever some have imagined and pretended about promises made to natural men's earnest seeking and knocking, it is plain and manifest, that whatever pains a natural man takes in religion, whatever prayers he makes, till he believes in Christ, God is under no manner of obligation to keep him a moment from eternal destruction.

So that, thus it is that natural men are held in the hand of God, over the pit of hell; they have deserved the fiery pit, and are already sentenced to it; and God is dreadfully provoked, his anger is as great towards them as to those that are actually suffering the executions of the fierceness of his wrath in hell, and they have done nothing in the least to appease or abate that anger, neither is God in the least bound by any promise to hold them up one moment; the devil is waiting for them, hell is gaping for them, the flames gather and flash about them, and would fain lay hold on them, and swallow them up; the fire pent up in their own hearts is struggling to break out: and they have no interest in any Mediator, there are no means within reach that can be any security to them. In short, they have no refuge, nothing to take hold of; all that preserves them every moment is the mere arbitrary will, and uncovenanted, unobliged forbearance of an incensed God.

APPLICATION

The use of this awful subject may be for awakening unconverted persons in this congregation. This that you have heard is the case of every one of you that are out of Christ.—That world of misery, that take of burning brimstone, is extended abroad under you. There is the dreadful pit of the glowing flames of the wrath of God; there is hell's wide gaping mouth open; and you have nothing to stand upon, nor any thing to take hold of; there is nothing between you and hell but the air; it is only the power and mere pleasure of God that holds you up.

You probably are not sensible of this; you find you are kept out of hell, but do not see the hand of God in it; but look at other things, as the good state of your bodily constitution, your care of your own life, and the means you use for your own preservation. But indeed these things are nothing; if God should withdraw his hand, they would avail no more to keep you from falling, than the thin air to hold up a person that is suspended in it.

Your wickedness makes you as it were heavy as lead, and to tend downwards with great weight and pressure towards hell; and if God should let you go, you would immediately sink and swiftly descend and plunge into the bottomless gulf, and your healthy constitution, and your own care and prudence, and best contrivance, and all your righteousness, would have no more influence to uphold you and keep you out of hell, than a spider's web would have to stop a falling rock. Were it not for the sovereign pleasure of God, the earth would not bear you one moment; for you are a burden to it; the creation groans with you; the creature is made subject to the bondage of your corruption, not willingly;

the sun does not willingly shine upon you to give you light to serve sin and Satan; the earth does not willingly yield her increase to satisfy your lusts; nor is it willingly a stage for your wickedness to be acted upon; the air does not willingly serve you for breath to maintain the flame of life in your vitals, while you spend your life in the service of God's enemies. God's creatures are good, and were made for men to serve God with, and do not willingly subserve to any other purpose, and groan when they are abused to purposes so directly contrary to their nature and end. And the world would spew you out, were it not for the sovereign hand of him who hath subjected it in hope. There are the black clouds of God's wrath now hanging directly over your heads, full of the dreadful storm, and big with thunder; and were it not for the restraining hand of God, it would immediately burst forth upon you. The sovereign pleasure of God, for the present, stays his rough wind; otherwise it would come with fury, and your destruction would come like a whirlwind, and you would be like the chaff of the summer threshing floor.

The wrath of God is like great waters that are dammed for the present; they increase more and more, and rise higher and higher, till an outlet is given; and the longer the stream is stopped, the more rapid and mighty is its course, when once it is let loose. It is true, that judgment against your evil works has not been executed hitherto; the floods of God's vengeance have been withheld; but your guilt in the mean time is constantly increasing, and you are every day treasuring up more wrath; the waters are constantly rising, and waxing more and more mighty; and there is nothing but the mere pleasure of God, that holds the waters back, that are unwilling to be stopped, and press hard to go forward. If God should only withdraw his hand from the flood-gate, it would immediately fly open, and the fiery floods of the fierceness and wrath of God, would rush forth with inconceivable fury, and would come upon you with omnipotent power; and if your strength were ten thousand times greater than it is, yea, ten thousand times greater than the strength of the stoutest, sturdiest devil in hell, it would be nothing to withstand or endure it.

The bow of God's wrath is bent, and the arrow made ready on the string, and justice bends the arrow at your heart, and strains the bow, and it is nothing but the mere pleasure of God, and that of an angry God, without any promise or obligation at all, that keeps the arrow one moment from being made drunk with your blood. Thus all you that never passed under a great change of heart, by the mighty power of the

Spirit of God upon your souls; all you that were never born again, and made new creatures, and raised from being dead in sin, to a state of new, and before altogether unexperienced light and life, are in the hands of an angry God. However you may have reformed your life in many things, and may have had religious affections, and may keep up a form of religion in your families and closets, and in the house of God, it is nothing but his mere pleasure that keeps you from being this moment swallowed up in everlasting destruction. However unconvinced you may now be of the truth of what you hear, by and by you will be fully convinced of it. Those that are gone from being in the like circumstances with you, see that it was so with them; for destruction came suddenly upon most of them; when they expected nothing of it, and while they were saying, Peace and safety: now they see, that those things on which they depended for peace and safety, were nothing but thin air and empty shadows.

The God that holds you over the pit of hell, much as one holds a spider, or some loathsome insect over the fire, abhors you, and is dreadfully provoked: his wrath towards you burns like fire; he looks upon you as worthy of nothing else, but to be cast into the fire; he is of purer eyes than to bear to have you in his sight; you are ten thousand times more abominable in his eyes, than the most hateful venomous serpent is in ours. You have offended him infinitely more than ever a stubborn rebel did his prince; and yet it is nothing but his hand that holds you from falling into the fire every moment. It is to be ascribed to nothing else, that you did not go to hell the last night; that you was suffered to awake again in this world, after you closed your eyes to sleep. And there is no other reason to be given, why you have not dropped into hell since you arose in the morning, but that God's hand has held you up. There is no other reason to be given why you have not gone to hell, since you have sat here in the house of God, provoking his pure eyes by your sinful wicked manner of attending his solemn worship. Yea, there is nothing else that is to be given as a reason why you do not this very moment drop down into hell.

O sinner! Consider the fearful danger you are in: it is a great furnace of wrath, a wide and bottomless pit, full of the fire of wrath, that you are held over in the hand of that God, whose wrath is provoked and incensed as much against you, as against many of the damned in hell. You hang by a slender thread, with the flames of divine wrath flashing about it, and ready every moment to singe it, and burn it asunder; and you have no interest in any Mediator, and nothing to lay hold of to save yourself, nothing to keep off the flames of wrath, nothing of your own, nothing that you ever have done, nothing that you can do, to induce God to spare you one moment.—And consider here more particularly,

1. Whose wrath it is: it is the wrath of the infinite God. If it were only the wrath of man, though it were of the most potent prince, it would be comparatively little to be regarded. The wrath of kings is very much dreaded, especially of absolute monarchs, who have the possessions and lives of their subjects wholly in their power, to be disposed of at their mere will. Prov. 20:2. "The fear of a king is as the roaring of a lion: Whoso provoketh him to anger, sinneth against his own soul." The subject that very much enrages an arbitrary prince, is liable to suffer the most extreme torments that human art can invent, or human power can inflict. But the greatest earthly potentates in their greatest majesty and strength, and when clothed in their greatest terrors, are but feeble, despicable worms of the dust, in comparison of the great and almighty Creator and King of heaven and earth. It is but little that they can do, when most enraged, and when they have exerted the utmost of their fury. All the kings of the earth, before God, are as grasshoppers; they are nothing, and less than nothing: both their love and their hatred is to be despised. The wrath of the great King of kings, is as much more terrible than theirs, as his majesty is greater. Luke 12:4,5. "And I say unto you, my friends, Be not afraid of them that kill the body, and after that, have no more that they can do. But I will forewarn you whom you shall fear: fear him, which after he hath killed, hath power to cast into hell: yea, I say unto you, Fear him."

2. It is the fierceness of his wrath that you are exposed to. We often read of the fury of God; as in Isa. 59:18. "According to their deeds, accordingly he will repay fury to his adversaries." So Isa. 66:15. "For behold, the Lord will come with fire, and with his chariots like a whirlwind, to render his anger with fury, and his rebuke with flames of fire." And in many other places. So, Rev. 19:15, we read of "the wine press of the fierceness and wrath of Almighty God." The words are exceeding terrible. If it had only been said, "the wrath of God," the words would have implied that which is infinitely dreadful: but it is "the fierceness and wrath of God." The fury of God! the fierceness of Jehovah! Oh, how dreadful that must be! Who can utter or conceive what such expressions carry in them! But it is also "the fierceness and wrath of almighty God." As though there would be a very great manifestation of his al-

mighty power in what the fierceness of his wrath should inflict, as though omnipotence should be as it were enraged, and exerted, as men are wont to exert their strength in the fierceness of their wrath. Oh! then, what will be the consequence! What will become of the poor worms that shall suffer it! Whose hands can be strong? And whose heart can endure? To what a dreadful, inexpressible, inconceivable depth of misery must the poor creature be sunk who shall be the subject of this!

Consider this, you that are here present, that yet remain in an unregenerate state. That God will execute the fierceness of his anger, implies, that he will inflict wrath without any pity. When God beholds the ineffable extremity of your case, and sees your torment to be so fastly disproportioned to your strength, and sees how your poor soul is crushed, and sinks down, as it were, into an infinite gloom; he will have no compassion upon you, he will not forbear the executions of his wrath, or in the least lighten his hand; there shall be no moderation or mercy, nor will God then at all stay his rough wind; he will have no regard to your welfare, nor be at all careful lest you should suffer too much in any other sense, than only that you shall not suffer beyond what strict justice requires. Nothing shall be withheld, because it is so hard for you to bear. Ezek. 8:18. "Therefore will I also deal in fury: mine eye shall not spare, neither will I have pity; and though they cry in mine ears with a loud voice, yet I will not hear them." Now God stands ready to pity you; this is a day of mercy; you may cry now with some encouragement of obtaining mercy. But when once the day of mercy is past, your most lamentable and dolorous cries and shrieks will be in vain; you will be wholly lost and thrown away of God, as to any regard to your welfare. God will have no other use to put you to, but to suffer misery; you shall be continued in being to no other end; for you will be a vessel of wrath fitted to destruction; and there will be no other use of this vessel, but to be filled full of wrath. God will be so far from pitying you when you cry to him, that it is said he will only "laugh and mock," Prov. 1:25,26,&c.

How awful are those words, Isa. 63:3, which are the words of the great God. "I will tread them in mine anger, and will trample them in my fury, and their blood shall be sprinkled upon my garments, and I will stain all my raiment." It is perhaps impossible to conceive of words that carry in them greater manifestations of these three things, viz. contempt, and hatred, and fierceness of indignation. If you cry to God to pity you, he will be so far from pitying you in your doleful case, or showing you the least regard or favour, that instead of that, he will only tread you under foot. And though he will know that you cannot bear the weight of omnipotence treading upon you, yet he will not regard that, but he will crush you under his feet without mercy; he will crush out your blood, and make it fly, and it shall be sprinkled on his garments, so as to stain all his raiment. He will not only hate you, but he will have you in the utmost contempt: no place shall be thought fit for you, but under his feet to be trodden down as the mire of the streets.

3. The misery you are exposed to is that which God will inflict to that end, that he might show what that wrath of Jehovah is. God hath had it on his heart to show to angels and men, both how excellent his love is, and also how terrible his wrath is. Sometimes earthly kings have a mind to show how terrible their wrath is, by the extreme punishments they would execute on those that would provoke them. Nebuchadnezzar, that mighty and haughty monarch of the Chaldean empire, was willing to show his wrath when enraged with Shadrach, Meshach, and Abednego; and accordingly gave orders that the burning fiery furnace should be heated seven times hotter than it was before; doubtless, it was raised to the utmost degree of fierceness that human art could raise it. But the great God is also willing to show his wrath, and magnify his awful majesty and mighty power in the extreme sufferings of his enemies. Rom. 9:22. "What if God, willing to show his wrath, and to make his power known, endured with much long-suffering the vessels of wrath fitted to destruction?" And seeing this is his design, and what he has determined, even to show how terrible the unrestrained wrath, the fury and fierceness of Jehovah is, he will do it to effect. There will be something accomplished and brought to pass that will be dreadful with a witness. When the great and angry God hath risen up and executed his awful vengeance on the poor sinner, and the wretch is actually suffering the infinite weight and power of his indignation, then will God call upon the whole universe to behold that awful majesty and mighty power that is to be seen in it. Isa. 33:12–14. "And the people shall be as the burnings of lime, as thorns cut up shall they be burnt in the fire. Hear ye that are far off, what I have done; and ye that are near, acknowledge my might. The sinners in Zion are afraid; fearfulness hath surprised the hypocrites," &c.

Thus it will be with you that are in an unconverted state, if you continue in it; the infinite might, and majesty, and terribleness of the omnipotent God shall be magnified upon you, in the ineffable strength of your torments. You shall be tormented in the presence of the holy angels, and in the presence of the Lamb; and when you shall be in this state of suffering, the glorious inhabitants of heaven shall go forth and look on the awful spectacle, that they may see what the wrath and fierceness of the Almighty is; and when they have seen it, they will fall down and adore that great power and majesty. Isa. 66:23,24. "And it shall come to pass, that from one new moon to another, and from one sabbath to another, shall all flesh come to worship before me, saith the Lord. And they shall go forth and look upon the carcasses of the men that have transgressed against me; for their worm shall not die, neither shall their fire be quenched, and they shall be an abhorring unto all flesh."

4. It is everlasting wrath. It would be dreadful to suffer this fierceness and wrath of Almighty God one moment; but you must suffer it to all eternity. There will be no end to this exquisite horrible misery. When you look forward, you shall see a long for ever, a boundless duration before you, which will swallow up your thoughts, and amaze your soul; and you will absolutely despair of ever having any deliverance, any end, any mitigation, any rest at all. You will know certainly that you must wear out long ages, millions of millions of ages, in wrestling and conflicting with this almighty merciless vengeance; and then when you have so done, when so many ages have actually been spent by you in this manner, you will know that all is but a point to what remains. So that your punishment will indeed be infinite. Oh, who can express what the state of a soul in such circumstances is! All that we can possibly say about it, gives but a very feeble, faint representation of it; it is inexpressible and inconceivable: For "who knows the power of God's anger?"

How dreadful is the state of those that are daily and hourly in the danger of this great wrath and infinite misery! But this is the dismal case of every soul in this congregation that has not been born again, however moral and strict, sober and religious, they may otherwise be. Oh that you would consider it, whether you be young or old! There is reason to think, that there are many in this congregation now hearing this discourse, that will actually be the subjects of this very misery to all eternity. We know not who they are, or in what seats they sit, or what thoughts they now have. It may be they are now at ease, and hear all these things without much disturbance, and are now flattering themselves that they are not the persons, promising themselves that they shall escape. If we knew that there was one person, and but one, in the whole congregation, that was to be the subject of this misery, what an awful thing would it be to think of! If we knew who it was, what an awful sight would it be to see such a person! How might all the rest of the congregation lift up a lamentable and bitter cry over him! But, alas! instead of one, how many is it likely will remember this discourse in hell? And it would be a wonder, if some that are now present should not be in hell in a very short time, even before this year is out. And it would be no wonder if some persons, that now sit here, in some seats of this meeting-house, in health, quiet and secure, should be there before tomorrow morning. Those of you that finally continue in a natural condition, that shall keep out of hell longest will be there in a little time! your damnation does not slumber; it will come swiftly, and, in all probability, very suddenly upon many of you. You have reason to wonder that you are not already in hell. It is doubtless the case of some whom you have seen and known, that never deserved hell more than you, and that heretofore appeared as likely to have been now alive as you. Their case is past all hope; they are crying in extreme misery and perfect despair; but here you are in the land of the living and in the house of God, and have an opportunity to obtain salvation. What would not those poor damned hopeless souls give for one day's opportunity such as you now enjoy!

And now you have an extraordinary opportunity, a day wherein Christ has thrown the door of mercy wide open, and stands in calling and crying with a loud voice to poor sinners; a day wherein many are flocking to him, and pressing into the kingdom of God. Many are daily coming from the east, west, north and south; many that were very lately in the same miserable condition that you are in, are now in a happy state, with their hearts filled with love to him who has loved them, and washed them from their sins in his own blood, and rejoicing in hope of the glory of God. How awful is it to be left behind at such a day! To see so many others feasting, while you are pining and perishing! To see so many rejoicing and singing for joy of heart, while you have cause to mourn for sorrow of heart, and howl for vexation of spirit! How can you rest one moment in such a condition? Are not your souls as precious as the souls of the people at Suffield, where they are flocking from day to day to Christ?

Are there not many here who have lived long in the world, and are not to this day born again? and so are aliens from the commonwealth of Israel, and have done nothing ever since they have lived, but treasure up wrath against the day of wrath? Oh, sirs, your case, in an especial manner, is extremely dangerous. Your guilt and hardness of heart is extremely great. Do you not see how generaity persons of your years are passed over and left, in the present remarkable and wonderful dispensation of God's mercy? You had need to consider yourselves, and awake thoroughly out of sleep. You cannot bear the fierceness and wrath of the infinite God.—And you, young men, and young women, will you neglect this precious season which you now enjoy, when so many others of your age are renouncing all youthful vanities, and flocking to Christ? You especially have now an extraordinary opportunity; but if you neglect it, it will soon be with you as with those persons who spent all the precious days of youth in sin, and are now come to such a dreadful pass in blindness and hardness.—And you, children, who are unconverted, do not you know that you are going down to hell, to bear the dreadful wrath of that God, who is now angry with you every day and every night? Will you be content to be the children of the devil, when so many other children in the land are converted, and are become the holy and happy children of the King of kings?

And let every one that is yet out of Christ, and hanging over the pit of hell, whether they be old men and women, or middle aged, or young people, or little children, now hearken to the loud calls of God's word and providence. This acceptable year of the Lord, a day of such great favour to some, will doubtless be a day of as remarkable vengeance to others. Men's hearts harden, and their guilt increases apace at such a day as this, if they neglect their souls; and never was there so great danger of such persons being given up to hardness of heart and blindness of mind. God seems now to be hastily gathering in his elect in all parts of the land; and probably the greater part of adult persons that ever shall be saved, will be brought in now in a little time, and that it will be as it was on the great out-pouring of the Spirit upon the Jews in the apostles' days; the election will obtain, and the rest will be blinded. If this should be the case with you, you will eternally curse this day, and will curse the day that ever you was born, to see such a season of the pouring out of God's Spirit, and will wish that you had died and gone to hell before you had seen it. Now undoubtedly it is, as it was in the days of John the Baptist, the axe is in an extraordinary manner laid at the root of the trees, that every tree which brings not forth good fruit, may be hewn down and cast into the fire.

A DIVINE
AND
SUPERNATURAL
LIGHT

A DIVINE AND SUPERNATURAL LIGHT

Immediately imparted to the soul, by the Spirit of God, shown to be both a scriptural and rational doctrine

Preached in Northampton, and published at the desire of the hearers, in the year 1734.—Dated August 1733

And Jesus answered and said unto him, Blessed art thou, Simon Barjona: for flesh and blood hath not revealed it unto thee, but my Father which is in heaven.—Matthew 16:17

S ubject: That there is such a thing as a spiritual and divine light, immediately imparted to the soul by God, of a different nature from any that is obtained by natural means.

Christ addresses these words to Peter upon occasion of his professing his faith in him as the Son of God. Our Lord was inquiring of his disciples, whom men said that he was: not that he needed to be informed, but only to introduce and give occasion to what follows. They answer, that some said he was John the Baptist, and some Elias, and others Jeremias, or one of the Prophets. When they had thus given an account who others said that he was, Christ asks them, whom they said he was? Simon Peter, whom we find always zealous and forward, was the first

21

to answer. He readily replied to the question, Thou art Christ, the Son of the living God.

Upon this occasion, Christ says as he does to him, and of him in the text: in which we may observe,

1. That Peter is pronounced blessed on this account.—Blessed art thou—"Thou art a happy man, that thou art not ignorant of this, that I am Christ, the Son of the living God. Thou art distinguishingly happy. Others are blinded and have dark and deluded apprehensions, as you have now given an account, some thinking that I am Elias, and some that I am Jeremias, and some one thing, and some another, but none of them thinking right, all of them misled. Happy art thou, that art so distinguished as to know the truth in this matter."

2. The evidence of this his happiness declared; viz., that God, and he only, had revealed it to him. This is an evidence of his being blessed,

First, as it shows how peculiarly favored he was of God above others: q.d. "How highly favored art thou, that others, wise and great men, the scribes, Pharisees, and Rulers, and the nation in general, are left in darkness, to follow their own misguided apprehensions; and that thou shouldst be singled out, as it were, by name, that my heavenly Father should thus set his love, on thee, Simon Barjona.—This argues thee blessed, that thou shouldst thus be the object of God's distinguishing love."

Secondly, it evidences his blessedness also, as it intimates that this knowledge is above any that flesh and blood can reveal. "This is such knowledge as only my Father which is in heaven can give: it is too high and excellent to be communicated by such means as other knowledge is. Thou art blessed, that thou knowest that which God alone can teach thee."

The original of this knowledge is here declared, both negatively and positively. Positively, as God is here declared the author of it. Negatively, as it is declared, that flesh and blood had not revealed it. God is the author of all knowledge and understanding whatsoever. He is the author of all moral prudence, and of the skill that men have in their secular business. Thus it is said of all in Israel that were wise-hearted, and skillful in embroidering, that God had filled them with the spirit of wisdom, Exo. 28:3.

God is the author of such knowledge, yet so that flesh and blood reveals it. Mortal men are capable of imparting the knowledge of human arts and sciences, and skill in temporal affairs. God is the author of such knowledge by those means: flesh and blood is employed as the mediate or second cause of it. He conveys it by the power and influence of natural means. But this spiritual knowledge spoken of in the text, is what God is the author of, and none else. He reveals it, and flesh and blood reveals it not. He imparts this knowledge immediately, not making use of any intermediate natural causes, as he does in other knowledge.

What had passed in the preceding discourse naturally occasioned Christ to observe this, because the disciples had been telling how others did not know him, but were generally mistaken about him, and divided and confounded in their opinions of him. But Peter had declared his assured faith, that he was the Son of God. Now it was natural to observe, how it was not flesh and blood that had revealed it to him, but God. For if this knowledge were dependent on natural causes or means, how came it to pass that they, a company of poor fishermen, illiterate men, and persons of low education, attained to the knowledge of the truth, while the scribes and Pharisees, men of vastly higher advantages, and greater knowledge and sagacity in other matters, remained in ignorance? This could be owing only to the gracious distinguishing influence and revelation of the Spirit of God. Hence, what I would make the subject of my present discourse from these words, is this

DOCTRINE

That there is such a thing as a spiritual and divine light, immediately imparted to the soul by God, of a different nature from any that is obtained by natural means.—And on this subject I would,

I. Show what this divine light is.

II. How it is given immediately by God, and not obtained by natural means.

III. Show the truth of the doctrine.

And then conclude with a brief improvement.

I. I would show what this spiritual and divine light is. And in order to it, would show,

First, in a few things, what it is not. And here,

1. Those convictions that natural men may have of their sin and misery, is not this spiritual and divine light. Men in a natural condition may have convictions of the guilt that lies upon them, and of the anger

of God, and their danger of divine vengeance. Such convictions are from light of truth. That some sinners have a greater conviction of their guilt and misery than others, is because some have more light, or more of an apprehension of truth, than others. And this light and conviction may be from the Spirit of God. The Spirit convinces men of sin, but yet nature is much more concerned in it than in the communication of that spiritual and divine light that is spoken of in the doctrine. It is from the Spirit of God only as assisting natural principles, and not as infusing any new principles. Common grace differs from special, in that it influences only by assisting of nature, and not by imparting grace, or bestowing anything above nature. The light that is obtained is wholly natural, or of no superior kind to what mere nature attains to, though more of that kind be obtained than would be obtained if men were left wholly to themselves. Or, in other words, common grace only assists the faculties of the soul to do that more fully which they do by nature, as natural conscience or reason will by mere nature make a man sensible of guilt, and will accuse and condemn him when he has done amiss. Conscience is a principle natural to men, and the work that it does naturally, or of itself, is to give an apprehension of right and wrong, and to suggest to the mind the relation that there is between right and wrong, and a retribution. The Spirit of God, in those convictions which unregenerate men sometimes have, assists conscience to do this work in a further degree than it would do if they were left to themselves. He helps it against those things that tend to stupefy it, and obstruct its exercise. But in the renewing and sanctifying work of the Holy Ghost, those things are wrought in the soul that are above nature, and of which there is nothing of the like kind in the soul by nature. They are caused to exist in the soul habitually, and according to such a stated constitution or law that lays such a foundation for exercises in a continued course, as is called a principle of nature. Not only are remaining principles assisted to do their work more freely and fully, but those principles are restored that were utterly destroyed by the fall. The mind thenceforward habitually exerts those acts that the dominion of sin had made it as wholly destitute of, as a dead body is of vital acts.

The Spirit of God acts in a very different manner in the one case, from what he does in the other. He may indeed act upon the mind of a natural man, but he acts in the mind of a saint as an indwelling vital principle. He acts upon the mind of an unregenerate person as an extrinsic, occasional agent, for in acting upon them, he does not unite himself to them. For notwithstanding all his influences that they may possess, they are still sensual, having not the Spirit, Jude 19. But he unites himself with the mind of a saint, takes him for his temple, actuates and influences him as a new supernatural principle of life and action. There is this difference, that the Spirit of God, in acting in the soul of a godly man, exerts and communicates himself there in his own proper nature. Holiness is the proper nature of the Spirit of God. The Holy Spirit operates in the minds of the godly, by uniting himself to them, and living in them, and exerting his own nature in the exercise of their faculties. The Spirit of God may act upon a creature, and yet not in acting communicate himself. The Spirit of God may act upon inanimate creatures, as the Spirit moved upon the face of the waters, in the beginning of the creation. So the Spirit of God may act upon the minds of men many ways, and communicate himself no more than when he acts upon an inanimate creature. For instance, he may excite thoughts in them, may assist their natural reason and understanding, or may assist other natural principles, and this without any union with the soul, but may act, as it were, upon an external object. But as he acts in his holy influences and spiritual operations, he acts in a way of peculiar communication of himself, so that the subject is thence denominated spiritual.

2. This spiritual and divine light does not consist in any impression made upon the imagination. It is no impression upon the mind, as though one saw anything with the bodily eyes. It is no imagination or idea of an outward light or glory, or any beauty of form or countenance, or a visible luster or brightness of any object. The imagination may be strongly impressed with such things, but this is not spiritual light. Indeed when the mind has a lively discovery of spiritual things, and is greatly affected by the power of divine light, it may, and probably very commonly does, much affect the imagination, so that impressions of an outward beauty or brightness may accompany those spiritual discoveries. But spiritual light is not that impression upon the imagination, but an exceeding different thing. Natural men may have lively impressions on their imaginations, and we cannot determine but the devil, who transforms himself into an angel of light, may cause imaginations of an outward beauty, or visible glory, and of sounds and speeches, and other such things. But these are things of a vastly inferior nature to spiritual light.

3. This spiritual light is not the suggesting of any new truths or propositions not contained in the Word of God. This suggesting of new

truths or doctrines to the mind, independent of any antecedent revelation of those propositions, either in word or writing, is inspiration, such as the prophets and apostles had, and such as some enthusiasts pretend to. But this spiritual light that I am speaking of, is quite a different thing from inspiration. It reveals no new doctrine, it suggests no new proposition to the mind, it teaches no new thing of God, or Christ, or another world, not taught in the Bible, but only gives a due apprehension of those things that are taught in the Word of God.

4. It is not every affecting view that men have of religious things that is this spiritual and divine light. Men by mere principles of nature are capable of being affected with things that have a special relation to religion as well as other things. A person by mere nature, for instance, may be liable to be affected with the story of Jesus Christ, and the sufferings he underwent, as well as by any other tragic story. He may be the more affected with it from the interest he conceives mankind to have in it. Yea, he may be affected with it without believing it, as well as a man may be affected with what he reads in a romance, or sees acted in a stage play. He may be affected with a lively and eloquent description of many pleasant things that attend the state of the blessed in heaven, as well as his imagination be entertained by a romantic description of the pleasantness of fairy land, or the like. And a common belief of the truth of such things, from education or otherwise, may help forward their affection. We read in Scripture of many that were greatly affected with things of a religious nature, who yet are there represented as wholly graceless, and many of them very ill men. A person therefore may have affecting views of the things of religion, and yet be very destitute of spiritual light. Flesh and blood may be the author of this: one man may give another an affecting view of divine things with but common assistance, but God alone can give a spiritual discovery of them.—But I proceed to show,

Secondly, positively what this spiritual and divine light is.

And it may be thus described: A true sense of the divine excellency of the things revealed in the Word of God, and a conviction of the truth and reality of them thence arising. This spiritual light primarily consists in the former of these, viz. A real sense and apprehension of the divine excellency of things revealed in the Word of God. A spiritual and saving conviction of the truth and reality of these things, arises from such a sight of their divine excellency and glory, so that this conviction of their truth is an effect and natural consequence of this sight of their divine glory. There is therefore in this spiritual light,

. 1. A true sense of the divine and superlative excellency of the things of religion: a real sense of the excellency of God and Jesus Christ, and of the work of redemption, and the ways and works of God revealed in the gospel. There is a divine and superlative glory in these things, an excellency that is of a vastly higher kind and more sublime nature than in other things, [and] a glory greatly distinguishing them from all that is earthly and temporal. He that is spiritually enlightened truly apprehends and sees it, or has a sense of it. He does not merely rationally believe that God is glorious, but he has a sense of the gloriousness of God in his heart. There is not only a rational belief that God is holy, and that holiness is a good thing, but there is a sense of the loveliness of God's holiness. There is not only a speculatively judging that God is gracious, but a sense how amiable God is on account of the beauty of this divine attribute.

There is a twofold knowledge of good of which God has made the mind of man capable. The first, that which is merely notional, as when a person only speculatively judges that anything is, which by the agreement of mankind, is called good or excellent, viz., that which is most to general advantage, and between which and a reward there is a suitableness,—and the like. And the other is, that which consists in the sense of the heart, as when the heart is sensible of pleasure and delight in the presence of the idea of it. In the former is exercised merely the speculative faculty, or the understanding, in distinction from the will or disposition of the soul. In the latter, the will, or inclination, or heart, is mainly concerned.

Thus there is a difference between having an opinion, that God is holy and gracious, and having a sense of the loveliness and beauty of that holiness and grace. There is a difference between having a rational judgment that honey is sweet, and having a sense of its sweetness. A man may have the former that knows not how honey tastes, but a man cannot have the latter unless he has an idea of the taste of honey in his mind. So there is a difference between believing that a person is beautiful, and having a sense of his beauty. The former may be obtained by hearsay, but the latter only by seeing the countenance. When the heart is sensible of the beauty and amiableness of a thing, it necessarily feels pleasure in the apprehension. It is implied in a person's being heartily sensible of the loveliness of a thing, that the idea of it is pleasant to his soul, which is a far different thing from having a rational opinion that it is excellent.

2. There arises from this sense of divine excellency of things contained in the Word of God, a conviction of the truth and reality of them; and that either indirectly or directly.

(1.) Indirectly, and that two ways.

1. As the prejudices of the heart, against the truth of divine things, are hereby removed, so that the mind becomes susceptive of the due force of rational arguments for their truth. The mind of man is naturally full of prejudices against divine truth. It is full of enmity against the doctrines of the gospel, which is a disadvantage to those arguments that prove their truth, and causes them to lose their force upon the mind. But when a person has discovered to him the divine excellency of Christian doctrines, this destroys the enmity, removes those prejudices, sanctifies the reason, and causes it to lie open to the force of arguments for their truth.

Hence was the different effect that Christ's miracles had to convince the disciples, from what they had to convince the scribes and Pharisees. Not that they had a stronger reason, or had their reason more improved, but their reason was sanctified, and those blinding prejudices, that the scribes and Pharisees were under, were removed by the sense they had of the excellency of Christ, and his doctrine.

2. It not only removes the hindrances of reason, but positively helps reason. It makes even the speculative notions more lively. It engages the attention of the mind, with more fixedness and intensity to that kind of objects, which causes it to have a clearer view of them, and enables it more clearly to see their mutual relations, and occasions it to take more notice of them. The ideas themselves that otherwise are dim and obscure, are by this means impressed with the greater strength, and have a light cast upon them, so that the mind can better judge of them. As he that beholds the objects on the face of the earth, when the light of the sun is cast upon them, is under greater advantage to discern them in their true forms and mutual relations, than he that sees them in a dim twilight.

The mind being sensible of the excellency of divine objects, dwells upon them with delight. The powers of the soul are more awakened and enlivened to employ themselves in the contemplation of them, and exert themselves more fully and much more to the purpose. The beauty of the objects draws on the faculties, and draws forth their exercises, so that reason itself is under far greater advantages for its proper and free exercises, and to attain its proper end, free of darkness and delusion.—But,

(2.) A true sense of the divine excellency of the things of God's Word does more directly and immediately convince of the truth of them, and that because the excellency of these things is so superlative. There is a beauty in them that is so divine and God-like, that it greatly and evidently distinguishes them from things merely human, or that of which men are the inventors and authors. [There is] a glory that is so high and great, that when clearly seen, commands assent to their divine reality. When there is an actual and lively discovery of this beauty and excellency, it will not allow of any such thought as that it is the fruit of men's invention. This is a kind of intuitive and immediate evidence. They believe the doctrines of God's Word to be divine, because they see a divine, and transcendent, and most evidently distinguishing glory in them. Such a glory as, if clearly seen, does not leave room to doubt of their being of God, and not of men.

Such a conviction of the truths of religion as this, arising from a sense of the divine excellency, is included in saving faith. And this original of it, is that by which it is most essentially distinguished from that common assent, of which unregenerate men are capable.

II. I proceed now to the second thing proposed, viz. To show how this light is immediately given by God, and not obtained by natural means. And here,

First, it is not intended that the natural faculties are not used of in it. They are the subject of this light, and in such a manner that they are not merely passive, but active in it. God, in letting in this light into the soul, deals with man according to his nature, and makes use of his rational faculties. But yet this light is not the less immediately from God for that. The faculties are made use of as the subject and not as the cause. As the use that we make of our eyes in beholding various objects, when the sun arises, is not the cause of the light that discovers those objects to us.

Second, it is not intended that outward means have no concern in this affair. It is not in this affair, as in inspiration, where new truths are suggested. For by this light is given only a due apprehension of the same truths that are revealed in the Word of God, and therefore it is not given without the Word. The gospel is employed in this affair. This light is the "light of the glorious gospel of Christ," 2 Cor. 4:4. The gospel is as a glass, by which this light is conveyed to us, 1 Cor. 13:12. Now we see through a glass.—But,

Third, when it is said that this light is given immediately by God, and not obtained by natural means, hereby is intended that it is given by God without making use of any means that operate by their own power, or a natural force. God makes use of means, but it is not as mediate causes to produce this effect. There are not truly any second causes of it, but it is produced by God immediately. The Word of God is no proper cause of this effect, but is made use of only to convey to the mind the subject matter of this saving instruction, and this indeed it does convey to us by natural force or influence. It conveys to our minds these doctrines. It is the cause of the notion of them in our heads, but not of the sense of their divine excellency in our hearts. Indeed a person cannot have spiritual light without the Word. But that does not argue, that the Word properly causes that light. The mind cannot see the excellency of any doctrine, unless that doctrine be first in the mind. But the seeing of the excellency of the doctrine may be immediately from the Spirit of God, though the conveying of the doctrine or proposition itself may be by the Word. So that the notions which are the subject matter of this light, are conveyed to the mind by the Word of God, but that due sense of the heart, wherein this light formally consists, is immediately by the Spirit of God. As for instance, that notion that there is a Christ, and that Christ is holy and gracious, is conveyed to the mind by the Word of God. But the sense of the excellency of Christ by reason of that holiness and grace, is nevertheless immediately the work of the Holy Spirit.—I come now,

III. To show the truth of the doctrine; that is, to show that there is such a thing as that spiritual light that has been described, thus immediately let into the mind by God. And here I would show briefly, that this doctrine is both scriptural and rational.

First, it is scriptural. My text is not only full to the purpose, but it is a doctrine with which the Scripture abounds. We are there abundantly taught, that the saints differ from the ungodly in this: that they have the knowledge of God, and a sight of God, and of Jesus Christ. I shall mention but few texts of many. 1 John 3:6, "Whosoever sinneth, has not seen him, nor known him." 3 John 11, "He that doth good, is of God: but he that doth evil, hath not seen God." John 14:19, "The world seeth me no more; but ye see me." John 17:3, "And this is eternal life, that they might know thee, the only true God, and Jesus Christ whom thou hast sent." This knowledge, or sight of God and Christ, cannot be a mere speculative knowledge, because it is spoken of that wherein they differ from the ungodly. And by these Scriptures it must not only be a different knowledge in degree and circumstances, and different in its effects, but it must be entirely different in nature and kind.

And this light and knowledge is always spoken of as immediately given of God, Mat. 11:25, 26, 27, "At that time Jesus answered and said, I thank thee, O Father, Lord of heaven and earth, because thou hast hid these things from the wise and prudent, and hast revealed them unto babes. Even so, Father, for so it seemed good in thy sight. All things are delivered unto me of my Father: and no man knoweth the Son, but the Father: neither knoweth any man the Father, save the Son, and he to whomsoever the Son will reveal him." Here this effect is ascribed alone to the arbitrary operation, and gift of God, bestowing this knowledge on whom he will, and distinguishing those with it who have the least natural advantage or means for knowledge, even babes, when it is denied to the wise and prudent. And imparting this knowledge is here appropriated to the Son of God, as his sole prerogative. And again, 2 Cor. 4:6, "For God, who commanded the light to shine out of darkness, hath shined in our hearts, to give the light of the knowledge of the glory of God, in the face of Jesus Christ." This plainly shows that there is a discovery of the divine superlative glory and excellency of God and Christ, peculiar to the saints, and also, that it is as immediately from God, as light from the sun, and that it is the immediate effect of his power and will. For it is compared to God's creating the light by his powerful Word in the beginning of the creation, and is said to be by the Spirit of the Lord, in the 18th verse of the preceding chapter. God is spoken of as giving the knowledge of Christ in conversion, as of what before was hidden and unseen. Gal. 1:15, 16, "But when it pleased God, who separated me from my mother's womb, and called me by his grace, to reveal his Son in me."—The Scripture also speaks plainly of such a knowledge of the Word of God, as has been described, as the immediate gift of God, Psa. 119:18: "Open thou mine eyes, that I may behold wondrous things out of thy law." What could the Psalmist mean, when he begged of God to open his eyes? Was he ever blind? Might he not have resort to the law and see every word and sentence in it when he pleased? And what could he mean by those wondrous things? Were they wonderful stories of the creation, and deluge, and Israel's passing through the Red Sea, and the like? Were not his eyes open to read these strange things when he would? Doubtless by wondrous things in God's law, he had respect to those distinguishing and wonderful excellencies, and marvelous manifestations of the divine perfections and glory, contained in the commands and doctrines of the Word, and those works and counsels of God that were revealed. So the Scripture speaks of a knowledge of God's dispensation, and covenant of mercy, and way of grace towards his people, as peculiar to the saints, and given only by God, Psa. 25:14: "The secret of the Lord is with them that fear him; and he will show them his covenant."

And that a true and saving belief of the truth of religion is that which arises from such a discovery, is also what the Scripture teaches. As John 6:40, "And this is the will of him that sent me, that everyone who seeth the Son, and believeth on him, may have everlasting life;" where it is plain that a true faith is what arises from a spiritual sight of Christ. And John 17:6, 7, 8, "I have manifested thy name unto the men which thou gavest me out of the world.—Now they have known that all things whatsoever thou hast given me, are of thee. For I have given unto them the words which thou gavest me; and they have received them, and have known surely that I came out from thee, and they have believed that thou didst send me;" where Christ's manifesting God's name to the disciples, or giving them the knowledge of God, was that whereby they knew that Christ's doctrine was of God, and that Christ himself proceeded from him, and was sent by him. Again, John 12:44, 45, 46, "Jesus cried and said, He that believeth on me, believeth not on me, but on him that sent me. And he that seeth me, seeth him that sent me. I am come a light into the world, that whosoever believeth on me, should not abide in darkness." Their believing in Christ, and spiritually seeing him, are spoken of as running parallel.

Christ condemns the Jews, that they did not know that he was the Messiah, and that his doctrine was true, from an inward distinguishing taste and relish of what was divine, in Luke 12:56, 57. He having there blamed the Jews that though they could discern the face of the sky and of the earth, and signs of the weather, that yet they could not discern those times—or as it is expressed in Matthew, the signs of those times—adds, "yea, and why even of your own selves, judge ye not what is right?" i.e., without extrinsic signs. Why have ye not that sense of true excellency, whereby ye may distinguish that which is holy and divine? Why have ye not that savor of the things of God, by which you may see the distinguishing glory, and evident divinity of me and my doctrine?

The apostle Peter mentions it as what gave them him and his companions good and well grounded assurance of the truth of the gospel, that they had seen the divine glory of Christ.—2 Pet. 1:16, "For we have not followed cunningly devised fables, when we made known unto you the power and coming of our Lord Jesus Christ, but were eyewitnesses of his majesty." The apostle has respect to that visible glory of Christ which they saw in his transfiguration: that glory was so divine, having such an ineffable appearance and semblance of divine holiness, majesty and grace, that it evidently denoted him to be a divine person. But if a sight of Christ's outward glory might give a rational assurance of his divinity, why may not an apprehension of his spiritual glory do so too? Doubtless Christ's spiritual glory is in itself as distinguishing, and as plainly showing his divinity, as his outward glory,—nay a great deal more. For his spiritual glory is that wherein his divinity consists, and the outward glory of his transfiguration showed him to be divine, only as it was a remarkable image or representation of that spiritual glory. Doubtless, therefore, he that has had a clear sight of the spiritual glory of Christ, may say, I have not followed cunningly devised fables, but have been an eyewitness of his majesty, upon as good grounds as the apostle, when he had respect to the outward glory of Christ that he had seen. But this brings me to what was proposed next, viz., to show that,

Secondly, this doctrine is rational.

1. It is rational to suppose that there is really such an excellency in divine things—so transcendent and exceedingly different from what is in other things—that if it were seen, would most evidently distinguish them. We cannot rationally doubt but that things that are divine, which appertain to the Supreme Being, are vastly different from things that are human: that there is a high, glorious, and God-like excellency in them that does most remarkably difference them from the things that are of men, insomuch that if the difference were but seen, it would have a convincing, satisfying influence upon anyone that they are divine. What reason can be offered against it, unless we would argue that God is not remarkably distinguished in glory from men.

If Christ should now appear to anyone as he did on the mount at his transfiguration. Or if he should appear to the world in his heavenly glory, as he will do at the day of judgment, without doubt, the glory and majesty would be such as would satisfy everyone that he was a divine person, and that religion was true. It would be a most reasonable, and well-grounded conviction too. And why may there not be that stamp of divinity, or divine glory, on the Word of God, on the scheme and doctrine of the gospel, that may be in like manner distinguishing and as rationally convincing, provided it be but seen? It is rational to suppose, that when God speaks to the world, there should be something in his Word vastly different from man's word. Supposing that God never had spoken to the world, but we had notice that he was about to reveal himself from heaven, and speak to us immediately himself, or that he should give us a book of his own inditing: after what manner should we expect that he would speak? Would it not be rational to suppose, that his speech would be exceeding different from man's speech, that there should be such an excellency and sublimity in his speech or word, such a stamp of wisdom, holiness, majesty and other divine perfections, that the word of man, yea of the wisest of men, should appear mean and base in comparison of it? Doubtless it would be thought rational to expect this, and unreasonable to think otherwise. When a wise man speaks in the exercise of his wisdom, there is something in everything he says that is very distinguishable from the talk of a little child. So, without doubt, and much more, is the speech of God to be distinguished from that of the wisest of men; agreeably to Jer. 23:28, 29. God having there been reproving the false prophets that prophesied in his name, and pretended that what they spoke was his Word, when indeed it was their own word, says, "The prophet that hath a dream, let him tell a dream; and he that hath my word, let him speak my word faithfully: what is the chaff to the wheat? saith the Lord. Is not my word like as a fire? saith the Lord: and like a hammer that breaketh the rock in pieces?"

2. If there be such a distinguishing excellency in divine things, it is rational to suppose that there may be such a thing as seeing it. What should hinder but that it may be seen? It is no argument that there is no such thing as such a distinguishing excellency, or that it cannot be seen, because some do not see it, though they may be discerning men in temporal matters. It is not rational to suppose, if there be any such excellency in divine things, that wicked men should see it. Is it rational to suppose, that those whose minds are full of spiritual pollution, and under the power of filthy lusts, should have any relish or sense of divine beauty or excellency, or that their minds should be susceptive of that light that is in its own nature so pure and heavenly? It need not seem at all strange, that sin should so blind the mind, seeing that men's particular natural tempers and dispositions will so much blind them in secular mat-

ters, as when men's natural temper is melancholy, jealous, fearful, proud, or the like.

3. It is rational to suppose that this knowledge should be given immediately by God, and not be obtained by natural means. Upon what account should it seem unreasonable that there should be any immediate communication between God and the creature? It is strange that men should make any matter of difficulty of it. Why should not he that made all things, still have something immediately to do with the things that he has made? Where lies the great difficulty, if we own the being of a God, and that he created all things out of nothing, of allowing some immediate influence of God on the creation still? And if it be reasonable to suppose it with respect to any part of the creation, it is especially so with respect to reasonable, intelligent creatures, who are next to God in the gradation of the different orders of beings, and whose business is most immediately with God. Reason teaches that man was made to serve and glorify his Creator. And if it be rational to suppose that God immediately communicates himself to man in any affair, it is in this. It is rational to suppose that God would reserve that knowledge and wisdom, which is of such a divine and excellent nature, to be bestowed immediately by himself, and that it should not be left in the power of second causes. Spiritual wisdom and grace is the highest and most excellent gift that ever God bestows on any creature: in this the highest excellency and perfection of a rational creature consists. It is also immensely the most important of all divine gifts. It is that wherein man's happiness consists, and on which his everlasting welfare depends. How rational is it to suppose that God, however he has left lower gifts to second causes, and in some sort in their power, yet should reserve this most excellent, divine, and important of all divine communications, in his own hands, to be bestowed immediately by himself, as a thing too great for second causes to be concerned in! It is rational to suppose that this blessing should be immediately from God, for there is no gift or benefit that is in itself so nearly related to the divine nature. Nothing which the creature receives is so much a participation of the Deity. It is a kind of emanation of God's beauty, and is related to God as the light is to the sun. It is therefore congruous and fit that when it is given of God, it should be immediately from himself, and by himself, according to his own sovereign will.

It is rational to suppose that it should be beyond a man's power to obtain this light by the mere strength of natural reason, for it is not a thing that belongs to reason, to see the beauty and loveliness of spiritual things. It is not a speculative thing, but depends on the sense of the heart. Reason indeed is necessary in order to it, as it is by reason only that we are become the subjects of the means of it, which means I have already shown to be necessary in order to it, though they have no proper causal influence in the affair. It is by reason that we become possessed of a notion of those doctrines that are the subject matter of this divine light or knowledge. Reason may many ways be indirectly and remotely an advantage to it. Reason has also to do in the acts that are immediately consequent on this discovery. For seeing the truth of religion from hence, is by reason, though it be but by one step, and the inference be immediate. So reason has to do in that accepting of, and trusting in Christ, that is consequent on it. But if we take reason strictly—not for the faculty of mental perception in general, but for ratiocination, or a power of inferring by arguments—the perceiving of spiritual beauty and excellency no more belongs to reason, than it belongs to the sense of feeling to perceive colors, or the power of seeing to perceive the sweetness of food. It is out of reason's province to perceive the beauty or loveliness of anything: such a perception does not belong to that faculty. Reason's work is to perceive truth and not excellency. It is not ratiocination that gives men the perception of the beauty and amiableness of a countenance, though it may be many ways indirectly an advantage to it. Yet it is no more reason that immediately perceives it, than it is reason that perceives the sweetness of honey: it depends on the sense of the heart.—Reason may determine that a countenance is beautiful to others, it may determine that honey is sweet to others, but it will never give me a perception of its sweetness.

I will conclude with a brief improvement of what has been said.

First, this doctrine may lead us to reflect on the goodness of God, that has so ordered it, that a saving evidence of the truth of the gospel is such, as is attainable by persons of mean capacities and advantages, as well as those that are of the greatest parts and learning. If the evidence of the gospel depended only on history, and such reasonings as learned men only are capable of, it would be above the reach of far the greatest part of mankind. But persons with but an ordinary degree of knowledge are capable, without a long and subtle train of reasoning, to see the divine excellency of the things of religion. They are capable of being taught by the Spirit of God, as well as learned men. The evidence that is this way obtained, is vastly better and more satisfying, than all that can be obtained by the arguings of those that are most learned, and greatest masters of reason. And babes are as capable of knowing these things, as the wise and prudent, and they are often hid from these when they are revealed to those. 1 Cor. 1:26, 27, "For ye see your calling, brethren, how that not many wise men, after the flesh, not many mighty, nor many noble, are called. But God hath chosen the foolish things of the world.—"

Secondly, this doctrine may well put us upon examining ourselves, whether we have ever had this divine light let into our souls. If there be such a thing indeed, doubtless it is of great importance whether we have thus been taught by the Spirit of God; whether the light of the glorious gospel of Christ, who is the image of God, has shined unto us, giving us the light of the knowledge of the glory of God in the face of Jesus Christ; [and] whether we have seen the Son, and believed on him, or have that faith of gospel doctrines which arises from a spiritual sight of Christ.

Thirdly, all may hence be exhorted, earnestly to seek this spiritual light. To influence and move to it, the following things may be considered.

1. This is the most excellent and divine wisdom that any creature is capable of. It is more excellent than any human learning. It is far more excellent than all the knowledge of the greatest philosophers or statesmen. Yea, the least glimpse of the glory of God in the face of Christ does more exalt and ennoble the soul, than all the knowledge of those that have the greatest speculative understanding in divinity without grace. This knowledge has the most noble object that is or can be, viz. the divine glory and excellency of God and Christ. The knowledge of these objects is that wherein consists the most excellent knowledge of the angels, yea, of God himself.

2. This knowledge is that which is above all others sweet and joyful. Men have a great deal of pleasure in human knowledge, in studies of natural things, but this is nothing to that joy which arises from this divine light shining into the soul. This light gives a view of those things that are immensely the most exquisitely beautiful, and capable of delighting the eye of the understanding. This spiritual light is the dawning of the light of glory in the heart. There is nothing so powerful as this to support persons in affliction, and to give the mind peace and brightness in this stormy and dark world.

3. This light is such as effectually influences the inclination, and

changes the nature of the soul. It assimilates our nature to the divine nature, and changes the soul into an image of the same glory that is beheld. 2 Cor. 3:18, "But we all with open face, beholding as in a glass the glory of the Lord, are changed into the same image, from glory to glory, even as by the Spirit of the Lord." This knowledge will wean from the world, and raise the inclination to heavenly things. It will turn the heart to God as the fountain of good, and to choose him for the only portion. This light, and this only, will bring the soul to a saving close with Christ. It conforms the heart to the gospel, mortifies its enmity and opposition against the scheme of salvation therein revealed. It causes the heart to embrace the joyful tidings, and entirely to adhere to, and acquiesce in the revelation of Christ as our Savior. It causes the whole soul to accord and symphonize with it, admitting it with entire credit and respect, cleaving to it with full inclination and affection, and it effectually disposes the soul to give up itself entirely to Christ.

4. This light, and this only, has its fruit in a universal holiness of life. No merely notional or speculative understanding of the doctrines of religion will ever bring to this. But this light, as it reaches the bottom of the heart, and changes the nature, so it will effectually dispose to a universal obedience. It shows God as worthy to be obeyed and served. It draws forth the heart in a sincere love to God, which is the only principle of a true, gracious, and universal obedience, and it convinces of the reality of those glorious rewards that God has promised to them that obey him.

GOD'S
SOVEREIGNTY
IN THE
SALVATION
OF MEN

GOD'S SOVEREIGNTY IN THE SALVATION OF MEN

Therefore hath he mercy on whom he will have mercy, and whom he will he hardeneth.—Romans 9:18

The apostle, in the beginning of this chapter, expresses his great concern and sorrow of heart for the nation of the Jews, who were rejected of God. This leads him to observe the difference which God made by election between some of the Jews and others, and between the bulk of that people and the Christian Gentiles. In speaking of this he enters into a more minute discussion of the sovereignty of God in electing some to eternal life, and rejecting others, than is found in any other part of the Bible; in the course of which he quotes several passages from the Old Testament, confirming and illustrating this doctrine. In the ninth verse he refers us to what God said to Abraham, showing his election of Isaac before Ishmael—"For this is the word of promise; At this time will I come, and Sarah shall have a son:" then to what God had said to Rebecca, showing his election of Jacob before Esau; "The elder shall serve the younger:" in the thirteenth verse, to a passage from Malachi, "Jacob have I loved, but Esau have I hated:" in the fifteenth verse, to what God said to Moses, "I will have mercy on whom I will have mercy; and I will have compassion on whom I will have compassion:" and the verse preceding the text, to what God says to Pharaoh, "For the scripture saith unto Pharaoh, Even for this same purpose have I raised thee up, that I might show my power in thee, and that my name might be declared throughout all the earth." In what the apostle says in the text, he seems to have respect especially to the two last-cited passages: to what God said to Moses in the fifteenth verse, and to what he said to Pharaoh in the verse immediately preceding. God said to Moses, "I will have mercy on whom I will have mercy." To this the apostle refers in the former part of the text. And we know how often it is said of Pharaoh, that God hardened his heart. And to this the apostle seems to have respect in the latter part of the text; "and whom he will he hardeneth." We may observe in the text,

1. God's different dealing with men. He hath mercy on some, and hardeneth others. When God is here spoken of as hardening some of the children of men, it is not to be understood that God by any positive efficiency hardens any man's heart. There is no positive act in God, as though he put forth any power to harden the heart. To suppose any such thing would be to make God the immediate author of sin. God is said to harden men in two ways: by withholding the powerful influences of his Spirit, without which their hearts will remain hardened, and grow harder and harder; in this sense he hardens them, as he leaves them to hardness. And again, by ordering those things in his providence which, through the abuse of their corruption, become the occasion of their hardening. Thus God sends his word and ordinances to men which, by their abuse, prove an occasion of their hardening. So the apostle said, that he was unto some "a savour of death unto death." So God is represented as sending Isaiah on this errand, to make the hearts of the people fat, and to make their ears heavy, and to shut their eyes; lest they should see with their eyes, and hear with their ears, and understand with their heart, and convert, and be healed. Isa. 6:10. Isaiah's preaching was, in itself, of a contrary tendency, to make them better. But their abuse of it rendered it an occasion of their hardening. As God is here said to harden men, so he is said to put a lying spirit in the mouth of the false prophets. 2 Chron. 18:22. That is, he suffered a lying spirit to enter into them. And thus he is said to have bid Shimei curse David. 2 Sam. 16:10. Not that he properly commanded him; for it is contrary to God's commands. God expressly forbids cursing the ruler of the people. Exod. 22:28. But he suffered corruption at that time so to work in Shimei, and ordered

that occasion of stirring it up, as a manifestation of his displeasure against David.

2. The foundation of his different dealing with mankind; viz. his sovereign will and pleasure. "He hath mercy on whom he will have mercy, and whom he will he hardeneth." This does not imply, merely, that God never shows mercy or denies it against his will, or that he is always willing to do it when he does it. A willing subject or servant, when he obeys his lord's commands, may never do any thing against his will, nothing but what he can do cheerfully and with delight; and yet he cannot be said to do what he wills in the sense of the text. But the expression implies that it is God's mere will and sovereign pleasure, which supremely orders this affair. It is the divine will without restraint, or constraint, or obligation.

DOCTRINE

God exercises his sovereignty in the eternal salvation of men.

He not only is sovereign, and has a sovereign right to dispose and order in that affair; and he not only might proceed in a sovereign way, if he would, and nobody could charge him with exceeding his right; but he actually does so; he exercises the right which he has. In the following discourse, I propose to show,

    I. What is God's sovereignty.
    II. What God's sovereignty in the salvation of men implies.
    III. That God actually doth exercise his sovereignty in this matter.
    IV. The reasons for this exercise.

I. I would show what is God's sovereignty.

The sovereignty of God is his absolute, independent right of disposing of all creatures according to his own pleasure. I will consider this definition by the parts of it.

The will of God is called his mere pleasure,

1. In opposition to any constraint. Men may do things voluntarily, and yet there may be a degree of constraint. A man may be said to do a thing voluntarily, that is, he himself does it; and, all things considered, he may choose to do it; yet he may do it out of fear, and the thing in itself considered be irksome to him, and sorely against his inclination.

When men do things thus, they cannot be said to do them according to their mere pleasure.

2. In opposition to its being under the will of another. A servant may fulfil his master's commands, and may do it willingly, and cheerfully, and may delight to do his master's will; yet when he does so, he does not do it of his own mere pleasure. The saints do the will of God freely. They choose to do it; it is their meat and drink. Yet they do not do it of their mere pleasure and arbitrary will; because their will is under the direction of a superior will.

3. In opposition to any proper obligation. A man may do a thing which he is obliged to do, very freely; but he cannot be said to act from his own mere will and pleasure. He who acts from his own mere pleasure, is at full liberty; but he who is under any proper obligation, is not at liberty, but is bound. Now the sovereignty of God supposes, that he has a right to dispose of all his creatures according to his mere pleasure in the sense explained. And his right is absolute and independent. Men may have a right to dispose of some things according to their pleasure. But their right is not absolute and unlimited. Men may be said to have a right to dispose of their own goods as they please. But their right is not absolute; it has limits and bounds. They have a right to dispose of their own goods as they please, provided they do not do it contrary to the law of the state to which they are subject, or contrary to the law of God. Men's right to dispose of their things as they will, is not absolute, because it is not independent. They have not an independent right to what they have, but in some things depend on the community to which they belong, for the right they have; and in every thing depend on God. They receive all the right they have to any thing from God. But the sovereignty of God imports that he has an absolute, and unlimited, and independent right of disposing of his creatures as he will. I proposed to inquire,

II. What God's sovereignty in the salvation of men implies. In answer to this inquiry, I observe, it implies that God can either bestow salvation on any of the children of men, or refuse it, without any prejudice to the glory of any of his attributes, except where he has been pleased to declare, that he will or will not bestow it. It cannot be said absolutely, as the case now stands, that God can, without any prejudice to the honour of any of his attributes, bestow salvation on any of the children of men, or refuse it; because, concerning some, God has been pleased to declare either that he will or that he will not bestow salvation on them; and thus to bind himself by his own promise. And concerning some he has been pleased to declare, that he never will bestow salvation upon them; viz. those who have committed the sin against the Holy Ghost. Hence, as the case now stands, he is obliged; he cannot bestow salvation in one case, or refuse it in the other, without prejudice to the honour of his truth. But God exercised his sovereignty in making these declarations. God was not obliged to promise that he would save all who believe in Christ; nor was he obliged to declare, that he who committed the sin against the Holy Ghost should never be forgiven. But it pleased him so to declare. And had it not been so that God had been pleased to oblige himself in these cases, he might still have either bestowed salvation, or refused it, without prejudice to any of his attributes. If it would in itself be prejudicial to any of his attributes to bestow or refuse salvation, then God would not in that matter act as absolutely sovereign. Because it then ceases to be a merely arbitrary thing. It ceases to be a matter of absolute liberty, and is become a matter of necessity or obligation. For God cannot do any thing to the prejudice of any of his attributes, or contrary to what is in itself excellent and glorious. Therefore,

1. God can, without prejudice to the glory of any of his attributes, bestow salvation on any of the children of men, except on those who have committed the sin against the Holy Ghost. The case was thus when man fell, and before God revealed his eternal purpose and plan for redeeming men by Jesus Christ. It was probably looked upon by the angels as a thing utterly inconsistent with God's attributes to save any of the children of men. It was utterly inconsistent with the honour of the divine attributes to save any one of the fallen children of men, as they were in themselves. It could not have been done had not God contrived a way consistent with the honour of his holiness, majesty, justice, and truth. But since God in the gospel has revealed that nothing is too hard for him to do, nothing beyond the reach of his power, and wisdom, and sufficiency; and since Christ has wrought out the work of redemption, and fulfilled the law by obeying, there is none of mankind whom he may not save without any prejudice to any of his attributes, excepting those who have committed the sin against the Holy Ghost. And those he might have saved without going contrary to any of his attributes, had he not been pleased to declare that he would not. It was not because he could not have saved them consistently with his justice, and consistently with his law, or because his attribute of mercy was not great enough, or the blood of Christ not sufficient to cleanse from that

sin. But it has pleased him for wise reasons to declare that that sin shall never be forgiven in this world, or in the world to come. And so now it is contrary to God's truth to save such. But otherwise there is no sinner, let him be ever so great, but God can save him without prejudice to any attribute; if he has been a murderer, adulterer, or perjurer, or idolater, or blasphemer, God may save him if he pleases, and in no respect injure his glory. Though persons have sinned long, have been obstinate, have committed heinous sins a thousand times, even till they have grown old in sin, and have sinned under great aggravations: let the aggravations be what they may; if they have sinned under ever so great light; if they have been backsliders, and have sinned against ever so numerous and solemn warnings and strivings of the Spirit, and mercies of his common providence: though the danger of such is much greater than of other sinners, yet God can save them if he pleases, for the sake of Christ, without any prejudice to any of his attributes. He may have mercy on whom he will have mercy. He may have mercy on the greatest of sinners, if he pleases, and the glory of none of his attributes will be in the least sullied. Such is the sufficiency of the satisfaction and righteousness of Christ, that none of the divine attributes stand in the way of the salvation of any of them. Thus the glory of any attribute did not at all suffer by Christ's saving some of his crucifiers.

1. God may save any of them without prejudice to the honour of his holiness. God is an infinitely holy being. The heavens are not pure in his sight. He is of purer eyes than to behold evil, and cannot look on iniquity. And if God should in any way countenance sin, and should not give proper testimonies of his hatred of it, and displeasure at it, it would be a prejudice to the honour of his holiness. But God can save the greatest sinner without giving the least countenance to sin. If he saves one, who for a long time has stood out under the calls of the gospel, and has sinned under dreadful aggravations; if he saves one who, against light, has been a pirate or blasphemer, he may do it without giving any countenance to their wickedness; because his abhorrence of it and displeasure against it have been already sufficiently manifested in the sufferings of Christ. It was a sufficient testimony of God's abhorrence against even the greatest wickedness, that Christ, the eternal Son of God, died for it. Nothing can show God's infinite abhorrence of any wickedness more than this. If the wicked man himself should be thrust into hell, and should endure the most extreme torments which are ever

suffered there, it would not be a greater manifestation of God's abhorrence of it, than the sufferings of the Son of God for it.

2. God may save any of the children of men without prejudice to the honour of his majesty. If men have affronted God, and that ever so much, if they have cast ever so much contempt on his authority; yet God can save them, if he pleases, and the honour of his majesty not suffer in the least. If God should save those who have affronted him, without satisfaction, the honour of his majesty would suffer. For when contempt is cast upon infinite majesty, its honour suffers, and the contempt leaves an obscurity upon the honour of the divine majesty, if the injury is not repaired. But the sufferings of Christ do fully repair the injury. Let the contempt be ever so great, yet if so honourable a person as Christ undertakes to be a Mediator for the offender, and in the mediation suffer in his stead, it fully repairs the injury done to the majesty of heaven by the greatest sinner.

3. God may save any sinner whatsoever consistently with his justice. The justice of God requires the punishment of sin. God is the Supreme Judge of the world, and he is to judge the world according to the rules of justice. It is not the part of a judge to show favour to the person judged; but he is to determine according to a rule of justice without departing to the right hand or left. God does not show mercy as a judge, but as a sovereign. And therefore when mercy sought the salvation of sinners, the inquiry was how to make the exercise of the mercy of God as a sovereign, and of his strict justice as a judge, agree together. And this is done by the sufferings of Christ, in which sin is punished fully, and justice answered. Christ suffered enough for the punishment of the sins of the greatest sinner that ever lived. So that God, when he judges, may act according to a rule of strict justice, and yet acquit the sinner, if he be in Christ. Justice cannot require any more for any man's sins, than those sufferings of one of the persons in the Trinity, which Christ suffered. Rom. 3:25,26. "Whom God hath set forth to be a propitiation through faith in his blood; to declare his righteousness, that he might be just, and the justifier of him which believeth in Christ."

4. God can save any sinner whatsoever, without any prejudice to the honour of his truth. God passed his word, that sin should be punished with death, which is to be understood not only of the first, but of the second death. God can save the greatest sinner consistently with his truth in this threatening. For sin is punished in the sufferings of Christ, inasmuch as he is our surety, and so is legally the same person, and

sustained our guilt, and in his sufferings bore our punishment. It may be objected, that God said, If thou eatest, thou shalt die; as though the same person that sinned must suffer; and therefore why does not God's truth oblige him to that? I answer, that the word then was not intended to be restrained to him, that in his own person sinned. Adam probably understood that his posterity were included, whether they sinned in their own person or not. If they sinned in Adam, their surety, those words, "if thou eatest," meant, if thou eatest in thyself, or in thy surety. And therefore, the latter words, "thou shalt die," do also fairly allow of such a construction as, thou shalt die in thyself, or in thy surety. Isa. 42:21. "The Lord is well pleased for his righteousness' sake, he will magnify the law and make it honourable." But,

II. God may refuse salvation to any sinner whatsoever, without prejudice to the honour of any of his attributes.

There is no person whatever in a natural condition, upon whom God may not refuse to bestow salvation without prejudice to any part of his glory. Let a natural person be wise or unwise, of a good or ill natural temper, of mean or honourable parentage, whether born of wicked or godly parents; let him be a moral or immoral person, whatever good he may have done, however religious he has been, how many prayers soever he has made, and whatever pains he has taken that he may be saved; whatever concern and distress he may have for fear he shall be damned; or whatever circumstances he may be in; God can deny him salvation without the least disparagement to any of his perfections. His glory will not in any instance be the least obscured by it.

1. God may deny salvation to any natural person without any injury to the honour of his righteousness. If he does so, there is no injustice nor unfairness in it. There is no natural man living, let his case be what it will, but God may deny him salvation, and cast him down to hell, and yet not be chargeable with the least unrighteous or unfair dealing in any respect whatsoever. This is evident, because they all have deserved hell: and it is no injustice for a proper judge to inflict on any man what he deserves. And as he has deserved condemnation, so he has never done any thing to remove the liability, or to atone for the sin. He never has done any thing whereby he has laid any obligations on God not to punish him as he deserved.

2. God may deny salvation to any unconverted person whatever without any prejudice to the honour of his goodness. Sinners are sometimes ready to flatter themselves, that though it may not be contrary to

the justice of God to condemn them, yet it will not consist with the glory of his mercy. They think it will be dishonourable to God's mercy to cast them into hell, and have no pity or compassion upon them. They think it will be very hard and severe, and not becoming a God of infinite grace and tender compassion. But God can deny salvation to any natural person without any disparagement to his mercy and goodness. That, which is not contrary to God's justice, is not contrary to his mercy. If damnation be justice, then mercy may choose its own object. They mistake the nature of the mercy of God, who think that it is an attribute, which, in some cases, is contrary to justice. Nay, God's mercy is illustrated by it, as in the twenty-third verse of the context. "That he might make known the riches of his glory on the vessels of mercy, which he had afore prepared unto glory."

3. It is in no way prejudicial to the honour of God's faithfulness. For God has in no way obliged himself to any natural man by his word to bestow salvation upon him. Men in a natural condition are not the children of promise; but lie open to the curse of the law, which would not be the case if they had any promise to lay hold of.

III. God does actually exercise his sovereignty in men's salvation.

We shall show how he exercises this right in several particulars.

1. In calling one people or nation, and giving them the means of grace, and leaving others without them. According to the divine appointment, salvation is bestowed in connexion with the means of grace. God may sometimes make use of very unlikely means, and bestow salvation on men who are under very great disadvantages; but he does not bestow grace wholly without any means. But God exercises his sovereignty in bestowing those means. All mankind are by nature in like circumstances towards God. Yet God greatly distinguishes some from others by the means and advantages which he bestows upon them. The savages, who live in the remote parts of this continent, and are under the grossest heathenish darkness, as well as the inhabitants of Africa, are naturally in exactly similar circumstances towards God with us in this land. They are no more alienated or estranged from God in their natures than we; and God has no more to charge them with. And yet what a vast difference has God made between us and them! In this he has exercised his sovereignty. He did this of old, when he chose but one people, to make them his covenant people, and to give them the means of grace, and left all others, and gave them over to heathenish darkness and the tyranny of the devil, to perish from generation to generation for many hundreds of

years. The earth in that time was peopled with many great and mighty nations. There were the Egyptians, a people famed for their wisdom. There were also the Assyrians and Chaldeans, who were great, and wise, and powerful nations. There were the Persians, who by their strength and policy subdued a great part of the world. There were the renowned nations of the Greeks and Romans, who were famed over the whole world for their excellent civil governments, for their wisdom and skill in the arts of peace and war, and who by their military prowess in their turns subdued and reigned over the world. Those were rejected. God did not choose them for his people, but left them for many ages under gross heathenish darkness, to perish for lack of vision; and chose one only people, the posterity of Jacob, to be his own people, and to give them the means of grace. Psal. 147:19,20. "He showeth his word unto Jacob, his statutes and his judgments unto Israel. He hath not dealt so with any nation; and as for his judgments, they have not known them." This nation were a small, inconsiderable people in comparison with many other people. Deut. 7:7. "The Lord did not set his love upon you, nor choose you, because ye were more in number than any people; for ye were the fewest of all people." So neither was it for their righteousness; for they had no more of that than other people. Deut. 9:6. "Understand therefore, that the Lord thy God giveth thee not this good land to possess it for thy righteousness; for thou art a stiff-necked people." God gives them to understand, that it was from no other cause but his free electing love, that he chose them to be his people. That reason is given why God loved them; it was because he loved them. Deut. 7:8. Which is as much as to say, it was agreeable to his sovereign pleasure, to set his love upon you.

God also showed his sovereignty in choosing that people, when other nations were rejected, who came of the same progenitors. Thus the children of Isaac were chosen, when the posterity of Ishmael and other sons of Abraham were rejected. So the children of Jacob were chosen, when the posterity of Esau were rejected: as the apostle observes in the seventh verse, "Neither because they are the seed of Abraham, are they all children; but in Isaac shall thy seed be called:" and again in verses 10, 11, 12, 13. "And not only this; but when Rebekah also had conceived by one, even by our father Isaac; the children moreover being not yet born, neither having done any good or evil, that the promise of God according to election might stand, not of works, but of him that calleth; it was said unto her, The elder shall serve the younger. As it is written, Jacob have I loved, but Esau have I hated." The apostle has not respect merely to the election of the persons of Isaac and Jacob before Ishmael and Esau; but of their posterity. In the passage, already quoted from Malachi, God has respect to the nations, which were the posterity of Esau and Jacob; Mal. 1:2,3. "I have loved you, saith the Lord. Yet ye say, Wherein hast thou loved us? Was not Esau Jacob's brother? saith the Lord: yet I loved Jacob; and I hated Esau, and laid his mountains and his heritage waste for the dragons of the wilderness." God showed his sovereignty, when Christ came, in rejecting the Jews, and calling the Gentiles. God rejected that nation who were the children of Abraham according to the flesh, and had been his peculiar people for so many ages, and who alone possessed the one true God, and chose idolatrous heathen before them, and called them to be his people. When the Messiah came, who was born of their nation, and whom they so much expected, he rejected them. He came to his own, and his own received him not. John 1:11. When the glorious dispensation of the gospel came, God passed by the Jews, and called those who had been heathens, to enjoy the privileges of it. They were broken off, that the Gentiles might be grafted on. Rom. 11:17. She is now called beloved, that was not beloved. And more are the children of the desolate, than the children of the married wife. Isa. 54:1. The natural children of Abraham are rejected, and God raises up children to Abraham of stones. That nation, which was so honoured of God, has now been for many ages rejected, and remain dispersed all over the world, a remarkable monument of divine vengeance. And now God greatly distinguishes some Gentile nations from others, and all according to his sovereign pleasure.

2. God exercises his sovereignty in the advantages he bestows upon particular persons. All need salvation alike, and all are, naturally, alike undeserving of it; but he gives some vastly greater advantages for salvation than others. To some he assigns their place in pious and religious families, where they may be well instructed and educated, and have religious parents to dedicate them to God, and put up many prayers for them. God places some under a more powerful ministry than others, and in places where there are more of the outpourings of the Spirit of God. To some he gives much more of the strivings and the awakening influences of the Spirit, than to others. It is according to his mere sovereign pleasure.

3. God exercises his sovereignty in sometimes bestowing salvation upon the low and mean, and denying it to the wise and great. Christ in

his sovereignty passes by the gates of princes and nobles, and enters some cottage and dwells there, and has communion with its obscure inhabitants. God in his sovereignty withheld salvation from the rich man, who fared sumptuously every day, and bestowed it on poor Lazarus, who sat begging at his gate. God in this way pours contempt on princes, and on all their glittering splendour. So God sometimes passes by wise men, men of great understanding, learned and great scholars, and bestows salvation on others of weak understanding, who only comprehend some of the plainer parts of Scripture, and the fundamental principles of the christian religion. Yea, there seem to be fewer great men called, than others. And God in ordering it thus manifests his sovereignty. 1 Cor. 1:26,27,28. "For ye see your calling, brethren, how that not many wise men after the flesh, not many mighty, not many noble, are called. But God hath chosen the foolish things of the world to confound the wise; and God hath chosen the weak things of the world to confound the things which are mighty; and base things of the world, and things which are despised, hath God chosen, yea, and things which are not, to bring to nought things that are."

4. In bestowing salvation on some who have had few advantages. God sometimes will bless weak means for producing astonishing effects, when more excellent means are not succeeded. God sometimes will withhold salvation from those who are the children of very pious parents, and bestow it on others, who have been brought up in wicked families. Thus we read of a good Abijah in the family of Jeroboam, and of a godly Hezekiah, the son of wicked Ahaz, and of a godly Josiah, the son of a wicked Amon. But on the contrary, of a wicked Amnon and Absalom, the sons of holy David, and that vile Manasseh, the son a good Hezekiah. Sometimes some, who have had eminent means of grace, are rejected, and left to perish, and others, under far less advantages, are saved. Thus the scribes and Pharisees, who had so much light and knowledge of the Scriptures, were mostly rejected, and the poor ignorant publicans saved. The greater part of those, among whom Christ was much conversant, and who heard him preach, and saw him work miracles from day to day, were left; and the woman of Samaria was taken, and many other Samaritans at the same time, who only heard Christ preach, as he occasionally passed through their city. So the woman of Canaan was taken, who was not of the country of the Jews, and but once saw Jesus Christ. So the Jews, who had seen and heard Christ, and saw his miracles, and with whom the apostles laboured so much, were not saved.

But the Gentiles, many of them, who, as it were, but transiently heard the glad tidings of salvation, embraced them, and were converted.

5. God exercises his sovereignty in calling some to salvation, who have been very heinously wicked, and leaving others, who have been moral and religious persons. The Pharisees were a very strict sect among the Jews. Their religion was extraordinary. Luke 18:11. They were not as other men, extortioners, unjust, or adulterers. There was their morality. They fasted twice a week, and gave tithes of all that they possessed. There was their religion. But yet they were mostly rejected, and the publicans, and harlots, and openly vicious sort of people, entered into the kingdom of God before them. Matt. 21:31. The apostle describes his righteousness while a Pharisee. Philip. 3:6. "Touching the righteousness which is of the law, blameless." The rich young man, who came kneeling to Christ, saying, Good Master, what shall I do, that I may have eternal life, was a moral person. When Christ bade him keep the commandments, he said, and in his own view with sincerity, "All these have I kept from my youth up." He had obviously been brought up in a good family, and was a youth of such amiable manners and correct deportment, that it is said, "Jesus beholding him, loved him." Still he was left; while the thief, that was crucified with Christ, was chosen and called, even on the cross. God sometimes shows his sovereignty by showing mercy to the chief of sinners, on those who have been murderers, and profaners, and blasphemers. And even when they are old, some are called at the eleventh hour. God sometimes shows the sovereignty of his grace by showing mercy to some, who have spent most of their lives in the service of Satan, and have little left to spend in the service of God.

6. In saving some of those who seek salvation, and not others. Some who seek salvation, as we know both from Scripture and observation, are soon converted; while others seek a long time, and do not obtain at last. God helps some over the mountains and difficulties which are in the way; he subdues Satan, and delivers them from his temptations: but others are ruined by the temptations with which they meet. Some are never thoroughly awakened; while to others God is pleased to give thorough convictions. Some are left to backsliding hearts; others God causes to hold out to the end. Some are brought off from a confidence in their own righteousness; others never get over that obstruction in their way, as long as they live. And some are converted and saved, who never had so great strivings as some who, notwithstanding, perish.

53

IV. I come now to give the reasons, why God does thus exercise his sovereignty in the eternal salvation of the children of men.

1. It is agreeable to God's design in the creation of the universe to exercise every attribute, and thus to manifest the glory of each of them. God's design in the creation was to glorify himself, or to make a discovery of the essential glory of his nature. It was fit that infinite glory should shine forth; and it was God's original design to make a manifestation of his glory, as it is. Not that it was his design to manifest all his glory to the apprehension of creatures; for it is impossible that the minds of creatures should comprehend it. But it was his design to make a true manifestation of his glory, such as should represent every attribute. If God glorified one attribute, and not another, such manifestation of his glory would be defective; and the representation would not be complete. If all God's attributes are not manifested, the glory of none of them is manifested as it is: for the divine attributes reflect glory on one another. Thus if God's wisdom be manifested, and not his holiness, the glory of his wisdom would not be manifested as it is; for one part of the glory of the attribute of divine wisdom is, that it is a holy wisdom. So if his holiness were manifested, and not his wisdom, the glory of his holiness would not be manifested as it is; for one thing which belongs to the glory of God's holiness is, that it is a wise holiness. So it is with respect to the attributes of mercy and justice. The glory of God's mercy does not appear as it is, unless it is manifested as a just mercy, or as a mercy consistent with justice. And so with respect to God's sovereignty, it reflects glory on all his other attributes. It is part of the glory of God's mercy, that it is sovereign mercy. So all the attributes of God reflect glory on one another. The glory of one attribute cannot be manifested, as it is, without the manifestation of another. One attribute is defective without another, and therefore the manifestation will be defective. Hence it was the will of God to manifest all his attributes. The declarative glory of God in Scripture is often called God's name, because it declares his nature. But if his name does not signify his nature as it is, or does not declare any attribute, it is not a true name. The sovereignty of God is one of his attributes, and a part of his glory. The glory of God eminently appears in his absolute sovereignty over all creatures, great and small. If the glory of a prince be his power and dominion, then the glory of God is his absolute sovereignty. Herein appear God's infinite greatness and highness above all creatures. Therefore it is the will of God to manifest his sovereignty. And his sovereignty, like his other attributes, is mani-

fested in the exercises of it. He glorifies his power in the exercise of power. He glorifies his mercy in the exercise of mercy. So he glorifies his sovereignty in the exercise of sovereignty.

2. The more excellent the creature is over whom God is sovereign, and the greater the matter in which he so appears, the more glorious is his sovereignty. The sovereignty of God in his being sovereign over men, is more glorious than in his being sovereign over the inferior creatures. And his sovereignty over angels is yet more glorious than his sovereignty over men. For the nobler the creature is, still the greater and higher doth God appear in his sovereignty over it. It is a greater honour to a man to have dominion over men, than over beasts; and a still greater honour to have dominion over princes, nobles, and kings, than over ordinary men. So the glory of God's sovereignty appears in that he is sovereign over the souls of men, who are so noble and excellent creatures. God therefore will exercise his sovereignty over them. And the further the dominion of any one extends over another, the greater will be the honour. If a man has dominion over another only in some instances, he is not therein so much exalted, as in having absolute dominion over his life, and fortune, and all he has. So God's sovereignty over men appears glorious, that it extends to every thing which concerns them. He may dispose of them with respect to all that concerns them, according to his own pleasure. His sovereignty appears glorious, that it reaches their most important affairs, even the eternal state and condition of the souls of men. Herein it appears that the sovereignty of God is without bounds or limits, in that it reaches to an affair of such infinite importance. God, therefore, as it is his design to manifest his own glory, will and does exercise his sovereignty towards men, over their souls and bodies, even in this most important matter of their eternal salvation. He has mercy on whom he will have mercy, and whom he will he hardens.

APPLICATION

1. Hence we learn how absolutely we are dependent on God in this great matter of the eternal salvation of our souls. We are dependent not only on his wisdom to contrive a way to accomplish it, and on his power to bring it to pass, but we are dependent on his mere will and pleasure in the affair. We depend on the sovereign will of God for every thing belonging to it, from the foundation to the top-stone. It was of the

sovereign pleasure of God, that he contrived a way to save any of mankind, and gave us Jesus Christ, his only-begotten Son, to be our Redeemer. Why did he look on us, and send us a Saviour, and not the fallen angels? It was from the sovereign pleasure of God. It was of his sovereign pleasure what means to appoint. His giving us the Bible, and the ordinances of religion, is of his sovereign grace. His giving those means to us rather than to others, his giving the awakening influences of his Spirit, and his bestowing saving grace, are all of his sovereign pleasure. When he says, "Let there be light in the soul of such an one," it is a word of infinite power and sovereign grace.

2. Let us with the greatest humility adore the awful and absolute sovereignty of God. As we have just shown, it is an eminent attribute of the Divine Being, that he is sovereign over such excellent beings as the souls of men, and that in every respect, even in that of their eternal salvation. The infinite greatness of God, and his exaltation above us, appears in nothing more, than in his sovereignty. It is spoken of in Scripture as a great part of his glory. Deut. 32:39. "See now that I, even I, am he, and there is no God with me. I kill, and I make alive; I wound, and I heal; neither is there any that can deliver out of my hand." Psal. 115:3. "Our God is in the heavens; he hath done whatsoever he pleased." Daniel 4:34,35. "Whose dominion is an everlasting dominion, and his kingdom is from generation to generation. And all the inhabitants of the earth are reputed as nothing; and he doeth according to his will in the armies of heaven, and among the inhabitants of the earth; and none can stay his hand, or say unto him, What doest thou?" Our Lord Jesus Christ praised and glorified the Father for the exercise of his sovereignty in the salvation of men. Matt. 11:25,26. "I thank thee, O Father, Lord of heaven and earth, because thou hast hid these things from the wise and prudent, and hast revealed them unto babes. Even so, Father, for so it seemed good in thy sight." Let us therefore give God the glory of his sovereignty, as adoring him, whose sovereign will orders all things, beholding ourselves as nothing in comparison with him. Dominion and sovereignty require humble reverence and honour in the subject. The absolute, universal, and unlimited sovereignty of God requires, that we should adore him with all possible humility and reverence. It is impossible that we should go to excess in lowliness and reverence of that Being, who may dispose of us to all eternity, as he pleases.

3. Those who are in a state of salvation are to attribute it to sovereign grace alone, and to give all the praise to him, who maketh them to differ

from others. Godliness is no cause for glorying, except it be in God. 1 Cor. 1:29,30,31. "That no flesh should glory in his presence. But of him are ye in Christ Jesus, who of God is made unto us wisdom, and righteousness, and sanctification, and redemption. That, according as it is written, He that glorieth, let him glory in the Lord." Such are not, by any means, in any degree to attribute their godliness, their safe and happy state and condition, to any natural difference between them and other men, or to any strength or righteousness of their own. They have no reason to exalt themselves in the least degree; but God is the being whom they should exalt. They should exalt God the Father, who chose them in Christ, who set his love upon them, and gave them salvation, before they were born, and even before the world was. If they inquire, why God set his love on them, and chose them rather than others, if they think they can see any cause out of God, they are greatly mistaken. They should exalt God the Son, who bore their names on his heart, when he came into the world, and hung on the cross, and in whom alone they have righteousness and strength. They should exalt God the Holy Ghost, who of sovereign grace has called them out of darkness into marvellous light; who has by his own immediate and free operation, led them into an understanding of the evil and danger of sin, and brought them off from their own righteousness, and opened their eyes to discover the glory of God, and the wonderful riches of God in Jesus Christ, and has sanctified them, and made them new creatures. When they hear of the wickedness of others, or look upon vicious persons, they should think how wicked they once were, and how much they provoked God, and how they deserved for ever to be left by him to perish in sin, and that it is only sovereign grace which has made the difference. 1 Cor. 6:10. Many sorts of sinners are there enumerated; fornicators, idolaters, adulterers, effeminate, abusers of themselves with mankind. And then in the eleventh verse, the apostle tells them, "Such were some of you; but ye are washed, but ye are sanctified, but ye are justified, in the name of the Lord Jesus, and by the Spirit of our God." The people of God have the greater cause of thankfulness, more reason to love God, who hath bestowed such great and unspeakable mercy upon them of his mere sovereign pleasure.

4. Hence we learn what cause we have to admire the grace of God, that he should condescend to become bound to us by covenant; that he, who is naturally supreme in his dominion over us, who is our absolute proprietor, and may do with us as he pleases, and is under no obligation

to us; that he should, as it were, relinquish his absolute freedom, and should cease to be merely sovereign in his dispensations towards believers, when once they have believed in Christ, and should, for their more abundant consolation, become bound. So that they can challenge salvation of this Sovereign; they can demand it through Christ, as a debt. And it would be prejudicial to the glory of God's attributes, to deny it to them; it would be contrary to his justice and faithfulness. What wonderful condescension is it in such a Being, thus to become bound to us, worms of the dust, for our consolation! He bound himself by his word, his promise. But he was not satisfied with that; but that we might have stronger consolation still, he hath bound himself by his oath. Heb. 6:13, etc. "For when God made promise to Abraham, because he could swear by no greater, he sware by himself; saying, Surely blessing I will bless thee, and multiplying I will multiply thee. And so, after he had patiently endured, he obtained the promise. For men verily swear by the greater; and an oath for confirmation is to them an end of all strife. Wherein God, willing more abundantly to show unto the heirs of promise the immutability of his counsel, confirmed it by an oath; that by two immutable things, in which it was impossible for God to lie, we might have a strong consolation, who have fled for refuge to lay hold upon the hope set before us. Which hope we have as an anchor of the soul, both sure and stedfast, and which entereth into that within the veil; whither the forerunner is for us entered, even Jesus, made an high priest for ever after the order of Melchisedec."

Let us, therefore, labour to submit to the sovereignty of God. God insists, that his sovereignty be acknowledged by us, and that even in this great matter, a matter which so nearly and infinitely concerns us, as our own eternal salvation. This is the stumbling-block on which thousands fall and perish; and if we go on contending with God about his sovereignty, it will be our eternal ruin. It is absolutely necessary that we should submit to God, as our absolute sovereign, and the sovereign over our souls; as one who may have mercy on whom he will have mercy, and harden whom he will.

5. And lastly. We may make use of this doctrine to guard those who seek salvation from two opposite extremes—presumption and discouragement. Do not presume upon the mercy of God, and so encourage yourself in sin. Many hear that God's mercy is infinite, and therefore think, that if they delay seeking salvation for the present, and seek it hereafter, that God will bestow his grace upon them. But consider, that

though God's grace is sufficient, yet he is sovereign, and will use his own pleasure whether he will save you or not. If you put off salvation till hereafter, salvation will not be in your power. It will be as a sovereign God pleases, whether you shall obtain it or not. Seeing, therefore, that in this affair you are so absolutely dependent on God, it is best to follow his direction in seeking it, which is to hear his voice to-day: "To-day if ye will hear his voice, harden not your heart." Beware also of discouragement. Take heed of despairing thoughts, because you are a great sinner, because you have persevered so long in sin, have backslidden, and resisted the Holy Ghost. Remember that, let your case be what it may, and you ever so great a sinner, if you have not committed the sin against the Holy Ghost, God can bestow mercy upon you without the least prejudice to the honour of his holiness, which you have offended, or to the honour of his majesty, which you have insulted, or of his justice, which you have made your enemy, or of his truth, or of any of his attributes. Let you be what sinner you may, God can, if he pleases, greatly glorify himself in your salvation.

AN ESSAY
ON THE
TRINITY

An Essay on the Trinity

I t is common when speaking of the Divine happiness to say that God is infinitely happy in the enjoyment of Himself, in perfectly beholding and infinitely loving, and rejoicing in, His own essence and perfection, and accordingly it must be supposed that God perpetually and eternally has a most perfect idea of Himself, as it were an exact image and representation of Himself ever before Him and in actual view, and from hence arises a most pure and perfect act or energy in the Godhead, which is the Divine love, complacence and joy. The knowledge or view which God has of Himself must necessarily be conceived to be something distinct from His mere direct existence. There must be something that answers to our reflection. The reflection as we reflect on our own minds carries something of imperfection in it. However, if God beholds Himself so as thence to have delight and joy in Himself He must become his own object. There must be a duplicity. There is God and the idea of God, if it be proper to call a conception of that that is purely spiritual an idea.

If a man could have an absolutely perfect idea of all that passed in his mind, all the series of ideas and exercises in every respect perfect as to order, degree, circumstance and for any particular space of time past, suppose the last hour, he would really to all intents and purpose be over again what he was that last hour. And if it were possible for a man by reflection perfectly to contemplate all that is in his own mind in an hour, as it is and at the same time that it is there in its first and direct existence; if a man, that is, had a perfect reflex or contemplative idea of every thought at the same moment or moments that that thought was and of every exercise at and during the same time that that exercise was, and so through a whole hour, a man would really be two during that time, he would be indeed double, he would be twice at once. The idea he has of himself would be himself again.

Note, by having a reflex or contemplative idea of what passes in our own minds I don't mean consciousness only. There is a great difference between a man's having a view of himself, reflex or contemplative idea of himself so as to delight in his own beauty or excellency, and a mere direct consciousness. Or if we mean by consciousness of what is in our own minds anything besides the mere simple existence in our minds of what is there, it is nothing but a power by reflection to view or contemplate what passes.

Therefore as God with perfect clearness, fullness and strength, understands Himself, views His own essence (in which there is no distinction of substance and act but which is wholly substance and wholly act), that idea which God hath of Himself is absolutely Himself. This representation of the Divine nature and essence is the Divine nature and essence again: so that by God's thinking of the Deity must certainly be generated. Hereby there is another person begotten, there is another Infinite Eternal Almighty and most holy and the same God, the very same Divine nature.

And this Person is the second person in the Trinity, the Only Begotten and dearly Beloved Son of God; He is the eternal, necessary, perfect, substantial and personal idea which God hath of Himself; and that it is so seems to me to be abundantly confirmed by the Word of God.

Nothing can more agree with the account the Scripture gives us of the Son of God, His being in the form of God and His express and perfect image and representation: (II Cor. 4:4) "Lest the light of the glorious Gospel of Christ Who is the image of God should shine unto them." (Phil. 2:6) "Who being in the form of God." (Col. 1:15) "Who is the image of the invisible God." (Heb. 1:3) "Who being the brightness of His glory and the express image of His person."

Christ is called the face of God (Exod. 33:14): the word [A.V. presence] in the original signifies face, looks, form or appearance. Now what can be so properly and fitly called so with respect to God as God's own perfect idea of Himself whereby He has every moment a view of His own essence: this idea is that "face of God" which God sees as a man sees his own face in a looking glass. 'Tis of such form or appearance whereby God eternally appears to Himself. The root that the original word comes from signifies to look upon or behold: now what is that which God looks upon or beholds in so eminent a manner as He doth on His own idea or that perfect image of Himself which He has in view. This is what is eminently in God's presence and is therefore called the angel of God's presence or face (Isa. 63:9). But that the Son of God is God's own eternal and perfect idea is a thing we have yet much more expressly revealed in God's Word. First, in that Christ is called "the wisdom of God." If we are taught in the Scripture that Christ is the same with God's wisdom or knowledge, then it teaches us that He is the same with God's perfect and eternal idea. They are the same as we have already observed and I suppose none will deny. But Christ is said to be the wisdom of God (I Cor. 1:24, Luke 11:49, compare with Matt. 23:34); and how much doth Christ speak in Proverbs under the name of Wisdom especially in the 8th chapter.

The Godhead being thus begotten by God's loving an idea of Himself and shewing forth in a distinct subsistence or person in that idea, there proceeds a most pure act, and an infinitely holy and sacred energy arises between the Father and Son in mutually loving and delighting in each other, for their love and joy is mutual, (Prov. 8:30) "I was daily His delight rejoicing always before Him." This is the eternal and most perfect and essential act of the Divine nature, wherein the Godhead acts to an infinite degree and in the most perfect manner possible. The Deity becomes all act, the Divine essence itself flows out and is as it were breathed forth in love and joy. So that the Godhead therein stands forth in yet another manner of subsistence, and there proceeds the third Person in the Trinity, the Holy Spirit, viz., the Deity in act, for there is no other act but the act of the will.

We may learn by the Word of God that the Godhead or the Divine nature and essence does subsist in love. (I John 4:8) "He that loveth not knoweth not God; for God is love." In the context of which place I think it is plainly intimated to us that the Holy Spirit is that Love, as in the 12th and 13th verses. "If we love one another, God dwelleth in us, and His love is perfected in us; hereby know we that we dwell in Him . . . because He hath given us of His Spirit." 'Tis the same argument in both verses. In the 12th verse the apostle argues that if we have love dwelling in us we have God dwelling in us, and in the 13th verse He clears the force of the argument by this that love is God's Spirit. Seeing we have God's Spirit dwelling in us, we have God dwelling in [in us], supposing it as a thing granted and allowed that God's Spirit is God. 'Tis evident also by this that God's dwelling in us and His love or the love that He hath exerciseth, being in us, are the same thing. The same is intimated in the same manner in the last verse of the foregoing chapter. The apostle was, in the foregoing verses, speaking of love as a sure sign of sincerity and our acceptance with God, beginning with the 18th verse, and he sums up the argument thus in the last verse, "and hereby do we know that He abideth in us by the Spirit that He hath given us."

The Scripture seems in many places to speak of love in Christians as if it were the same with the Spirit of God in them, or at least as the prime and most natural breathing and acting of the Spirit in the soul. (Phil. 2:1) "If there be therefore any consolation in Christ, any comfort of love, any fellowship of the Spirit, if any bowels of mercies, fulfil ye my joy that ye be likeminded, having the same love, being of one accord, of one mind." (II Cor. 6:6) "By kindness, by the Holy Ghost, by love unfeigned." (Romans 15:30) "Now I beseech you, brethren, for the Lord Jesus Christ's sake, and for the love of the Spirit." (Col. 1:8) "Who declared unto us your love in the Spirit." (Rom. 5:5) "Having the love of God shed abroad in our hearts by the Holy Ghost which is given to us." (Gal. 5:13–16) "Use not liberty for an occasion to the flesh, but by love serve one another. For all the law is fulfilled in one word, even in this: Thou shalt love thy neighbour as thyself. But if ye bite and devour one another, take heed that ye be not consumed one of another. This I say then, Walk in the Spirit, and ye shall not fulfill the lusts of the flesh." The Apostle argues that Christian liberty does not make way for fulfilling the lusts of the flesh in biting and devouring one another and the like, because a principle of love which was the fulfilling of the law would prevent it, and in the 16th verse he asserts the same thing in other words: "This I say then walk in the Spirit and ye shall not fulfill the lusts of the flesh."

The third and last office of the Holy Spirit is to comfort and delight the souls of God's people, and thus one of His names is the Comforter, and thus we have the phrase of "joy in the Holy Ghost." (I Thess. 1:6) "Having received the Word in much affliction with joy of the Holy Ghost." (Rom. 14:17) "The kingdom of God is . . . righteousness, and peace, and joy in the Holy Ghost." (Acts 9:31) "Walking in the fear of the Lord and in the comfort of the Holy Ghost." But how well doth this agree with the Holy Ghost being God's joy and delight, (Acts 13:52) "And the disciples were filled with joy and with the Holy Ghost"— meaning as I suppose that they were filled with spiritual joy.

This is confirmed by the symbol of the Holy Ghost, viz., a dove, which is the emblem of love or a lover, and is so used in Scripture, and especially often so in Solomon's Song, (1:15) "Behold thou art fair; my love, behold thou art fair; thou hast dove's eyes:" i.e. "Eyes of love," and again 4:1, the same words; and 5:12, "His eyes are as the eyes of doves," and 5:2, "My love, my dove," and 2:14 and 6:9; and this I believe to be the reason that the dove alone of all birds (except the sparrow in the single case of the leprosy) was appointed to be offered in sacrifice because of its innocence and because it is the emblem of love, love being the most acceptable sacrifice to God. It was under this similitude that the Holy Ghost descended from the Father on Christ at His baptism, signifying the infinite love of the Father to the Son, Who is the true David, or beloved, as we said before.

The same was signified by what was exhibited to the eye in the appearance there was of the Holy Ghost descending from the Father to the Son in the shape of a dove, as was signified by what was exhibited to the eye in the voice there was at the same time, viz., "This is My well Beloved Son in Whom I am well pleased."

(That God's love or His loving kindness is the same with the Holy Ghost seems to be plain by Psalm 36:7-9, "How excellent (or how precious as 'tis in the Hebrew) is Thy loving-kindness O God, therefore the children of men put their trust under the shadow of Thy wings, they shall be abundantly satisfied (in the Hebrew "watered") with the fatness of Thy house and Thou shalt make them to drink of the river of Thy pleasures; for with Thee is the fountain of life and in Thy light shall we see light."

Doubtless that precious loving-kindness and that fatness of God's house and river of His pleasures and the water of the fountain of life and God's light here spoken [of] are the same thing; by which we learn that the Holy anointing oil that was kept in the House of God, which was a type of the Holy Ghost, represented God's love, and that the "River of water of life" spoken of in the 22nd [chapter] of Revelation, which proceeds out of the throne of God and of the Lamb, which is the same with Ezekiel's vision of Living and life-giving water, which is here [in Ps. 36] called the "Fountain of life and river of God's pleasures," is God's loving-kindness.

But Christ Himself expressly teaches us that by spiritual fountains and rivers of water of life is meant the Holy Ghost. (John 4:14; 7:38,39). That by the river of God's pleasures here is meant the same thing with the pure river of water of life spoken of in Revelation 22:1, will be much confirmed if we compare those verses with Revelation 21:23, 24; 22:1,5. (See the notes on chapters 21, 23, 24) I think if we compare these places and weigh them we cannot doubt but that it is the same happiness that is meant in this Psalm which is spoken of there.

So this well agrees with the similitudes and metaphors that are used about the Holy Ghost in Scripture, such as water, fire, breath, wind, oil, wine, a spring, a river, a being poured out and shed forth, and a being breathed forth. Can there any spiritual thing be thought, or anything belonging to any spiritual being to which such kind of metaphors so naturally agree, as to the affection of a Spirit. The affection, love or joy, may be said to flow out as water or to be breathed forth as breath or wind. But it would [not] sound so well to say that an idea or judgment flows out or is breathed forth.

It is no way different to say of the affection that it is warm, or to compare love to fire, but it would not seem natural to say the same of perception or reason. It seems natural enough to say that the soul is poured out in affection or that love or delight are shed abroad: (Rom. 5:5) "The love of God is shed abroad in our hearts," but it suits with nothing else belonging to a spiritual being.

This is that "river of water of life" spoken of in the 22nd [chapter] of Revelation, which proceeds from the throne of the Father and the Son, for the rivers of living water or water of life are the Holy Ghost, by the same apostle's own interpretation (John 7:38, 39); and the Holy Ghost being the infinite delight and pleasure of God, the river is called the river of God's pleasures (Ps. 36:8), not God's river of pleasures, which I suppose signifies the same as the fatness of God's House, which they that trust in God shall be watered with, by which fatness of God's House I suppose is signified the same thing which oil typifies.

It is a confirmation that the Holy Ghost is God's love and delight, because the saints' communion with God consists in their partaking of the Holy Ghost. The communion of saints is twofold: 'tis their communion with God and communion with one another, (I John 1:3) "That ye also may have fellowship with us, and truly our fellowship is with the Father and with His Son, Jesus Christ." Communion is a common partaking of good, either of excellency or happiness, so that when it is said the saints have communion or fellowship with the Father and with the Son, the meaning of it is that they partake with the Father and the Son of their good, which is either their excellency and glory (II Peter 1:4), "Ye are made partakers of the Divine nature"; Heb. 12:10, "That we might be partakers of His holiness;" John 17:22, 23, "And the glory which Thou hast given Me I have given them, that they may be one, even as we are one, I in them and Thou in Me"); or of their joy and happiness: (John 17:13) "That they might have My joy fulfilled in themselves."

But the Holy Ghost being the love and joy of God is His beauty and happiness, and it is in our partaking of the same Holy Spirit that our communion with God consists: (II Cor. 13:14) "The grace of the Lord Jesus Christ, and the love of God, and the communion of the Holy Ghost, be with you all, Amen." They are not different benefits but the same that the Apostle here wisheth, viz., the Holy Ghost: in partaking of the Holy Ghost, we possess and enjoy the love and grace of the Father and the Son, for the Holy Ghost is that love and grace, and therefore I suppose it is that in that forementioned place, (I John 1:3). We are said to have fellowship with the Son and not with the Holy Ghost, because therein consists our fellowship with the Father and the Son, even in partaking with them of the Holy Ghost.

In this also eminently consists our communion with the Son that we drink into the same Spirit. This is the common excellency and joy and happiness in which they all are united; 'tis the bond of perfectness by which they are one in the Father and the Son as the Father is in the Son.

I can think of no other good account that can be given of the apostle Paul's wishing grace and peace from God the Father and the Lord Jesus Christ in the beginning of his Epistles, without ever mentioning the Holy Ghost,—as we find it thirteen times in his salutations in the beginnings of his Epistles,—but [i.e., except] that the Holy Ghost is Himself love and grace of God the Father and the Lord Jesus Christ; and in his blessing at the end of his second Epistle to the Corinthians where all three Persons are mentioned he wishes grace and love from the Son and the Father [except that] in the communion or the partaking of the Holy Ghost, the blessing is from the Father and the Son in the Holy Ghost. But the blessing from the Holy Ghost is Himself, the communication of Himself. Christ promises that He and the Father will love believers (John 14:21,23), but no mention is made of the Holy Ghost, and the love of Christ and the love of the Father are often distinctly mentioned, but never any mention of the Holy Ghost's love.

(This I suppose to be the reason why we have never any account of the Holy Ghost's loving either the Father or the Son, or of the Son's or the Father's loving the Holy Ghost, or of the Holy Ghost's loving the saints, tho these things are so often predicated of both the other Persons.)

And this I suppose to be that blessed Trinity that we read of in the Holy Scriptures. The Father is the Deity subsisting in the prime, un-originated and most absolute manner, or the Deity in its direct existence. The Son is the Deity generated by God's understanding, or having an idea of Himself and subsisting in that idea. The Holy Ghost is the Deity subsisting in act, or the Divine essence flowing out and breathed forth in God's Infinite love to and delight in Himself. And I believe the whole Divine essence does truly and distinctly subsist both in the Divine idea and Divine love, and that each of them are properly distinct Persons.

It is a maxim amongst divines that everything that is in God is God which must be understood of real attributes and not of mere modalities. If a man should tell me that the immutability of God is God, or that the omnipresence of God and authority of God is God, I should not be able to think of any rational meaning of what he said. It hardly sounds to me proper to say that God's being without change is God, or that God's being everywhere is God, or that God's having a right of government over creatures is God.

But if it be meant that the real attributes of God, viz., His understanding and love are God, then what we have said may in some measure explain how it is so, for Deity subsists in them distinctly; so they are distinct Divine Persons.

One of the principal objections that I can think of against what has been supposed is concerning the Personality of the Holy Ghost—that this scheme of things does not seem well to consist with [the fact] that a person is that which hath understanding and will. If the three in the Godhead are Persons they doubtless each of them have understanding, but this makes the understanding one distinct person and love another. How therefore can this love be said to have understanding, (Here I would observe that divines have not been wont to suppose that these three had three distinct understandings, but all one and the same understanding.)

In order to clear up this matter let it be considered that the whole Divine office is supposed truly and properly to subsist in each of these three, viz., God and His understanding and love, and that there is such a wonderful union between them that they are, after an ineffable and inconceivable manner, One in Another, so that One hath Another and they have communion in One Another and are as it were predicable One of Another; as Christ said of Himself and the Father "I am in the Father and the Father in Me," so may it be said concerning all the Persons in the Trinity, the Father is in the Son and the Son in the Father, the Holy Ghost is in the Father, and the Father in the Holy Ghost, the Holy Ghost is in the Son, and the Son in the Holy Ghost, and the Father understands because the Son Who is the Divine understanding is in Him, the Father loves because the Holy Ghost is in Him, so the Son loves because the Holy Ghost is in Him and proceeds from Him, so the Holy Ghost or the Divine essence subsisting is Divine, but understands because the Son the Divine Idea is in Him.

Understanding may be predicated of this love because it is the love of the understanding both objectively and subjectively. God loves the understanding and that understanding also flows out in love so that the Divine understanding is in the Deity subsisting in love. It is not a blind love. Even in creatures there is consciousness included in the very nature of the will or act of the soul, and tho perhaps not so that it can so properly be said that it is a seeing or undemanding will, yet it may truly and properly be said so in God by reason of God's infinitely more perfect manner of acting so that the whole Divine essence flows out and subsists in this act, and the Son is in the Holy Spirit tho it does not proceed from Him by reason (of the fact) that the understanding must be considered as prior in the order of nature to the will or love or act, both in creatures and in the Creator. The understanding is so in the Spirit that the Spirit may be said to know, as the Spirit of God is truly and perfectly said to know and to search all things, even the deep things of God.

(All the Three are Persons for they all have understanding and will. There is understanding and will in the Father, as the Son and the Holy Ghost are in Him and proceed from Him. There is understanding and will in the Son, as He is understanding and as the Holy Ghost is in Him and proceeds from Him. There is understanding and will in the Holy Ghost as He is the Divine will and as the Son is in Him.

Nor is it to be looked upon as a strange and unreasonable figment that the Persons should be said to have an understanding or love by another person's being in them, for we have Scripture ground to conclude so concerning the Father's having wisdom and understanding or reason that it is by the Son's being in Him; because we are there informed

71

that He is the wisdom and reason and truth of God, and hereby God is wise by His own wisdom being in Him. Understanding and wisdom is in the Father as the Son is in Him and proceeds from Him. Understanding is in the Holy Ghost because the Son is in Him, not as proceeding from Him but as flowing out in Him.)

But I don't pretend fully to explain how these things are and I am sensible a hundred other objections may be made and puzzling doubts and questions raised that I can't solve. I am far from pretending to explaining the Trinity so as to render it no longer a mystery. I think it to be the highest and deepest of all Divine mysteries still, notwithstanding anything that I have said or conceived about it. I don't intend to explain the Trinity. But Scripture with reason may lead to say something further of it than has been wont to be said, tho there are still left many things pertaining to it incomprehensible.

It seems to me that what I have here supposed concerning the Trinity is exceeding analogous to the Gospel scheme and agreeable to the tenor of the whole New Testament and abundantly illustrative of Gospel doctrines, as might be particularly shown, would it not exceedingly lengthen out this discourse.

I shall only now briefly observe that many things that have been wont to be said by orthodox divines about the Trinity are hereby illustrated. Hereby we see how the Father is the fountain of the Godhead, and why when He is spoken of in Scripture He is so often, without any addition or distinction, called God, which has led some to think that He only was truly and properly God. Hereby we may see why in the economy of the Persons of the Trinity the Father should sustain the dignity of the Deity, that the Father should have it as His office to uphold and maintain the rights of the Godhead and should be God not only by essence, but as it were, by His economical office.

Hereby is illustrated the doctrine of the Holy Ghost. Proceeding [from] both the Father and the Son. Hereby we see how that it is possible for the Son to be begotten by the Father and the Holy Ghost to proceed from the Father and Son, and yet that all the Persons should be Co-eternal. Hereby we may more clearly understand the equality of the Persons among themselves, and that they are every way equal in the society or family of the three.

They are equal in honor: besides the honor which is common to them all, viz., that they are all God, each has His peculiar honor in the society or family. They are equal not only in essence, but the Father's honor is that He is, as it were, the Author of perfect and Infinite wisdom. The Son's honor is that He is that perfect and Divine wisdom itself the excellency of which is that from whence arises the honor of being the author or Generator of it. The honor of the Father and the Son is that they are infinitely excellent, or that from them infinite excellency proceeds; but the honor of the Holy Ghost is equal for He is that Divine excellency and beauty itself.

'Tis the honor of the Father and the Son that they are infinitely holy and are the fountain of holiness, but the honor of the Holy Ghost is that holiness itself. The honor of the Father and the Son is [that] they are infinitely happy and are the original and fountain of happiness and the honor of the Holy Ghost is equal for He is infinite happiness and joy itself.

The honor of the Father is that He is the fountain of the Deity as He from Whom proceed both the Divine wisdom and also excellency and happiness. The honor of the Son is equal for He is Himself the Divine wisdom and is He from Whom proceeds the Divine excellency and happiness, and the honor of the Holy Ghost is equal for He is the beauty and happiness of both the other Persons.

By this also we may fully understand the equality of each Person's concern in the work of redemption, and the equality of the Redeemed's concern with them and dependence upon them, and the equality and honor and praise due to each of them. Glory belongs to the Father and the Son that they so greatly loved the world: to the Father that He so loved that He gave His Only Begotten Son: to the Son that He so loved the world as to give up Himself.

But there is equal glory due to the Holy Ghost for He is that love of the Father and the Son to the world. Just so much as the two first Persons glorify themselves by showing the astonishing greatness of their love and grace, just so much is that wonderful love and grace glorified Who is the Holy Ghost. It shows the Infinite dignity and excellency of the Father that the Son so delighted and prized His honor and glory that He stooped infinitely low rather than [that] men's salvation should be to the injury of that honor and glory.

It showed the infinite excellency and worth of the Son that the Father so delighted in Him that for His sake He was ready to quit His anger and receive into favor those that had [deserved?] infinitely ill at His Hands, and what was done shows how great the excellency and worth of the Holy Ghost Who is that delight which the Father and the Son have in each other: it shows it to be Infinite. So great as the worth of a thing delighted in is to any one, so great is the worth of that delight and joy itself which he has in it.

Our dependence is equally upon each in this office. The Father appoints and provides the Redeemer, and Himself accepts the price and grants the thing purchased; the Son is the Redeemer by offering Himself and is the price; and the Holy Ghost immediately communicates to us the thing purchased by communicating Himself, and He is the thing purchased. The sum of all that Christ purchased for men was the Holy Ghost: (Gal. 3:13,14) "He was made a curse for us . . . that we might receive the promise of the Spirit through faith."

What Christ purchased for us was that we have communion with God [which] is His good, which consists in partaking of the Holy Ghost: as we have shown, all the blessedness of the Redeemed consists in their partaking of Christ's fullness, which consists in partaking of that Spirit which is given not by measure unto him: the oil that is poured on the head of the Church runs down to the members of His body and to the skirts of His garment (Ps. 133:2). Christ purchased for us that we should have the favor of God and might enjoy His love, but this love is the Holy Ghost.

Christ purchased for us true spiritual excellency, grace and holiness, the sum of which is love to God, which is [nothing] but the indwelling of the Holy Ghost in the heart. Christ purchased for us spiritual joy and comfort, which is in a participation of God's joy and happiness, which joy and happiness is the Holy Ghost as we have shown. The Holy Ghost is the sum of all good things. Good things and the Holy Spirit are synonymous expressions in Scripture: (Matt. 7:11) "How much more shall your Heavenly Father give the Holy Spirit to them that ask Him." The sum of all spiritual good which the finite have in this world is that spring of living water within them which we read of (John 4:10), and those rivers of living water flowing out of them which we read of (John 7:38,39), which we are there told means the Holy Ghost; and the sum of all happiness in the other world is that river of water of life which proceeds out of the throne of God and the Lamb, which we read of (Rev. 22:1), which is the River of God's pleasures and is the Holy Ghost and therefore the sum of the Gospel invitation to come and take the water of life (verse 17).

The Holy Ghost is the purchased possession and inheritance of the saints, as appears because that little of it which the saints have in this world is said to be the earnest of that purchased inheritance. (Eph. 1:14) Tis an earnest of that which we are to have a fullness of hereafter. (II Cor. 1:22; 5:5) The Holy Ghost is the great subject of all Gospel promises and therefore is called the Spirit of promise. (Eph. 1:13) This is called the promise of the Father (Luke 24:49), and the like in other places. (If the Holy Ghost be a comprehension of all good things promised in the Gospel, we may easily see the force of the Apostle's arguing (Gal. 3:2), "This only would I know, Received ye the Spirit by the works of the law or by the hearing of faith?") So that it is God of Whom our good is purchased and it is God that purchases it and it is God also that is the thing purchased.

Thus all our good things are of God and through God and in God, as we read in Romans 11:36: "For of Him and through Him and to Him (or in Him as *eis* is rendered, I Cor. 8:6) are all things." "To Whom be glory forever." All our good is of God the Father, it is all through God the Son, and all is in the Holy Ghost as He is Himself all our good. God is Himself the portion and purchased inheritance of His people. Thus God is the Alpha and the Omega in this affair of redemption.

If we suppose no more than used to be supposed about the Holy Ghost, the concern of the Holy Ghost in the work of redemption is not equal with the Father's and the Son's, nor is there an equal part of the glory of this work belonging to Him: merely to apply to us or immediately to give or hand to us the blessing purchased, after it was purchased, as subservient to the other two Persons, is but a little thing [compared] to the purchasing of it by the paying an Infinite price, by Christ offering up Himself in sacrifice to procure it, and it is but a little thing to God the Father's giving His infinitely dear Son to be a sacrifice for us and upon His purchase to afford to us all the blessings of His purchased.

But according to this there is an equality. To be the love of God to the world is as much as for the Father and the Son to do so much from love to the world, and to be the thing purchased was as much as to be the price. The price and the thing bought with that price are equal. And it is as much as to afford the thing purchased, for the glory that belongs to Him that affords the thing purchased arises from the worth of that thing that He affords and therefore it is the same glory and an equal glory; the glory of the thing itself is its worth and that is also the glory of him that affords it.

There are two more eminent and remarkable images of the Trinity among the creatures. The one is in the spiritual creation, the soul of man. There is the mind, and the understanding or idea, and the spirit of the mind as it is called in Scripture, i.e., the disposition, the will or affection. The other is in the visible creation, viz., the Sun. The father is as the substance of the Sun. (By substance I don't mean in a philosophical sense, but the Sun as to its internal constitution.) The Son is as the brightness and glory of the disk of the Sun or that bright and glorious form under which it appears to our eyes. The Holy Ghost is the action of the Sun which is within the Sun in its intestine heat, and, being diffusive, enlightens, warms, enlivens and comforts the world. The Spirit as it is God's Infinite love to Himself and happiness in Himself, is as the internal heat of the Sun, but as it is that by which God communicates Himself, it is as the emanation of the sun's action, or the emitted beams of the sun.

The various sorts of rays of the sun and their beautiful colors do well represent the Spirit. They well represent the love and grace of God and were made use of for this purpose in the rainbow after the flood, and I suppose also in that rainbow that was seen round about the throne by Ezekiel (Ezek. 1:28; Rev. 4:3) and round the head of Christ by John (Rev. 10:1), or the amiable excellency of God and the various beautiful graces and virtues of the Spirit. These beautiful colors of the sunbeams we find made use of in Scripture for this purpose, viz., to represent the graces of the Spirit, as (Ps. 68:13) "Though ye have lien among the pots, yet shall be as the wings of a dove covered with silver, and her feathers with yellow gold," i.e., like the light reflected in various beautiful colors from the feathers of a dove, which colors represent the graces of the Heavenly Dove.

The same I suppose is signified by the various beautiful colors reflected from the precious stones of the breastplate, and that these spiritual ornaments of the Church are what are represented by the various colors of the foundation and gates of the new Jerusalem (Rev. 21; Isaiah 54:11, etc.) and the stones of the Temple (I Chron. 29: 2); and I believe the variety there is in the rays of the Sun and their beautiful colors was designed by the Creator for this very purpose, and indeed that the whole visible creation which is but the shadow of being is so made and ordered by God as to typify and represent spiritual things, for which I could give many reasons. (I don't propose this merely as an hypothesis but as a part of Divine truth sufficiently and fully ascertained by the revelation God has made in the Holy Scriptures.)

I am sensible what kind of objections many will be ready to make against what has been said, what difficulties will be immediately found, How can this be? And how can that be!

I am far from affording this as any explication of this mystery, that unfolds and renews the mysteriousness and incomprehensibleness of it, for I am sensible that however by what has been said some difficulties are lessened, others that are new appear, and the number of those things that appear mysterious, wonderful and incomprehensible, is increased by it. I offer it only as a farther manifestation of what of Divine truth the Word of God exhibits to the view of our minds concerning this great mystery.

I think the Word of God teaches us more things concerning it to be believed by us than have been generally believed, and that it exhibits many things concerning it exceeding [i.e., more] glorious and wonderful than have been taken notice of; yea, that it reveals or exhibits many more wonderful mysteries than those which have been taken notice of; which mysteries that have been overvalued are incomprehensible things and yet have been exhibited in the Word of God tho they are an addition to the number of mysteries that are in it. No wonder that the more things we are told concerning that which is so infinitely above our reach, the number of visible mysteries increases.

When we tell a child a little concerning God he has not an hundredth part so many mysteries in view on the nature and attributes of God and His works of creation and Providence as one that is told much concerning God in a Divinity School; and yet he knows much more about God and has a much clearer understanding of things of Divinity and is able more clearly to explicate some things that were dark and very unintelligible to him; I humbly apprehend that the things that have been observed increase the number of visible mysteries in the Godhead in no other manner than as by them we perceive that God has told us much more about it than was before generally observed.

Under the Old Testament the Church of God was not told near so much about the Trinity as they are now. But what the New Testament has revealed, tho it has more opened to our view the nature of God, yet it has increased the number of visible mysteries and they thus appear to us exceeding wonderful and incomprehensible. And so also it has come to pass in the Church being told [i.e., that the churches are told] more about the incarnation and the satisfaction of Christ and other Gospel doctrines.

It is so not only in Divine things but natural things. He that looks on a plant, or the parts of the bodies of animals, or any other works of nature, at a great distance where he has but an obscure sight of it, may see something in it wonderful and beyond his comprehension, but he that is near to it and views them narrowly indeed understands more about them, has a clearer and distinct sight of them, and yet the number of things that are wonderful and mysterious in them that appear to him are much more than before, and, if he views them with a microscope, the number of the wonders that he sees will be increased still but yet the microscope gives him more a true knowledge concerning them.

God is never said to love the Holy Ghost nor are any epithets that betoken love anywhere given to Him, tho so many are ascribed to the Son, as God's Elect, The Beloved, He in Whom God's soul delights, He in Whom He is well pleased, etc. Yea such epithets seem to be ascribed to the Son as tho He were the object of love exclusive of all other persons, as tho there were no person whatsoever to share the love of the Father with the Son. To this purpose evidently He is called God's Only Begotten Son, at the time that it is added, "In Whom He is well pleased." There is nothing in Scripture that speaks of any acceptance of the Holy Ghost or any reward or any mutual friendship between the Holy Ghost and either of the other Persons, or any command to love the Holy Ghost or to delight in or have any complacence in [the Holy Ghost], tho such commands are so frequent with respect to the other Persons.

That knowledge or understanding in God which we must conceive of as first is His knowledge of every thing possible. That love which must be this knowledge is what we must conceive of as belonging to the essence of the Godhead in its first subsistence. Then comes a reflex act of knowledge and His viewing Himself and knowing Himself and so knowing His own knowledge and so the Son is begotten. There is such a thing in God as knowledge of knowledge, an idea of an idea. Which can be nothing else than the idea or knowledge repeated.

The world was made for the Son of God especially. For God made the world for Himself from love to Himself; but God loves Himself only in a reflex act. He views Himself and so loves Himself, so He makes the world for Himself viewed and reflected on, and that is. The same with Himself repeated or begotten in His own idea, and that is His Son. When God considers of making any thing for Himself He presents Himself before Himself and views Himself as His End, and that viewing Himself is the same as reflecting on Himself or having an idea of Himself, and to make the world for the Godhead thus viewed and understood is to make the world for the Godhead begotten and that is to make the world for the Son of God.

The love of God as it flows forth as extra is wholly determined and directed by Divine wisdom, so that those only are the objects of it that Divine wisdom chooses, so that the creation of the world is to gratify Divine love as that is exercised by Divine wisdom. But Christ is Divine wisdom so that the world is made to gratify Divine love as exercised by Christ or to gratify the love that is in Christ's heart, or to provide a spouse for Christ. Those creatures which wisdom chooses for the object of Divine love as Christ's elect spouse and especially those elect creatures that wisdom chiefly pitches upon and makes the end of the rest of creatures.

A
FAREWELL
SERMON

A FAREWELL SERMON

Preached at the First Church in Northampton, Massachusetts,
after being voted out as the Pastor July 1, 1750,

As also you have acknowledged us in part, that we are your rejoicing,
even as ye also are ours in the day of the Lord Jesus.—2 Corinthians
1:14

Subject: Ministers and people that are under their care, must meet one another before Christ's tribunal at the day of judgment.

The apostle, in the preceding part of the chapter, declares what great troubles he met with in the course of his ministry. In the text, and two foregoing verses, he declares what were his comforts and supports under the troubles he met with. There are four things in particular.

1. That he had approved himself to his own conscience, verse 12, "For our rejoicing is this, the testimony of our conscience, that in simplicity and godly sincerity, not with fleshly wisdom, but by the grace of God, we have had our conversation in the world, and more abundantly to you-wards."

2. Another thing he speaks of as matter of comfort, is that as he had approved himself to his own conscience, so he had also to the con-

sciences of his hearers, the Corinthians, to whom he now wrote, and that they should approve of him at the day of judgment.

3. The hope he had of seeing the blessed fruit of his labors and sufferings in the ministry, in their happiness and glory, in that great day of accounts.

4. That in his ministry among the Corinthians, he had approved himself to his Judge, who would approve and reward his faithfulness in that day.

These three last particulars are signified in my text, and the preceding verse, and indeed all the four are implied in the text. It is implied that the Corinthians had acknowledged him as their spiritual father, and as one that had been faithful among them, and as the means of their future joy and glory at the day of judgment. It is implied that the apostle expected at that time to have a joyful meeting with them before the Judge, and with joy to behold their glory, as the fruit of his labors, and so they would be his rejoicing. It is implied also that he then expected to be approved of the great Judge, when he and they should meet together before him, and that he would then acknowledge his fidelity, and that this had been the means of their glory, and that thus he would, as it were, give them to him as his crown of rejoicing. But this the apostle could not hope for, unless he had the testimony of his own conscience in his favor. And therefore the words do imply, in the strongest manner, that he had approved himself to his own conscience.

There is one thing implied in each of these particulars, and in every part of the text, which I shall make the subject of my present discourse, viz.

DOCTRINE

Ministers, and the people that have been under their care, must meet one another before Christ's tribunal at the day of judgment.

Ministers, and the people that have been under their care, must be parted in this world, how wellsoever they have been united. If they are not separated before, they must be parted by death, and they may be separated while life is continued. We live in a world of change, where nothing is certain or stable, and where a little time, a few revolutions of the sun, brings to pass strange things, surprising alterations, in particular persons in families, in towns and churches, in countries and nations. It often happens, that those who seem most united, in a little time are most disunited, and at the greatest distance. Thus ministers and people, between whom there has been the greatest mutual regard and strictest union, may not only differ in their judgments, and be alienated in affection, but one may rend from the other, and all relation between them be dissolved. The minister may be removed to a distant place, and they may never have any more to do one with another in this world. But if it be so, there is one meeting more that they must have, and that is in the last great day of accounts. Here I would show,

I. In what manner ministers, and the people which have been under their care, shall meet one another at the day of judgment.

II. For what purposes.

III. For what reasons God has so ordered it, that ministers and their people shall then meet together in such a manner, and for such purposes.

I. I would show, in some particulars, in what manner ministers and the people which have been under their care, shall meet one another at the day of judgment.

First, they shall not meet at the day merely as all the world must then meet together. I would observe a difference in two things.

1. As to a clear actual view, and distinct knowledge and notice, of each other.

Although the whole world will be then present, all mankind of all generations gathered in one vast assembly, with all of the angelic nature, both elect and fallen angels, yet we need not suppose that everyone will have a distinct and particular knowledge of each individual of the whole assembled multitude, which will undoubtedly consist of many millions of millions. Though it is probable that men's capacities will be much greater than in their present state, yet they will not be infinite. Though their understanding and comprehension will be vastly extended, yet men will not be deified. There will probably be a very enlarged view that particular persons will have of the various parts and members of that vast assembly, and so of the proceedings of that great day. But yet it must needs be, that according to the nature of finite minds, some persons and some things, at that day, shall fall more under the notice of particular persons than others. This (as we may well suppose) according as they shall have a nearer concern with some than others in the transactions of the day. There will be special reason why those who have had special concerns together in this world, in their state of probation, and whose mutual affairs will be then to be tried and judged, should especially be set in one another's view. Thus we may suppose, that rulers and subjects, earthly judges and those whom they have judged, neighbors who have had mutual converse, dealings, and contests, heads of families and their children and servants, shall then meet, and in a peculiar distinction be set together. And especially will it be thus with ministers and their people. It is evident by the text, that these shall be in each other's view, shall distinctly know each other, and shall have particular notice one of another at that time.

2. They shall meet together, as having special concern one with another in the great transactions of that day.

Although they shall meet the whole world at that time, yet they will not have any immediate and particular concern with all. Yea, the far greater part of those who shall then be gathered together, will be such as they have had no intercourse with in their state of probation, and so will have no mutual concerns to be judged of. But as to ministers and the people that have been under their care, they will be such as have had much immediate concern one with another, in matters of the greatest moment. Therefore they especially must meet, and be brought together before the Judge, as having special concern one with another in the design and business of that great day of accounts.—Thus their meeting, as to the manner of it, will be diverse from the meeting of mankind in general.

Second, their meeting at the day of judgment will be very diverse from their meetings one with another in this world.

Ministers and their people, while their relation continues, often meet together in this world. They are wont to meet from sabbath to sabbath, and at other times, for the public worship of God, and administration of ordinances, and the solemn services of God's house. And besides these meetings, they have also occasions to meet for the determining and managing their ecclesiastical affairs, for the exercise of church discipline, and the settling and adjusting those things which concern the purity and good order of public administrations. But their meeting at the day of judgment will be exceeding diverse, in its manner and circumstances, from any meetings and interviews they have one with another in the present state. I would observe how, in a few particulars.

1. Now they meet together in a preparatory mutable state, but then in an unchangeable state.

Now sinners in the congregation meet their minister in a state wherein they are capable of a saving change, capable of being turned, through God's blessing on the ministrations and labors of their pastor, from the power of Satan unto God; and being brought out of a state of guilt, condemnation, and wrath, to a state of peace and favor with God, to the enjoyment of the privileges of his children, and a title to their eternal inheritance. And saints now meet their minister with great remains of corruption, and sometimes under great spiritual difficulties and affliction: and therefore are yet the proper subjects of means for a happy alteration of their state, which they have reason to hope for in the attendance on ordinances, and of which God is pleased commonly to make his ministers the instruments. Ministers and their people now meet in order to the bringing to pass such happy changes: they are the great benefits sought in their solemn meetings.

But when they shall meet together at the day of judgment, it will be far otherwise. They will all meet in an unchangeable state. Sinners will be in an unchangeable state. They who then shall be under the guilt and power of sin, and have the wrath of God abiding on them, shall be beyond all remedy or possibility of change, and shall meet their ministers without any hopes of relief or remedy, or getting any good by their means. And as for the saints, they will be already perfectly delivered from all their corruption, temptation, and calamities of every kind, and set forever out of their reach; and no deliverance, no happy alteration, will remain to be accomplished in the use of means of grace, under the administrations of ministers. It will then be pronounced, "He that is unjust, let him be unjust still; and he that is filthy, let him be filthy still; and he that is righteous, let him be righteous still; and he that is holy, let him be holy still."

2. Then they shall meet together in a state of clear, certain, and infallible light.

Ministers are set as guides and teachers, and are represented in Scripture as lights set up in the churches, and in the present state meet their people, from time to time, in order to instruct and enlighten them, to correct their mistakes, and to be a voice behind them, when they turn aside to the right hand or the left, saying, "This is the way, walk ye in it;" to evince and confirm the truth by exhibiting the proper evidences of it. They are to refute errors and corrupt opinions, to convince the erroneous, and establish the doubting. But when Christ shall come to judgment, every error and false opinion shall be detected. All deceit and delusion shall vanish away before the light of that day, as the darkness of the night vanishes at the appearance of the rising sun. Every doctrine of the Word of God shall then appear in full evidence, and none shall remain unconvinced. All shall know the truth with the greatest certainty, and there shall be no mistakes to rectify.

Now ministers and their people may disagree in their judgments concerning some matters of religion, and may sometimes meet to confer together concerning those things wherein they differ, and to hear the reasons that may be offered on one side and the other; and all may be ineffectual as to any conviction of the truth. They may meet and part again, no more agreed than before, and that side which was in the wrong may remain so still. Sometimes the meetings of ministers with their people, in such a case of disagreeing sentiments, are attended with unhappy debate and controversy, managed with much prejudice and want of candor; not tending to light and conviction, but rather to confirm and increase darkness, and establish opposition to the truth, and alienation of affection one from another. But when they shall meet together at the day of judgment, before the tribunal of the great Judge, the mind and will of Christ will be made known, and there shall no longer be any debate or difference of opinions. The evidence of the truth shall appear beyond all dispute, and all controversies shall be finally and forever decided.

Now ministers meet their people in order to enlighten and awaken the consciences of sinners: setting before them the great evil and danger of sin, the strictness of God's law, their own wickedness of heart and practice, the great guilt they are under, the wrath that abides upon them, and their impotence, blindness, poverty, and helpless and undone condition. But all is often in vain. They remain still, notwithstanding all their ministers can say, stupid and unawakened, and their consciences unconvinced. But it will not be so at their last meeting at the day of judgment. Sinners, when they shall meet their minister before their great Judge, will not meet him with a stupid conscience. They will then be fully convinced of the truth of those things which they formerly heard from him, concerning the greatness and terrible majesty of God, his holiness and hatred of sin, his awful justice in punishing it, the strictness of his law and the dreadfulness and truth of his threatenings, and their own unspeakable guilt and misery. And they shall never more be insensible of these things. The eyes of conscience will now be fully enlightened, and never shall be blinded again. The mouth of conscience shall now be opened, and never shall be shut any more.

Now ministers meet with their people, in public and private, in order to enlighten them concerning the state of their souls; to open and apply the rules of God's Word to them, in order to their searching their own hearts, and discerning their state. But now ministers have no infallible discernment of the state of their people; and the most skillful of them are liable to mistakes, and often are mistaken in things of this nature. Nor are the people able certainly to know the state of their minister, or one another's state: very often those pass among them for saints, and it may be eminent saints, that are grand hypocrites. And on the other hand, those are sometimes censured, or hardly received into their charity, that are indeed some of God's jewels. And nothing is more common than for men to be mistaken concerning their own state. Many that are abominable to God, and the children of his wrath, think highly of themselves, as his precious saints and dear children. Yea, there is reason to think that often some that are most bold in their confidence of their safe and happy state, and think themselves not only true saints, but the most eminent saints in the congregation, are in a peculiar manner a smoke in God's nostrils. And thus it undoubtedly often is in those congregations where the Word of God is most faithfully dispensed, notwithstanding all that ministers can say in their clearest explications, and most searching applications of the doctrines and rules of God's Word to the souls of their hearers. But in the day of judgment they shall have another sort of meeting. Then the secrets of every heart shall be made manifest, and every man's state shall be perfectly known. 1 Cor. 4:5, "Therefore judge nothing before the time, until the Lord come, who both will bring to light the hidden things of darkness, and will make manifest the counsels of the hearts: and then shall every man have praise of God." Then none shall be deceived concerning his own state, nor shall be any more in doubt about it. There shall be an eternal end to all the self-conceit and vain hopes of deluded hypocrites, and all the doubts and fears of sincere Christians. And then shall all know the state of one another's souls. The people shall know whether their minister has been sincere and faithful, and the minister shall know the state of every one of their people, and to who the word and ordinances of God have been a savor of life unto life, and to whom a savor of death unto death.

Now in this present state it often happens that when ministers and people meet together to debate and manage their ecclesiastical affairs, especially in a state of controversy, they are ready to judge and censure with regard to each other's views, designs, and the principles and ends by which each is influenced, and are greatly mistaken in their judgment and wrong one another in their censures. But at that future meeting, things will be set in a true and perfect light, and the principles and aims that everyone has acted from, shall be certainly known. There will be an end to all errors of this kind, and all unrighteous censures.

3. In this world, ministers and their people often meet together to hear of and wait upon an unseen Lord. But at the judgment, they shall meet in his most immediate and visible presence.

Ministers, who now often meet their people to preach to them the King eternal, immortal, and invisible, to convince them that there is a God and declare to them what manner of being he is, and to convince them that he governs and will judge the world, and that there is a future state of rewards and punishments, and to preach to them a Christ in heaven, at the right hand of God, in an unseen world—shall then meet their people in the most immediate sensible presence of this great God, Savior, and Judge, appearing in the most plain, visible, and open manner, with great glory, with all his holy angels, before them and the whole world. They shall not meet them to hear about an absent Christ, an unseen Lord, and future Judge; but to appear before that Judge—being set together in the presence of that supreme Lord—in his immense glory and awful majesty, of whom they have heard so often in their meetings together on earth.

4. The meeting at the last day, of ministers and the people that have been under their care, will not be attended by anyone with a careless, heedless heart.

With such a heart are their meetings often attended in this world by many persons, having little regard to him whom they pretend unitedly to adore in the solemn duties of his public worship, taking little heed to their own thoughts or frame of their minds, not attending to the business they are engaged in, or considering the end for which they are come together. But at that great day there will not be one careless heart: no sleeping, no wandering of mind from the great concern of the meeting, no inattentiveness to the business of the day, no regardlessness of the presence they are in or of those great things which they shall hear from Christ, or that they formerly heard from him, and of him, by their ministers in their state of trial, or which they shall now hear their ministers declaring concerning them before their Judge.

Having observed these things, concerning the manner and circumstances of this future meeting, before the tribunal of Christ at the day of judgment, I now proceed,

II. To observe to what purposes they shall then meet.

First, to give an account, before the great Judge, of their behavior one to another, in the relation they bore to each other in this world.

Ministers are sent forth by Christ to their people on his business. They are his servants and messengers; and, when they have finished their service, they must return to their master to give him an account of what they have done, and of the entertainment they have had in performing their ministry. Thus we find, in Luke 14:16–21, that when the servant who was sent forth to call the guests to the great supper, had finished his appointed service, he returned to his master, and gave him an account of what he had done, and of the entertainment he had received. And when the master, being angry, sent his servant to others, he returns again and gives his master an account of his conduct and success. So we read, in Heb. 13:17, of ministers or rulers in the house of God, that "they watch for souls, as those that must give account." And we see by the forementioned Luke 14 that ministers must give an account to their master, not only of their own behavior in the discharge of their office, but also of their people's reception of them, and of the treatment they have met with among them.

Faithful ministers will then give an account with joy, concerning those who have received them well, and made a good improvement of their ministry; and these will be given them, at that day, as their crown of rejoicing. And, at the same time, they will give an account of the ill treatment of such as have not well received them and their messages from Christ. They will meet these, not as they used to do in this world, to counsel and warn them, but to bear witness against them, as their judges and assessors with Christ, to condemn them. And, on the other hand, the people will at that day rise up in judgment against wicked and unfaithful ministers, who have sought their own temporal interest more than the good of the souls of their flock.

Second, at that time ministers, and the people who have been under their care, shall meet together before Christ, that he may judge between them, as to any controversies which have subsisted between them in this world.

It often comes to pass in this evil world, that great differences and controversies arise between ministers and the people under their pastoral care. Though they are under the greatest obligations to live in peace, above persons in almost any relation whatever, and although contests and dissensions between persons so related are the most unhappy and terrible in their consequences on many accounts of any sort of contentions, yet how frequent have such contentions been! Sometimes a people contest with their ministers about their doctrine, sometimes about their administrations and conduct, and sometimes about their maintenance. Sometimes such contests continue a long time, and sometimes they are decided in this world, according to the prevailing interest of one party or the other, rather than by the Word of God, and the reason of things. And sometimes such controversies never have any proper determination in this world.

But at the day of judgment there will be a full, perfect, and everlasting decision of them. The infallible Judge, the infinite fountain of light, truth, and justice, will judge between the contending parties, and will declare what is the truth, who is in the right, and what is agreeable to his mind and will. And in order hereto, the parties must stand together before him at the last day, which will be the great day of finishing and determining all controversies, rectifying all mistakes, and abolishing all unrighteous judgments, errors, and confusions, which have before subsisted in the world of mankind.

Third, ministers, and the people that have been under their care, must meet together at that time to receive an eternal sentence and retribution from the Judge, in the presence of each other, according to their behavior in the relation they stood in one to another in the present state.

The Judge will not only declare justice, but he will do justice between ministers and their people. He will declare what is right between them, approving him that has been just and faithful, and condemning the unjust. Perfect truth and equity shall take place in the sentence which he passes, in the rewards he bestows, and the punishments which he inflicts. There shall be a glorious reward to faithful ministers, to those who have been successful. Dan. 12:3, "And they that be wise shall shine as the brightness of the firmament, and they that turn many to righteousness, as the stars for ever and ever:" and also to those who have been faithful, and yet not successful, Isa. 49:4, "Then I said, I have laboured in vain, I have spent my strength for nought; yet surely my judgment is with the Lord, and my reward with my God." And those who have well received and entertained them shall be gloriously rewarded, Mat. 10:40, 41, "He that receiveth you, receiveth me; and he that receiveth me, receiveth him that sent me. He that receiveth a prophet in the name of a prophet, shall receive a prophet's reward, and he that receiveth a righteous man, in the name of a righteous man, shall receive a righteous man's reward." Such people, and their faithful ministers, shall be each other's crown of rejoicing, 1 Thes. 2:19, 20, "For what is our hope, or joy, or crown of rejoicing? Are not even ye in the presence of our Lord Jesus Christ at his coming? For ye are our glory and joy." And in the text, "We are your rejoicing, as ye also are ours, in the day of the Lord Jesus." But they that evil entreat Christ's faithful ministers, especially in that wherein they are faithful, shall be severely punished; Mat. 10:14, 15, "And whosoever shall not receive you, nor hear your words, when ye depart out of that house or city, shake off the dust of your feet. Verily I say unto you, it shall be more tolerable for the sinners of Sodom and Gomorrah, in the day of judgment, than for that city." Deu. 33:8–11, "And of Levi he said, Let thy Thummin and thy Urim be with thy holy one. They shall teach Jacob thy judgments, and Israel thy law. Bless, Lord, his substance, and accept the work of his hands; smite through the loins of them that rise against him, and of them that hate him, that they rise not again." On the other hand, those ministers who are found to have been unfaithful, shall have a most terrible punishment. See Eze. 33:6; Mat. 23:1–33.

Thus justice shall be administered at the great day to ministers and their people: and to that end they shall meet together, that they may not only receive justice to themselves, but see justice done to the other party. For this is the end of that great day, to reveal or declare the righteous judgment of God; Rom. 2:5. Ministers shall have justice done them, and they shall see justice done to their people. And the people shall receive justice themselves from their Judge, and shall see justice done to their minister. And so all things will be adjusted and settled forever between them: everyone being sentenced and recompensed according to his works, either in receiving and wearing a crown of eternal joy and glory, or in suffering everlasting shame and pain.—I come now to the next thing proposed, viz.

III. To give some reasons why we may suppose God has so ordered it, that ministers, and the people that have been under their care, shall meet together at the day of judgment, in such a manner and for such purposes.

There are two things which I would now observe.

First, the mutual concerns of ministers and their people are of the greatest importance.

The Scripture declares that God will bring every work into judgment, with every secret thing, whether it be good or whether it be evil. It is fit that all the concerns and all the behavior of mankind, both public and private, should be brought at last before God's tribunal, and finally determined by an infallible judge. But it is especially requisite that it should be thus, as to affairs of very great importance.

Now the mutual concerns of a Christian minister and his church and congregation, are of the vastest importance: in many respects, of much greater moment than the temporal concerns of the greatest earthly monarchs, and their kingdoms or empires. It is of vast consequence how ministers discharge their office, and conduct themselves towards their people in the work of the ministry, and in affairs appertaining to it. It is also a matter of vast importance, how a people receive and entertain a faithful minister of Christ, and what improvement they make of his ministry. These things have a more immediate and direct respect to the great and last end for which man was made, and the eternal welfare of mankind, than any of the temporal concerns of men, whether private or public. And therefore it is especially fit that these affairs should be brought into judgment, and openly determined and settled, in truth and righteousness, and that to this end, ministers and their people should meet together before the omniscient and infallible Judge.

Second, the mutual concerns of ministers and their people have a special relation to the main things appertaining to the day of judgment.

They have a special relation to that great and divine person who will then appear as Judge. Ministers are his messengers, sent forth by him, and in their office and administrations among their people, represent his person, stand in his stead, as those that are sent to declare his mind, to do his work, and to speak and act in his name. And therefore it is especially fit that they should return to him to give an account of their work and success. The king is judge of all his subjects, they are all accountable to him. But it is more especially requisite that the king's ministers, who are especially entrusted with the administrations of his kingdom, and who are sent forth on some special negotiation, should return to him, to give an account of themselves, and their discharge of their trust, and the reception they have met with.

Ministers are not only messengers of the person who at the last day will appear as Judge, but the errand they are sent upon, and the affairs they have committed to them as his ministers, most immediately concern his honor, and the interest of his kingdom. The work they are sent upon is to promote the designs of his administration and government, therefore their business with their people has a near relation to the day of judgment. For the great end of that day is completely to settle and establish the affairs of his kingdom, to adjust all things that pertain to it, that everything that is opposite to the interests of his kingdom may be removed, and that everything which contributes to the completeness and glory of it may be perfected and confirmed, that this great King may receive his due honor and glory.

Again, the mutual concerns of ministers and their people have a direct relation to the concerns of the day of judgment, as the business of ministers with their people is to promote the eternal salvation of the souls of men, and their escape from eternal damnation. The day of judgment is the day appointed for that end, openly to decide and settle men's eternal state, to fix some in a state of eternal salvation, and to bring their salvation to its utmost consummation, and to fix others in a state of everlasting damnation and most perfect misery. The mutual concerns of ministers and people have a most direct relation to the day of judgment, as the very design of the work of the ministry is the people's preparation for that day. Ministers are sent to warn them of the approach of that day, to forewarn them of the dreadful sentence then to be pronounced on the wicked, and declare to them the blessed sentence then to be pronounced on the righteous, and to use means with them that they may escape the wrath which is then to come on the ungodly, and obtain the reward then to be bestowed on the saints.

And as the mutual concerns of ministers and their people have so near and direct a relation to that day, it is especially fit that those concerns should there settled and issued, and that in order to this, ministers and their people should meet and appear together before the great Judge at that day.

APPLICATION

The improvement I would make of the subject is to lead the people here present, who have been under my pastoral care, to some reflections, and give them some advice suitable to our present circumstances, relating to what has been lately done in order to our being separated, but expecting to meet each other before the great tribunal at the day of judgment.

The deep and serious consideration of our future most solemn meeting, is certainly most suitable at such a time as this. There having so lately been that done, which, in all probability, will (as to the relation we have heretofore stood in) be followed with an everlasting separation.

How often have we met together in the house of God in this relation! How often have I spoke to you, instructed, counseled, warned, directed, and fed you, and administered ordinances among you, as the people which were committed to my care, and of whose precious souls I had the charge! But in all probability this never will be again.

The prophet Jeremiah, chap. 25:3, puts the people in mind how long he had labored among them in the work of the ministry: "From the thirteenth year of Josiah, the son of Amon, king of Judah, even unto this day (that is, the three and twentieth year), the word of the Lord came unto me, and I have spoken unto you, rising early and speaking." I am not about to compare myself with the prophet Jeremiah, but in this respect I can say as he did that "I have spoken the Word of God to you, unto the three and twentieth year, rising early and speaking." It was three and twenty years, the 15th day of last February, since I have labored in the work of the ministry, in the relation of a pastor to this church and congregation. And though my strength has been weakness, having always labored under great infirmity of body, besides my insufficiency for so great a charge in other respects, yet I have not spared my feeble strength, but have exerted it for the good of your souls. I can appeal to you, as the apostle does to his hearers, Gal. 4:13, "Ye know how through infirmity of the flesh, I preached the gospel unto you." I have spent the prime of my life and strength in labors for your eternal welfare. You are my witnesses that what strength I have had I have not neglected in idleness, nor laid out in prosecuting worldly schemes, and managing temporal affairs, for the advancement of my outward estate, and aggrandizing myself and family. But [I] have given myself to the work of the ministry, laboring in it night and day, rising early and applying myself to this great business to which Christ appointed me. I have found the work of the ministry among you to be a great work indeed, a work of exceeding care, labor and difficulty. Many have been the heavy burdens that I have borne in it, to which my strength has been very unequal. God called me to bear these burdens; and I bless his name that he has so supported me as to keep me from sinking under them, and that his power herein has been manifested in my weakness. So that although I have often been troubled on every side, yet I have not been distressed; perplexed, but not in despair; cast down, but not destroyed.—But now

I have reason to think my work is finished which I had to do as your minister: you have publicly rejected me, and my opportunities cease.

How highly therefore does it now become us to consider of that time when we must meet one another before the chief Shepherd! When I must give an account of my stewardship, of the service I have done for, and the reception and treatment I have had among the people to whom he sent me. And you must give an account of your own conduct towards me, and the improvement you have made of these three and twenty years of my ministry. For then both you and I must appear together, and we both must give an account, in order to an infallible, righteous and eternal sentence to be passed upon us, by him who will judge us with respect to all that we have said or done in our meeting here, and all our conduct one towards another in the house of God and elsewhere. [He] will try our hearts, and manifest our thoughts, and the principles and frames of our minds. He will judge us with respect to all the controversies which have subsisted between us, with the strictest impartiality, and will examine our treatment of each other in those controversies. There is nothing covered that shall not be revealed, nor hid which shall not be known. All will be examined in the searching, penetrating light of God's omniscience and glory, and by him whose eyes are as a flame of fire. Truth and right shall be made plainly to appear, being stripped of every veil. And all error, falsehood, unrighteousness, and injury shall be laid open, stripped of every disguise. Every specious pretense, every cavil, and all false reasoning shall vanish in a moment, as not being able to bear the light of that day. And then our hearts will be turned inside out, and the secrets of them will be made more plainly to appear than our outward actions do now. Then it shall appear what the ends are which we have aimed at, what have been the governing principles which we have acted from, and what have been the dispositions we have exercised in our ecclesiastical disputes and contests. Then it will appear whether I acted uprightly, and from a truly conscientious, careful regard to my duty to my great Lord and Master, in some former ecclesiastical controversies, which have been attended with exceeding unhappy circumstances and consequences. It will appear whether there was any just cause for the resentment which was manifested on those occasions. And then our late grand controversy, concerning the qualifications necessary for admission to the privileges of members, in complete standing, in the visible church of Christ, will be examined and judged in all its parts and circumstances, and the whole set forth in a clear, certain, and perfect light. Then it will appear whether the doctrine which I have preached and published concerning this matter be Christ's own doctrine, whether he will not own it as one of the precious truths which have proceeded from his own mouth, and vindicate and honor as such before the whole universe. Then it will appear what is meant by "the man that comes without the wedding garment;" for that is the day spoken of, Mat. 22:13, wherein such a one shall be "bound hand and foot, and cast into outer darkness, where shall be weeping and gnashing of teeth." And then it will appear whether, in declaring this doctrine, and acting agreeable to it, and in my general conduct in the affair, I have been influenced from any regard to my own temporal interest, or honor, or desire to appear wiser than others, or have acted from any sinister, secular views whatsoever, and whether what I have done has not been from a careful, strict, and tender regard to the will of my Lord and Master, and because I dare not offend him, being satisfied what his will was, after a long, diligent, impartial, and prayerful inquiry. Then it will be seen whether I had this constantly in view and prospect, to engage me to great solicitude not rashly to determine the question, that such a determination would not be for my temporal interest, but every way against it, bringing a long series of extreme difficulties, and plunging me into an abyss of trouble and sorrow. And then it will appear whether my people have done their duty to their pastor with respect to this matter; whether they have shown a right temper and spirit on this occasion; whether they have done me justice in hearing, attending to and considering what I had to say in evidence of what I believed and taught as part of the counsel of God; whether I have been treated with that impartiality, candor, and regard which the just Judge esteemed due; and whether, in the many steps which have been taken, and the many things that have been said and done in the course of this controversy, righteousness, and charity, and Christian decorum have been maintained; or, if otherwise, to how great a degree these things have been violated. Then every step of the conduct of each of us in this affair, from first to last, and the spirit we have exercised in all, shall be examined and manifested, and our own consciences shall speak plain and loud, and each of us shall be convinced, and the world shall know; and never shall there be any more mistake, misrepresentation, or misapprehension of the affair to eternity.

This controversy is now probably brought to an issue between you and me as to this world. It has issued in the event of the week before last, but it must have another decision at that great day, which certainly will come, when you and I shall meet together before the great judgment seat. Therefore I leave it to that time, and shall say no more about it at present.—But I would now proceed to address myself particularly to several sorts of persons.

I. To those who are professors of godliness amongst us.

I would now call you to a serious consideration of that great day wherein you must meet him who has heretofore been your pastor, before the Judge whose eyes are as a flame of fire.—I have endeavored, according to my best ability, to search the Word of God, with regard to the distinguishing notes of true piety, those by which persons might best discover their state, and most surely and clearly judge of themselves. And these rules and marks I have from time to time applied to you, in the preaching of the Word to the utmost of my skill, and in the most plain and search manner that I have been able, in order to the detecting the deceived hypocrite, and establishing the hopes and comforts of the sincere. And yet it is to be feared, that after all that I have done, I now leave some of you in a deceived, deluded state. For it is not to be supposed that among several hundred professors, none are deceived.

Henceforward I am like to have no more opportunity to take the care and charge of your souls, to examine and search them. But still I entreat you to remember and consider the rules which I have often laid down to you during my ministry, with a solemn regard to the future day when you and I must meet together before our Judge, when the uses of examination you have heard from me must be rehearsed again before you, and those rules of trial must be tried, and it will appear whether they have been good or not. It will also appear whether you have impartially heard them, and tried yourselves by them. The Judge himself, who is infallible, will try both you and me. And after this none will be deceived concerning the state of their souls.

I have often put you in mind, that whatever your pretenses to experiences, discoveries, comforts, and joys have been, at that day everyone will be judged according to his works, and then you will find it so. May you have a minister of greater knowledge of the Word of God, and better acquaintance with soul cases, and of greater skill in applying himself to souls, whose discourses may be more searching and convincing, that such of you as have held fast deceit under my preaching, may have your eyes opened by his: that you may be undeceived before that great day.

What means and helps for instruction and self-examination you may hereafter have is uncertain. But one thing is certain: that the time is short, your opportunity for rectifying mistakes in so important a concern will soon come to an end. We live in a world of great changes. There is now a great change come to pass. You have withdrawn yourselves from my ministry, under which you have continued for so many years. But the time is coming, and will soon come, when you will pass out of time into eternity, and so will pass from under all means of grace whatsoever.

The greater part of you who are professors of godliness have (to use the phrase of the apostle) "acknowledged me, in part:" you have heretofore acknowledged me to be your spiritual father, the instrument of the greatest good to you that can be obtained by any of the children of men. Consider of that day when you and I shall meet before our Judge, when it shall be examined whether you have had from me the treatment which is due to spiritual children, and whether you have treated me as you ought to have treated a spiritual father.—As the relation of a natural parent brings great obligations on children in the sight of God, so much more, in many respects, does the relation of a spiritual father bring great obligations on such of whose conversation and eternal salvation they suppose God has made them the instruments, 1 Cor. 4:15, "For though you have ten thousand instructors in Christ, yet have ye not many fathers: for in Christ Jesus, I have begotten you through the gospel."

II. Now I am taking my leave of this people I would apply myself to such among them as I leave in a Christless, graceless condition, and would call on such seriously to consider of that solemn day when they and I must meet before the Judge of the world.

My parting with you is, in some respects, in a peculiar manner a melancholy parting, inasmuch as I leave you in most melancholy circumstances, because I leave you in the gall of bitterness and bond of iniquity, having the wrath of God abiding on you, and remaining under condemnation to everlasting misery and destruction. Seeing I must leave you, it would have been a comfortable and happy circumstance of our parting, if I had left you in Christ, safe and blessed in that sure refuge and glorious rest of the saints. But it is otherwise. I leave you far off, aliens and strangers, wretched subjects and captives of sin and Satan, and prisoners of vindictive justice: without Christ, and without God in the world.

Your consciences bear me witness that while I had opportunity, I have not ceased to warn you, and set before you your danger. I have studied to represent the misery and necessity of your circumstances in the clearest manner possible. I have tried all ways that I could think of tending to awaken your consciences, and make you sensible of the necessity of your improving your time, and being speedy in flying from the wrath to come, and thorough in the use of means for your escape and safety. I have diligently endeavored to find out and use the most powerful motives to persuade you to take care for your own welfare and salvation. I have not only endeavored to awaken you, that you might be moved with fear, but I have used my utmost endeavors to win you: I have sought out acceptable words, that if possible I might prevail upon you to forsake sin, and turn to God, and accept of Christ as your Savior and Lord. I have spent my strength very much in these things. But yet, with regard to you whom I am addressing, I have not been successful, but have this day reason to complain in those words, Jer. 6:29: "The bellows are burnt, the lead is consumed of the fire, the founder melteth in vain, for the wicked are not plucked away." It is to be feared that all my labors, as to many of you, have served no other purpose but to harden you, and that the word which I have preached, instead of being a savor of life unto life, has been a savor of death unto death. Though I shall not have any account to give for the future of such as have openly and resolutely renounced my ministry, as of a trust committed to me, yet remember you must give account for yourselves, of your care of your own souls, and your improvement of all means past and future, through your whole lives. God only knows what will become of your poor perishing souls, what means you may hereafter enjoy, or what disadvantages and temptations you may be under. May God in his mercy grant that however all past means have been unsuccessful, you may have future means which may have a new effect, and that the Word of God, as it shall be hereafter dispensed to you, may prove as the fire and the hammer that breaketh the rock in pieces. However, let me now at parting exhort and beseech you not wholly to forget the warnings you have had while under my ministry. When you and I shall meet at the day of judgment, then you will remember them. The sight of me, your former minister, on that occasion, will soon revive them in your memory; and that in a very affecting manner. O do not let that be the first time that they are so revived.

You and I are now parting one from another as to this world. Let us labor that we may not be parted after our meeting at the last day. If I have been your faithful pastor (which will that day appear whether I have or no), then I shall be acquitted, and shall ascend with Christ. O do your part that in such a case, you may not be forced eternally to part from me, and all that have been faithful in Christ Jesus. This is a sorrowful parting, but that would be a more sorrowful.—This you may perhaps bear without being much affected with it, if you are not glad of it, but such a parting in that day will most deeply, sensibly, and dreadfully affect you.

III. I would address myself to those who are under some awakenings.

Blessed be God that there are some such, and that (although I have reason to fear I leave multitudes in this large congregation in a Christless state) yet I do not leave them all in total stupidity and carelessness about their souls. Some of you that I have reason to hope are under some awakenings, have acquainted me with your circumstances, which has a tendency to cause me, now I am leaving you, to take my leave with peculiar concern for you. What will be the issue of your present exercise of mind, I know not, but it will be known at that day, when you and I shall meet before the judgment seat of Christ. Therefore now be much in consideration of that day.

Now I am parting with this flock, I would once more press upon you the counsels I have heretofore given, to take heed of slighting so great a concern, to be thorough and in good earnest in the affair, and to beware of backsliding, to hold on and hold out to the end. And cry mightily to God, that these great changes which pass over this church and congregation do not prove your overthrow. There is great temptation in them, and the devil will undoubtedly seek to make his advantage of them, if possible to cause your present convictions and endeavors to be abortive. You had need to double your diligence, and watch and pray, lest you be overcome by temptation.

Whoever may hereafter stand related to you as your spiritual guide, my desire and prayer is that the great Shepherd of the sheep would have a special respect to you, and be your guide (for there is none teacheth like him), and that he who is the infinite fountain of light, would "open your eyes, and turn you from darkness unto light, and from the power of Satan unto God; that you may receive forgiveness of sins, and inheritance among them that are sanctified, through faith that is in Christ;" that so in that great day, when I shall meet you again before your Judge and mine, we may meet in joyful and glorious circumstances, never to be separated any more.

IV. I would apply myself to the young people of the congregation.

Since I have been settled in the work of the ministry in this place, I have ever had a peculiar concern for the souls of the young people, and a desire that religion might flourish among them; and have especially exerted myself in order to it. Because I knew the special opportunity they had beyond others, and that ordinarily those for whom God intended mercy, were brought to fear and love him in their youth. And it has ever appeared to me a peculiarly amiable thing, to see young people walking in the ways of virtue and Christian piety, having their hearts purified and sweetened with a principle of divine love. How exceeding beautiful, and conducive to the adorning and happiness of the town, if the young people could be persuaded, when they meet together, to converse as Christians and as the children of God, avoiding impurity, levity and extravagance, keeping strictly to rules of virtue and conversing together of the things of God, and Christ, and heaven! This is what I have longed for, and it has been exceeding grievous to me when I have heard of vice, vanity and disorder among our youth. And so far as I know my own heart, it was from hence that I formerly led this church to some measures, for the suppressing vice among our young people, which gave so great offense, and by which I became so obnoxious. I have sought the good, and not the hurt of our young people. I have desired their truest honor and happiness, and not their reproach: knowing that true virtue and religion tended not only to the glory and felicity of young people in another world, but their greatest peace and prosperity, and highest dignity and honor in this world, and above all things to sweeten, and render pleasant and delightful, even the days of youth.

But whether I have loved you, and sought your good more or less, now committing your souls to him who once committed the pastoral care of them to me—nothing remains, but only (as I am now taking my leave of you) earnestly to beseech you, from love to yourselves, if you have none to me, not to despise and forget the warnings and counsels I have so often given you. Remember the day when you and I must meet again before the great Judge of quick and dead, when it will appear whether the things I have taught you were true, whether the counsels I have given you were good, and whether I truly sought your welfare, and whether you have well improved my endeavors.

I have, from time to time, earnestly warned you against frolicking (as it is called), and some other liberties commonly taken by young people in the land. And whatever some may say in justification of such liberties and customs, and may laugh at warnings against them, I now leave you my parting testimony against such things, not doubting but God will approve and confirm it in that day when we shall meet before him.

V. I would apply myself to the children of the congregation, the lambs of this flock, who have been so long under my care.

I have just now said that I have had a peculiar concern for the young people, and in so saying I did not intend to exclude you. You are in youth, and in the most early youth. Therefore I have been sensible that if those that were young had a precious opportunity for their souls' good, you who are very young had, in many respects, a peculiarly precious opportunity. And accordingly I have not neglected you. I have endeavored to do the part of a faithful shepherd, in feeding the lambs as well as the sheep. Christ did once commit the care of your souls to me as your minister; and you know, dear children, how I have instructed you, and warned you from time to time. You know how I have often called you together for that end, and some of you, sometimes, have seemed to be affected with what I have said to you. But I am afraid it has had no saving effect as to many of you, but that you remain still in an unconverted condition, without any real saving work wrought in your souls, convincing you thoroughly of your sin and misery, causing you to see the great evil of sin, and to mourn for it, and hate it above all things, and giving you a sense of the excellency of the Lord Jesus Christ, bringing you with all your hearts to cleave to him as your Savior, weaning your hearts from the world, and causing you to love God above all, and to delight in holiness more than in all the pleasant things of this earth. And I must now leave you in a miserable condition, having no interest in Christ, and so under the awful displeasure and anger of God, and in danger of going down to the pit of eternal misery.—Now I must bid you farewell. I must leave you in the hands of God. I can do no more for you than to pray for you. Only I desire you not to forget, but often think of the counsels and warnings I have given you, and the endeavors I have used, that your souls might be saved from everlasting destruction.

Dear children, I leave you in an evil world, that is full of snares and temptations. God only knows what will become of you. This the Scripture has told us that there are but few saved, and we have abundant confirmation of it from what we see. This we see, that children die as well as others. Multitudes die before they grow up, and of those that grow up, comparatively few ever give good evidence of saving conversion to God. I pray God to pity you, and take care of you, and provide for you the best means for the good of your souls, and that God himself would undertake for you to be your heavenly Father, and the mighty Redeemer of your immortal souls. Do not neglect to pray for yourselves. Take heed you be not of the number of those who cast off fear, and restrain prayer before God. Constantly pray to God in secret, and often remember that great day when you must appear before the judgment seat of Christ, and meet your minister there, who has so often counseled and warned you.

FREEDOM
OF THE WILL

the will, is that power, or principle of mind, by which it is capable of choosing: an act of the will is the same as an act of choosing or choice.

If any think it is a more perfect definition of the will, to say, that it is that by which the soul either chooses or refuses, I am content with it; though I think it enough to say, it is that by which the soul chooses: for in every act of will whatsoever, the mind chooses one thing rather than another; it chooses something rather than the contrary or rather than the want or non-existence of that thing. So in every act of refusal, the mind chooses the absence of the thing refused; the positive and the negative are set before the mind for its choice, and it chooses the negative; and the mind's making its choice in that case is properly the act of the Will: the Will's determining between the two, is a voluntary determination; but that is the same thing as making a choice. So that by whatever names we call the act of the Will, choosing, refusing, approving, disapproving, liking, disliking, embracing, rejecting, determining, directing, commanding, forbidding, inclining, or being averse, being pleased or displeased with; all may be reduced to this of choosing. For the soul to act voluntarily, is evermore to act electively. Mr. Locke (1) says, " The Will signifies nothing but a power or ability to prefer or choose." And, in the foregoing page, he says, "The word preferring seems best to express the act of volition;" but adds, that "it does it not precisely; for, though a man would prefer flying to walking, yet who can say he ever wills it?" But the instance he mentions, does not prove that there is any thing else in willing, but merely preferring: for it should be considered what is the immediate object of the will, with respect to a man's walking, or any other external action; which is not being removed from one place to another; on the earth or through the air; these are remoter objects of preference; but such or such an immediate exertion of himself. The thing next chosen, or preferred, when a man wills to walk is not his being removed to such a place where he would be, but such an exertion and motion of his legs and feet &c, in order to it. And his willing such an alteration in his body in the present moment, is nothing else but his choosing or preferring such an alteration in his body at such a moment, or his liking it better than the forbearance of it. And God has so made and established the human nature, the soul being united to a body in proper state that the soul preferring or choosing such an immediate exertion or alteration of the body, such an alteration instantaneously follows. There is nothing else in the actions of my mind, that I am conscious of while I walk, but only my preferring or choosing, through successive moments that there should be such alterations of my external sensations and motions; together with a concurring habitual expectation that it will be so; having ever found by experience, that on such an immediate preference, such sensations and motions do actually, instantaneously, and constantly arise. But it is not so in the case of flying; though a man may be said remotely to choose or prefer flying; yet he does not prefer, or desire, under circumstances in view, any immediate exertion of the members of his body in order to it; because he has no expectation that he should obtain the desired end by any such exertion and he does not prefer, or incline to, any bodily exertion under this apprehended circumstance, of its being wholly in vain. So that if we carefully distinguish the proper objects of the several acts of the will, it will not appear by this, and such like instances, that there is any difference between volition and preference; or that a man's choosing liking best, or being pleased with a thing, are not the same with his willing that thing. Thus an act of the will is commonly expressed by its pleasing a man to do thus or thus ; and a man doing as he wills, and doing as he pleases are in common speech the same thing.

Mr. Locke (2) says, "The Will is perfectly distinguished from desire; which in the very same action may have quite contrary tendency from that which our wills sets us upon. A man, says he, whom I cannot deny, may oblige me to use persuasions to another, which, at the same time I am speaking, I may wish not prevail on him. In this case, it is plain the Will and Desire run counter." I do not suppose, that Will and Desire are words of precisely the same signification: Will seems to be a word of more general signification, extending to things present and absent. Desire respects something absent. I may prefer my present situation and posture, suppose sitting still, or having my eyes open, and so may will it. But yet I cannot think they are so entirely distinct, that they can ever be properly said to run counter. A man never, in any instance, wills any thing contrary to his desires, or desires any thing contrary to his will. The forementioned instance, which Mr. Locke produces, is no proof that ever does. He may, on some consideration or other will to utter speeches which have a tendency to persuade another and still may desire that they may not persuade him; but yet his Will and Desire do not run counter all: the thing which he wills, the very same he desires; and he does not will a thing, and desire the contrary, in any particular. In this instance, it is not carefully observed, what is the thing willed, and what is the thing desired: if it were, it would be found, that Will and Desire do not clash in the least. The thing willed on some consideration, is to utter such words; and certainly, the same consideration so influences him, that he does not desire the contrary; all things considered, he chooses to utter such words, and does not desire not to utter them. And so as to the thing which Mr. Locke speaks of as desired, viz. That the words, though they tend to persuade, should not be effectual to that end, his Will is not contrary to this; he does not will that they should be effectual, but rather wills that they should not, as he desires. In order to prove that the Will and Desire may run counter, it should be shown that they may be contrary one to the other in the same thing, or with respect to the very same object of Will or Desire: but here the objects are two; and in each, taken by themselves, the Will and Desire agree. And it is no wonder that they should not agree in different things, though but little distinguished in their nature. The Will may not agree with the Will, nor Desire agree with Desire, in different things. As in this very instance which Mr. Locke mentions, a person may, on some consideration, desire to use persuasions, and at the same time may desire they may not prevail; but yet nobody will say, that Desire runs counter to Desire; or that this proves that Desire is perfectly a distinct thing from Desire.—The like might be observed of the other instance Mr. Locke produces, of a man's desiring to be eased of pain, &c.

But, not to dwell any longer on this, whether Desire and Will, and whether Preference and Volition be precisely the same things, I trust It will he allowed by all, that in every act of Will there is an act of choice; that in every volition there is a preference, or a prevailing inclination of the soul, whereby at that instant, it is out of a state of perfect indifference, with respect to the direct object of the volition. So that in every act, or going forth of the Will; there is some preponderation of the mind, one way rather than another; and the soul had rather have or do one thing, than another, or than not to have or do that thing; and that where there is absolutely no preferring or choosing, but a perfect, continuing equilibrium, there is no volition.

PART I. SECTION II. CONCERNING THE DETERMINATION OF THE WILL.

By determining the Will, if the phrase be used with any meaning, must be intended, causing that the act of the Will or choice should be thus, and not otherwise: and the Will is said to be determined, when, in consequence of some action, or influence, its choice is directed to, and fixed upon a particular object. As when we speak of the determination of motion, we mean causing the motion of the body to be in such a direction, rather than another.

The Determination of the Will, supposes an effect, which must have a cause. If the Will be determined, there is a Determiner. This must be supposed to be intended even by them that say, The Will determines itself. If it be so, the Will is both Determiner and determined; it is a cause that acts and produces effects upon itself, and is the object of its own influence and action.

With respect to that grand inquiry, "What determines the Will?" it would be very tedious and unnecessary, at present, to examine all the various opinions, which have been advanced concerning this matter; nor is it needful that I should enter into a particular discussion of all points debated in disputes on that other question, "Whether the Will always follows the last dictate of the understanding?" It is sufficient to my present purpose to say, It is that motive, which, as it stands in view of the mind, is the strongest, that determines the will. But may be necessary that I should a little explain my meaning.

By motive I mean the whole of that which moves, excites, or invites the mind to volition, whether that be one thing singly, or many things conjunctly. Many particular things may concur, and unite their strength, to induce the mind; and when it is so, all together are as one complex motive. And when I speak of the strongest motive, I have respect to the strength of the whole that operates to induce a particular act of volition, whether that be the strength of one thing alone, or of many together.

Whatever is objectively a motive, in this sense, must, be something that is extant in the view or apprehension of the understanding, or perceiving faculty. Nothing can induce or invite the mind to will or act any thing, any further than it is perceived, or is some way or other in the mind's view; for what is wholly unperceived and perfectly out of the mind's view, cannot affect the mind at all. It is most evident, that nothing is in the mind, or reaches it, or takes any hold of it, any otherwise than as it is perceived or thought of.

And I think it must also be allowed by all, that every thing that is properly called a motive, excitement, or inducement to a perceiving, willing agent, has some sort and degree of tendency, or advantage to move or excite the Will, previous to the effect, or to the act of the will excited. This previous tendency of the motive is what I call the strength of the motive. That motive which has a less degree of previous advantage, or tendency to move the Will, or which appears less inviting, as it stands in the view of the mind, is What I call a weaker motive. On the contrary, that which appears most inviting, and has, by what appears concerning it to the understanding or apprehension, the greatest degree of previous tendency to excite and induce the choice, is what I call the strongest motive. And in this sense, I suppose the will is always determined by the strongest motive.

Things that exist in the view of the mind have their strength, tendency, or advantage to move, or excite its Will, from many things appertaining to the nature and circumstances of the thing viewed, the nature and circumstances of the mind the mind that views, and the degree and manner of its view; of which it would perhaps be hard to make a perfect enumeration. But so much I think may be determined in general, without room for controversy, that whatever is perceived or apprehended by an intelligent and voluntary agent, which has the nature and influence of a motive to volition or choice, is considered or viewed as good; nor has it any tendency to engage the election of the soul in any further degree than it appears such. For to say otherwise, would be to say, that things that appear, have a tendency, by the appearance they make, to engage the mind to elect them, some other way than by their appearing eligible to it; which is absurd. And therefore it must be true, in some sense, that the will always is, as the greatest apparent good is. But only, for the right understanding of this, two things must be well and distinctly observed.

1. It must be observed in what sense I use the term "good;" namely, as of the same import with "agreeable." To appear good to the mind, as I use the phrase, is the same as to appear agreeable, or seem pleasing to the mind. Certainly, nothing appears inviting and eligible to the mind, or tending to engage its inclination and choice, considered as evil or disagreeable; nor indeed, as indifferent, and neither agreeable nor disagreeable. But if it tends to draw the inclination, and move the Will, it must be under the notion of that which suits the mind. And therefore that must have the greatest tendency to attract and engage it, which as it stands in the mind's view, suits it best, and pleases it most; and in that sense, is the greatest apparent good: to say otherwise, is little, if any thing, short of a direct and plain contradiction.

The word "good," in this sense, includes in its signification, the removal or avoiding of evil, or of that which is disagreeable and uneasy.

It is agreeable and pleasing, to avoid what is disagreeable and displeasing, and to have uneasiness removed. So that here is included what Mr. Locke supposes determines the will. For when he speaks of "uneasiness," as determining the will, he must be understood as supposing that the end or aim which governs in the volition or act of preference, is the avoiding or the removal of that uneasiness; and that is the same thing as choosing and seeking what is more easy and agreeable.

2. When I say, that the will is as the greatest apparent good, or, (as I have explained it,) that volition has always for its object the thing which appears most agreeable; it must be carefully observed, to avoid confusion and needless objection, that I speak of the direct and immediate object of the act of volition; and not some object to which the act of will has only an indirect and remote respect. Many acts of volition have some remote relation to an object, that is different from the thing most immediately willed and chosen. Thus, when a drunkard has his liquor before him, and he has to choose whether to drink it, or no; the immediate objects, about which his present volition is conversant, and between which his choice now decides, are his own nets, in drinking the liquor, or letting it alone; and this will certainly be done according to what, in the present view of his mind, taken in the whole of it, is most agreeable to him. If he chooses to drink it, and not to let it alone, then this action, as it stands in the view of his mind, with all that belongs to its appearance there, is more agreeable and pleasing than letting it alone.

But the objects to which this act of volition may relate more remotely, and between which his choice may determine more indirectly, are the present pleasure the man expects by drinking, and the future misery which he judges will be the consequence of it: he may judge that this future misery, when it comes, will be more disagreeable and unpleasant, than refraining from drinking now would be. But these two things are not the proper objects that the act of volition spoken of is next conversant about. For the act of Will spoken of, is concerning present drinking, or forbearing to drink. If he wills to drink, then drinking is the proper object of the act of his Will; and drinking, on some account or other, now appears most agreeable to him, and suits him best. If he chooses to refrain, then refraining is immediate object of his Will, and is most pleasing to him. If in the choice he makes in the case, he prefers a present pleasure to a future advantage, which he judges will be greater when it comes; then a lesser present pleasure appears more agreeable to him than a greater advantage at a distance. If on the contrary a future advantage is preferred, then that appears most agreeable, and suits him best. And so still, the present volition is, as the greatest apparent good at present is.

I have rather chosen to express myself thus, "that the Will always is as the greatest apparent good," or "as what appears most agreeable," than to say "that the will is determined by the greatest apparent good," or " by what seems most agreeable;" because an appearing most agreeable to the mind, and the mind's preferring, seem scarcely distinct. If strict propriety of speech be insisted on, it may more properly be said, that the voluntary action, which is the immediate consequence of the mind's choice, is determined by that which appears most agreeable, than the choice itself; but that volition itself is always determined by that in or about the mind's view of the object, which causes it to appear most agreeable. I say, "in or about the mind's view of the object;" because what has influence to render an object in view agreeable, is not only what appears in the object viewed, but also the manner of the view and the state and circumstances of the mind that views. Particularly to enumerate all things pertaining to the mind's view of the objects of volition, which have influence in their appearing agreeable to the mind, would be a matter of no small difficulty, and might require a treatise by itself, and is not necessary to my present purpose. I shall therefore only mention some things in general.

I. One thing that makes an object proposed to choice agreeable, is the apparent nature and circumstances of the object. And there are various things of this sort, that have influence in rendering the object more or less agreeable; as, 1. That which appears in the object, rendering it beautiful and pleasant, or deformed and irksome to the mind; viewing it as it is in itself.

2. The apparent degree of pleasure or trouble attending the object, or the consequence of it. Such concomitants and consequences being viewed as circumstances of the object, are to be considered as belonging to it; and as it were parts of it, as it stands in the mind's view a proposed object of choice.

3. The apparent state of the pleasure or trouble that appears, with respect to distance of time; being either nearer or farther off. It is a thing in itself agreeable to the mind, to have pleasure speedily; and disagreeable, to have it delayed: so that if there be two equal degrees of pleasure set in the mind's view, and all other things are equal, but one is beheld as near, and the other afar off; the nearer will appear most

agreeable, and so will be chosen. Because, though the agreeableness of the objects be exactly equal, as viewed in themselves, yet not as viewed in their circumstances; one of them having the additional agreeableness of the circumstance of nearness.

II. Another thing that contributes to the agreeableness of an object of choice, as it stands in the mind's view, is the manner of view. If the object be something which appears connected with future pleasure, not only will the degree of apparent pleasure have influence, but also the manner of the view, especially in two respects.

1. With respect to the degree of assent, with which the mind judges the pleasure to be future. Because it is more agreeable to have a certain happiness, than an uncertain one; and a pleasure viewed as more probable, all other things being equal, is more agreeable to the mind, than that which is viewed as less probable.

2. With respect to the degree of the idea or apprehension of the future pleasure. With regard to things which are the subject of our thoughts, either past, present, or future, we have much more of an idea or apprehension of some things than others; that is, our idea is much more clear, lively, and strong. Thus the ideas we have of sensible things by immediate sensation, are usually much more lively than those we have by mere imagination, or by contemplation of them when absent. My idea of the sun when I look upon it is more vivid, than when I only think I of it. Our idea of the sweet relish of a delicious fruit is usually stronger when we taste it, than when we only imagine it. And sometimes, the idea we have of things by contemplation, are much stronger and clearer, than at other times. Thus, a man at one time has a much stronger idea of the pleasure which is to be enjoyed in eating some sort of food that he loves, than at another. Now the strength of the idea or the sense that men have of future good or evil, is one thing that has great influence on their minds to excite volition. When two kinds of future pleasure are presented for choice, though both are supposed exactly equal by the judgment, and both equal certain, yet of one the mind has a far more lively sense, than of the other; this last has the greatest advantage by far to affect and attract the mind, and move the will. It is now more agreeable to the mind, to take the pleasure of which it has a strong and lively sense, than that of which it has only a faint idea. The view of the former is attended with the strongest appetite, and the greatest uneasiness attends the want of it; and it is agreeable to the mind to have uneasiness removed, and its appetite gratified. And if several

future enjoyments are presented together, as competitors for the choice of the mind, some of them judged to be greater, and others less; the mind also having a more lively idea of the good of some, and of others a less; and some are viewed as of greater certainty or probability than others; and those enjoyments that appear most agreeable in one of these respects, appear least so in others: in this case, all other things being equal, the agreeableness of a proposed object of choice will be in a degree some way compounded of the degree of good supposed by the judgment, the degree of apparent probability or certainty of that good, and the degree of the liveliness of the idea the mind has of that good; because all together concur to constitute the degree in which the object appears at present agreeable; and accordingly will volition be determined.

I might further observe, that the the state of the mind which views a proposed object of choice, is another thing that contributes to the agreeableness or disagreeableness of that object; the particular temper which the mind has by nature, or that has been introduced and established by education, example, custom, or some other means; or the frame or state that the mind is in on a particular occasion. That object which appears agreeable to one, does not so to another. And the same object does not always appear alike agreeable to the same person, at different times. It is most agreeable to some men, to follow their reason; and to others, to follow their appetites: to some men, it is more agreeable to deny a vicious inclination, than to gratify it; others it suits best to gratify the vilest appetites. It is more disagreeable to some men than others, to counteract a former resolution. In these respects, and many others which might be mentioned, different things will be most agreeable to different persons; and not only so, but to the same persons at different times.

But possibly it is needless to mention the "state of the mind," as a ground of the agreeableness of objects distinct from the other two mentioned before; viz. The apparent nature and circumstances of the objects viewed, and the manner of the view. Perhaps, if we strictly consider the matter, the different temper and state of the mind makes no alteration as to the agreeableness of objects, any other way, than as it makes the objects themselves appear differently beautiful or deformed, having apparent pleasure or pain attending them; and, as it occasions the manner of the view to be different, causes the idea of beauty or deformity, pleasure or uneasiness, to be more or less lively. However, I think so much is certain, that volition, in no one instance that can be mentioned, is otherwise than the greatest apparent good is, in the manner which has been explained. The choice of the mind never departs from that which, at the time, and with respect to the direct and immediate objects of decision, appears most agreeable and pleasing, all things considered. If the immediate objects of the will are a man's own actions, then those actions which appear most agreeable to him he wills. If it be now most agreeable to him, all things considered, to walk, then he now wills to walk. If it be now, upon the whole of what at present appears to him, most agreeable to speak, then he chooses to speak; if it suits him best to keep silence, then he chooses to keep silence. There is scarcely a plainer and more universal dictate of the sense and experience of mankind, than that, when men act voluntarily, and do what they please, then they do what suits them best, or what is most agreeable to them. To say, that they do what pleases them, but yet not what is agreeable to them, is the same thing as to say, they do what they please, but do not act their pleasure; and that is to say, that they do what they please and yet do not what they please.

It appears from these things, that in some sense, the will always follows the last dictate of the understanding. But then the understanding must be taken in a large sense, as including the whole faculty of perception or apprehension, and not merely what is called reason or judgment. If by the dictate of the understanding is meant what reason declares to be best, or most for the person's happiness, taking in the whole of its duration, it is not true, that the Will always follows the last dictate of the understanding. Such a dictate of reason is quite a different matter from things appearing now most agreeable, all things being put together which pertain to the mind's present perceptions in any respect: although that dictate of reason, when it takes place, has concern in the compound influence which moves Will; and should be considered in estimating the degree of that appearance of good which the Will always follows; either as having its influence added to other things, or subducted from them. When such dictate of reason concurs with other things, then its weight is added to them, as put into the same scale; but when it is against them, it is as a weight in the opposite scale, resisting the influence of other things: yet its resistance is often overcome by their greater weight, and so the act of the Will is determined in opposition to it.

These things may serve, I hope, in some measure, illustrate and confirm the position laid down in the beginning of this section, viz. "That the Will is always determined by the strongest motive," or by that view the mind which has the greatest degree of previous tendency to excite volition. But whether I have been so happy as rightly to explain the thing wherein consists the strength of motives, or not, yet my failing in this will not overthrow the position itself; which carries much of its own evidence with it, and is a point of chief importance to the purpose of the ensuing discourse: And the truth of it, I hope, will appear with great clearness, before I have finished what I have to say on the subject of human liberty.

PART I. SECTION III. CONCERNING THE MEANING OF THE TERMS, NECESSITY, IMPOSSIBILITY, INABILITY, &C. AND OF CONTINGENCE

The words necessary, impossible, &c. are abundantly used in controversies about Free-Will and Moral Agency; and therefore the sense in which they are used should clearly be understood.

Here I might say, that a thing is then said to be necessary when it must be, and cannot be otherwise. But this would not properly be a definition of Necessity, any more than I explained the word must, by the phrase, there being Necessity. The words must, can, and cannot, need explication as much as the words necessary, and impossible; excepting that the former are words that in earliest life we more commonly use.

The word necessary, as used in common speech, is a relative term; and relates to some supposed opposition made to the existence of a thing, which opposition is overcome, or proves insufficient to hinder or alter it. That is necessary, in the original and proper sense of the word, which is, or will be, notwithstanding all supposable opposition. To say, that a thing is necessary, is the same thing as to say, that it is impossible that it should not be. But the word impossible is manifestly a relative term, and has reference to supposed power exerted to bring a thing to pass, which is insufficient for the effect; as the word unable is relative and has relation to ability, or endeavor, which is insufficient. Also the word irresistible is relative, and has always reference to resistance which is made, or may be made, to some force or power tending to an effect, and is insufficient to withstand the power, or hinder the effect. The common notion of Necessity and Impossibility Implies something that frustrates endeavor or desire. Here several things are to be noted.

1. Things are said to be necessary in general, which are or will be notwithstanding any supposable opposition from whatever quarter. But

things are said to be necessary to us, which are or will be notwithstanding all opposition supposable in the case from us. The same may be observed of the word impossible, and other such like terms.

2. These terms necessary, impossible, irresistible, &c. more especially belong to controversies about liberty and moral agency, as used in the latter of the two senses now mentioned, viz. as necessary or impossible to us, and with relation to any supposable opposition or endeavor of ours.

3. As the word Necessity, in its vulgar and common use, is relative, and has always reference to some supposable insufficient opposition; so when we speak of anything as necessary to us, it is with relation to some supposable opposition of our Wills, or some voluntary exertion or effort of ours to the contrary. For we do not properly make opposition to an event, any otherwise than as we voluntarily oppose it. Things are said to be what must be, or necessarily are, as to us, when they are, or will be, though we desire or endeavor the contrary, or try to prevent or remove their existence: but such opposition of ours always either consists in, or implies, opposition of our wills.

It is manifest that all such like words and phrases, as vulgarly used, are understood in this manner. A thing is said to be necessary, when we cannot help it, let us do what we will. So any thing is said to be impossible to us, when we would do it, or would have it brought to pass, and endeavor it; or at least may be supposed to desire and seek it; but all our desires and endeavors are, or would be, vain. And that is said to be irresistible, which overcomes all our opposition, resistance, and endeavor to the contrary. And we are said to be unable to do a thing when our supposable desires and endeavors are insufficient.

We are accustomed, in the common use of language, thus to apply and understand these phrases: we grow up with such a habit; which, by the daily use of these terms from our childhood, becomes fixed and settled; so that the idea of a relation to a supposed will, desire, and endeavor of ours, is strongly connected with these terms, whenever we hear the words used. Such ideas, and these words, are so associated, that they unavoidably go together, one suggests the other, and never can be easily separated as long as we live. And though we use the words, as terms of art, in another sense, get, unless we are exceedingly circumspect, we shall insensibly slide into the vulgar use of them, and so apply the words in a very inconsistent manner, which will deceive and confound us in our reasonings and discourses, even when we pretend to use them as terms of art.

4. It follows from what has been observed, that when these terms necessary, impossible, irresistible, unable, &c. are used in cases wherein no insufficient will is supposed, or can be supposed, but the very nature of the supposed case itself excludes any opposition, will, or endeavor; they are then not used in their proper signification. The reason is manifest; in such cases we cannot use the words with reference to a supposable opposition, will, or endeavor. And therefore if any man uses these terms in such cases, he either uses them nonsensically, or in some new sense, diverse from their original and proper meaning. As for instance; if any one should affirm after this manner, That it is necessary for a man, or what must be, that he should choose virtue rather than vice, during the time that he prefers virtue to vice; and that it is a thing impossible and irresistible, that it should be otherwise than that he should have this choice, so long as this choice continues; such a one would use the terms must, irresistible, &c. with either insignificance, or in some new sense, diverse from their common use; which is with reference, as has been observed, to supposable opposition, unwillingness, and resistance; whereas, here, the very supposition excludes and denies any such thing: for the case supposed is that of being willing, and choosing.

5. It appears from what has been said, that these terms necessary, impossible, &c. are often used by philosophers and metaphysicians in a sense quite diverse from their common and original signification; for they apply them to man cases in which no opposition is supposable. Thus they use them with respect to God's existence before the creation of the world, when there was no other being; with regard to many of the dispositions and acts of the divine Being, such as his loving himself, his loving righteousness, hating sin, &c. So they apply them to many cases of the inclinations and actions of created intelligent beings wherein all opposition of the Will is excluded in the very supposition of the case.

Metaphysical or philosophical Necessity is nothing different from their certainty. I speak not now of the certainty of knowledge, but the certainty that is in things themselves, which is the foundation of the certainty of the knowledge, or that wherein lies the ground of the infallibility of the proposition which affirms them.

What is sometimes given as the definition of philosophical Necessity, namely, "That by which a thing cannot but be," or "where by it cannot be otherwise," fails of being a proper explanation of it, on two accounts:

First, the words can, or cannot, need explanation as much as the word Necessity; and the former may as well be explained by the latter, as the latter by the former. Thus, if any one asked us what we mean, when we say, a thing cannot but be, we might explain ourselves by saying, it must necessarily be so; as well as explain Necessity, by saying, it is that by which a thing cannot but be. And Secondly, this definition is liable to the fore-mentioned great inconvenience; the words cannot, or unable, are properly relative, and have relation to power exerted, or that may be exerted, in order to the thing spoken of; to which as I have now observed, the word Necessity, as used by philosophers, has no reference.

Philosophical Necessity is really nothing else than the FULL AND FIXED CONNECTION BETWEEN THE THINGS SIGNIFIED BY THE SUBJECT AND PREDICATE OF A PROPOSITION, which affirms something to be true. When there is such a connection, then the thing affirmed in the proposition is necessary, in a philosophical sense; whether any opposition or contrary effort be supposed, or no. When the subject and predicate of the proposition, which affirms the existence of any thing, either substance, quality, act, or circumstance, have a full and CERTAIN CONNECTION, then the existence or being of that thing is said to be necessary in a metaphysical sense. And in this sense I use the word necessity, in the following discourse, when I endeavor to prove that necessity is not inconsistent with liberty.

The subject and predicate of a proposition, which affirms existence of something, may have a full, fixed, and certain connection several ways.

(1.) They may have a full and perfect connection in and themselves; because it may imply a contradiction, or gross absurdity, to suppose them not connected. Thus many things are necessary in their own nature. So the eternal existence of being generally considered, is necessary in itself: because it would be in itself the greatest absurdity, to deny the existence of being in general, or to say there was absolute and universal nothing; and is as it were the sum of all contradictions; as might be shown if this were a proper place for it. So God's infinity and other attributes are necessary. So it is necessary in its own nature, that two and two should be four; and it is necessary that all right lines drawn from the center of a circle to the circumference should be equal. It is necessary, fit and suitable, that men should do to others, as they would that they should do to them. So innumerable metaphysical and mathematical truths are necessary in themselves: the subject and predicate of the proposition which affirm them, are perfectly connected of themselves.

(2.) The connection of the subject and predicate of; proposition, which affirms the existence of something, may be fixed and made certain, because the existence of that thing is already come to pass; and either now is, or has been; and so has, as it were, made sure of existence. And therefore, the proposition which affirms present and past existence of it, may by this means be made certain and necessarily and unalterably true; the past event has fixed and decided the matter, as to its existence; and has made it impossible but that existence should be truly predicated of it. Thus the existence of whatever is already come to pass, is now become necessary; it is become impossible it should be otherwise than true, that such a thing has been.

(3.) The subject and predicate of a proposition which affirms something to be, may have a real and certain connection consequently; and so the existence of the thing may be consequently necessary; as it may be surely and firmly connected with something else, that is necessary in one of the former respects. As it is either fully and thoroughly connected with that which is absolutely necessary in its own nature, or with something which has already received and made sure of existence. This Necessity lies in, or may be explained by, the connection of two or more propositions one with another.—Things which are perfectly connected with other things that are necessary, are necessary themselves, by a Necessity of consequence.

And here it may be observed, that all things which are future, or which will hereafter begin to be, which can be said to be necessary, are necessary only in this last way. Their existence is not necessary in itself; for if so, the always would have existed. Nor is their existence become necessary by being already come to pass. Therefore, the only way that any thing that is to come to pass hereafter is or can be necessary, is by a connection with something that is necessary in its own nature, or something that already is, or has been; so that the one being supposed the other certainly follows.—And this also is the only way that all things past, excepting those which were from eternity, could be necessary before they come to pass; and therefore the only way in which any effect or event, or any thing whatsoever that ever has had or will have a beginning, has come into being necessarily, or will hereafter necessarily exist. And therefore this is the Necessity which especially belongs to controversies about the acts of the will.

It may be of some use in these controversies, further to observe concerning, metaphysical Necessity, that (agreeable to the distinction before observed of Necessity, as vulgarly understood) things that exist may be said to be necessary, either with a general or particular Necessity. The existence of a thing may be said to be necessary with a general Necessity, when, all things considered, there is a foundation for the certainty of their existence; or when in the most general and universal view of things, the subject and predicate of the proposition, which affirms its existence, would appear with an infallible connection.

An event, or the existence of a thing, may be said to be necessary with a particular Necessity, when nothing that can be taken into consideration, in or about a person, thing, or time, alters the case at all, as to the certainty of an event, or the existence of a thing; or can be of any account at all, in determining the infallibility of the connection of the subject and predicate in the proposition which affirms the existence of the things; so that it is all one, as to that person, or thing, at least, at that time, as if the existence were necessary with a Necessity that is most universal and absolute. Thus there are many things that happen to particular persons, in the existence of which no will of theirs has any concern, at least, at that time; which, whether they are necessary or not, with regard to things in general, yet are necessary to them, and with regard to any volition of theirs at that time; as they prevent all acts of the will about the affair.—I shall have occasion to apply this observation to particular instances in the following discourse.—Whether the same things that are necessary with a particular Necessity, be not also necessary with a general Necessity, may be a matter of future consideration. Let that be as it will, it alters not the case, as to the use of this distinction of the kinds of Necessity.

These things may be sufficient for the explaining of the terms necessary and Necessity, as terms of art, and as often used by metaphysicians, and controversial writers in divinity, in a sense diverse from, and more extensive than, their original meaning, in common language, which was before explained.

What has been said to show the meaning of the terms necessary and necessity, may be sufficient for the explaining of the opposite terms, impossible and impossibility. For there is no difference, but only the latter are negative, and the former positive. Impossibility is the same as negative necessity, or a Necessity that a thing should not be. And it is used as a term of art in a like diversity from the original and vulgar meaning, with Necessity.

The same may be observed concerning the words unable and inability. It has been observed, that these terms, in their original and common use, have relation to will and endeavor, as supposable in the case, and as insufficient for the bringing to pass the thing willed and endeavored. But as these terms are often used by philosophers and divines, especially writers on controversies about Free Will, they are used in a quite different and far more extensive sense, and are applied to many cases wherein no will or endeavor for the bringing of the thing to pass is or can be supposed.

As the words necessary, impossible, unable, &c. are used by polemic writers, in a sense diverse from their common signification, the like has happened to the term contingent. Any thing is said to be contingent, or to come to pass by chance or accident, in the original meaning of such words, when its connection with its causes or antecedents, according to the established course of things, is not discerned; and so is what we have no means of foreseeing. And especially is any thing said to be contingent, or accidental, with regard to us, when it comes to pass without our foreknowledge, and besides our design and scope.

But the word contingent is abundantly used in a very different sense; not for that whose connection with the series of things we cannot discern, so as to foresee the event, but for something which has absolutely no previous ground or reason, with which its existence has any fixed and certain connection.

PART I. SECTION IV. OF THE DISTINCTION OF NATURAL AND MORAL NECESSITY, AND INABILITY.

That Necessity which has been explained, consisting in an infallible connexion of the things signified by the subject and predicate of a proposition, as intelligent beings are the subjects of it, is distinguished into moral and natural Necessity.

I shall not now stand to inquire whether this distinction be a proper and perfect distinction; but shall only explain how these two sorts of Necessity are understood, as the terms are sometimes used, and as they are used in the following discourse.

The phrase, moral Necessity, is used variously: sometimes it is used for a Necessity of moral obligation. So we say, a man is under Necessity, when he is under bonds of duty and conscience, from which he cannot be discharged. Again, the word Necessity is often used for great obligation in point of interest. Sometimes by moral Necessity is meant that apparent connexion of things, which is the ground of moral evidence; and so is distinguished from absolute Necessity, or that sure connexion of things, that is a foundation for infallible certainty. In this sense, moral Necessity signifies much the same as that high degree of probability, which is ordinarily sufficient to satisfy mankind, in their conduct and behavior in the world, as they would consult their own safety and interest, and treat others properly as members of society. And sometimes by moral Necessity is meant that Necessity of connexion and consequence, which arises from such moral causes, as the strength of inclination, or motives, and the connexion which there is in many cases between these and such certain volitions and actions. And it is in this sense, that I use the phrase, moral necessity, in the following discourse.

By natural necessity, as applied to men, I mean such Necessity as men are under through the force of natural causes; as distinguished from what are called moral causes, such as habits and dispositions of the heart, and moral motives and inducements. Thus men, placed in certain circumstances, are the subjects of particular sensations by Necessity: they feel pain when their bodies are wounded; they see the objects presented before them in a clear light, when their eyes are opened: so they assent to the truth of certain propositions, as soon as the terms are understood; as that two and two make four, that black is not white, that two parallel lines can never cross one another; so by a natural Necessity men's bodies move downwards, when there is nothing to support them.

But here several things may be noted concerning these two kinds of Necessity.

1. Moral Necessity may be as absolute as natural Necessity. That is, the effect may be as perfectly connected with its moral cause, as a natural, necessary effect is with its natural cause. Whether the Will in every case is necessarily determined by the strongest motive, or whether the Will ever makes any resistance to such a motive, or can ever oppose the strongest present inclination, or not; if that matter should be controverted, yet I suppose none will deny, but that, in some cases, a previous bias and inclination, or the motive presented, may be so powerful, that the act of the will may be certainly and indissolubly connected therewith.

When motives or previous bias are very strong, all will allow that there is some difficulty in going against them. And if they were yet stronger, the difficulty would be still greater. And therefore, if more were still added to their strength, to a certain degree, it would make the difficulty so great, that it would be wholly impossible to surmount it; for this plain reason, because whatever power men may be supposed to have to surmount difficulties, yet that power is not infinite; and so goes not beyond certain limits. If a man can surmount ten degrees of difficulty of this kind with twenty degrees of strength, because the degrees of strength are beyond the degrees of difficulty; yet if the difficulty be increased to thirty, or an hundred, or a thousand degrees, and his strength not also increased, his strength will be wholly insufficient to surmount the difficulty. As therefore it must be allowed, that there may be such a thing as a sure and perfect connexion between moral causes and effects; so this only is what I call by the name of moral Necessity.

2. When I use this distinction of moral and natured Necessity, I would not he understood to suppose, that if any thing come to pass by the former kind of Necessity, the nature of things is not concerned in it, as well as in the latter. I do not mean to determine, that when a moral habit or motive is so strong, that the act of the Will infallibly follows, this is not owing to the nature of things. But natural and moral are the terms by which thee two kinds of Necessity have usually been called; and they must be distinguished by some names, for there is a difference between them, that is very important in its consequences. This difference, however, does not lie so much in the nature of the connexion, as in the two terms connected. The cause with which the effect is connected, is of a particular kind; viz. that which is of a moral nature; either some previous habitual disposition, or some motive exhibited to the under-standing. And the effect is also of a particular kind; being likewise of a moral nature; consisting in some inclination or volition of the soul, or voluntary action.

I suppose, that Necessity which is called natural in distinction from moral Necessity, is so called, because mere nature, as the word is vulgarly used, is concerned, without any thing of choice. The word nature is often used in opposition to choice; not because nature has indeed never any hand in our choice; but, probably, because we first get our notion of nature from that obvious course of events, which we observe in many things where our choice has no concern; and especially in the material world; which, in very many parts of it, we easily perceive to be in a settled course; the stated order, and manner of succession, being very apparent. But where we do not readily discern the rule and connexion, (though there be a connexion, according to an established law, truly taking place,) we signify the manner of event by some other name. Even in many things which are seen in the material and inanimate world, which do not obviously come to pass according to any settled course, men do not call the manner of the event by the name of nature, but by such names as accident, chance, contingence, &c. So men make a distinction between nature and choice; as if they were completely and universally distinct. Whereas, I suppose none will deny but that choice, in many cases, arises from nature, as truly as other events. But the connexion between acts of choice, and their causes, according to established laws, is not so obvious. And we observe that choice is, as it were, a new principle of motion and action, different from that established order of things which is most obvious, and seen especially in corporeal things. The choice also often interposes, interrupts, and alters the chain of events in these external objects, and causes them to proceed otherwise than they would do, if let alone. Hence it is spoken of as if it were a principle of motion entirely distinct from nature, and properly set in opposition to it. Names being commonly given to things, according to what is most obvious, and is suggested by what appears to the senses without reflection and research.

3. It must be observed, that in what has been explained, as signified by the name of moral Necessity, the word Necessity is not used according to the original design and meaning of the word: for, as was observed before, such terms, necessary, impossible, irresistible, &c. in common speech, and their most proper sense, are always relative; having reference to some supposable voluntary opposition or endeavour, that is insufficient. But no such opposition, or contrary will and endeavour, is supposable in the case of moral Necessity; which is a certainty of the inclination and will itself; which does not admit of the supposition of a will to oppose and resist it. For it is absurd, to suppose the same individual will to oppose itself, in its present act; or the present choice to be opposite to and resisting present choice: as absurd as it is to talk of two contrary motions, in the same moving body, at the same time.—And therefore the very case supposed never admits of any trial, whether an opposing or resisting will can overcome this Necessity.

What has been said of natural and moral Necessity, may serve to explain what is intended by natural and moral Inability. We are said to be naturally unable to do a thing, when we cannot do it if we will, because what is most commonly called nature does not allow of it, or because of some impeding defect or obstacle that is extrinsic to the Will; either in the Faculty of understanding, constitution of body, or external objects. Moral Inability consists not in any of these things; but either in the want of inclination; or the strength of a contrary inclination; or the want of sufficient motives in view, to induce and excite the act of the Will, or the strength of apparent motives to the contrary. Or both these may be resolved into one; and it may be said in one word, that moral Inability consists in the opposition or want of inclination. For when a person is unable to will or choose such a thing, through a defect of motives, or prevalence of contrary motives, it is the same thing as his being unable through the want of an inclination, or the prevalence of a contrary inclination, in such circumstances, and under the influence of such views.

To give some instances of this moral Inability.—A woman of great honour and chastity may have a moral Inability to prostitute herself to her slave. A child of great love and duty to his parents, may be thus unable to kill his father. A very lascivious man, in case of certain opportunities and temptations, and in the absence of such and such restraints, may be unable to forbear gratifying his lust. A drunkard, under such and such circumstances, may be unable to forbear taking strong drink. A very malicious man may be unable to exert benevolent acts to an enemy, or to desire his prosperity; yea, some may be so under the power of a vile disposition, that they may be unable to love those who are most worthy of their esteem and affection. A strong habit of virtue, and a great degree of holiness, may cause a moral Inability to love wickedness in general, and may render a man unable to take complacence in wicked persons or things; or to choose a wicked in preference to a virtuous life. And on the other hand, a great degree of habitual wickedness may lay a man under an Inability to love and choose holiness; and render him utterly unable to love an infinitely holy Being, or to choose and cleave to him as his chief good.

Here it may be of use to observe this distinction of moral Inability, viz. of that which is general and habitual, and that which is particular and occasional. By a general and habitual moral Inability, I mean an Inability in the heart to all exercises or acts of will of that kind, through a fixed and habitual inclination, or an habitual and stated defect, or want of a certain kind of inclination. Thus a very ill-natured man may be unable to exert such acts of benevolence, as another, who is full of good nature, commonly exerts; and a man whose heart is habitually void of gratitude, may be unable to exert grateful acts through that stated defect of a grateful inclination. By particular and occasional moral Inability, I mean an Inability of the will or heart to a particular act, through the strength or defect of present motives, or of inducements presented to the view of the understanding, on this occasion.—If it be so, that the Will is always determined by the strongest motive, then it must always have an Inability, in this latter sense, to act otherwise than it does; it not being possible, in any case, that the Will should, at present, go against the motive which has now, all things considered, the greatest advantage to induce it.—The former of these kinds of moral inability is most commonly called by the name of Inability; because the word, in its most proper and original signification, has respect to some stated defect. And this especially obtains the name of Inability also upon another account:— . because, as before observed, the word Inability, in its original and most common use, is a relative term; and has respect to will and endeavor, as supposable in the case, and as insufficient to bring to pass the thing desired and endeavored. Now there may be more of an appearance and shadow of this, with respect to the acts which arise from a fixed and strong habit, than others that arise only from transient occasions and causes. Indeed will and endeavour against, or diverse from present acts of the Will are in no case supposable, whether those acts be occasional or habitual; for that would be to suppose the Will, at present, to be otherwise than, at present, it is. But yet their may be will and endeavour against future acts of the Will, or volitions that are likely to take place, as viewed at a distance. It is no contradiction, to suppose that the acts of the Will at one time, may be against the acts of the Will at another time; and there may be desires and endeavors to prevent or excite future acts of the will; but such desires and endeavors are, in many cases, rendered insufficient and vain, through fixedness of habit: when the occasion returns, the strength of habit overcomes and baffles all such opposition. In this respect, a man may be in miserable slavery and bondage to a strong habit. But it may be comparatively easy to make an alteration, with respect to such future acts, as are only occasional and transient; because the occasion or transient cause, if foreseen, may often easily be prevented or avoided. On this account, the moral Inability that attends fixed habits, especially obtains the name of Inability. And then, as the will may remotely and indirectly resist itself, and do it in vain, in the case of strong habits; so reason may resist present acts of the Will, and its resistance be insufficient; and this is more commonly the case also, when the acts arise from strong habit.

But it must be observed concerning moral Inability, in each kind of it, that the word Inability is used in a sense very diverse from its original import. The word signifies only a natural Inability, in the proper use of it; and is applied to such cases only wherein a present will or inclination to the thing, with respect to which a person is said to be unable, is supposable. It cannot be truly said, according to the ordinary use of language, that a malicious man, let him be never so malicious, cannot hold his hand from striking, or that he is not able to show his neighbor kindness; or that a drunkard, let his appetite be never so strong, cannot keep the cup from his mouth. In the strictest propriety of speech, a man has a thing in his power, if he has it in his choice, or at his election: and a man cannot be truly said to be unable to do a thing, when he can do it if he will. It is improperly said, that a person cannot perform those external actions, which are dependent on the act of the Will, and which would be easily performed, if the act of the Will were present. And if it be improperly said, that he cannot perform those external voluntary actions, which depend on the Will, it is in some respect more improperly said, that he is unable to exert the acts of the Will themselves; because it is more evidently false, with respect to these, that he cannot if he will: for to say so, is a downright contradiction; it is to say, he cannot will, if he does will. And in this case, not only is it true, that it is easy for a man to do the thing if he will, but the very willing is the doing; when once he has willed, the thing is performed; and nothing else remains to be done. Therefore, in these things, to ascribe a non-performance to the want of power or ability, is not just; because the thing wanting, is not a being able, but a being willing. There are faculties of mind, and a capacity of nature, and every thing else, sufficient, but a disposition: nothing is wanting but a will.

PART I. SECTION V. CONCERNING THE NOTION OF LIBERTY, AND OF MORAL AGENCY.

The plain and obvious meaning of the words Freedom and Liberty, in common speech, is The power, opportunity, or advantage, that any one has, to do as he pleases. Or in other words, his being free from hindrance or impediment in the way of doing, or conducting in any respect, as he wills.—And the contrary to Liberty, whatever name we call that by, is a person's being hindered or unable to conduct as he will, or being necessitated to do otherwise.

If this which I have mentioned be the meaning of the word Liberty, in the ordinary use of language; as I trust that none that has ever learned to talk, and is unprejudiced, will deny; then it will follow, that in propriety of speech, neither Liberty, nor its contrary, can properly be ascribed to any being or thing, but that which has such a faculty, power or property, as is called will. For that which is possessed of no will, cannot have any power or opportunity of doing according to its will, nor be necessitated to act contrary to its will, nor be restrained from acting agreeably to it. And therefore to talk of Liberty, or the contrary, as belonging to the very Will itself, is not to speak good sense; if we judge of sense, and nonsense, by the original and proper signification of words.—For the Will itself is not an Agent that has a will: the power of choosing, itself, has not a power of choosing. That which has the power of volition is the man, or the soul, and not the power of volition itself. And he that has the Liberty of doing according to his will, is the Agent who is possessed of the Will; and not the Will which he is possessed of. We say with propriety, that a bird let loose has power and liberty to fly; but not that the bird's power of flying has a power and Liberty of flying. To be free is the property of an Agent, who is possessed of powers and faculties, as much as to be cunning, valiant, bountiful, or zealous. But these qualities are the properties of persons; and not the properties of properties.

There are two things contrary to what is called Liberty in common speech. One is constraint; otherwise called force, compulsion, and coaction; which is a person's being necessitated to do a thing contrary to his will. The other is restraint; which is, his being hindered, and not having power to do according to his will. But that which has no will, cannot be the subject of these things.—I need say the less on this head, Mr. Locke having set the same thing forth, with so great clearness, in his Essay on the Human Understanding.

But one thing more I would observe concerning what is vulgarly called Liberty; namely, that power and opportunity for one to do and conduct as he will, or according to his choice, is all that is meant by it; without taking into the meaning of the word, any thing of the cause of that choice; or at all considering how the person came to have such a volition; whether it was caused by some external motive, or internal habitual bias; whether it was determined by some internal antecedent volition, or whether it happened without a cause; whether it was necessarily connected with something foregoing, or not connected. Let the person come by his choice any how, yet, if he is able, and there is nothing in the way to hinder his pursuing and executing his will, the man is perfectly free, according to, the primary and common notion of freedom.

What has been said may be sufficient to show what is meant by Liberty, according to the common notions of mankind, and in the usual and primary acceptation of the word: but the word, as used by Arminians, Pelagians, and others, who oppose the Calvinists, has an entirely different signification.—These several things belong to their notion of Liberty. 1. That it consists in a self-determining power in the Will, or a certain sovereignty the Will has over itself, and its own acts, whereby it determines its own volitions; so as not to be dependent, in its determinations, on any cause without itself, nor determined by any thing prior to its own acts. 2. Indifference belongs to Liberty in their notion of it, or that the mind, previous to the act of volition, be in equilibria. 3. Contingence is another thing that belongs and is essential to it; not in the common acceptation of the word, as that has been already explained, but as opposed to all necessity, or any fixed and certain connexion with some previous ground or reason of its existence. They suppose the essence of Liberty so much to consist in these things, that unless the will of man be free in this sense, he has no real freedom, how much soever, he may be at Liberty to act according to his will.

A moral agent is a being that is capable of those actions that have a moral quality, and which can properly be denominated good or evil in a moral sense, virtuous or vicious, commendable or faulty. To moral Agency belongs a moral faculty, or sense of moral good and evil, or of such a thing as desert or worthiness, of praise or blame, reward or punishments; and a capacity which an Agent has of being influenced in his actions by moral inducements or motives, exhibited to the view of understanding and reason, to engage to a conduct agreeable to the moral faculty.

The sun is very excellent and beneficial in its action and influence on the earth, in warming and causing it to bring forth its fruit; but it is not a moral agent: its action, though good, is not virtuous or meritorious. Fire that breaks out in a city, and consumes great part of it, is very mischievous in its operation; but is not a moral Agent: what it does is not faulty or sinful, or deserving of any punishment. The brute creatures are not moral Agents: the actions of some of them are very profitable and pleasant; others are very hurtful: yet seeing they have no moral faculty, or sense of desert, and do not act from choice guided by understanding, or with a capacity of reasoning and reflecting, but only from instinct, and are not capable of being influenced by moral inducements, their actions are not properly sinful or virtuous, nor are they properly the subjects of any such moral treatment for what they do, as moral Agents are for their faults or good deeds.

Here it may be noted, that there is a circumstantial difference between the moral Agency of a ruler and a subject. I call it circumstantial, because it lies only in the difference of moral inducements, by which they are capable of being influenced, arising from the difference of circumstance. A ruler, acting in that capacity only, is not capable of being influenced by a moral law, and its sanctions of threatenings and promises, rewards and punishments, as the subject is; though both may be influenced by a knowledge of moral good and evil. And therefore the moral Agency of the Supreme Being, who acts only in the capacity of a ruler towards his creatures, and never as an adjunct, differs in that respect from the moral Agency of created intelligent beings. God's actions, and particularly those which he exerts as a moral governor, have moral qualifications, and are morally good in the highest degree. They are most perfectly holy and righteous; and we must conceive of Him as influenced, in the highest degree, by that which, above all others, is properly a moral inducement; viz. the moral good which He sees in such and such things: and therefore He is, in the most proper sense, a moral Agent, the source of all moral ability and Agency, the fountain and rule of all virtue and moral good; though by reason of his being supreme over all, it is not possible He should be under the influence of law or command, promises or threatenings, rewards or punishments, counsels or warnings. The essential qualities of a moral Agent are in God, in the greatest possible perfection; such as understanding to perceive the difference between moral good and evil; a capacity of discerning that moral worthiness and demerit, by which some things are praiseworthy, others deserving of blame and punishment; and also a capacity of choice, and choice guided by understanding, and a power of acting according to his choice or pleasure, and being capable of doing those things which are in the highest sense praiseworthy. And herein does very much consist that image of God wherein he made man, (which we read of, Gen. 1:26, 27, and chap. 9:6.) by which God distinguished man from the beasts, viz. in those faculties and principles of nature, whereby He is capable of moral Agency. Herein very much consists the natural image of God; whereas the spiritual and moral image, wherein man was made at first, consisted in that moral excellency with which he was endowed.

Part II. WHEREIN IT IS CONSIDERED WHETHER THERE IS OR CAN BE ANY SORT OF FREEDOM OF WILL, AS THAT WHEREIN ARMINIANS PLACE THE ESSENCE OF THE LIBERTY OF ALL MORAL AGENTS; AND WHETHER ANY SUCH THING EVER WAS OR CAN BE CONCEIVED OF.

1. Showing the manifest inconsistence of the Arminian notion of Liberty of Will, consisting in the Will's self-determining Power.

2. Several supposed ways of evading the foregoing reasoning considered.

3. Whether any event whatsoever, and Volition in particular, can come to pass without a Cause of its existence.

4. Whether Volition can arise without a Cause, through the activity of the nature of the soul.

5. Showing, that if the things asserted in these Evasions should be supposed to be true, they are altogether impertinent, and cannot help the cause of Arminian Liberty; and how, this being the state of the case, Arminian writers are obliged to talk inconsistently.

6. Concerning the Will determining in things which are perfectly indifferent in the view of the mind.

7. Concerning the Notion of Liberty of Will, consisting in Indifference.

8. Concerning the supposed Liberty of the will, as opposite to all Necessity.

9. Of the Connexion of the Acts of the Will with the Dictates of the Understanding.

10. Volition necessarily connected with the influence of Motives: with particular observations on the great inconsistence of Mr. Chubb's assertions and reasonings about the Freedom of the Will.

11. The evidence of God's certain Foreknowledge of the volitions of moral Agents.

12. God's certain foreknowledge of the future volitions of moral

agents, inconsistent with such a contingence of those volitions as is without all necessity.

13. Whether we suppose the volitions of moral Agents to be connected with any thing antecedent, or not, yet they must be necessary in such a sense as to overthrow Arminian liberty.

PART II. SECTION I. SHOWING THE MANIFEST INCONSISTENCE OF THE ARMINIAN NOTION OF LIBERTY OF WILL, CONSISTING IN THE WILL'S SELF-DETERMINING POWER.

Having taken notice of those things which may be necessary to be observed, concerning the meaning of the principal terms and phrases made use of in controversies concerning human liberty, and particularly observed what Liberty is according to the common language and general apprehension of mankind, and what it is as understood and maintained by Arminians; I proceed to consider the Arminian notion of the Freedom of the Will, and the supposed necessity of it in order to moral agency, or in order to any one's being capable of virtue or vice, and properly the subject of command or counsel, praise or blame, promises or threatenings, rewards or punishments; or whether that which has been described, as the thing meant by Liberty in common speech, be not sufficient, and the only Liberty, which make, or can make any one a moral agent, and so properly the subject of these things. In this Part, I shall consider whether any such thing be possible or conceivable, as that Freedom of Will which Arminians insist on; and shall inquire, whether any such sort of Liberty be necessary to moral agency, &c. in the next part.

And first of all, I shall consider the notion of a self-determining Power in the Will: wherein, according to the Arminians, does most essentially consist the Will's freedom; and shall particularly inquire, whether it be not plainly absurd, and a manifest inconsistence, to suppose that the Will itself determines all the free acts of the will.

Here I shall not insist on the great impropriety of such ways of speaking as the Will determining itself; because actions are to be ascribed to agents, and not properly to the powers of agents; which improper way of speaking leads to many mistakes, and much confusion, as Mr. Locke observes. But I shall suppose that the Arminians, when they speak of the Will's determining itself, do by the Will mean the soul willing. I shall take it for granted, that when they speak of the will, as the determiner, they mean the soul in the exercise of a power of willing, or acting voluntarily. I shall suppose this to be their meaning, because nothing else can be meant, without the grossest and plainest absurdity. In all cases when we speak of the powers or principles of acting, or doing such things we mean that the agents which have these Powers of acting, do them, in the exercise of those Powers. So where we say, valor fights courageously, we mean, the man who is under the influence of valor fights courageously. Where we say, love seeks the object loved, we mean, the person loving seeks that object. When we say, the understanding discerns, we mean the soul in the exercise of that faculty. So when it is said, the will decides or determines, this meaning must be, that the person, in the exercise of: Power of willing and choosing, or the soul, acting voluntarily, determines.

Therefore, if the Will determines all its own free acts the soul determines them in the exercise of a Power of willing and choosing; or, which is the same thing, it determines them of choice; it determines its own acts, by choosing its own acts. If the Will determines the Will then choice orders and determines the choice; and acts choice are subject to the decision, and follow the conduct of other acts of choice. And therefore if the Will deter mines all its own free acts, then every free act of choice is determined by a preceding act of choice, choosing that act. And if that preceding act of the will be also a free act. then by these principles, in this act too, the will is self-determined: that is, this, in like manner, is an act that the soul voluntarily chooses; or, which is the same thing, it is an act determined still by a preceding act of the will, choosing that. Which brings us directly to a contradiction: for it supposes an act of the Will preceding the first act in the whole train, dieting and determining the rest; or a free act of the Will, before the first free act of the Will. Or else we must come at last to an act of the will, determining the consequent acts, wherein the Will is not self-determined, and so is not a free act, in this notion of freedom: but if the first act in the train, determining and fixing the rest, be not free, none of them all can be free; as is manifest at first view, but shall be demonstrated presently.

If the Will, which we find governs the members of the body, and determines their motions, does also govern itself, and determines its own actions, it doubtless determines them the same way, even by antecedent volitions. The Will determines which way the hands and feet shall move, by an act of choice: and there is no other way of the Will's determining, directing, or commanding any thing at all. Whatsoever the will commands, it commands by an act of the Will. And if it has itself under its command, and determines itself in its own actions, it doubtless does it the same way that it determines other things which are under its command. So that if the freedom of the will consists in this, that it has itself and its own actions under its command and direction, and its own volitions are determined by itself, it will follow, that every free volition arises from another antecedent volition, directing and commanding that: and if that directing volition be also free, in that also the will is determined; that is to say, that directing volition is determined by another going before that; and so on, till we come to the first volition in the whole series: and if that first volition be free, and the will self-determined in it, then that is determined by another volition preceding that. Which is a contradiction; because by the supposition, it can have none before it, to direct or determine it, being the first in the train. But if that first volition is not determined by any preceding act of the Will, then that act is not determined by the Will, and so is not free in the Arminian notion of freedom, which consists in the Will's self-determination. And if that first act of the will which determines and fixes the subsequent acts, be not free, none of the following acts which are determined by it can be free.—If we suppose there are five acts in the train, the fifth and last determined by the fourth, and the fourth by the third, the third by the second, and the second by the first; if the first is not determined by the Will, and so not free, then none of them are truly determined by the Will: that is, that each of them are as they are, and not otherwise, is not first owing to the will, but to the determination of the first in the series, which is not dependent on the will, and is that which the will has no hand in determining. And this being that which decides what the rest shall be, and determines their existence; therefore the first determination of their existence is not from the Will. The case is just the same, if instead of a chain of five acts of the Will, we should suppose a succession of ten, or an hundred, or ten thousand. If the first act be not free, being determined by something out of the will, and this determines the next to be agreeable to itself, and that the next, and so on; none of them are free, but all originally depend on, and are determined by, some cause out of the Will; and so all freedom in the case is excluded, and no act of the will can be free, according to this notion of freedom. If we should suppose a long chain of ten thousand links, so connected, that if the first link moves, it will move the next, and that the next; and so the whole chain must be determined to motion, and in the direction of its motion, by the motion of the first link; and that is moved by something else; in this case, though all the links, but one, are moved by other parts of the same chain, yet it appears that the motion of no one, nor the direction of its motion, is from any self-moving or self-determining power in the chain, any more than if every link were immediately moved by something that did not belong to the chain.—If the Will be not free in the first act, which causes the next, then neither is it free in the next, which is caused by that first act; for though indeed the Will caused it, yet it did not cause it freely; because the preceding act, by which it was caused, was not free. And again, if the Will be not free in the second act, so neither can it be in the third, which is caused by that; because in like manner, that third was determined by an act of the Will that was not free. And so we may go on to the next act, and from that to the next; and how long soever the succession of acts is, it is all one: if the first on which the whole chain depends, and which determines all the rest, be not a free act, the Will is not free in causing or determining any one of those acts; because the act by which it determines them all is not a free act; and therefore the Will is no more free in determining them, than if it did not cause them at all.—Thus, this Arminian notion of Liberty of the Will, consisting in the will's Self-determination, is repugnant to itself, and shuts itself wholly out of the world.

PART II. SECTION II. SEVERAL SUPPOSED WAYS OF EVADING THE FOREGOING REASONING CONSIDERED.

Is to evade the force of what has been observed, it should be said, that when the Arminians speak of the Will determining its own acts, they do not mean that the Will determines them by any preceding act, or that one act of the will determines another; but only that the faculty or power of Will, or the soul in the use of that power, determines its own volitions; and that it does it without any act going before the act determined; such an evasion would be full of the most gross absurdity.— I confess, it is an evasion of my own inventing; and I do not know but I should wrong the Arminians, in supposing that any of them would make use of it. Bur, it being as good a one as I can invent, I would observe upon it a few things.

First, If the power of the will determines an act of volition, or the soul in the use or exercise of that power determines it, that is the same thing as for the soul to determine volition by an act of will, For an exercise of the power of will, and an art of that power, are the same thing. Therefore to say, that the power of will, or the soul in the use or exercise of that power, determines volition, without an act of will preceding the volition determined, is a contradiction.

Secondly, If a power of will determines the act of the Will, then a power of choosing determines it. For, as was before observed, in every act of will, there is choice, and a power of willing is a power of choosing. But if a power of choosing determines the act of volition, it determines it by choosing it. For it is most absurd to say, that a power of choosing determines one thing rather than another, without choosing any thing. But if a power of choosing determines volition by choosing it, then here is the act of volition determined by an antecedent choice, choosing that volition.

Thirdly, To say, that the faculty, or the soul, determines its own volition, but not by any act, is a contradiction. Because for the soul to direct, decide, or determine any thing, is to act; and this is supposed: for the soul is here spoken of as being a cause in this affair, doing something; or, which is the same thing, exerting itself in order to an effect, which effect is the determination of volition, or the particular kind and manner of an act of will. But certainly, this action is not the same with the effect, in order to the production of which it is exerted; but must be something prior to it.

The advocates for this notion of the freedom of the Will, speak of a certain sovereignty in the will, whereby it has power to determine its own volition. And therefore the determination of volition must itself be an act of the will; for otherwise it can be no exercise of that supposed power and sovereignty. Again, if the Will determines itself, then either the will is active in determining its volitions, or it is not. If active, then the determination is an act of the will; and so there is one act of the will determining another. But if the Will is not active in the determination, then how does it exercise any liberty in it? These gentlemen suppose that the thing wherein the Will exercises liberty, is in its determining its own acts. But how can this be, if it be not active in determining? Certainly the will, or the soul, cannot exercise any liberty in that wherein it doth not act, or wherein it doth not exercise itself. So that if either part of this dilemma be taken, this scheme of liberty, consisting in self-determining power, is overthrown. If there be an act of the Will in determining all its own free acts, then one free act of the Will is determined by another; and so we have the absurdity of every free act, even the very first, determined by a foregoing free act. But if there be no act or exercise of the Will in determining its own acts, then no liberty is exercised in determining them. From whence it follows, that no liberty consists in the Will's power to determine its own acts: or, which is the same thing, that there is no such thing as liberty consisting in a self-determining power of the Will.

If it should be said, That although it be true, if the soul determines its own volitions, it must be active in so doing, and the determination itself must be an act; yet there is no need of supposing this act to be prior to the volition determined; but the will or soul determines the act of the Will in willing; it determines its own volition, in the very act of volition; it directs and limits the act of the will, causing it to be so and not otherwise, in exerting the act, without any preceding act to exert that. If any should say after this manner, they must mean one of these three things: either, (1.) That the determining act, though it be before the act determined in the order of nature, yet is not before it in order of time. Or, (2.) That the determining act is not before the act determined, either in the order of time or nature, nor is truly distinct from it; but that the soul's determining the act of volition is the same thing with its exerting the act of volition: the mind's exerting such a particular act, is its causing and determining the act. Or, (3.) That volition has no cause, and is no effect; but comes into existence, with such a particular determination, without any ground or reason of its existence and determination.—I shall consider these distinctly.

(1.) If all that is meant, be, that the determining act is not before the act determined in order of time, it will not help the case at all, though it should be allowed. If it be before the determined act in the order of nature, being the cause or ground of its existence, this as much proves it to be distinct from, and independent on it, as if it were before in the order of time. As the cause of the particular motion of a natural body in a certain direction, may have no distance as to time, yet cannot be the same with the motion effected by it, but must be as distinct from it, as any other cause, that is before its effect in the order of time: as the architect is distinct from the house which he builds, or the father distinct from the son which he begets. And if the act of the Will determining be distinct from the act determined, and before it in the order of nature, then we can go back from one to another, till we come to the first in the series, which has no act of the will before it in the order of nature, determining it; and consequently is an act not determined by the will, and so not a free act, in this notion of freedom. And this being the act which determines all the rest, none of them are free acts. As when there is a chain of many links, the first of which only is taken hold of and drawn by hand; all the rest may follow and be moved at the same instant, without any distance of time; but yet the motion of one link is before that of another in the order of nature; the last is moved by the next, and that by the next, and so till we come to the first; which not being moved by any other, but by something distinct from the whole chain, this as much proves that no part is moved by any self-moving power in the chain, as if the motion of one link followed that of another in the order of time.

(2.) If any should say, that the determining act is not before the determined act, either in the order of time, or of nature, nor is distinct from it; but that the exertion of the act is the determination of the act; that for the soul to exert a particular volition, is for it to cause and determine that act of volition: I would on this observe, that the thing in question seems to be forgotten, or kept out of sight in a darkness and unintelligibleness of speech; unless such an objector would mean to contradict himself.—The very act of volition itself is doubtless a determination of mind; i.e. it is the mind's drawing up a conclusion, or coming to a choice between two or more things proposed to it. But determining among external objects of choice, is not the same with determining the act of choice itself, among various possible acts of choice.—The question is, What influences, directs, or determines the mind or Will to come to such a conclusion or choice as it does? Or what is the cause, ground, or reason, why it concludes thus, and not otherwise? Now it must be answered, according to the Arminian notion of freedom, that the Will influences, orders, and determines itself thus to act. And if it does, I say, it must be by some antecedent act. To say, it is caused, influenced, and determined by something, and yet not determined by any thing antecedent, either in order of time or nature, is a contradiction. For that is what is meant by a thing's being prior in the order of nature, that it is someway the cause or reason of the thing, with respect to which it is said to be prior.

If the particular act or exertion of will, which comes into existence, be any thing properly determined at all, then it has some cause of existing, and of existing in such a particular determinate manner, and not another; some cause, whose influence decides the matter: which cause is distinct from the effect, and prior to it. But to say, that the Will or mind orders, influences, and determines itself to exert an act by the very exertion itself, is to make the exertion both cause and effect; or the exerting such an act, to be a cause of the exertion of such an act. For the question is, What is the cause and reason of the soul's exerting such an act? To which the answer is, The soul exerts such an act, and that is the cause of it. And so, by this, the exertion must be distinct from, and in the order of nature prior to, itself.

(3.) If the meaning be, that the soul's exertion of such a particular act of will, is a thing that comes to pass of itself, without any cause; and that there is absolutely no reason of the soul being determined to exert such a volition, and make such a choice, rather than another; I say, if this be the meaning of Arminians, when they contend so earnestly for the Will determining its own acts, and for liberty of Will consisting in self-determining power; they do nothing but confound themselves and others with words without a meaning. In the question, What determines the will? and in their answer, that the Will determines itself; and in all the dispute, it seems to be taken for granted, that something determines the Will; and the controversy on this head is not, whether its determination has any cause or foundation at all; but where the foundation of it is, whether in the will itself, or somewhere else. But if the thing intended be what is above mentioned, then nothing at all determines the Will; volition having absolutely no cause or foundation of its existence, either within or without.—There is a great noise made about self-determining power, as the source of all free acts of the Will: but when the matter comes to be explained, the meaning is, that no power at all is the source of these acts, neither self-determining power, nor any other, but they arise from nothing; no cause, no power, no influence, being at all concerned in the matter.

However, this very thing, even that the free acts of the Will are events which come to pass without a cause, is certainly implied in the Arminian notion of liberty of Will; though it be very inconsistent with many other things in their scheme, and repugnant to some things implied in their notion of liberty. Their opinion implies, that the particular determination of volition is without any cause; because they hold the free acts of the will to be contingent events; and contingence is essential to freedom in their notion of it. But certainly, those things which have a prior ground and reason of their particular existence, a cause which antecedently determines them to be, and determines them to be just as they are, do not happen contingently. If something foregoing, by a casual influence and connexion, determines and fixes precisely their coming to pass, and the manner of it, then it does not remain a contingent thing whether they shall come to pass or no.

And because it is a question in many respects very important in this controversy, Whether the free acts of the Will are events which come to pass without a cause; I shall be particular in examining this point in the two following sections.

PART II. SECTION III. WHETHER ANY EVENT WHATSOEVER, AND VOLITION IN PARTICULAR, CAN COME TO PASS WITHOUT A CAUSE OF ITS EXISTENCE.

Before I enter on any argument on this subject, I would explain how I would be understood, when I use the word Cause in this discourse; since, for want of a better word, I shall have occasion to use it in a sense which is more extensive than that in which it is sometimes used. The word is often used in so restrained a sense as to signify only that which has a positive efficiency or influence to produce a thing, or bring it to pass. But there are many things which have no such positive productive influence; which yet are Causes in this respect, that they have truly the nature of a reason why some things are, rather than others; or why they are thus, rather than otherwise. Thus the absence of the sun in the night, is not the Cause of the fall of dew at that time, in the same manner as its beams are the cause of the ascent of vapors in the day-time; and its withdrawment in the winter, is not in the same manner the Cause of the freezing of the waters, as its approach in the spring is the cause of their thawing. But yet the withdrawment or absence of the sun is an antecedent, with which these effects in the night and winter are connected, and on which they depend; and is one thing that belongs to the ground and reason why they come to pass at that time, rather than at other times; though the absence of the sun is nothing positive, nor has any positive influence.

It may be further observed, that when I speak of connexion of Causes and effects, I have respect to moral Causes, as well as those that are called natural in distinction from them. Moral Causes may be Causes in as proper a sense as any Causes whatsoever; may have as real an influence, and may as truly be the ground and reason of an Event's coming to pass.

Therefore I sometimes use the word Cause, in this inquiry, to signify any antecedent, either natural or moral, positive or negative, on which an Event, either a thing, or the manner and circumstance of a thing, so depends, that it is the ground and reason, either in whole, or in part, why it is, rather than not; or why it is as it is, rather than otherwise; or, in other words, any antecedent with which a consequent event is so connected, that it truly belongs to the reason why the proposition which affirms that Event is true; whether it has any positive influence, or not. And agreeably to this, I sometimes use the word effect for the consequence of another thing, which is perhaps rather an occasion than a Cause, most properly speaking.

I am the more careful thus to explain my meaning, that I may cut off occasion, from any that might seek occasion to cavil and object against some things which I may say concerning the dependence of all things which come to pass, on some Cause, and their connexion with their Cause.

Having thus explained what I mean by Cause, I assert, that nothing ever comes to pass without a Cause. What is self-existent must be from eternity, and must be unchangeable: but as to all things that begin to be, they are not self-existent, and therefore must have some foundation of their existence without themselves.—That whatsoever begins to be, which before was not, must have a Cause why it then begins to exist, seems to be the first dictate of the common and natural sense which God hath implanted in the minds of all mankind, and the main foundation of all our reasonings about the existence of things, past, present, or to come.

And this dictate of common sense equally respects substances and modes, or things and the manner and circumstances of things. Thus, if we see a body which has hitherto been at rest, start out of a state of rest, and begin to move, we do as naturally and necessarily suppose there is some Cause or reason of this new mode of existence, as of the existence of a body itself which had hitherto not existed. And so if a body, which had hitherto moved in a certain direction, should suddenly change the direction of its motion; or if it should put off its old figure, and take a new one; or change its color: the beginning of these new modes is a new Event, and the human mind necessarily supposes that there is some Cause or reason of them.

If this grand principle of common sense be taken away, all arguing from effects to causes ceaseth, and so all knowledge of any existence, besides what we have by the most direct and immediate intuition, particularly all our proof of the being of God, ceases: we argue His being from our own being, and the being of other things, which we are sensible once were not, but have begun to be; and from the being of the world, with all its constituent parts, and the manner of their existence; all which we see plainly are not necessary in their own nature, and so not self-existent, and therefore must have a Cause. But if things, not in themselves necessary, may begin to be without a Cause, all this arguing is vain.

Indeed, I will not affirm, that there is in the nature of things no foundation for the knowledge of the Being of God, without any evidence of it from his works. I do suppose there is a great absurdity in denying Being in general, and imagining an eternal, absolute, universal nothing: and therefore that there would be, in the nature of things, a foundation of intuitive evidence, that there must be an eternal, infinite, most perfect Being; if we had strength and comprehension of mind sufficient, to have a clear idea of general and universal Being. But then we should not properly come to the knowledge of the Being of God by arguing; our evidence would be intuitive: we should see it, as we see other things that are necessary in themselves, the contraries of which are in their own nature absurd and contradictory; as we see that twice two is four; and as we see that a circle has no angles. If we had as clear an idea of universal, infinite entity, as we have of these other things, I suppose we should most intuitively see the absurdity of supposing such Being not to be; should immediately see there is no room for the question, whether it is possible that Being, in the most general, abstracted notion of it should not be. But we have not that strength and extent of mind, to know this certainly in this intuitive, independent manner: but the way that mankind come to the knowledge of the Being of God, is that which the apostle speaks of, Rom. 1:20. The invisible things of him from the creation of the world, are clearly seen; being understood by the things that are made; even his eternal power and Godhead. We first ascend, and prove a posteriori, or from effects, that there must be an eternal Cause; and then secondly, prove by argumentation, not intuition, that this Being must be necessarily existent; and then thirds, from the proved necessity of his existence, we may descend, and prove many of his perfections a priori.

But if once this grand principle of common sense be given up, that what is not necessary in itself, must have a Cause; and we begin to maintain, that things which heretofore have not been, may come into existence, and begin to be of themselves, without any cause; all our means of ascending in our arguing from the creature to the Creator, and all our evidence of the Being of God, is cut off at one blow. In this case, we cannot prove that there is a God, either from the Being of the world, and the creatures in it, or from the manner of their Being, their order, beauty, and use. For if things may come into existence without any Cause at all, then they doubtless may without any Cause answerable to the effect. Our minds do alike naturally suppose and determine both these things; namely, that what begins to be has a Cause, and also that it has a Cause proportionable to the effect. The same principle which leads us to determine, that there cannot be any thing coming to pass without a Cause, leads us to determine that there cannot be more in the effect than in the Cause.

Yea, if once it should be allowed, that things may come to pass without a Cause, we should not only have no proof Of the Being of God, but we should be without evidence of the existence of any thing whatsoever, but our own immediately present ideas and consciousness. For we have no way to prove any thing else, but by arguing from effects to Causes: from the ideas now immediately in view, we argue other things not immediately in view; from sensations now excited in us, we infer the existence of things without us, as the Causes of these sensations; and from the existence of these things, we argue other things, on which they depend, as effects on Causes. We infer the past existence of ourselves, or any thing else, by memory; only as we argue, that the ideas, which are now in our minds, are the consequences of past ideas and sensations. We immediately perceive nothing else but the ideas which are this moment extant in our minds. We perceive or know other things only by means of these, as necessarily connected with others, and dependent on them. But if things may be without Causes, all this necessary connexion and dependence is dissolved, and so all means of our knowledge is gone. If there be no absurdity or difficulty in supposing one thing to start out of non-existence into being, of itself without a Cause; then there is no absurdity or difficulty in supposing the same of millions of millions. For nothing, or no difficulty, multiplied, still is nothing, or no difficulty: nothing multiplied by nothing, does not increase the sum.

And indeed, according to the hypothesis I am opposing, of the acts of the Will coming to pass without a Cause, it is the cause in fact, that millions of millions of Events are continually coming into existence contingently, without any Cause or reason why they do so, all over the world, every day and hour, through all ages. So it is in a constant succession, in every moral agent. This contingency, this efficient nothing, this effectual No-Cause, is always ready at hand, to produce this sort of effects, as long as the agent exists, and as often as he has occasion.

If it were so, that things only of one kind, viz. acts of the Will, seemed to come to pass of themselves; and it were an Event that was continual, and that happened in a course, wherever were found subjects capable of such Events; this very thing would demonstrate that there was some Cause of them, which made such a difference between this Event and others, and that they did not really happen contingently. For contingence is blind, and does not pick and choose a particular sort of Events. Nothing has no choice. This No-Cause, which causes no existence, cannot cause the existence which comes to pass, to be of one particular sort only, distinguished from all others. Thus, that only one sort of matter drops out of the heavens, even water, and that this comes so often, so constantly and plentifully, all over the world, in all ages, shows that there is some Cause or reason of the falling of water out of the heavens; and that something besides mere contingence has a hand in the matter.

If we should suppose Non-entity to be about to bring forth; and things were coming into existence, without any Cause or antecedent, on which the existence, or kind, or manner of existence depends; or which could at all determine whether the things should be stones, or stars, or beasts, or angels, or human bodies, or souls, or only some new motion or figure in natural bodies, or some new sensations in animals, or new ideas in the human understanding, or new volitions in the Will; or any thing else of all the infinite number of possibles; then certainly it would not be expected, although many millions of millions of things were coming into existence in this manner, all over the face of the earth, that they should all be only of one particular kind, and that it should be thus in all ages, and that this sort of existences should never fail to come to pass where there is room for them, or a subject capable of them, and that constantly, whenever there is occasion.

If any should imagine, there is something in the sort of Event that renders it possible for it to come into existence without a Cause, and should say, that the free acts of the Will are existences of an exceeding different nature from other things; by reason of which they may come into existence without any previous ground or reason of it, though other things cannot: if they make this objection in good earnest, it would be an evidence of their strangely forgetting themselves; for they would be giving an account of some ground of the existence of a thing, when at the same time they would maintain there is no ground of its existence. Therefore I would observe, that the particular nature of existence, be it never so diverse from others, can lay no foundation for that thing coming into existence without a Cause; because to suppose this, would be to suppose the particular nature of existence to be a thing prior to the existence, and so a thing which makes way for existence, without a cause or reason of existence. But that which in any respect makes way for a thing coming into being, or for any manner or circumstance of its first existence, must, be prior to the existence. The distinguished nature of the effect, which is something belonging to the effect, cannot have influence backward, to act before it is. The peculiar nature of that thing called Volition, can do nothing, can have no influence, while it is not. And afterwards it is too late for its influence: for then the thing has made sure of existence already, without its help.

So that it is indeed as repugnant to reason, to suppose that an act of the Will should come into existence without a Cause, as to suppose the human soul, or an angel, or the globe of the earth, or the whole universe, should come into existence without a Cause. And if once we allow, that such a sort of effect as a Volition may come to pass without a Cause, how do we know but that many other sorts of effects may do so too? It is not the particular kind of effect that makes the absurdity of supposing it has being without a Cause, but something which is common to all things that ever begin to be, viz. That they are not self-existent, or necessary in the nature of things.

PART II. SECTION IV. WHETHER VOLITION CAN ARISE WITHOUT A CAUSE, THROUGH THE ACTIVITY OF THE NATURE OF THE SOUL.

The author of the Essay on the Freedom of the Will in God and the Creatures, in answer to that objection against his doctrine of a self-determining power in the will, (p. 68–69.) That nothing is, or comes to pass, without a sufficient reason why it is, and why it is in this manner rather than another, allows that it is thus in corporeal things, which are, properly and philosophically speaking, passive being; but denies it is thus in spirits, which are beings of an active nature, who have the spring of action within themselves, and can determine themselves. By which it is plainly supposed, that such an event as an act of the Will, may come to pass in a spirit, without a sufficient reason why it comes to pass, or why it is after this manner, rather than another. But certainly this author, in this matter, must be very unwary and inadvertent. For:

1. The objection or difficulty proposed by him seems to be forgotten in his answer or solution. The very difficulty, as he himself proposes it, is this: How an event can come to pass without a sufficient reason why it is, or why it is in this manner rather than another? Instead of solving this difficulty, with regard to Volition, as he proposes, he forgets himself, and answers another question quite diverse, viz. What is a sufficient reason why it is, and why it is in this manner rather than another! And he assigns the active being's own determination as the Cause, and a Cause sufficient for the effect; and leaves all the difficulty unresolved, even, How the soul's own determination, which he speaks of, came to exist, and to be what it was, without a Cause? The activity of the soul may enable it to be the Cause of effects; but it does not at all enable it to be the subject of effects which have no Cause; which is the thing this author supposes concerning acts of the Will. Activity of nature will no more enable a being to produce effects, and determine the manner of their existence, within itself, without a Cause, than out of itself, in some other being. But if an active being should, through its activity, produce and determine an effect in some external object, how absurd would it be to say, that the effect was produced without a Cause!

2. The question is not so much, How a spirit endowed with activity comes to act, as why it exerts such an act, and not another; or why it acts with such a particular determination? If activity of nature be the Cause why a spirit (the soul of man, for instance) acts, and does not lie still; yet that alone is not the Cause why its action is thus and thus limited, directed, and determined. Active nature is a general thing; it is an ability or tendency of nature to action, generally taken; which may be a Cause why the soul acts as occasion or reason is given; but this alone cannot be a sufficient Cause why the soul exerts such a particular act, at such a time, rather than others. In order to this there must be something besides a general tendency to action; there must also be a particular tendency to that individual action.—If it should be asked, why the soul of man uses its activity, in such a manner as it does; and it

should be answered, that the soul uses its activity thus, rather than otherwise, because it has activity; would such an answer satisfy a rational man? Would it not rather be looked upon as a very impertinent one?

3. An active being can bring no effects to pass by his activity, but what are consequent upon his acting: he produces nothing by his activity, any other way than by the exercise of his activity, and so nothing but the fruits of its exercise: he brings nothing to pass by a dormant activity. But the exercise of his activity is action; and so his action, or exercise of his activity, must be prior to the effects of his activity. If an active being produces an effect in another being, about which his activity is conversant, the effect being the fruit of his activity, his activity must be first exercised or exerted, and the effect of it must follow. So it must be, with equal reason, if the active being is his own object, and his activity is conversant about himself, to produce and determine some effect in himself; still the exercise of his activity must go before the effect, which he brings to pass and determines by it. And therefore his activity cannot be the Cause of the determination of the first action, or exercise of activity itself, whence the effects of activity arise; for that would imply a contradiction; it would be to say, the first exercise of activity is before the first exercise of activity, and is the Cause of it.

4. That the soul, though an active substance, cannot diversify its own acts, but by first acting; or be a determining Cause of different acts, or any different effects, sometimes of one kind, and sometimes of another, any other way than in consequence of its own diverse acts, is manifest by this; that if so, then the same Cause, the same causal influence, without variation in any respect, would produce different effects at different times. For the same substance of the soul before it acts, and the same active nature of the soul before it is exerted, i. e. before in the order of nature, would be the Cause of different effects, viz. different Volitions at different times. But the substance of the soul before it acts, and its active nature before it is exerted, are the same without variation. For it is some act that makes the first variation in the Cause, as to any causal exertion, force, or influence. But if it be so, that the soul has no different causality, or diverse causal influence, in producing these diverse effects; then it is evident, that the soul has no influence in the diversity of the effect; and that the difference of the effect cannot be owing to any thing in the soul; or which is the same thing, the soul does not determine the diversity of the effect; which is contrary to the supposition.—It is true, the substance of the soul before it acts, and before there is any

difference in that respect, may be in a different state and circumstances: but those whom I oppose, will not allow the different circumstances of the soul to be the determining Causes of the acts of the will; as being contrary to their notion of self-determination.

5. Lt us suppose, as these divines do, that there are no acts of the soul, strictly speaking, but free Volitions; then it will follow, that the soul is an active being in nothing further than it is a voluntary or elective being; and when ever it produces effects actively, it produces effects voluntarily and electively. But to produce effects thus, is the same thing as to produce effects in consequence of, and according to its own choice. And if so, then surely the soul does not by its activity produce all its own acts of will or choice themselves; for this, by the supposition, is to produce all its free acts of choice voluntarily and electively or in consequence of its own free acts of choice, which brings the matter directly to the forementioned contradiction, of a free act of choice before the first free act of choice.—According to these gentlemen's own notion of action, if there arises in the mind a Volition without a free act of the Will to produce it, the mind is not the voluntary Cause of that Volition; because it does not arise from, nor is regulated by choice or design. And therefore it cannot be, that the mind should be the active, voluntary, determining Cause of the first and leading Volition that relates to the afffair.—The mind being a designing Cause, only enables it to produce effects in consequence of its design; it will not enable it to be the designing Cause of all its own designs. The mind being an elective Cause, will enable it to produce effects only in consequence of its elections, and according to them; but cannot enable it to be the elective Cause of all its own elections; because that supposes an election before the first election. So the mind being an active Cause enables it to produce effects in consequence of its own acts, but cannot enable it to be the determining Cause of all its own acts; for that is, in the same manner, a contradiction; as it supposes a determining act conversant about the first act, and prior to it, having a causal influence on its existence, and manner of existence.

I can conceive of nothing else that can be meant by the soul having power to cause and determine its own Volitions, as a being to whom God has given a power of action, but this; that God has given power to the soul, sometimes at least, to excite Volitions at its pleasure, or according as it chooses. And this certainly supposes, in all such cases, a choice preceding all Volitions which are thus caused, even the first of them. Which runs into the forementioned great absurdity.

Therefore the activity of the nature of the soul affords no relief from the difficulties with which the notion of a self-determining power in the Will is attended, nor will it help, in the least, its absurdities and inconsistences.

PART II. SECTION V. SHOWING, THAT IF THE THINGS ASSERTED IN THESE EVASIONS SHOULD BE SUPPOSED TO BE TRUE, THEY ARE ALTOGETHER IMPERTINENT, AND CANNOT HELP THE CAUSE OF ARMINIAN LIBERTY; AND HOW, THIS BEING THE STATE OF THE CASE, ARMINIAN WRITERS ARE OBLIGED TO TALK INCONSISTENTLY.

What was last observed in the preceding section, may show—not only that the active nature of the soul cannot be a reason why an act of the Will is, or why it is in this manner rather than another, but also—that if it could be proved, that volitions are contingent events, their being and manner of being not fixed or determined by any cause, or any thing antecedent; it would not at all serve the purpose of Arminians, to establish their notion of freedom, as consisting in the Will's determination of itself, which supposes every free act of the Will to be determined by some act of the will going before; inasmuch as for the Will to determine a thing, is the same as for the soul to determine a thing by willing; and there is no way that the Will can determine an act of the Will, than by willing that act of the Will, or, which is the same thing, choosing it. So that here must be two acts of the Will in the case, one going before another, one conversant about the other, and the latter the object of the former, and chosen by the former. If the Will does not cause and determine the act by choice, it does not cause or determine it at all; for that which is not determined by choice, is not determined voluntarily or willingly: and to say, that the Will determines something which the soul does not determine willingly, is as much as to say, that something is done by the will, which the soul doth not with its Will.

So that if Arminian liberty of will, consisting in the Will determining its own acts, be maintained, the old absurdity and contradiction must be maintained, that every free act of Will is caused and determined by a foregoing free act of will. Which doth not consist with the free acts arising without any cause, and being so contingent, as not to be fixed by any thing foregoing. So that this evasion must be given up, as not at all relieving this sort of liberty, but directly destroying it.

And if it should be supposed, that the soul determines its own acts of Will some other way, than by a foregoing act of Will; still it will help not their cause if it determines them by an act of the understanding, or some other power, then the Will does not determine itself; and so the self-determining power of the will is given up. And what liberty is there exercised, according to their own opinion of liberty, by the soul being determined by something besides its own choice? The acts of the Will, it is true, may be directed, and effectually determined and fixed; but it is not done by the soul's own Will and pleasure: there is no exercise at all of choice or Will in producing the effect: and if Will and choice are not exercised in it, how is the liberty of the Will exercised in it?

So that let Armninians turn which way they please with their notion of liberty, consisting in the Will determining its own acts, their notion destroys itself. If they hold every free act of Will to be determined by the soul's own free choice, or foregoing free act of Will; foregoing, either in the order of time, or nature; it implies that gross contradiction, that the first free act belonging to the affair, is determined by a free act which is before it. Or if they say, that the free acts of the Will are determined by some other art of the soul, and not an act of will or choice; this also destroys their notion of liberty consisting in the acts of the Will being determined by the will itself; or if they hold that the acts of the Will are determined by nothing at all that is prior to them, but that they are contingent in that sense, that they are determined and fixed by no cause at all; this also destroys their notion of liberty, consisting in the Will determining its own acts.

This being the true state of the Arminian notion of liberty, the writers who defend it are forced into gross inconsistences, in what they say upon this subject. To instance in Dr. Whitby; he, in his discourse on the freedom of the Will, opposes the opinion of the Calvinists, who place man's liberty only in a power of doing what he will, as that wherein they plainly agree with Mr. Hobbes. And yet he himself mentions the very same notion of liberty, as the dictate of the sense and common reason of mankind, and a rule laid down by the light of nature; viz. that liberty is a power of acting from ourselves, or DOING WHAT WE WILL. This is indeed, as he says, a thing agreeable to the sense and common reason of mankind; and therefore it is not so much to be wondered at, that he unawares acknowledges it against himself: for if liberty does not consist in this, what else can be devised that it should consist in? If it be said, as Dr. Whitby elsewhere insists, that it does not only consist in liberty of doing what we will, but also a liberty of willing without necessity; still the question returns, what does that liberty of willing without necessity consist in, but in a power of willing as we please, without being impeded by a contrary necessity? or in other words, a liberty for the soul in its willing to act according to its own choice? Yea, this very thing the same author seems to allow, and suppose again and again, in the use he makes of sayings of the fathers, whom he quotes as his vouchers. Thus he cites the words of Origen, which he produces as a testimony on his side; "The soul acts by HER OWN CHOICE, and it is free for her to incline to whatever part SHE WILL." And those of Justin Martyr; "The doctrine of the Christians is this, that nothing is done or suffered according to fate, but that every man doth good or evil ACCORDING TO HIS OWN FREE CHOICE." And from Eusebius, these words; "If fate be established, philosophy and piety are overthrown.—All these things depending upon the necessity intro-duced by the stars, aloud not upon meditation and exercise PROCEED-ING FROM OUR OWN FREE CHOICE. And again, the words of MACCARIUS; "God, to preserve the liberty of man's Will, suffered their bodies to die, that it might be IN THEIR CHOICE to turn to good or evil."—"They who are acted by the Holy Spirit, are not held under any necessity, but have liberty to turn themselves, and DO WHAT THEY WILL in this life."

Thus, the Doctor in effect comes into that very notion of liberty, which the Calvinists have; which he at the same time condemns, as agreeing with the opinion of Mr. Hobbes, namely, "The soul acting by its own choice, men doing good or evil according to their own free choice, their being in that exercise which proceeds from their own free choice, having it in their choice to turn to good or evil, and doing what they will." So that if men exercise this liberty in the acts of the will themselves, it must be in exerting acts of Will according to their own free choice; or, exerting acts of will that proceed from their choice. And if it be so, then let every one judge whether this does not suppose a free choice going before the free act of will, or whether an act of choice does not go before that act of the will which proceeds from it. And if it be thus with all free acts of the Will, then let every one judge, whether it will not follow that there is a free choice going before the first free act of the Will exerted in the case! And finally, let every one judge whether in the scheme of these writers there be any possibility of avoiding these absurdities.

If liberty consists, as Dr. Whitby himself says, in a man's doing what he will; and a man exercises this liberty, not only in external actions, but in the acts of the will themselves; then so far as liberty is exercised in the latter, it consists in willing what he wills: and if any say so, one of these two things must be meant, either, 1. That a man has power to will, as he does will; because what he wills, he wills; and therefore power to will what he has power to will. If this be their meaning, then all this mighty controversy about freedom of the Will and self-determining power, comes wholly to nothing; all that is contended for being no more than this, that the mind of man does what it does, and is the subject of what it is the subject, or that what is, is; wherein none has any controversy with them. Or, 2. The meaning must be, that a man has power to will as he chooses to will: that is, he has power by one act of choice to choose another; by an antecedent act of Will to choose a consequent act: and therein to execute his own choice. And if this be their meaning, it is nothing but shuffling with those they dispute with, and baffling their own reason. For still the question returns, wherein lies man's liberty in that antecedent act of will which chose the consequent act? The answer according to the same principles must be, that his liberty in this also lies in his willing as he would, or as he chose, or agreeable to another act of choice preceding that. And so the question returns in infinitum, and the like answer must be made in infinitum: in order to support their opinion, there must be no beginning, but free acts of Will must have been chosen by foregoing free acts of will in the soul of every man, without beginning.

PART II. SECTION VI. CONCERNING THE WILL DETERMINING IN THINGS WHICH ARE PERFECTLY INDIFFERENT IN THE VIEW OF THE MIND.

A great argument for self-determining power, is the supposed experience we universally have of an ability to determine our Wills, in cases wherein no prevailing motive is presented: the Will, as is supposed, has its choice to make between two or more things, that are perfectly equal in the view of the mind; and the Will is apparently, altogether indifferent; and yet we find no difficulty in coming to a choice; the Will can instantly determine itself to one, by a sovereign power which it has over itself, without being moved by any preponderating inducement.

Thus the fore-mentioned author of an Essay on the Freedom of the will, &c. (p. 25, 26, 27.) supposes, "That there are many instances, wherein the will is determined neither by present uneasiness, nor by the greatest apparent good, nor by the last dictate of the understanding, nor by any thing else, but merely by itself, as a sovereign self-determining power of the soul; and that the soul does not will this or that action, in some cases, by any other influence but because it will. Thus, says he, I can turn my face to the south, or the north; I can point with my finger upward, or downward.—And thus, in some cases, the will determines itself in a very sovereign manner, because it will, without a reason borrowed from the understanding: and hereby it discovers its own perfect power of choice, rising from within itself, and free from all influence or restraint of any kind." And (p. 66, 70, 73, 74.) this author very expressly supposes the will in many cases to be determined by no motive at all, and acts altogether without motive, or ground of preference.—Here I would observe,

1. The very supposition which is here made, directly contradicts and overthrows itself. For the thing supposed, wherein this grand argument consists, is, that among several things the Will actually chooses one before another, at the same time that it is perfectly indifferent; which is the very same thing as to say, the mind has a preference, at the same time that it has no preference. What is meant cannot be, that the mind is indifferent before it comes to have a choice, or until it has a preference; for certainly this author did not imagine he had a controversy with any person in supposing this. Besides, it appears in fact, that the thing which he supposes, is—not that the Will chooses one thing before another, concerning which it is indifferent before it chooses, but that the Will is indifferent when it chooses; and that it being otherwise than indifferent is not until afterwards, in consequence of its choice; that the chosen thing appearing preferable, and more agreeable than another, arises from its choice already made. His words are, (p. 30.)"Where the objects which are proposed appear equally fit or good, the Will is left without a guide or director; and therefore must take its own choice, by its own determination; it being properly a self-determining power. And in such cases the Will does as it were make a good to itself by its own choice, i.e. creates its own pleasure or delight in this self-chosen good. Even as a man by seizing upon a spot of unoccupied land, in an uninhabited country, makes it his own possession and property, and as such rejoices in it.

Where things were indifferent before, the Will finds nothing to make them more agreeable, considered merely in themselves, but the pleasure it feels arising from its own choice, and its perseverance therein. We love many things which we have chosen, and purely because we chose them."

This is as much as to say, that we first begin to prefer many things, purely because we have preferred and chosen them before.—These things must needs be spoken inconsiderately by this author. Choice or preference cannot be before itself in the same instance, either in the order of time or nature: It cannot be the foundation of itself, or the consequence of itself. The very act of choosing one thing rather than another, is preferring that thing, and that is setting a higher value on that thing. But that the mind sets a higher value on one thing than another, is not, in the first place, the fruit of its setting a higher value on that thing.

This author says, (p. 36.) "The Will may be perfectly indifferent, and yet the Will may determine itself to choose one or the other." And again, in the same page, "I am entirely indifferent to either; and yet my Will may determine itself to choose." And again, "Which I shall choose must be determined by the mere act of my Will." If the choice is determined by a mere act of Will, then the choice is determined by a mere act of choice. And concerning this matter, viz. That the act of the Will itself is determined by act of choice, this writer is express. (p. 72.) Speaking of the case, where there is no superior fitness in objects presented, he has these words: "There it must act by its own choice, and determine itself as it PLEASES." Where it is supposed that the very determination, which is the ground and spring of the Will's act, is an act of choice and pleasure, wherein one act is more agreeable than another: and this preference and superior pleasure is the ground of all it does in the case. And if so, the mind is not indifferent when it determines itself, but had rather determine itself one way than another. And therefore the Will does not act at all in indifference; not so much as in the first step it takes. If it be possible for the understanding to act in indifference, yet surely the Will never does; because the Will beginning to act is the very same thing as it beginning to choose or prefer. And if in the very first act of the Will, the mind prefers something, then the idea of that thing preferred, does at that time preponderate, or prevail in the mind; or, which is the same thing, the idea of it has a prevailing influence on the Will. So that this wholly destroys the thing supposed, viz. That the mind can by a sovereign power choose one of two or more things, which in the view of the mind are, in every respect, perfectly equal, one of which does not at all preponderate, nor has any prevailing influence on the mind above another.

So that this author, in his grand argument for the ability of the Will to choose one of two or more things, concerning which it is perfectly indifferent, does at the same time, in effect, deny the thing he supposes, even that the Will, in choosing, is subject to no prevailing influence of the view of the thing chosen. And indeed it is impossible to offer this argument without overthrowing it; the thing supposed in it being that which denies itself. To suppose the Will to act at all in a state of perfect indifference, is to assert that the mind chooses without choosing. To say that when it is indifferent, it can do as it pleases, is to say that it can follow its pleasure, when it has no pleasure to follow. And therefore if there be any difficulty in the instances of two cakes, or two eggs, &c. which are exactly alike, one as good as another; concerning which this author supposes the mind in fact has a choice, and so in effect supposes that it has a preference; it as much concerned himself to solve the difficulty, as it does those whom he opposes. For if these instances prove any thing to his purpose, they prove that a man chooses without choice. And yet this is not to his purpose; because if this is what he asserts, his own words are as much against him, and does as much contradict him, as the words of those he disputes against can do.

2. There is no great difficulty in showing, in such instances as are alleged, not only that it must needs be so, that the mind must be influenced in its choice by something that has a preponderating influence upon it, but also how it is so. A little attention to our own experience, and a distinct consideration of the acts of our own minds, in such cases, will be sufficient to clear up the matter.

Thus, supposing I have a chess-board before me; and because I am required by a superior, or desired by a friend, or on some other consideration, I am determined to touch some one of the spots or squares on the board with my finger. Not being limited or directed, in the first proposal, to any one in particular; and there being nothing in the squares, in themselves considered, that recommends any one of all the sixty-four, more than another; in this case, my mind determines to give itself up to what is vulgarly called accident, by determining to touch that square which happens to be most in view, which my eye is especially upon at that moment, or which happens to be then most in my mind, or which I shall be directed to by some other such like accident. Here are several steps of the mind proceeding (though all may be done, as it were, in a moment). The first step is its general determination that it will touch one of the squares. The next step is another general determination to give itself up to accident, in some certain way; as to touch that which shall be most in the eye or mind at that time, or to some other such like accident. The third and last step is a particular determination to touch a certain individual spot, even that square, which, by that sort of accident the mind has pitched upon, has actually offered itself beyond others. Now it is apparent that in none of these several steps does the mind proceed in absolute indifference, but in each of them is influenced by a preponderating inducement. So it is in the first step, the mind's general determination to touch one of the sixty-four spots: the mind is not absolutely indifferent whether it does so or no; it is induced to it, for the sake of making some experiment, or by the desire of a friend, or some other motive that prevails. So it is in the second step, the mind determining to give itself up to accident, by touching that which shall be most in the eye, or the idea of which shall be most prevalent in the mind, &c. The mind is not absolutely indifferent whether it proceeds by this rule or no; but chooses it, because it appears at that time a convenient and requisite expedient in order to fulfil the general purpose. And so it is in the third and last step, which is determining to touch that individual spot which actually does prevail in the mind's view. The mind is not indifferent concerning this; but is influenced by a prevailing inducement and reason; which is, that this is a prosecution of the preceding determination, which appeared requisite, and was fixed before in the second step.

Accident will ever serve a man, without hindering him a moment, in such a case. Among a number of objects in view, one will prevail in the eye, or in idea, beyond others. When we have our eyes open in the clear sunshine, many objects strike the eye at once, and innumerable images may be at once painted in it by the rays of light; but the attention of the mind is not equal to several of them at once; or if it be, it does not continue so for any time. And so it is with respect to the ideas of the mind in general: several ideas are not in equal strength in the mind's view and notice at once; or at least, does not remain so for any sensible continuance. There is nothing in the world more constantly varying, than the ideas of the mind; they do not remain precisely in the same state for the least perceivable space of time; as is evident by this:—That all time is perceived by the mind, only by the successive changes of its own ideas. Therefore while the perceptions of the mind remain precisely in the same state, there is no perceivable length of time, because no sensible succession at all.

As the acts of the Will, in each step of the forementioned procedure, do not come to pass without a particular cause, but every act is owing to a prevailing inducement; so the accident, as I have called it, or that which happens in the unsearchable course of things, to which the mind yields itself, and by which it is guided, is not any thing that comes to pass without a cause. The mind in determining to be guided by it, is not determined by something that has no cause; any more than if it be determined to be guided by a lot, or the casting of a die. For though the die falling in such a manner be accidental to him that casts it, yet none will suppose that there is no cause why it falls as it does. The involuntary changes in the succession of our ideas, though the cause may not be observed, have as much a cause, as the changeable motions of the motes that float in the air, or the continual, infinitely various, successive changes of the unevennesses on the surface of the water.

There are two things especially, which are probably the occasions of confusion in the minds of them who insist upon it, that the Will acts in a proper indifference, and without being moved by any inducement, in its determinations in such cases as have been mentioned.

1. They seem to mistake the point in question, or at least not to keep it distinctly in view. The question they dispute about, is, Whether the mind be indifferent about the objects presented, one of which is to be taken, touched, pointed to, &c. as two eggs, two cakes, which appear equally good. Whereas the question to be considered, is, Whether the person be indifferent with respect to his own actions; whether he does not, on some consideration or other, prefer one act with respect to these objects before another. The mind in its determination and choice, in these cases, is not most immediately and directly conversant about the objects presented; but the acts to be done concerning these objects. The objects may appear equal, and the mind may never properly make any choice between them; but the next act of the Will being about the external actions to be performed, taking, touching, &c. these may not appear equal, and one action may properly be chosen before another. In each step of the mind's progress, the determination is not about the objects, unless indirectly and improperly, but about the actions, which it chooses for other reasons than any preference of the objects, and for reasons not taken at all from the objects.

There is no necessity of supposing, that the mind does ever at all properly choose one of the objects before another: either before it has taken, or afterwards. Indeed the man chooses to take or touch one rather than another; but not because it chooses the thing taken, or touched, but from foreign considerations. The case may be so, that of two things offered, a man may, for certain reasons, prefer taking that which he undervalues, and choose to neglect that which his mind prefers. In such a case, choosing the thing taken, and choosing to take, are diverse: and so they are in a case where the things presented are equal in the mind's esteem, and neither of them preferred. All that fact and experience makes evident, is, that the mind chooses one action rather than another. And therefore the arguments which they bring, in order to be to their purpose, should be to prove that the mind chooses the action in perfect indifference, with respect to that action; and not to prove that the mind chooses the action in perfect indifference with respect to the object; which is very possible, and yet the Will not act at all without prevalent inducement, and proper preponderation.

2. Another reason of confusion and difficulty in this matter, seems to be, not distinguishing between a general indifference, or an indifference with respect to what is to be done in a more distant and general view of it, and a particular indifference, or an indifference with respect to the next immediate act, viewed with its particular and present circumstances. A man may be perfectly indifferent with respect to his own actions, in the former respect; and yet not in the latter. Thus in the foregoing instance of touching one of the squares of a chess-board; when it is first proposed that I should touch one of them, I may be perfectly indifferent which I touch; because as yet I view the matter remotely and generally, being but in the first step of the mind's progress in the affair. But yet, when I am actually come to the last step, and the very next thing to be determined is which, is to be touched, having already determined that I will touch that which happens to be most in my eye or mind, and my mind being now fixed on a particular one, the act of touching that, considered thus immediately, and in these particular present circumstances, is not what my mind is absolutely indifferent about.

PART II. SECTION VII. CONCERNING THE NOTION OF LIBERTY OF WILL, CONSISTING IN INDIFFERENCE.

What has been said in the foregone section, has a tendency in some measure to evince the absurdity of the opinion of such as place Liberty in Indifference, or in that equilibrium whereby the will is without all antecedent bias; that the determination of the Will to either side may be entirely from itself, and that it may be owing only to its own power, and the sovereignty which it has over itself, that it goes this way rather than that.

But inasmuch as this has been of such long standing, and has been so generally received, and so much insisted on by Pelagians, Semi-Pelagians, Jesuits, Socinians, Arminians, and others, it may deserve a more full consideration. And therefore I shall now proceed to a more particular and thorough inquiry into this notion.

Now lest some should suppose that I do not understand those that place Liberty in Indifference, or should charge me with misrepresenting their opinion, I would signify, that I am sensible, there are some, who, when they talk of Liberty of the Will as consisting in Indifference, express themselves as though they would not be understood to mean the Indifference of the inclination or tendency of the Will, but an Indifference of the soul's power, of willing; or that the will, with respect to its power or ability to choose, is indifferent, can go either way indifferently, either to the right hand or left, either act or forbear to act, one as well as the other. This indeed seems to be a refining of some particular writers only, and newly invented, which will by no means consist with the manner of expression used by the defenders of Liberty of Indifference in general. I wish such refiners would thoroughly consider, whether they distinctly know their own meaning, when they make a distinction between an Indifference of the soul as to its power or ability of choosing, and the soul's Indifference as to the preference or choice itself; and whether they do not deceive themselves in imagining that they have any distinct meaning at all. The Indifference of the soul as to its ability or power to will, must be the same thing as the Indifference of the state of the power or faculty of the will, or the indifference of the state which the soul itself, which has that power or faculty, hitherto remains in, as to the exercise of that power, in the choice it shall by and by make.

But not to insist any longer on the inexplicable abstruseness of this distinction; let what will be supposed concerning the meaning of them that use it, this much must at least be intended by Arminians when they talk of Indifference as essential to Liberty of Will, if they intend any thing, in any respect to their purpose, viz. That it is such an Indifference as leaves the will not determined already; but free from actual possession, and vacant of predetermination, so far, that there may be room for the exercise of the self-determining power of the Will; and that the Will's freedom consists in, or depends upon, this vacancy and opportunity that is left for the will itself to be the determiner of the act that is to be the free act.

And here I would observe in the first place, that to make out this scheme of Liberty, the Indifference must be perfect and absolute; there must be a perfect freedom from all antecedent preponderation or inclination. Because if the Will be already inclined, before it exerts its own sovereign power on itself, then its inclination is not wholly owing to itself: if when two opposites are proposed to the soul for its choice, the proposal does not find the soul wholly in a state of Indifference, then it is not found in a state of Liberty for mere self-determination.—The least degree of an antecedent bias must be inconsistent with their notion of liberty. For so long as prior inclination possesses the will, and is not removed, the former binds the latter, so that it is utterly impossible that the Will should act otherwise than agreeably to it. Surely the Will cannot act or choose contrary to a remaining prevailing inclination of the Will. To suppose otherwise, would be the same thing as to suppose that the Will is inclined contrary to its present prevailing inclination, or contrary to what it is inclined to. That which the will prefers, to that, all things considered, it preponderates and inclines. It is equally impossible for the Will to choose contrary to its own remaining and present preponderating inclination, as it is to prefer contrary to its own present preference, or choose contrary to its own present choice. The Will, therefore, so long as it is under the influence of an old preponderating inclination, is not at Liberty for a new free act; if any, that shall now be an act of self-determination. That which is a self-determined free act, must be one which the will determines in the possession and use of a peculiar sort of liberty; such as consists in a freedom from every thing, which, if it were there, would make it impossible that the Will, at that time, should be otherwise than that way to which it tends.

If any one should say, there is no need that the Indifference should be perfect; but although a former inclination still remains, yet, if it be not very strong, possibly the strength of the Will may oppose and overcome it:—This is grossly absurd; for the strength of the will, let it be ever so great, gives it no such sovereignty and command, as to cause itself to prefer and not to prefer at the same time, or to choose contrary to its own present choice.

Therefore, if there be the least degree of antecedent preponderation of the Will, it must be perfectly abolished, before the Will can be at liberty to determine itself the contrary way. And if the Will determines itself the same way, it was not a free determination, because the Will is not wholly at liberty in so doing; its determination is not altogether from itself, but it was partly determined before, in its prior inclination: and all the freedom the will exercises in the case, is in an increase of inclination, which it gives itself, added to what it had by a foregoing bias; so much is from itself, and so much is from perfect indifference. For though the Will had a previous tendency that way, yet as to that additional degree of inclination, it had no tendency. Therefore the previous tendency is of no consideration, with respect to the act wherein the will is free. So that it comes to the same thing which was said at first, that as to the act of the will, wherein the will is free, there must be perfect indifference, or equilibrium.

To illustrate this: suppose a sovereign self-moving power in a natural body; but that the body is in motion already, by an antecedent bias; for instance, gravitation towards the centre of the earth; and has one degree of motion by virtue of that previous tendency; but by its self-moving power it adds one degree more to its motion, and moves so much more swiftly towards the centre of the earth than it would do by its gravity only: it is evident, all that is owing to a self-moving power in this case, is the additional degree of motion; and that the other degree which it had from gravity, is of no consideration in the case; the effect is just the same, as if the body had received from itself one degree of motion from a state of perfect rest. So, if we suppose a self-moving power given to the scale of a balance, which has a weight of one degree beyond the opposite scale; and if we ascribe to it an ability to add to itself another degree of force the same way, by its self-moving power; this is just the same thing as to ascribe to it a power to give itself one degree of preponderation from a perfect equilibrium; and so much power as the scale has to give itself an over-balance from a perfect equipoise, so much self-moving, self-preponderating power it has, and no more. So that its free power this way is always to be measured from perfect equilibrium.

I need say no more to prove, that if Indifference be essential to liberty, it must be perfect Indifference; and that so far as the Will is destitute of this, so far is it destitute of that freedom by which it is in a capacity of being its own determiner, without being at all passive, or subject to the power and sway of something else, in its motions and determinations.

Having observed these things, let us now try whether this notion of the Liberty of Will consisting in Indifference and equilibrium, and the Will's self-determination in such a state, be not absurd and inconsistent.

And here I would lay down this as an axiom of undoubted truth; that every free act is done IN a state of freedom, and not only after such a state, If an act of the Will be an act wherein the soul is free, it must be exerted in a state of freedom, and in the time of freedom. It will not suffice, that the act immediately follows a state of liberty; but Liberty must yet continue, and co-exist with the act; the soul remaining in possession of Liberty. Because that thing as the soul coming to a choice to do so. If the soul does not determine this of choice, or in the exercise of choice, then it does not determine it voluntarily. And if the soul does not determine it voluntarily, or of its own will, then in what sense does its Will determine it? And if the Will does not determine it, then how is the Liberty of the Will exercised in the determination? What sort of Liberty is exercised by the soul in those determinations, wherein there is no exercise of choice, which are not voluntary, and wherein the Will is not concerned? But if it be allowed, that this determination is an act of choice, and it be insisted on, that the soul, while it yet remains in a state of perfect Indifference, chooses to put itself out of that state, and to turn itself one way; then the soul is already come to a choice; and chooses that way. And so we have the very same absurdity which we had before. Here is the soul in a state of choice, and in a state of equilibrium, both at the same time: the soul already choosing one way, while it remains in a state of perfect Indifference, and has no choice of one way more than the other.—And indeed this manner of talking, though it may a little hide the absurdity, in the obscurity of expression, increases the inconsistence. To say, the free act of the Will, or the act which the will exerts in a state of freedom and Indifference, does not imply preference in it, but is what the will does in order to cause or produce a preference, is as much as to say, the soul chooses (for to will and to choose are the same thing) without choice, and prefers without preference, in order to cause or produce the beginning of a preference, or the first choice. And that is, that the first choice is exerted without choice, in order to produce itself!

If any, to evade these things, should own, that a state of liberty and a state of Indifference are not the same, and that the former may be without the latter; but should say, that Indifference is still essential to freedom, as it is necessary to go immediately before it; it being essential to the freedom of an act of Will that it should directly and immediately arise out of a state of Indifference; still this will not help the cause of Arminian Liberty, or make it consistent with itself. For if the act springs immediately out of a state of Indifference, then it does not arise from antecedent choice or preference. But if the act arises directly out of a state of Indifference, without any intervening choice to determine it, then the act not being determined by choice, is not determined by the will; the mind exercises no free choice in the affair, and free choice and free will have no hand in the determination of the act. Which is entirely inconsistent with their notion of the freedom of volition.

If any should suppose, that these absurdities may be avoided, by saying, that the Liberty of the mind consists in a power to suspend the act of the will, and so to keep it in a state of Indifference, until there has been opportunity for consideration; and so shall say, that however Indifference is not essential to Liberty in such a manner, that the mind must make its choice in a state of Indifference, which is an inconsistency, or that the act of will must spring immediately out of Indifference; yet Indifference may be essential to the Liberty of acts of the Will in this respect; viz. that Liberty consists in a power of the mind to forbear or suspend the act of volition, and keep the mind in a state of Indifference for the present, until there has been opportunity for proper deliberation: I say, if any one imagines that this helps the matter, it is a great mistake: it reconciles no inconsistency, and relieves no difficulty.—For here the following things must be observed:

1. That this suspending of volition, if there be properly any such thing, is itself an act of volition. If the mind determines to suspend its act, it determines it voluntarily; it chooses, on some consideration, to suspend it. And this choice or determination, is an act of the Will: And indeed it is supposed to be so in the very hypothesis; for it is supposed that the Liberty of the Will consists in its power to do this, and that its doing it is the very thing wherein the Will exercises its Liberty. But how can the Will exercise Liberty in it, if it be not an act of the Will? The Liberty of the Will is not exercised in any thing but what the Will does.

2. This determining to suspend acting is not only an act of the will, but it is supposed to be the only free act of the Will; because it is said, that this is the thing wherein the Liberty of the Will consists.—If so, then this is all the act of Will that we have to consider in this controversy. And now, the former question returns upon us; viz. Wherein consists the freedom of the will in those acts wherein it is free? And if this act

of determining a suspension be the only act in which the Will is free, then wherein consists the Will's freedom with respect to this act of suspension? And how is Indifference essential to this act? The answer must be, according to what is supposed in the ice evasion under consideration, that the liberty of the Will in this act of suspension, consists in a power to suspend even this act, until there has been opportunity for thorough deliberation. But this will be to plunge directly into the grossest nonsense: for it is the act of suspension itself that we are speaking of; and there is no room for a space of deliberation and suspension in order to determine whether we will suspend or no. For that supposes, that even suspension itself may be deferred: which is absurd; for the very deferring the determination of suspension, to consider whether we will suspend or no, will be actually suspending. For during the space of suspension, to consider whether to suspend, the act is, ipso facto, suspended. There is no medium between suspending to act, and immediately acting; and therefore no possibility of avoiding either the one or the other one moment.

And besides, this is attended with ridiculous absurdity another way: for now, it seems, Liberty consists wholly in the mind having power to suspend its determination whether to suspend or no; that there may be time for consideration, whether it be best to suspend. And if Liberty consists in this only, then this is the Liberty under consideration. We have to inquire now, how Liberty, with respect to this act of suspending a determination of suspension, consists in Indifference, or how Indifference is essential to it. The answer, according to the hypothesis we are upon, must be, that it consists in a power of suspending even this last-mentioned act, to have time to consider whether to suspend that. And then the same difficulties and inquiries return over again with respect to that; and so on for ever. Which, if it would show any thing, would show only that there is no such thing as a free act. It drives the exercise of freedom back in infinitum; and that is to drive it out of the world.

And besides all this, there is a delusion, and a latent gross contradiction in the affair another way; inasmuch as in explaining how, or in what respect, the Will is free, with regard to a particular act of volition, it is said, that its Liberty consists in a power to determine to suspend that act, which places Liberty not in that act of volition which the inquiry is about, but altogether in another antecedent act. Which contradicts the thing supposed in both the question and answer. The question is, wherein consists the mind's liberty in any particular act of volition? And the answer, in pretending to show wherein lies the mind's Liberty in that act, in effect says, it does not lie in that act at all, but in another, viz. a volition to suspend that act. And therefore the answer is both contradictory, and altogether impertinent and beside the purpose. For it does not show wherein the Liberty of the Will consists in the act in question; instead of that, it supposes it does not consist in that act at all, but in another distinct from it, even a volition to suspend that act, and take time to consider of it. And no account is pretended to be given wherein the mind is free with respect to that act, wherein this answer supposes the Liberty of the mind indeed consists, viz. the act of suspension, or of determining the suspension.

On the whole, it is exceeding manifest, that the Liberty of the mind does not consist in Indifference, and that Indifference is not essential or necessary to it, or at all belonging to it, as the Arminians suppose; that opinion being full of nothing but self-contradiction.

PART II. SECTION VIII. CONCERNING THE SUPPOSED LIBERTY OF THE WILL, AS OPPOSITE TO ALL NECESSITY.

It is chiefly insisted on by Arminians, in this controversy, as a thing most important and essential in human Liberty, that volitions, or the acts of the will, are contingent events; understanding contingence as opposite, not only to constraint, but to all Necessity. Therefore I would particularly consider this matter.

And, first, I would inquire, whether there is or can be any such thing, as a volition which is contingent in such a sense, as not only to come to pass without any Necessity of constraint or co-action, but also without a Necessity of consequence, or an infallible connexion with any thing foregoing.—Secondly, Whether, if it were so, this would at all help the cause of Liberty.

I. I would consider whether volition is a thing that ever does or can come to pass, in this manner, contingently.

And here it must be remembered, that it has been already shown, that nothing can ever come to pass without a cause, or a reason, why it exists in this manner rather than another; and the evidence of this has been particularly applied to the acts of the will. Now if this be so, it will demonstrably follow, that the acts of the will are never contingent, or without necessity, in the sense spoken of; inasmuch as those things which have a cause, or a reason of their existence, must be connected with their cause. This appears by the following considerations.

1. For an event to have a cause and ground of its existence, and yet not to be connected with its cause, is an inconsistence. For if the event be not connected with the cause, it is not dependent on the cause; its existence is as it were loose from its influence, and may attend it, or may not; it being a mere contingence, whether it follows or attends the influence of the cause, or not: And that is the same thing as not to he dependent on it. And to say, the event is not dependent on its cause, is absurd; it is the same thing as to say, it is not its cause, nor the event the effect of it; for dependence on the influence of a cause is the very notion of an effect. If there be no such relation between one thing and another, consisting in the connexion and dependence of one thing on the influence of another, then it is certain there is no such relation between them as is signified by the terms cause and effect. So far as an event is dependent on a cause, and connected with it, so much causality is there in the case, and no more. The cause does, or brings to pass, no more in any event, than is dependent on it. If we say, the connexion and dependence is not total, but partial, and that the effect, though it has some connexion and dependence, yet is not entirely dependent on it; that is the same thing as to say, that not all that is in the event is an effect of that cause, but that only part of it arises from thence, and part some other way.

2. If there are some events which are not necessarily connected with their causes, then it will follow, that there are some things which come to pass without any cause, contrary to the supposition. For if there be any event which was not necessarily connected with the influence of the cause under such circumstances, then it was contingent whether it would attend or follow the influence of the cause, or no; it might have followed, and it might not, when the cause was the same, its influence the same, and under the same circumstances. And if so, why did it follow, rather than not follow? Of this there is no cause or reason. Therefore here is something without any cause or reason why it is, viz. the following of the effect on the influence of the cause, with which it was not necessarily connected. If there be no necessary connexion of the effect on any thing antecedent, then we may suppose that sometimes the event will follow the cause, and sometimes not, when the cause is the same, and in every respect in the same state and circumstances. And what can be the cause and reason of this strange phenomenon, even this diversity, that in one

instance, the effect should follow, in another not? It is evident by the supposition, that this is wholly without any cause or ground. Here is something in the present manner of the existence of things, and state of the world, that is absolutely without a cause. Which is contrary to the supposition, and contrary to what has been before demonstrated.

3. To suppose there are some events which have a cause and ground of their existence, that yet are not necessarily connected with their cause, is to suppose that they have a cause which is not their cause. Thus; if the effect be not necessarily connected with the cause, with its influence, and influential circumstances; then, as I observed before, it is a thing possible and supposable, that the cause may sometimes exert the same influence, under the same circumstances, and yet the effect not follow. And if this actually happens in any instance, this instance is a proof, in fact, that the influence of the cause is not sufficient to produce the effect. For if it had been sufficient, it would have done it. And yet, by the supposition, in another instance, the same cause, with perfectly the same influence, and when all circumstances which have any influence are the same, it was followed with the effect. By which it is manifest, that the effect in this last instance was not owing to the influence of the cause, but must come to pass some other way. For it was proved before, that the influence of the cause was not sufficient to produce the effect. And if it was not sufficient to produce it, then the production of it could not be owing to that influence, but must be owing to something else, or owing to nothing. And if the effect be not owing to the influence of the cause, then it is not the cause. Which brings us to the contradiction of a cause, and no cause, that which is the ground and reason of the existence of a thing, and at the same time is NOT the ground and reason of its existence.

If the matter be not already so plain as to render any further reasoning upon it impertinent, I would say, that which seems to be the cause in the supposed case, can be no cause; its power and influence having, on a full trial, proved insufficient to produce such an effect: and if it be not sufficient to produce it, then it does not produce it. To say otherwise, is to say, there is power to do that which there is not power to do. If there be in a cause sufficient power exerted, and in circumstances sufficient to produce an effect, and so the effect be actually produced at one time; all these things concurring, will produce the effect at all times. And so we may turn it the other way; that which proves not sufficient at one time, cannot be sufficient at another, with precisely the same influential circumstances. And therefore if the effect follows, it is not owing to that cause; unless the different time be a circumstance which has influence: but that is contrary to the supposition; for it is supposed that all circumstances that have influence, are the same. And besides, this would be to suppose the time to be the cause; which is contrary to the supposition of the other thing being the cause. But if merely diversity of time has no influence, then it is evident that it is as much of an absurdity to say, the cause was sufficient to produce the effect at one time, and not at another; as to say, that it is sufficient to produce the effect at a certain time, and yet not sufficient to produce the same effect at the same time.

On the whole, it is clearly manifest, that every effect has a necessary connexion with its cause, or with that which is the true ground and reason of its existence. And therefore, if there be no event without a cause, as was proved before, then no event whatsoever is contingent, in the manner that Arminians suppose the free acts of the will to be contingent.

PART II. SECTION IX. OF THE CONNEXION OF THE ACTS OF THE WILL WITH THE DICTATES OF THE UNDERSTANDING.

It is manifest, that no Acts of the Will are contingent, in such a sense as to be without all necessity, or so as not to be necessary with a necessity of consequence and Connexion; because every Act of the Will is some way connected with the Understanding, and is as the greatest apparent good is, in the manner which has already been explained; namely, that the soul always wills or chooses that which, in the present view of the mind, considered in the whole of that view, and all that belongs to it, appears most agreeable. Because, as was observed before, nothing is more evident than that, when men act voluntarily, and do what they please, then they do what appears most agreeable to them; and to say otherwise, would be as much as to affirm, that men do not choose what appears to suit them best, or what seems most pleasing to them; or that they do not choose what they prefer. Which brings the matter to a contradiction.

And as it is very evident in itself, that the Acts of the will have some connexion with the dictates or views of the understanding, so this is allowed by some of the chief of the Arminian writers; particularly by

Dr. Whitby and Dr. Samuel Clark. Dr. Turnbull, though a great enemy to the doctrine of necessity, allows the same thing. In his Christian Philosophy, (p. 196.) he with much approbation cites another philosopher, as of the same mind, in these words: "No man (says an excellent philosopher) sets himself about any thing, but upon some view or other, which serves him for a reason for what he does; and whatsoever faculties he employs, the Understanding, with such light as it has, well or ill formed, constantly leads; and by that light, true or false, all her operative powers are directed. The Will itself, how absolute and incontrollable soever it may be thought, never fails in its obedience to the dictates of the understanding. Temples have their sacred images; and we see what influence they have always had over a great part of mankind; but in truth, the ideas and images in men's minds are the invisible powers that constantly govern them; and to these they all pay universally a ready submission." But whether this be in a just consistence with themselves, and their own notions of liberty, I desire may now be impartially considered.

Dr. Whitby plainly supposes, that the acts and determinations of the Will always follow the understanding's view of the greatest good to be obtained, or evil to be avoided; or, in other words, that the determinations of the Will constantly and infallibly follow these two things in the Understanding: 1. The degree of good to be obtained, and evil to be avoided, proposed to the understanding, and apprehended, viewed, and taken notice of by it. 2. The degree of the understanding's apprehension of that good or evil; which is increased by attention and consideration. That this is an opinion in which he is exceeding peremptory, (as he is in every opinion which he maintains in his controversy with the Calvinists,) with disdain of the contrary opinion, as absurd and self-contradictory, will appear by the following words, in his Discourse on the Five Points.

"Now, it is certain, that what naturally makes the Understanding to perceive, is evidence proposed, and apprehended, considered or adverted to: for nothing else can be requisite to make us come to the knowledge of the truth. Again, what makes the Will choose, is something approved by the Understanding; and consequently appearing to the soul as good. And whatsoever it refuseth, is something represented by the Understanding, and so appearing to the Will, as evil. Whence all that God requires of us is and can be only this; to refuse the evil, and choose the good. Wherefore, to say that evidence proposed, apprehended, and considered, is not sufficient to make the Understanding approve; or that the greatest good proposed, the greatest evil threatened, when equally believed and reflected on, is not sufficient to engage the Will to choose the good and refuse the evil, is in effect to say, that which alone doth move the Will to choose or to refuse, is not sufficient to engage it so to do; which being contradictory to itself, must of necessity be false. Be it then so, that we naturally have an aversion to the truths proposed to us in the gospel; that only can make us indisposed to attend to them, but cannot hinder our conviction, when we do apprehend them, and attend to them.—Be it, that there is in us also a renitency to the good we are to choose; that only can indispose us to believe it is, and to approve it as our chiefest good. Be it, that we are prone to the evil that we should decline; that only can render it the more difficult for us to believe it is the worst of evils. But yet, what we do really believe to be our chiefest good, will still be chosen; and what we apprehend to be the worst of evils, will, whilst we do continue under that conviction be refused by us. It therefore can be only requisite, in order to these ends, that the Good Spirit should so illuminate our Understandings, that we attending to and considering what lies before us, should apprehend and be convinced of our duty; and that the blessings of the gospel should be so propounded to us, as that we may discern them to be our chiefest good; and the miseries it threateneth, so as we may be convinced that they are the worst of evils; that we may choose the one, and refuse the other."

Here let it be observed, how plainly and peremptorily it is asserted, that the greatest good proposed, and the greatest evil threatened, when equally believed and reflected on, is sufficient to engage the will to choose the good, and refuse the evil, and is that alone which doth move the Will to choose or to refuse; and that it is contradictory to itself, to suppose otherwise; and therefore must of necessity be false; and then what we do really believe to be our chiefest good will still be chosen, and what we apprehend to be the worst of evils, will, whilst we continue under that conviction, be refused by us. Nothing could have been said more to the purpose, fully to signify, that the determinations of the Will must evermore follow the illumination, conviction, and notice of the Understanding, with regard to the greatest good and evil proposed, reckoning both the degree of good and evil understood, and the degree of Understanding, notice, and conviction of that proposed good and evil; and that it is thus necessarily, and can be otherwise in no instance: because it is asserted, that it implies a contradiction, to suppose it ever to be otherwise.

I am sensible, the Doctor's aim in these assertions is against the Calvinist; to show, in opposition to them, that there is no need of any physical operation of the Spirit of God on the Will, to change and determine that to a good choice, but that God's operation and assistance is only moral, suggesting ideas to the Understanding; which he supposes to be enough, if those ideas are attended to, infallibly to obtain the end. But whatever his design was, nothing can more directly and fully prove, that every determination of the Will, in choosing and refusing, is necessary; directly contrary to his own notion of the liberty of the Will. For if the determination of the Will, evermore, in this manner, follows the light, conviction, and view of the Understanding, concerning the greatest good and evil, and this be that alone which moves the Will, and it be a contradiction to suppose otherwise; then it is necessarily so, the Will necessarily follows this light or view of the understanding, not only in some of its acts, but in every act of choosing and refusing. So that the Will does not determine itself in any one of its own acts; but every act of choice and refusal depends on, and is necessarily connected with, some antecedent cause; which cause is not the Will itself, nor any act of its own, nor any thing pertaining to that faculty, but something belonging to another faculty, whose acts go before the will, in all its acts, and govern and determine them.

Here, if it should be replied, that although it be true, that according to the Doctor, the final determination of the Will always depends upon, and is infallibly connected with, the Understanding's conviction, and notice of the greatest good; yet the Acts of the will are not necessary; because that conviction of the Understanding is first dependent on a preceding Act of the Will, in determining to take notice of the evidence exhibited; by which means the mind obtains that degree of conviction, which is sufficient and effectual to determine the consequent and ultimate choice of the Will; and that the Will, with regard to that preceding act, whereby it determines whether to attend or no, is not necessary; and that in this, the liberty of the Will consists, that when God holds forth sufficient objective light, the Will is at liberty whether to command the attention of the mind to it or not.

Nothing can be more weak and inconsiderate than such a reply as this. For that preceding Act of the Will, in determining to attend and consider, still is an Act of the Will; if the Liberty of the Will consists in it, as is supposed, as if it be an Act of the Will, it is an act of choice or refusal. And therefore, if what the Doctor asserts be true, it is determined by some antecedent light in the Understanding concerning the greatest apparent good or evil. For he asserts, it is that light which alone doth move the will to choose or refuse. And therefore the Will must be moved by that, in choosing to attend to the objective light offered, in order to another consequent act of choice: so that this act is no less necessary than the other. And if we suppose another Act of the will, still preceding both these mentioned, to determine both, still that also must be an Act of the Will, an act of choice; and so must, by the same principles, be infallibly determined by some certain degree of light in the Understanding concerning the greatest good. And let us suppose as many Acts of the Will, one preceding another, as we please, yet are they every one of them necessarily determined by a certain degree of light in the understanding, concerning the greatest and most eligible good in that case; and so, not one of them free according to Dr. Whitby's notion of freedom. And if it be said, the reason why men do not attend to light held forth, is because of ill habits contracted by evil acts committed before, whereby their minds are indisposed to consider the truth held forth to them, the difficulty is not at all avoided: still the question returns, What determined the Will in those preceding evil acts? It must, by Dr. Whitby's principles, still be the view of the Understanding concerning the greatest good and evil. If this view of the Understanding be that alone which doth move the Will to choose or refuse, as the Doctor asserts, then every act of choice or refusal, from a man's first existence, is moved and determined by this view; and this view of the Understanding exciting and governing the act, must be before the act. And therefore the Will is necessarily determined, in every one of its acts, from a man's first existence, by a cause beside the will, and a cause that does not proceed from or depend on any act of the Will at all. Which at once utterly abolishes the Doctor's whole scheme of Liberty of Will; and he, at one stroke, has cut the sinews of all his arguments from the goodness, righteousness, faithfulness, and sincerity of God, in his commands, promises, threatenings, calls, invitations, and expostulations; which he makes use of, under the heads of reprobation, election, universal redemption, sufficient and effectual grace, and the freedom of the will of man; and has made vain all his exclamations against the doctrine of the Calvinists, as charging God with manifest unrighteousness, unfaithfulness, hypocrisy, fallaciousness, and cruelty.

Dr. Samuel Clark, in his Demonstration of the Being and Attributes of God, to evade the argument to prove the necessity of volition, from its necessary Connexion with the last Dictate of the Understanding, supposes the latter not to be diverse from the Act of the will itself. But if it be so, it will not alter the case as to the necessity of the Act. If the Dictate of the Understanding be the very same with the determination of the Will, as Dr. Clark supposes, then this determination is no fruit or effect of choice; and if so, no liberty of choice has any hand in it: it is necessary; that is, choice cannot prevent it. If the last Dictate of the Understanding be the same with the determination of volition itself, then the existence of that determination must be necessary as to volition; in as much as volition can have no opportunity to determine whether it shall exist or no, it having existence already before volition has opportunity to determine any thing. It is itself the very rise and existence of volition. But a thing after it exists, has no opportunity to determine as to its own existence; it is too late for that.

If liberty consists in that which Arminians suppose, viz. in the will determining its own acts, having free opportunity and being without all necessity; this is the same as to say, that liberty consists in the soul having power and opportunity to have what determinations of the will it pleases. And if the determinations of the Will, and the last Dictates of the Understanding, be the same thing, then liberty consists in the mind having power and opportunity to choose its own Dictates of understanding. But this is absurd; for it is to make the determination of choice prior to the Dictate of Understanding, and the ground of it; which cannot consist with the Dictate of the Understanding being the determination of choice itself.

Here is no alternative, but to recur to the old absurdity of one determination before another, and the cause of it; and another before, determining that; and so on in infinitum. If the last Dictate of the Understanding be the determination of the Will itself, and the soul be free with regard to that Dictate, in the Arminian notion of freedom; then the soul, before that dictate of its Understanding exists, voluntarily and according to its own choice determines, in every case, what that Dictate of the Understanding shall be; otherwise that Dictate, as to the will, is necessary; and the acts determined by it must also be necessary. So that there is a determination of the mind prior to that Dictate of the Understanding, an act of choice going before it, choosing and determining what that Dictate of the Understanding shall be: and this preceding act of choice, being a free Act of Will, must also be the same with another last Dictate of the Understanding: and if the mind also be free in that Dictate of

Understanding, that must be determined still by another; and so on for ever.

Besides, if the Dictate of the Understanding, and determination of the will be the same, this confounds the Understanding and will, and makes them the same. Whether they be the same or no, I will not now dispute; but only would observe, that if it be so, and the Arminian notion of liberty consists in a self-determining power in the Understanding, free of all necessity; being independent, undetermined by any thing prior to its own acts and determinations; and the more the Understanding is thus independent, and sovereign over its own determinations, the more free: then the freedom of the soul, as a moral agent, must consist in the independence of the Understanding of any evidence or appearance of things, or any thing whatsoever that stands forth to the view of the mind, prior to the Understanding's determination. And what a liberty is this! consisting in an ability, freedom, and easiness of judging, either according to evidence, or against it; having a sovereign command over itself at all times, to judge, either agreeably or disagreeably to what is plainly exhibited to its own view. Certainly, it is no liberty that renders persons the proper subjects of persuasive reasoning, arguments, expostulations, and such like moral means and inducements. The use of which with mankind is a main argument of the Arminians, to defend their notion of liberty without all necessity. For according to this, the more free men are, the less they are under the government of such means, less subject to the power of evidence and reason, and more independent of their influence, in their determinations.

And whether the Understanding and Will are the same or no, as Dr. Clark seems to suppose, yet in order to maintain the Arminian notion of liberty without necessity, the free Will is not determined by the Understanding, nor necessarily connected with the Understanding; and the further from such Connexion, the greater the freedom. And when the liberty is full and complete, the determinations of the will have no Connexion at all with the Dictates of the Understanding. And if so, in vain are all the applications to the Understanding, in order to induce to any free virtuous act; and so in vain are all instructions, counsels, invitations, expostulations, and all arguments and persuasive whatsoever: for these are but applications to the Understanding, and a clear and lively exhibition of the objects of choice to the mind's view. But if, after all, the will must be self-determined, and independent on the Understanding, to what purpose are things thus represented to the Understanding, in order to determine the choice?

PART II. SECTION X. VOLITION NECESSARILY CONNECTED WITH THE INFLUENCE OF MOTIVES: WITH PARTICULAR OBSERVATIONS ON THE GREAT INCONSISTENCE OF MR. CHUBB'S ASSERTIONS AND REASONINGS ABOUT THE FREEDOM OF THE WILL.

That every act of the Will has some cause, and consequently (by what has been already proved) has a necessary connexion with its cause, and so is necessary by a necessity of connexion and consequence, is evident by this, that every act of the Will whatsoever is excited by some motive: which is manifest, because, if the mind, in willing after the manner it does, is excited by no motive or inducement, then it has no end which it proposes to itself, or pursues in so doing; it aims at nothing, and seeks nothing. And if it seeks nothing, then it does not go after any thing, or exert any inclination or preference towards any thing, which brings the matter to a contradiction; because for the mind to will something, and for it to go after something by an act of preference and inclination, are the same thing.

But if every act of the Will is excited by a motive, then that Motive is the cause of the act. If the acts of the Will are excited by motives, then Motives are the causes of their being excited; or, which is the same thing, the cause of their existence. And if so, the existence of the acts of the will is properly the effect of their motives. Motives do nothing, as Motives or inducements, but by their influence; and so much as is done by their influence is the effect of them. For that is the notion of an effect, something that is brought to pass by the influence of something else.

And if volitions are properly the effects of their Motives, then they are necessarily connected with their Motives. Every effect and event being as was proved before, necessarily connected with that which is the proper ground and reason of its existence. Thus it is manifest, that volition is necessary, and is not from any self-determining power in the will: the volition, which is caused by previous motive and inducement, is not caused by the will exercising a sovereign power over itself, to determine, cause, and excite volitions in itself. This is not consistent with the will acting in a state of indifference and equilibrium, to determine itself to a preference; for the way in which Motives operate, is by biasing the will, and giving it a certain inclination or preponderation one way.

Here it may be proper to observe, that Mr. Chubb in his Collection of Tracts on Various Subjects, has advanced a scheme of liberty, which is greatly divided against itself, and thoroughly subversive of itself: and that many ways.

1. He is abundant in asserting, that the Will, in all its acts, is influenced by Motive and excitement; and that this is the previous ground and reason of all its acts, and that it is never otherwise in any instance. He says, (p. 262.) "No action can take place without some Motive to excite it." And, (p. 263,) "Volition cannot take place without SOME PREVIOUS reason or motive to induce it." And, (p. 310.) Action would not take place without some reason or motive to induce it; it being absurd to suppose, that the active faculty would be exerted without some PREVIOUS reason to dispose the mind to action." (So also p. 257.) And he speaks of these things, as what we may be absolutely certain of, and which are the foundation, the only foundation we have of certainty respecting God's moral perfections. (p. 252–255, 261–264.)

And yet, at the same time, by his scheme, the influence of Motives upon us to excite to action, and to be actually a ground of volition, is consequent on the volition or choice of the mind. For he very greatly insists upon it, that in all free actions, before the mind is the subject of those volitions, which motives excite, it chooses to be so. It chooses, whether it will comply with the Motive, which presents itself in view, or not; and when various Motives are presented, it chooses which it will yield to, and which it will reject. (p. 256.) "Every man has power to act, or to refrain from acting, agreeably with, or contrary to, any Motive that presents." (p. 257.) "Every man is at liberty to act, or refrain from acting, agreeably with, or contrary to, what each of these motives, considered singly, would excite him to.—Man has power, and is as much at liberty, to reject the Motive that does prevail, as he has power, and is at liberty, to reject those Motives that do not." (And so p. 310, 311.) "In order to constitute a moral agent, it is necessary, that he should have power to act, or to refrain from acting, upon such moral motives, as he pleases." And to the like purpose in many other places. According to these things, the Will acts first, and chooses or refuses to comply with the Motive that is presented, before it falls under its prevailing influence:

and it is first determined by the mind's pleasure or choice, what Motives it will be induced by, before it is induced by them.

Now, how can these things hang together? How can the mind First act, and by its act of volition and choice determine what motives shall be the ground and reason of its volition and choice? For this supposes, the choice is already made, before the Motive has its effect; and that the volition is already exerted, before the Motive prevails, so as actually to be the ground of the volition; and make the prevailing of the Motive, the consequence of the volition, of which yet it is the ground. If the mind has already chosen to comply with a motive, and to yield to its excitement, the excitement comes in too late, and is needless afterwards. If the mind has already chosen to yield to a Motive which invites to a thing, that implies, and in fact is, a choosing of the thing invited to; and the very act of choice is before the influence of the motive which induces, and is the ground of the choice; the son is beforehand with the father that begets him: the choice is supposed to be the ground of that influence of the Motive, which very influence is supposed to be the ground of the choice. And so vice versa, the choice is supposed to be the consequence of the influence of the Motive, which influence of the Motive is the consequence of that very choice.

And besides, if the Will acts first towards the motive before it falls under its influence, and the prevailing of the Motive upon it to induce it to act and choose, be the fruit and consequence of its act and choice, then how is the Motive "a PREVIOUS ground and reason of the act and choice, so that in the nature of the things, volition cannot take place without some PREVIOUS reason and Motive to induce it;" and that this act is consequent upon, and follows the Motive? Which things Mr. Chubb often asserts, as of certain and undoubted truth. So that the very same Motive is both previous and consequent, both before and after, both the ground and fruit of the very same thing!

II. Agreeable to the forementioned inconsistent notion of the Will first acting towards the motive, choosing whether it will comply with it, in order to it becoming a ground of the Will's acting, before any act of volition can take place, Mr. Chubb frequently calls Motives and excitements to the action of the will, "the passive ground or reason of that action." Which is a remarkable phrase; than which I presume there is none more unintelligible, and void of distinct and consistent meaning, in all the writings of Duns Scotus, or Thomas Aquinas. When he represents the Motive volition as passive, he must mean—passive in that affair, or passive with respect to that action, which he speaks of; otherwise it is nothing to the design of his argument: he must mean, (if that can be called a meaning,) that the Motive to volition is first acted upon or towards by the volition, choosing to yield to it, making it a ground of action, or determining to fetch its influence from thence; and so to make it a previous ground of its own excitation and existence. Which is the same absurdity, as if one should say, that the soul of man, previous to its existence, chose by what cause it would come into existence, and acted upon its cause, to fetch influence thence, to bring it into being; and so its cause was a passive ground of its existence!

Mr. Chubb very plainly supposes motive or excitement to be the ground of the being of volition. He speaks of it as the ground or reason of the EXERTION of an act of the will, (p. 391, and 392.) and expressly says, that "volition cannot TAKE PLACE without some previous ground or Motive to induce it," (p. 363.) And he speaks of the act as "FROM the motive, and FROM THE INFLUENCE of the motive," (p. 352.) "and from the influence that the Motive has on the man, for the PRODUCTION of an action," (p. 317.) Certainly there is no need of multiplying words about this; it is easily judged, whether motive can be the ground of volition taking place, so that the very production of it is from the influence of the motive, and yet the Motive, before it becomes the ground of the volition, is passive, or acted upon the volition. But this I will say, that a man, who insists so much on clearness of meaning in others, and is so much in blaming their confusion and inconsistence, ought, if he was able, to have explained his meaning in this phrase of "passive ground of action," so as to show it not to be confused and inconsistent.

If any should suppose, that Mr. Chubb, when he speaks of motive as a "passive ground of action," does not mean passive with regard to that volition which it is the ground of, but some other antecedent volition, (though his purpose and argument, and whole discourse, will by no means allow of such a supposition,) yet it would not help the matter in the least. For, (1.) If we suppose an act, by which the soul chooses to yield to the invitation of a Motive to another volition; both these supposed volitions are in effect the very same. A volition to yield to the force of a motive inviting to choose something, comes to just the same thing as choosing the thing which the motive invites to, as I observed before. So that here can be no room to help the matter, by a distinction of two volitions. (2.) If the Motive be passive, not with respect to the same volition to which the motive excites, but to one truly distinct and prior; yet, by Mr. Chubb, that prior volition cannot take place without a Motive or excitement, as a previous ground of its existence. For he insists, that "it is absurd to suppose any volition should take place without some previous motive to induce it," So that at last it comes to just the same absurdity: for if every volition must have a previous motive, then the very first in the whole series must be excited by a previous Motive; and yet the Motive to that first volition is passive; but cannot be passive with regard to another antecedent volition, because, by the supposition, it is the very first: therefore if it be passive with respect to any volition, it must be so with regard to that very volition of which it is the ground, and that is excited by it.

III. Though Mr. Chubb asserts, as above, that every volition has some motive, and that "in the nature of the thing, no volition can take place without some motive to induce it;" yet he asserts, that volition does not always follow the strongest Motive; or, in other words, is not governed by any superior strength of the motive that is followed, beyond Motives to the contrary, previous to the volition itself. His own words (p. 258.) are as follow: "Though with regard to physical causes, that which is strongest always prevails, yet it is otherwise with regard to moral causes. Of these, sometimes the stronger, sometimes the weaker, prevails. And the ground of this difference is evident, namely, that what we call moral causes, strictly speaking, are no causes at all, but barely passive reasons of or excitements to the action, or to the refraining from acting: which excitements we have power, or are at liberty, to comply with or reject, as I have showed above." And so throughout the paragraph, he in a variety of phrases insists, that the Will is not always determined by the strongest Motive, unless by strongest we preposterously mean actually prevailing in the event; which is not in the Motive, but in the Will; but that the will is not always determined by the Motive which is strongest, by any strength previous to the volition itself. And he elsewhere abundantly asserts, that the will is determined by no superior strength or advantage, that Motives have, from any constitution or state of things, or any circumstances whatsoever, previous to the actual determination of the will. And indeed his whole discourse on human liberty implies it, his whole scheme is founded upon it.

But these things cannot stand together. There is a diversity of strength in Motives to choice, previous to the choice itself. Mr. Chubb himself supposes, that they do previously invite, induce, excite, and dispose the mind to action. This implies, that they have something in themselves that is inviting, some tendency to induce and dispose to volition previous to volition itself. And if they have in themselves this nature and tendency, doubtless they have it in certain limited degrees, which are capable of diversity; and some have it in greater degrees, others in less; and they that have most of this tendency, considered with all their nature and circumstances, previous to volition, are the strongest Motives, and those that have least, are the weakest Motives.

Now if volition sometimes does not follow the motive which is strongest, or has most previous tendency or advantage, all things considered, to induce or excite it, but follows the weakest, or that which, as it stands previously in the mind's view, has least tendency to induce it; herein the will apparently acts wholly without Motive, without any previous reason to dispose the mind to it, contrary to what the same author supposes. The act, wherein the will must proceed without a previous motive to induce it, is the act of preferring the weakest Motive. For how absurd is it to say, the mind sees previous reason in the Motive, to prefer that Motive before the other; and at the same time to suppose, that there is nothing in the motive, in its nature, state, or any circumstance of it whatsoever, as it stands in the previous view of the mind, that gives it any preference: but on the contrary, the other Motive that stands in competition with it, in all these respects, has most belonging to it that is inviting and moving, and has most of a tendency to choice and preference. This is certainly as much as to say, there is previous ground and reason in the Motive for the act of preference, and yet no previous reason for it. By the supposition, as to all that is in the two rival Motives, which tends to preference, previous to the act of preference, it is not in that which is preferred, but wholly in the other: and yet Mr. Chubb supposes, that the act of preference is from previous ground and reason, in the motive which is preferred. But are these things consistent? Can there be previous ground in a thing for an event that takes place, and yet no previous tendency in it to that event? If one thing follows another, without any previous tendency to its following, then I should think it very plain, that it follows it without any manner of previous reason why it should follow.

Yea, in this case, Mr. Chubb supposes, that the event follows an antecedent, as the ground of its existence, which has not only no tendency to it, but a contrary tendency. The event is the preference, which the mind gives to that Motive, which is weaker, as it stands in the previous view of the mind; the immediate antecedent is the view the mind has of the two rival motives conjunctly; in which previous view of the mind, all the preferableness, or previous tendency to preference, is supposed to be on the other side, or in the contrary Motive; and all the unworthiness of preference, and so previous tendency to comparative neglect, or undervaluing, is on that side which is preferred: and yet in this view of the mind is supposed to be the previous ground or reason of this act of preference, exciting it, and disposing the mind to it. Which I leave the reader to judge, whether it be absurd or not. If it be not, then it is not absurd to say, that the previous tendency of an antecedent to a consequent, is the ground and reason why that consequent does not follow; and the want of a previous tendency to an event, yea, a tendency to the contrary, is the true ground and reason why that event does follow.

An act of choice or preference is a comparative act, wherein the mind acts with reference to two or more things that are compared, and stand in competition in the mind's view. If the mind, in this comparative act, prefers that which appears inferior in the comparison, then the mind herein acts absolutely without motive, or inducement, or any temptation whatsoever. Then, if a hungry man has the offer of two sorts of food, to both which he finds an appetite, but has a stronger appetite to one than the other; and there be no circumstances or excitements whatsoever in the case to induce him to take either the one or the other, but merely his appetite: if in the choice he makes between them, he chooses that which he has least appetite to, and refuse that to which he has the strongest appetite, this is a choice made absolutely without previous Motive, Excitement, Reason, or Temptation, as much as if he were perfectly without all appetite to either; because his volition in this case is a comparative act, following a comparative view of the food, which he chooses, in which view his preference has absolutely no previous ground, yea, is against all previous ground and motive. And if there be any principle in man, from whence an act of choice may arise after this manner, from the same principle volition may arise wholly without motive on either side. If the mind in its volition can go beyond Motive, then it can go without Motive: for when it is beyond the Motive, it is out of the reach of the Motive, out of the limits of its influence, and so without. Motive. If so, this demonstrates the independence of volition on Motive; and no reason can be given for what Mr. Chubb so often asserts, even that "in the nature of things volition cannot take place without a motive to induce it."

If the Most High should endow a balance with agency or activity of nature, in such a manner, that when unequaled weights are put into the scales, its agency could enable it to cause that scale to descend, which has the least weight, and so to raise the greater weight; this would clearly demonstrate, that the motion of the balance does not depend on weights in the scales; at least, as much as if the balance should move itself, when there is no weight in either scale. And the activity of the balance which is sufficient to move itself against the greater weight, must certainly be more than sufficient to move it when there is no weight at all.

Mr. Chubb supposes, that the Will cannot stir at all without some Motive; and also supposes, that if there be a Motive to one thing, and none to the contrary, volition will infallibly follow that motive. This is virtually to suppose an entire dependence of the Will on Motives; if it were not wholly dependent on them, it could surely help itself a little without them; or help itself a little against a Motive, without help from the strength and weight of a contrary Motive. And yet his supposing that the will, when it has before it various opposite Motives, can use them as it pleases, and choose its own influence from them, and neglect the strongest, and follow the weakest, supposes it to be wholly independent on Motives.

It further appears, on Mr. Chubb's hypothesis, that volition must be without any previous ground in any motive, thus: if it be, as he supposes, that the will is not determined by any previous superior strength of the motive, but determines and chooses its own Motive, then, when the rival Motives are exactly equal, in all respects, it may follow either; and may, in such a case, sometimes follow one, sometimes the other. And if so, this diversity which appears between the acts of the Will, is plainly without previous ground in either of the Motives; for all that is previously in the Motives, is supposed precisely and perfectly the same, without any diversity whatsoever. Now perfect identity, as to all that is previous in the antecedent, cannot be the ground and reason of diversity in the consequent. Perfect identity in the ground, cannot be a reason why it is not followed with the same consequence. And therefore the source of this diversity of consequence must be sought for elsewhere.

And lastly, it may be observed, that however much Mr. Chubb insists, that no volition can take place without some Motive to induce it, which previously disposes the mind to it; yet, as he also insists that the mind, without reference to any superior strength of motives, picks and chooses for its Motive to follow; he himself herein plainly supposes, that, with regard to the mind's preference of one Motive before another—it is not the motive that disposes the Will, but—the will disposes itself to follow the Motive.

IV. Mr. Chubb supposes necessity to be utterly inconsistent with agency; and that to suppose a being to be an agent in that which is necessary, is a plain contradiction, p. 311 and throughout his discourses on the subject of Liberty, he supposes, that necessity cannot consist with agency or freedom; and that to suppose otherwise, is to make Liberty and Necessity, Action and Passion, the same thing. And so he seems to suppose, that there is no action, strictly speaking, but volition; and that as to the effects of volition in body or mind, in themselves considered, being necessary, they are said to be free, only as they are the effects of an act that is not necessary.

And yet, according to him, volition itself is the effect of volition; yea, every act of free volition; and therefore every act of free volition must, by what has now been observed from him, be necessary. That every act of free volition is itself the effect of volition, is abundantly supposed by him. In p. 341, he says," If a man is such a creature as I have proved him to be, that is, if he has in him a power of Liberty of doing either good or evil, and either of these is the subject of his own free choice, so that he might, IF HE HAD PLEASED, have CHOSEN and done the contrary."—Here he supposes all that is good or evil in man is the effect of his choice; and so that his good or evil choice itself is the effect of his pleasure or choice, in these words, "he might if he had PLEASED, have CHOSEN the contrary." So in p. 356, "Though it be highly reasonable, that a man should always choose the greater good,—yet he may, if he PLEASES, CHOOSE otherwise." Which is the same thing as if he had said, he may if he chooses choose otherwise. And then he goes on,— "that is, he may, if he pleases, choose what is good for himself," &c. And again in the same page, "The Will is not confined by the understanding, to any particular sort of good, whether greater or less; but it is at liberty to choose what kind of good it pleases."—If there be any meaning in the last words, it must be this, that the Will is at liberty to choose what kind of good it chooses to choose; supposing the act of choice itself determined by an antecedent choice. The Liberty Mr. Chubb speaks of, is not only a man's power to move his body, agreeable to an antecedent act of choice, but to use or exert the faculties of his soul. Thus, (p. 379.) speaking of the faculties of the mind, he says, "Man has power, and is at liberty to neglect these faculties, to use them aright, or to abuse them, as he pleases." And that he supposes an act of choice or exercise of pleasure, properly distinct from, and antecedent to, those acts thus chosen, directing, commanding, and producing the chosen acts, and even the acts of choice themselves, is very plain in p. 283. "He can command his actions; and herein consists his Liberty; he can give or deny himself that pleasure, as he pleases. And p. 377. If the actions of men—are not the produce of a free choice, or election, but spring from a necessity of nature,—he cannot in reason be the object of reward or punishment on their account. Whereas, if action in man, whether good or evil, is the produce of will or free choice; so that a man in either case, had it in his power, and was at liberty to have CHOSEN the contrary, he is the proper object of reward or punishment, according as he chooses to behave himself." Here, in these last words, he speaks of Liberty of choosing according as he chooses. So that the behavior which he speaks of as subject to his choice, is his choosing itself, as well as his external conduct consequent upon it. And therefore it is evident, he means not only external actions, but the acts of choice themselves, when he speaks of all free actions, as the PRODUCE of free choice. And this is abundantly evident in what he says elsewhere, (p. 372, 373.)

Now these things imply a twofold great inconsistence. 1. To suppose, as Mr. Chubb plainly does, that every free act of choice is commanded by, and is the produce of, free choice, is to suppose the first free act of choice belonging to the case, yea, the first free act of choice that ever man exerted, to be the produce of an antecedent act of choice. But I hope I need not labor at all to convince my readers, that it is an absurdity to say, the very first act is the produce of another act that went before it.

2. If it were both possible and real, as Mr. Chubb insists, that every free act of choice were the produce or the effect of a free act of choice; yet even then, according to his principles, no one act of choice would be free, but every one necessary; because, every act of choice being the effect of a foregoing act, every act would be necessarily connected with that foregoing cause. For Mr. Chubb himself says, (p. 389.) "When the self-moving power is exerted, it becomes the necessary cause of its effects."—So that his notion of a free act, that is rewardable or punishable, is a heap of contradictions. It is a free act, and yet, by his own notion of freedom, is necessary; and therefore by him it is a contradiction, to suppose it to be free. According to him, every free act is the produce of a free act; so that there must be an infinite number of free acts in succession, without any beginning, in an agent that has a beginning.

And therefore here is an infinite number of free acts, every one of them free; and yet not any one of them free, but every act in the whole infinite chain a necessary effect. All the acts are rewardable or punishable, and yet the agent cannot, in reason, be the object of reward or punishment, on account of any one of these actions. He is active in them all, and passive in none; yet active in none, but passive in all, &c.

V. Mr. Chubb most strenuously denies, that Motives are causes of the acts of the Will; or that the moving principle in man is moved, or caused to be exerted by motives. His words, (p. 388 and 389.) are, "If the moving principle in man is Moved, or caused to be Exerted, by something external to man, which all Motives are, then it would not be a self-moving principle, seeing it would be moved by a principle external to itself. And to say, that a self-moving principle is moved, or caused to be exerted, by a cause external to itself; is absurd and a contradiction," &c.—And in the next page, it is particularly and largely insisted, that motives are causes in no case, that "they are merely passive in the production of action, and have no causality in the production of it,—no causality, to be the cause of the exertion of the will."

Now I desire it may be considered, how this can possibly consist with what he says in other places. Let it be noted here, 1. Mr. Chubb abundantly speaks of Motives as excitements of the acts of the Will; and says, that motives do excite volition, and induce it, and that they are necessary to this end; that in the reason and nature of things, volition cannot take place without motives to excite it. But now, if Motives excite the will, they move it; and yet he says, it is absurd to say, the Will is moved by motives. And again, if language is of any significancy at all, if Motives excite volition, then they are the cause of its being excited; and to cause volition to be excited, is to cause it to be put forth or excited. Yea, Mr. Chubb says himself, (p. 317.) motive is necessary to the exertion of the active faculty. To excite, is positively to do something; and certainly that which does something, is the cause of the thing done by it. To create, is to cause to be created; to make, is to cause to be made; to kill, is to cause to be killed; to quicken, is to cause to be quickened; and to excite, is to cause to be excited. To excite, is to be a cause, in the most proper sense, not merely a negative occasion, but a ground of existence by positive influence. The notion of exciting, is exerting influence to cause the effect to arise or come forth into existence.

2. Mr. Chubb himself (p. 317.) speaks of Motives as the ground and reason of action BY INFLUENCE, and BY PREVAILING INFLU-

ENCE. Now, what can be meant by a cause, but something that is the ground and reason of a thing by its influence, an influence that is prevalent and effectual?

3. This author not only speaks of Motives as the ground and reason of action, by prevailing influence; but expressly of their influence as prevailing for the production of an action, (p. 317.) which makes the inconsistency still more palpable and notorious. The production of an effect is certainly the causing of an effect; and production influence is causal influence, if any thing is; and that which has this influence prevalently, so as thereby to become the ground of another thing, is a cause of that thing, if there be any such thing as a cause. This influence, Mr. Chubb says, Motives have to produce an action; and yet, he says, it is absurd and a contradiction, to say they are causes.

4. In the same page, he once and again speaks of motives as disposing the Agent to action, by their influence. His words are these: "As Motive, which takes place in the understanding, and is the product of intelligence, is NECESSARY to action, that is, to the EXERTION of the active faculty, because that faculty would not be exerted without some PREVIOUS REASON TO DISPOSE the mind to action; so from hence it plainly appears, that when a man is said to be disposed to one action rather than another, this properly signifies the PREVAILING INFLUENCE that one motive has upon a man FOR THE PRODUCTION of an action, or for the being at rest, before all other Motives, for the production of the contrary. For as motive is the ground and reason of any action, so the Motive that prevails, disposes the agent to the performance of that action."

Now, if motives dispose the mind to action, then they cause the mind to be disposed; and to cause the mind to be disposed is to cause it to be willing; and to cause it to be willing is to cause it to will; and that is the same thing as to be the cause of an act of the Will. And yet this same Mr. Chubb holds it to be absurd, to support Motive to be a cause of the act of the Will.

And if we compare these things together, we have here again a whole heap of inconsistences. Motives are the previous ground and reason of the acts of the Will; yea, the necessary ground and reason of their exertion, without which they will not be exerted, and cannot, in the nature of things, take place; and they do excite these acts of the will, and do this by a prevailing influence; yea, an influence which prevails for the production of the act of the will, and for the disposing of the mind to it; and yet it is absurd, to suppose motive to be a cause of an act of the Will, or that a principle of Will is moved or caused to be exerted by it, or that it has any causality in the production of it, or any causality to be the cause of the exertion of the Will.

A due consideration of these things which Mr. Chubb has advanced, the strange inconsistences which his notion of Liberty—consisting in the Will's power of self-determination void of all necessity, united with that dictate of common sense, that there can be no volition without a Motive—drove him into, may be sufficient to convince us, that it is utterly impossible ever to make that notion of Liberty consistent with the influence of motives in volition. And as it is in a manner self-evident, that there can be no act of Will, or preference of the mind, without some motive or inducement, something in the mind's view which it aims at, or goes after; so it is most manifest, that there is no such Liberty in the universe as Arminians insist on; nor any such thing possible, or conceivable.

PART II. SECTION XI. THE EVIDENCE OF GOD'S CERTAIN FOREKNOWLEDGE OF THE VOLITIONS OF MORAL AGENTS.

That the acts of the Wills of moral Agents are not contingent events, in such a sense, as to be without all necessity, appears by God's certain Foreknowledge of such events.

In handling this argument, I would in the first place prove, that God has a certain Foreknowledge of the voluntary acts of moral Agents; and secondly, show the consequence, or how it follows from hence, that the Volitions of moral Agents are not contingent, so as to be without necessity of connexion and consequence.

First, I am to prove, that God has an absolute and certain Foreknowledge of the free actions of moral Agents.

One would think it wholly needless to enter on such an argument with any that profess themselves Christians: but so it is; God's certain Foreknowledge of the free acts of moral Agents, is denied by some that pretend to believe the Scriptures to be the Word of God; and especially of late. I therefore shall consider the evidence of such a prescience in the Most High, as fully as the designed limits of this essay will admit;—supposing myself herein to have to do with such as own the truth of the Bible.

Arg. I. My first argument shall be taken from God's prediction of such events. Here I would, in the first place, lay down these two things as axioms. 1. If God does not foreknow, He cannot foretell such events; that is, He cannot peremptorily and certainly foretell them. If God has no more than an uncertain guess concerning events of this kind, then He can declare no more than an uncertain guess. Positively to foretell, is to profess to foreknow, or declare positive Foreknowledge.

If God does not certainly foreknow the future Volitions of moral Agents, then neither can He certainly foreknow those events which are dependent on these Volitions. The existence of the one depending on the existence of the other, the knowledge of the existence of the one depends on the knowledge of the existence of the other; and the one cannot be more certain than the other.

Therefore, how many, how great, and how extensive soever the consequences of the Volitions of moral Agents may be; though they should extend to an alteration of the state of things through the universe, and should be continued in a series of successive events to all eternity, and should in the progress of things branch forth into an infinite number of series, each of them going on in an endless chain of events; God must be as ignorant of all these consequences, as He is of the Volition whence they first take their rise: and the whole state of things depending on them, how important, extensive, and vast soever, must be hid from him.

These positions being such as, I suppose, none will deny, I now proceed to observe the following things. 1. Men's moral conduct and qualities, their virtues and vices, their wickedness and good practice, things rewardable and punishable, have often been foretold by God.— Pharaoh's moral conduct, in refusing to obey God's command, in letting his people go, was foretold. God says to Moses, Exod. iii. 19. " I am sure that the king of Egypt will not let you go." Here. God professes not only to guess at, but to know Pharaoh's future disobedience. In chap. vii. 4. God says, " but Pharaoh shall not hearken unto you; that I may lay mine hand upon Egypt," &c. And chap. ix. 30. Moses says to Pharaoh, "as for thee, and thy servants, I Know that ye will not fear the Lord." See also chap. xi. 9.—The moral conduct of Josiah, by name, in his zealously exerting himself to oppose idolatry, in particular acts, was foretold above three hundred years before he was born, and the prophecy sealed by a miracle, and renewed and confirmed by the words of a second prophet, as what surely would not fail, (1 Kings xiii. 1–6, 32.) This prophecy was also in effect a prediction of the moral conduct of the people, in upholding their schismatical and idolatrous worship until that time, and the idolatry of those priests of the high places, which it is foretold Josiah should offer upon that altar of Bethel. Micah foretold the foolish and sinful conduct of Ahab, in refusing to hearken to the word of the Lord by him, and choosing rather to hearken to the false prophets, in going to RamothGilead to his ruin, (1 King's xxi. 20–22.) The moral conduct of Hazael was foretold, in that cruelty he should be guilty of; on which Hazael says, "what, is thy servant a dog, that he should do this thing!" The prophet speaks of the event as what he knew, and not what he conjectured, 2 Kings viii. 12. "I know the evil that thou wilt do unto the children of Israel: Thou wilt dash their children, and rip up their women with child." The moral conduct of Cyrus is foretold, long before he had a being, in his mercy to God's people, and regard to the true God, in turning the captivity of the Jews, and promoting the building of the temple, (Isa. xliv. 28. and lxv. 13. compare 2 Chron. xxxvi. 22, 23. and Ezra i. 1–4.) How many instances of the moral conduct of the kings of the North and South, particular instances of the wicked behaviour of the kings of Syria and Egypt, are foretold in the 11th chapter of Daniel! Their corruption, violence, robbery, treachery, and lies. And particularly, how much is foretold of the horrid wickedness of Antiochus Epiphanes, called there "a vile person," instead of Epiphones, or illustrious! In that chapter, and also in chap. viii. ver. 9, 14, 23, to the end, are foretold his flattery, deceit, and lies, his having "his heart set to do mischief," and set "against the holy covenant," his "destroying and treading under foot the holy people," in a marvellous manner, his "having indignation against the holy covenant, setting his heart against it, and conspiring against it," his "polluting the sanctuary of strength, treading it under foot, taking away the daily sacrifice, and placing the abomination that maketh desolate;" his great pride, " magnifying himself against God, and uttering marvellous blasphemies against Him," until God in indignation should destroy him. Withal, the moral conduct of the Jews, on occasion of his persecution, is predicted. It is foretold, that "he should corrupt many by flatteries," (chap. xi. 32–34.) But that others should behave with a glorious constancy and fortitude, in opposition to him, (ver. 32.) And that some good men should fall and repent, (ver. 35,) Christ foretold Peter's sin, in denying his Lord, with its circumstances, in a peremptory manner. And so, that great sin of Judas, in betraying his master, and its dreadful and eternal punishment in hell, was foretold in the like positive manner, Matt. xxvi. 21–25, and parallel places in the other Evangelists.

2. Many events have been foretold by God, which are dependent on the moral conduct of particular persons, and were accomplished, either by their virtuous or vicious actions. Thus, the children of Israel's going down into Egypt to dwell there, was foretold to Abraham,, (Gen. xv.) which was brought about by the wickedness of Joseph's brethren in selling him, and the wickedness of Joseph's mistress, and his own signal virtue in resisting her temptation. The accomplishment of the thing prefigured in Joseph's dream, depended on the same moral conduct. Jotham's parable and prophecy, (Judges ix. 15–20.) was accomplished by the wicked conduct of Abimelech, and the men of Shechem. The prophecies against the house of Eli, (1 Sam. chap. ii. and iii.) were accomplished by the wickedness of Doeg the Elomite, in accusing the priests; and the great impiety, and extreme cruelty of Saul in destroying the priests at Nob (1 Sam. xxii.) Nathan's prophecy against David, (2 Sam. xii. 11, 12.) was fulfilled by the horrible wickedness of Absalom, in rebelling against his father, seeking his life, and lying with his concubines in the sight of the sun. The prophecy against Solomon, (1 Kings xi. 11–13.) was fulfilled by Jeroboam's rebellion and usurpation, which are spoken of as his wickedness, (2 Chron. xiii. 5, 6; compare ver. 18.) The prophecy against Jeroboam's family, (1 Kings xiv.) was fulfilled by the conspiracy, treason, and cruel murders of Bassha, (2 Kings 15.27 &c.). The predictions of the prophet Jehu against the house of Bassha, (1 Kings xvi. at the beginning,) were fulfilled by the treason and parricide of Zimri, (1 Kings xvi. 9–13, 20.)

3. How often has God foretold the future moral conduct of nations and people, of numbers, bodies, and successions of men; with God's judicial proceedings, and many other events consequent and dependent on their virtues and vices; which could not be foreknown, if the Volitions of men, wherein they acted as moral Agents, had not been foreseen! The future cruelty of the Egyptians in oppressing Israel, and God's judging and punishing them for it, was foretold long before it came to pass, (Gen. xv. 13, 14.) The continuance of the iniquity of the Amorites, and the increase of it until it should be full, and they ripe for destruction, was foretold above four hundred years before, (Gen. xv. 16. Acts vii. 6, 7.) The prophecies of the destruction of Jerusalem, and the land of Judah, were absolute (2 Kings xx. 17–19. chap. xxii. 15, to the end). It was foretold in Hezekiah's time, and was abundantly insisted on in the book of the prophet Isaiah, who wrote nothing after Hezekiah's days. It was foretold in Josiah's time, in the beginning of a great reformation, (2 Kings

xxii.) And it is manifest by innumerable things in the predictions of the prophets, relating to this event, its time, its circumstances, its continuance, and end; the return from the captivity, the restoration of the temple, city, and land, &c. I say, these show plainly, that the prophecies of this great event were absolute. And yet this event was connected with, and dependent on, two things in men's moral conduct: first, the injurious rapine and violence of the king of Babylon and his people, as the efficient cause; which God often speaks of as what He Highly resented, and would severely punish; and secondly, the final obstinacy of the Jews. That great event is often spoken of as suspended on this, (Jer. iv. 1 and v. 1, vii. 1–7. xi. 1–6. xvii. 24, to the end, xxv. 1–7. xxvi. 1–8, 13. and xxxviii. 17, 18.) Therefore this destruction and captivity could not be foreknown, unless such a moral conduct of the Chaldeans and Jews had been foreknown. And then it was foretold, that the people should be finally obstinate, to the utter desolation of the city and land, (Isa. vi. 9–11. Jer. i. 18, 19. vii. 27–29. Ezek. iii. 7. and xxiv. 13, 14.)

The final obstinacy of those Jews who were left in the land of Israel, in their idolatry and rejection of the true God, was foretold by him, and the prediction confirmed with an oath, (Jer. xliv. 26, 27.) And God tells the people, (Isa. xlviii. 3, 4–8.) that he had predicted those things which should be consequent on their treachery and obstinacy, because he knew they would be obstinate; and that he had declared these things beforehand, for their conviction of his being the only true God, &c.

The destruction of Babylon, with many of the circumstances of it, was foretold, as the judgment of God for the exceeding pride and haughtiness of the heads of that monarchy, Nebuchadnezzar and his successors, and their wickedly destroying other nations, and particularly for their exalting themselves against the true God and his people, before any of these monarchs had a being; (Isa. chap. xiii. xiv. xlvii. compare Habak. ii. 5, to the end, and Jer. chap. l. and li.) That Babylon's destruction was to be "a recompense, according to the works of their own hands," appears by Jer. xxv. 14.—The immorality of which the people of Babylon, and particularly her princes and great men, were guilty, that very night that the city was destroyed, their reveling and drunkenness at Belshazzar's idolatrous feast, was foretold, Jer. li. 39, 57.)

The return of the Jews from the Babylonish captivity is often very particularly foretold, with many circumstances, and the promises of it are very peremptory (Jer. xxxi. 35–40. and xxxii. 6–15, 41–44. and xxxiii. 24–26.) And the very time of their return was prefixed; (Jer. xxv.

11, 12. and xxix. 10, 11. 2 Chron. xxxvi. 21. Ezek. iv. 6. and Dan. ix. 2.) And yet the prophecies represent their return as consequent on their repentance. And their repentance itself is very expressly and particularly foretold, (Jer. xxix. 12, 13, 14. xxxi. 8, 9, 18–31. xxxiii. 8. l. 4, 5. Ezek. vi. 8, 9, 10. vii. 16. xiv. 22, 23. and xx. 43, 44.)

It was foretold under the Old Testament, that the Messiah should suffer greatly through the malice and cruelty of men; as is largely and fully set forth, Psal. xxii. applied to Christ in the New Testament, (Matt. xxvii. 35, 43. Luke xxiii. 34. John xix. 24. Heb. ii. 12.) And likewise in Psal. lxix. which, it is also evident by the New Testament, is spoken of Christ; (John xv. 25. vii. 5, &c. and ii. 17. Rom. xv. 3. Matt. xxvii. 34, 48. Mark xv. 23. John xix. 29.) The same thing is also foretold, Isa. liii. and l. 6. and Mic. v. 1. This cruelty of men was their sin, and what they acted as moral Agents. It was foretold, that there should be an union of heathen and Jewish rulers against Christ, (Psal. ii. 1, 2. compared with Acts iv. 25–28.) It was foretold, that the Jew should generally reject and despise the Messiah, (Isa. xlix. 5, 6, 7. and liii. 1–3. Psal. xxii. 6, 7 and lxix. 4, 8, 19, 20.) And it was foretold, that the body of that nation should be rejected in the Messiah's days, from being God's people, for their obstinacy in sin (Isa. xlix. 4–7. and viii. 14, 15, 16. compared with Rom. x. 19. and Isa. lxv at the beginning, compared with Rom. x. 20, 21.) It was foretold, that Christ should be rejected by the chief priests and rulers among the Jews, (Psal. cxviii. 22. compared with Matt. xxi. 42. Acts iv. 11. 1 Pet. ii. 4, 7.)

Christ himself foretold his being delivered into the hands of the elders, chief priests, and scribes, and his being cruelly treated by them, and condemned to death; and that he by them should be delivered to the Gentiles: and that he should be mocked and scourged, and crucified, (Matt. xvi. 21. and xx. 17–19. Luke ix. 22. John viii. 28.) and that the people should be concerned in and consenting to his death, (Luke xx. 13–18.) especially the inhabitants of Jerusalem; (Luke xiii. 33–35.) He foretold, that the disciples should all be offended because of him, that night in which he was betrayed, and should forsake him; (Matt. xxvi. 31. John xvi. 32.) He foretold, that he should be rejected of that generation, even the body of the people, and that they should continue obstinate to their ruin; (Matt. xii. 45. xxi. 33–42. and xxii. 1–7. Luke xiii. 16, 21, 24. xvii. 25. xix. 14,27, 41 44. xx. 13–18. and xxiii. 34–39.)

As it was foretold in both the Old Testament and the New that the Jews should reject the Messiah, so it was foretold that the Gentiles should receive him, and so be admitted to the privileges of God's people; in places too many to be now particularly mentioned. It was foretold in the Old Testament, that the Jews should envy the Gentiles on this account; (Deut. xxxii. 21. compared with Rom. x. 19.) Christ himself often foretold, that the Gentiles would embrace the true religion, and become his followers and people; (Matt. viii. 10, 11, 12. xxi. 41–43. and xxii. 8–10. Luke xiii. 28. xiv. 16–24. and xx. 16. John x. 16.) He also foretold the Jew's envy of the Gentiles on this occasion; (Matt. xx. 12–16. Luke xv. 26, to the end.) He foretold, that they should continue in this opposition and envy, and should manifest it in the cruel persecutions of his followers, to their utter destruction; (Matt. xxi. 33–42. xxii. 6. and xxiii. 34–39 Luke xi. 49–51.) The obstinacy of the Jews is also foretold, (Acts xxii. 18.) Christ often foretold the great persecutions his followers should meet with, both from Jews and Gentiles; (Matt. x. 16–18, 21, 22, 34–36. and xxiv. 9. Mark xiii. 9. Luke x. 3. xii. 11, 49–53. and xxi. 12, 16, 17. John xv. 18–21. and xvi. 1–4, 20–22, 23.) He foretold the martyrdom of particular persons; (Matt. xx. 23. John xiii. 36. and xxi. 18, 19, 22.) He foretold the great success of the gospel in the city of Samaria, as near approaching; which afterwards was fulfilled by the preaching of Philip, (John iv. 35–38.) He foretold the rising of many deceivers after his departure, (Matt. xxiv. 4, 5, 11.) and the apostasy of many of his professed followers; (Matt. xxiv. 10, 12.)

The persecutions, which the apostle Paul was to meet with in the world, were foretold; (Acts ix. 16. xx. 23, and xxi. 11.) The apostle says, to the Christian Ephesians, (Acts xx. 29, 30.) "I know, that after my departure shall grievous wolves enter in among you, not sparing the Rock; also of your own selves shall men arise, speaking perverse things, to draw away disciples after them." The apostle says, he knew this: but he did not know it, if God did not know the future actions of moral Agents.

4. Unless God foreknows the future acts of moral Agents, all the prophecies we have in Scripture concerning the great Antichristian apostasy; the rise, reign, wicked qualities, and deeds of "the man of sin," and his instruments and adherents; the extent and long continuance of his dominion, his influence on the minds of princes and others, to corrupt them, and draw them away to idolatry, and other foul vices; his great and cruel persecutions; the behaviour of the saints under these great temptations, &c. &.c. I say, unless the Volitions of moral Agents are foreseen, all these prophecies are uttered without knowing the things foretold.

The predictions relating to this great apostasy are all of a moral nature, relating to men's virtues and vices, and their exercises, fruits, and consequences, and events depending on them; and are very particular; and most of them often repeated, with many precise characteristics, descriptions, and limitations of qualities, conduct, influence, effects, extent, duration, periods, circumstances, final issue, &c. which it would be tedious to mention particularly. And to suppose, that all these are predicted by God, without any certain knowledge of the future moral behaviour of free Agents, would be to the utmost degree absurd.

5. Unless God foreknow the future acts of men's Wills, and their behaviour as moral Agents, all those great things which are foretold both in the Old Testament and the New, concerning the erection, establishment, and universal extent of the kingdom of the Messiah, were predicted and promised while God was in ignorance whether any of these things would come to pass or no, and did but guess at them. For that kingdom is not of this world, it does not consist in things external, but is within men, and consists in the dominion of virtue in their hearts, in righteousness, and peace, and joy in the Holy Ghost; and in these things made manifest in practice, to the praise and glory of God. The Messiah came " to save men from their sins, and deliver them from their spiritual enemies; that they might serve him in righteousness and holiness before Him: he gave himself for us, that he might redeem us from all iniquity, and purify unto himself a peculiar people, zealous of good works." And therefore his success consists in gaining men's hearts to virtue, in their being made God's willing people in the day of his power. His conquest of his enemies consists in his victory over men's corruptions and vices. And such a victory, and such a dominion is often expressly foretold: that his kingdom shall fill the earth; that all people, nations, and languages should serve and obey him; and so that all nations should go up to the mountain of the house of the Lord, that he might teach them his ways, and that they might walk in his paths; and that all men should be drawn to Christ, and the earth be full of the knowledge of the Lord (true virtue and religion) as the waters cover the seas; that God's laws should be put into men's inward parts, and written in their hearts; and that God's people should be all righteous, &c. &c.

A very great part of the Old-Testament prophecies is taken up in such predictions as these.—And here I would observe, that the prophecies of the universal prevalence of the kingdom of the Messiah, and true religion of Jesus Christ, are delivered in the most peremptory manner, and confirmed by the oath of God, Isa. xlv. 22, to the end, "Look unto me, and be ye saved, all the ends of the earth; for I am God, and there is none else. I have SWORN by my Self, the word is gone out of my mouth in righteousness, and shall not return, that unto Me every knee shall bow, and every tongue shall swear. Surely, shall one say, in the Lord have I righteousness and strength: even to Him shall men come," &c. But, here, this peremptory declaration and great oath of the Most High, are delivered with such mighty solemnity, respecting things which God did not know, if he did not certainly foresee the Volitions of moral Agents.

And all the predictions of Christ and his apostles, to the like purpose, must be without knowledge: as those of our Saviour comparing the kingdom of God to a grain of mustard-seed, growing exceeding great, from a small beginning; and to leaven, hid in three measures of meal, until the whole was leavened, &c.—And the prophecies in the epistles concerning the restoration of the Jewish nation to the true church of God, and bringing in the fulness of the Gentiles; and the prophecies in all the Revelation concerning the glorious change in the moral state of the world of mankind, attending the destruction of Antichrist, "the kingdoms of the world becoming the kingdoms of our Lord and of his Christ;" and its being granted to the church to be "arrayed in that fine linen, white and clean, which is the righteousness of saints," &c.

Corol. 1. Hence that great promise and oath of God to Abraham, Isaac, and Jacob, so much celebrated in Scripture, both in the Old Testament and the New, namely, "That in their seed all the nations and families of the earth should be blessed," must be made on uncertainties, if God does not certainly foreknow the Volitions of moral Agents. For the fulfilment of this promise consists in that success of Christ in the work of redemption, and that setting up of his spiritual kingdom over the nations of the world, which has been spoken of. Men are "blessed in Christ" no otherwise than as they are brought to acknowledge him, trust in him, love and serve him, as is represented and predicted in Psal lxxii. 11. "All kings shall fall down before Him; all nations shall serve him." With ver. 17. "Men shall be blessed in him; all nations shall call him blessed." This oath to Jacob and Abraham is fulfilled in subduing men's iniquities; as is implied in that of the prophet Micah, chap. vii. 19, 20.

Corol. 2. Hence also it appears, that the first gospel promise that ever was made to mankind, that great prediction of the salvation of the Messiah, and his victory over Satan, made to our first parents, (Gen. iii. 15.) if there be no certain Prescience of the volitions of moral Agents, must have no better foundation than conjecture. For Christ's victory over Satan consists in men's being saved from sin, and in the victory of virtue and holiness over that vice and wickedness which Satan by his temptations has introduced, and wherein his kingdom consists.

6. If it be so, that God has not a Prescience of the future actions of moral Agents, it will follow, that the prophecies of Scripture in general are without Foreknowledge. For Scripture prophecies, almost all of them, if not universally, are either predictions of the actings and behaviour of moral Agents, or of events depending on them, or some way connected with them; judicial dispensations, judgments on men for their wickedness, or rewards of virtue and righteousness, remarkable manifestations of favour to the righteous, or manifestations of sovereign mercy to sinners, forgiving their iniquities, and magnifying the riches of divine grace; or dispensations of Providence, in some respect or other, relating to the conduct of the subjects of God's moral government, wisely adapted thereto; either providing for what should be in a future state of things, through the Volitions and voluntary actions of moral Agents, or consequent upon them, and regulated and ordered according to them. So that all events that are foretold, are either moral events, or others which are connected with and accommodated to them.

That the predictions of Scripture in general must be without knowledge, if God does not foresee the Volitions of men, will further appear, if it be considered, that almost all events belonging to the future state of the world of mankind, the changes and revolutions which come to pass in empires, kingdoms, and nations, and all societies, depend, in ways innumerable, on the acts of men's Wills; yea, on an innumerable multitude of millions of Volitions. Such is the state and course of things in the world of mankind, that one single event, which appears in itself exceeding inconsiderable, may, in the progress and series of things, occasion a succession of the greatest and most important and extensive events; causing the state of mankind to be vastly different from what it would otherwise have been, for all succeeding generations.

For instance, the coming into existence of those particular men, who have been the great conquerors of the world, which, under God, have had the main hand in all the consequent state of the world, in all after-ages; such as Nebuchadnezzar, Cyrus, Alexander, Pompey, Julius Caesar, &c. undoubtedly depended on many millions of acts of the will, in their parents. And perhaps most of these Volitions depended on millions of Volitions in their contemporaries of the same generation; and most of these on millions of millions of Volitions in preceding generations.—As we go back, still the number of Volitions, which were some way the occasion of the event, multiply as the branches of a river, until they come at last, as it were, to an infinite number. This will not seem strange to any one who well considers the matter; if we recollect what philosophers tell us of the innumerable multitudes of those things which are the principia, or stamina vitce, concerned in generation; the animalcula in semine masculo, and the ova in the womb of the female; the impregnation or animating of one of these in distinction from all the rest, must depend on things infinitely minute relating to the time and circumstances of the act of the parents, the state of their bodies, &c. which must depend on innumerable foregoing circumstances and occurrences; which must depend, infinite ways, on foregoing acts of their wills; which are occasioned by innumerable things that happen in the course of their lives, in which their own and their neighbor's behaviour must have a hand, an infinite number of ways. And as the Volitions of others must be so many ways concerned in the conception and birth of such men; so, no less, in their preservation, and circumstances of life, their particular determinations and actions, on which the great revolutions they were the occasions of, depended. As, for instance, when the conspirators in Persia, against the Magi, were consulting about a succession to the empire, it came into the mind of one of them, to propose, that he whose horse neighed first, when they came together the next morning, should be king. Now, such a thing coming into his mind, might depend on innumerable incidents, wherein the Volitions of mankind had been concerned. But, in consequence of this accident, Darius, the son of Hystaspes, was king. And if this had not been, probably his successor would not have been the same, and all the circumstances of the Persian empire might have been far otherwise: Then perhaps Alexander might never have conquered that empire; and then probably the circumstances of the world in all succeeding ages, might have been vastly otherwise. I might further instance in many other occurrences; such as those on which depended Alexander's preservation, in the many critical junctures of his life, wherein a small trifle would have turned the scale against him; and the preservation and success of the Roman people, in the infancy of their kingdom and commonwealth, and afterwards; upon which all the succeeding changes in their state, and the mighty revolutions that afterwards came to pass in the habitable world, depended. But these hints may be sufficient for every discerning considerate person, to convince him, that the whole state of the world of mankind, in all ages, and the very being of every person who has ever lived in it, in every age, since the times of the ancient prophets, has depended on more Volitions, or acts of the Wills of men, than there are sands on the sea-shore.

And therefore, unless God does most exactly and perfectly foresee the future acts of men's Wills, all the predictions which he ever uttered concerning David, Hezekiah, Josiah, Nebuchadnezzar, Cyrus, Alexander; concerning the four monarchies, and the revolutions in them; and concerning all the wars, commotions, victories, prosperity, and calamities, of any kingdoms, nations, or communities in the world, have all been without knowledge.

So that, according to this notion, God not foreseeing the Volitions and free actions of men, he could foresee nothing appertaining to the state of the world of mankind in future ages; not so much as the being of one person that should live in it: and could foreknow no events, but only such as he would bring to pass himself by the extraordinary interposition of his immediate power; or things which should come to pass in the natural material world, by the laws of motion, and course of nature, wherein that is independent of the actions or works of mankind: that is, as he might, like a very able mathematician and astronomer, with great exactness calculate the revolutions of the heavenly bodies, and the greater wheels of the machine of the external creation.

And if we closely consider the matter, there will appear reason to convince us, that he could not, with any absolute certainty, foresee even these. As to the first, namely, things done by the immediate and extraordinary interposition of God's power, these cannot be foreseen, unless it can be foreseen when there shall be occasion for such extraordinary interposition. And that cannot be foreseen, unless the state of the moral world can be foreseen. For whenever God thus interposes, it is with regard to the state of the moral world, requiring such divine interposition. Thus God could not certainly foresee the universal deluge, the calling of Abraham, the destruction of Sodom and Gomorrah, the plagues on Egypt, and Israel's redemption out of it, the expelling of the seven nations of Canaan, and the bringing Israel into that land; for these all are represented as connected with things belonging to the state of the moral world. Nor can God foreknow the most proper and convenient time of the day of judgment and general conflagration; for that chiefly depends on the course and state of things in the moral World.

Nor, secondly, can we on this supposition reasonably think, that God can certainly foresee what things shall come to pass, in the course of things, in the natural and material world, even those which in an ordinary state of things might be calculated by a good astronomer. For the moral world is the end of the natural world; and the course of things in the former, is undoubtedly subordinate to God's designs with respect to the latter. Therefore he, has seen cause, from regard to the state of things in the moral world, extraordinarily to interpose, to interrupt, and lay an arrest on the course of things in the natural world; and unless he can foresee the Volition of men, and so know something of the future state of the moral world, he cannot know but that he may still have as great occasion to interpose in this manner, as ever he had: nor can he foresee how, or when, he shall have occasion thus to interpose.

Corol. 1. It appears from the things observed, that unless God foresees the Volition of moral Agents, that cannot be true which is observed by the apostle James, (Acts xv. 18.) "Known unto God are all his works from the beginning of the world."

Corol. 2. It appears, that unless God foreknows the Volition of moral Agents, all the prophecies of Scripture have no better foundation than mere conjecture; and that, in most instances, a conjecture which must have the utmost uncertainty; depending on an innumerable multitude of Volition, which are all, even to God, uncertain events: however, these prophecies are delivered as absolute predictions, and very many of them in the most positive manner, with asseverations; and some of them with the most solemn oaths.

Corol. 3. It also follows, that if this notion of God's ignorance of future Volition's be true, in vain did Christ say, after uttering many great and important predictions, depending on men's moral actions, (Matt. xxiv. 35.) "Heaven and earth shall pass away; but my words shall not pass away."

Corol. 4. From the same notion of God's ignorance, it would follow, that in vain has he himself often spoken of the predictions of his word, as evidences of Foreknowledge; of that which is his prerogative as GOD, and his peculiar glory, greatly distinguishing him from all other beings; (as in Isa. xli. 22.-26 xliii. 9, 10. xliv. 8. xlv. 21. xlvi. 10. and xlviii. 14.)

Arg. II. If God does not foreknow the Volitions of moral Agents, then he did not foreknow the fall of man, nor of angels, and so could not foreknow the great things which are consequent on these events; such as his sending his Son into the world to die for sinners, and all things pertaining to the great work of redemption; all the things which were done for four thousand years before Christ came, to prepare the way for it; and the incarnation, life, death, resurrection, and ascension of Christ; setting Him at the head of the universe as King of heaven and earth, angels and men; and setting up his church and kingdom in this world, and appointing him the Judge of the world; and all that Satan should do in the world in opposition to the kingdom of Christ: and the great transactions of the day of judgment, &c. And if God was thus ignorant, the following scriptures, and others like them, must be without any meaning, or contrary to truth. (Eph. i. 4.) "According as he hath chosen us in him before the foundation of the world." (1 Pet. i. 20.) "Who verily was foreordained before the foundation of the world." (2 Tim. i. 9.) "who hath saved us, and called us with an holy calling; not according to our works, but according to his own purpose, and grace, which was given us in Christ Jesus before the world began." So (Eph. iii. 11.) speaking of the wisdom of God in the work of redemption, "according to the eternal purpose which he purposed in Christ Jesus." (Tit. i. 2.) "In hope of eternal life, which God that cannot lie, promised before the world began." (Rom. viii. 29.) "Whom he did foreknow, them he also did predestinate," &c. (1 Pet. i. 2.) "Elect, according to the foreknowledge of God the Father."

If God did not foreknow the fall of man, nor the redemption by Jesus Christ, nor the Volitions of man since the fall; then he did not foreknow the saints in any sense; neither as particular persons, nor as societies or nations; either by election, or by mere foresight of their virtue or good works; or any foresight of any thing about them relating to their salvation; or any benefit they have by Christ, or any manner of concern of theirs with a Redeemer.

Arg. III. On the supposition of God's ignorance of the future Volitions of free Agents, it will follow, that God must in many cases truly repent what he has done, so as properly to wish he had done otherwise: by reason that the event of things in those affairs which are most important, viz. the affairs of his moral kingdom, being uncertain and contingent, often happens quite otherwise than he was before aware of. And there would be reason to understand that, in the most literal sense, (Gen. vi. 6.) " It repented the Lord, that he had made man on the earth, and it grieved him at his heart," (and 1 Sam. xv. 11.) contrary to Num. xxiii. 19. "God is not the son of Man, that he should repent;" and 1 Sam. xv. 29. "Also the Strength of Israel will not lie, nor repent; for he is not a man that he should repent." Yea, from this notion it would follow, that God is liable to repent and be grieved at his heart, in a literal sense, continually; and is always exposed to an infinite number of real disappointments in governing the world; and to manifold, constant, great perplexity and vexation: but this is not very consistent with his title of "God over all, blessed for evermore;" which represents him as possessed of perfect, constant, and uninterrupted tranquillity and felicity, as God over the universe, and in his management of the affairs of the world, as supreme and universal ruler. (See Rom. i. 25. ix. 5. 2 Cor. xi. 31. 1 Tim. vi. 15.)

Arg. IV. It will also follow from this notion, that as God is liable to be continually repenting of what he has done; so he must be exposed to be constantly changing his mind and intentions, as to his future conduct; altering his measures, relinquishing his old designs, and forming new schemes and projects. For his purposes, even as to the main parts of his scheme, such as belong to the state of his moral kingdom, must be always liable to be broken, through want of foresight; and he must be continually putting his system to rights, as it gets out of order, through the contingence of the actions of moral Agents: he must. be a Being, who, instead of being absolutely immutable, must necessarily be the subject of infinitely the most numerous acts of repentance, and changes of intention, of any being whatsoever; for this plain reason, that his vastly extensive charge comprehends an infinitely greater number of those things which are to him contingent and uncertain. In such a situation, he must have little else to do, but to mend broken links as well as he can, and be rectifying his disjointed frame and disordered movements, in the best manner the case will allow, The Supreme Lord of all things must needs be under great and miserable disadvantages, in governing the world which he has made, and of which he has the care, through his being utterly unable to find out things of chief importance, which hereafter shall befall his system; for which, if he did but know, he might make seasonable provision. In many cases, there may be very great necessity that he should make provision, in the manner of his ordering and disposing things, for some great events which are to happen, of vast and extensive influence, and endless consequence to the universe; which he may see afterwards, when it is too late, and may wish in vain that he had known before, that he might have ordered his affairs accordingly. And it is in the power of man, on these principles, by his devices, purposes, and actions, thus to disappoint God, break his measures, make him continually change his mind, subject him to vexation, and bring him into confusion.

But how do these things consist with reason, or with the word of God? Which represents, that all God's works, all that he has ever to do, the whole scheme and series of his operations, are from the beginning perfectly in his view; and declares, that whatever devices and designs are in the hearts of men, "the counsel of the Lord shall stand, and the thoughts of his heart to all generations," (Prov. xix. 21. Psal. xxxiii. 10, 11.) And a "that which the Lord of hosts hath purposed, none shall disannul," (Isa. xiv. 27.) And that he cannot be frustrated in one design or thought, (Job xlii. 2.) And "that which God doth, it shall be for ever, that nothing can be put to it, or taken from it," (Eccl. iii. 14.) The stability and perpetuity of God's counsels are expressly spoken of as connected with his foreknowledge, (Isa. xlvi. 10.) "Declaring the end from the beginning, and from ancient times the things that are not yet done; saying, My counsel shall stand, and I will do my pleasure."—And how are these things consistent with what the Scripture says of God's immutability, which represents him as "without variableness, or shadow of turning;" and speaks of him, most particularly, as unchangeable with regard to his purposes, (Mal. iii. 6.) "I am the Lord; I change not; therefore ye sons of Jacob are not consumed." (Exod. iii. 14.) "I AM THAT I AM. (Job xxiii. 13, 14.) "He is in one mind; and who can turn him? And what his soul desireth, even that he doth: for he performeth the thing that is appointed for me."

Arg. V. If this notion of God's ignorance of future Volitions of moral Agents be thoroughly considered in its consequences, it will appear to follow from it, that God, after he had made the world, was liable to be wholly frustrated of his end in the creation of it; and so has been, in like manner, liable to be frustrated of his end in all the great works he had wrought. It is manifest, the moral world is the end of the natural: the rest of the creation is but a house which God hath built, with furniture, for moral Agents: and the good or bad state of the moral world depends on the improvement they make of their natural Agency, and so depends on their Volitions. And therefore, if these cannot be foreseen by God, because they are contingent, and subject to no kind of necessity, then the affairs of the moral world are liable to go wrong, to any assignable degree; yea, liable to be utterly ruined. As on this scheme, it may well be supposed to be literally said, when mankind, by the abuse of their mortal Agency, became very corrupt before the flood, "that the Lord repented that he had made man on the earth, and it grieved him at his heart;" so, when he made the universe, he did not know but that he might be so disappointed in it, that it might grieve him at his heart that he had made it. It actually proved, that all mankind became sinful, and a very great part of the angels apostatized: and how could God know before, that all of them would not? And how could God know but that all mankind, notwithstanding means used to reclaim them, being still left to the freedom of their own Will, would continue in their apostasy, and grow worse and worse, as they of the old world before the flood did?

According to the scheme I am endeavouring to confute, the Fall of neither men nor angels could be foreseen, and God must be greatly disappointed in these events; and so the grand contrivance for our redemption, and destroying the works of the devil, by the Messiah, and all the great things God has done in the prosecution of these designs, must be only the fruits of his own disappointment; contrivances to mend, as well as he could, his system, which originally was all very good, and perfectly beautiful; but was broken and confounded by the free Will of angels and men. And still he must be liable to be totally disappointed a second time: he could not know, that he should have his desired success, in the incarnation, life, death, resurrection, and exaltation of his only-begotten Son, and other great works accomplished to restore the state of things: he could not know, after all, whether there would actually be any tolerable measure of restoration; for this depended on the free Will of man. There has been a general great apostasy of almost all the Christian world, to that which was worse than heathenism; which continued for many ages. And how could God, without foreseeing men's Volitions, know whether ever Christendom would return from this apostasy? And which way would he foretell how soon it would begin? The apostle says, it began to work in his time; and how could it be known how far it would proceed in that age? Yea, how could it be known that the gospel which was not effectual for the reformation of the Jews, would ever be effectual for the turning of the heathen nations from their heathen apostasy, which they had been confirmed in for so many ages?

It is represented often in Scripture, that God, who made the world for himself, and created it for his pleasure, would infallibly obtain his end in the creation, and in all his works; that as all things are of him, so they would all be to him; and that in the final issue of things it would appear that he is "the first, and the last." (Rev. xxi. 6.) "And he said unto me, It is done. I am Alpha and Omega, the beginning and the end, the first and the last." But these things are not consistent with God's liability to be disappointed in all his works, nor indeed with his failing of his end in any thing that he has undertaken.

PART II. SECTION XII. GOD'S CERTAIN FOREKNOWLEDGE OF THE FUTURE VOLITIONS OF MORAL AGENTS, INCONSISTENT WITH SUCH A CONTINGENCE OF THOSE VOLITIONS AS IS WITHOUT ALL NECESSITY.

Having proved, that GOD has a certain and infallible Prescience of the voluntary acts of moral agents, I come now, in the second place, to show the consequence; how it follows from hence, that these events are necessary, with a Necessity of connexion or consequence.

The chief Arminian divines, so far as I have had opportunity to observe, deny this consequence; and affirm, that if such Foreknowledge be allowed, it is no evidence of any necessity of the event foreknown. Now I desire, that this matter may be particularly and thoroughly inquired into. I cannot but think that on particular and full consideration, it may be perfectly determined, whether it be indeed so or not.

In order to a proper consideration of this matter, I would observe the following things.

I. It is very evident, that, with regard to a thing whose existence is infallibly and indissolubly connected with something which already hath, or has had existence, the existence of that thing is necessary. Here may be noted the following particulars:

1. I observed before, in explaining the nature of Necessity, that in things which are past, their past existence is now necessary: having already made sure of existence, it is too late for any possibility of alteration in that respect; it is now impossible that it should be otherwise than true, that the thing has existed.

2. If there be any such thing as a divine Foreknowledge of the volitions of free agents, that Foreknowledge, by the supposition is a thing which already has, and long ago had existence; and so, now its existence is necessary; it is now utterly impossible to be otherwise, than that this Foreknowledge should be or should have been.

3. It is also very manifest, that those things which are indissolubly connected with other things that are necessary, are themselves necessary. As that proposition whose truth is necessarily connected with another proposition, which is necessarily true, is itself necessarily true. To say otherwise would be a contradiction: it would be in effect to say, that the connexion was indissoluble, and yet was not so, but might be broken. If that, the existence of which is indissolubly connected with something

209

whose existence is now necessary, is itself not necessary, then it may possibly not exist, notwithstanding that indissoluble connexion of its existence.—Whether the absurdity be not glaring, let the reader judge.

4. It is no less evident, that if there be a full, certain, and infallible Foreknowledge of the future existence of the volitions of moral agents, then there is a certain, infallible, and indissoluble connexion between those events and that Foreknowledge; and that therefore, by the preceding observations, those events are necessary events; being infallibly and indissolubly connected with that, whose existence already is, and so is now necessary, and cannot but have been.

To say, the Foreknowledge is certain and infallible, and yet the connexion of the event with that Foreknowledge is dissoluble and fallible, is very absurd. To affirm it, would be the same thing as to affirm, that there is no necessary connexion between a proposition being infallibly known to be true, and its being true indeed. So that it is perfectly demonstrable, that if there be any infallible knowledge of future volitions, the event is necessary; or, in other words, that it is impossible but the event should come to pass. For if it be not impossible but that it may be otherwise, then it is not impossible but that the proposition which affirms its future coming to pass, may not now be true. There is this absurdity in it, that it is not impossible, but that there now should be no truth in that proposition, which is now infallibly known to be true.

II. That no future event can be certainly foreknown, whose existence is contingent, and without all Necessity, may be proved thus; it is impossible for a thing to be certainly known to any intellect without evidence. To suppose otherwise, implies a contradiction: because for a thing to be certainly known to any understanding, is for it to be evident to that understanding: and for a thing to be evident to any understanding is the same thing, as for that understanding to see evidence of it: but no understanding, created or uncreated, can see evidence where there is none; for that is the same thing, as to see that to be which is not. And therefore, if there be any truth which is absolutely without evidence, that truth is absolutely unknowable, insomuch that it implies a contradiction to suppose that it is known.

But if there be any future event, whose existence is contingent, without all Necessity, the future existence of the event is absolutely without evidence. If there be any evidence of it, it must be one of these two sorts, either self-evidence or proof; an evident thing must be either evident in itself; or evident in something else: that is, evident by connexion with something else. But a future thing, whose existence is without all Necessity, can have neither of these sorts of evidence. It cannot be self-evident: for if it be, it may be now known, by what is now to be seen in the thing itself; its present existence, or the Necessity of its nature: but both these are contrary to the supposition. It is supposed, both that the thing has no present existence to be seen; and also that it is not of such a nature as to be necessarily existent for the future: so that its future existence is not self-evident. And secondly, neither is there any proof, or evidence in any thing else, or evidence of connexion with something else that is evident; for this is also contrary to the supposition. It is supposed that there is now nothing existent, with which the future existence of the contingent event is connected. For such a connexion destroys its contingence, and supposes Necessity. Thus it is demonstrated, that there is in the nature of things absolutely no evidence at all of the future existence of that event, which is contingent, without all Necessity, (if any such event there be,) neither self-evidence nor proof. And therefore the thing in reality is not evident; and so cannot be seen to be evident, or, which is the same thing, cannot be known.

Let us consider this in an example. Suppose that five thousand seven hundred and sixty years ago, there was no other being but the Divine Being; and then this world, or some particular body or spirit, all at once starts out of nothing into being, and takes on itself a particular nature and form; all in absolute Contingence, without any concern of God, or any other cause, in the matter; without any manner of ground or reason of its existence; or any dependence upon, or connexion at all with any thing foregoing: I say, that if this be supposed, there was no evidence of that event beforehand. There was no evidence of it to be seen in the thing itself; for the thing itself, as yet, was not. And there was no evidence of it to be seen in any thing else; for evidence in something else, is connexion with something else: but such connexion is contrary to the supposition. There was no evidence before, that this thing would happen; for by the supposition, there was no reason why it should happen, rather than something else, or rather than nothing. And if so, then all things before were exactly equal, and the same, with respect to that and other possible things; there was no preponderation, no superior weight or value; and therefore, nothing that could be of weight or value to determine any understanding. The thing was absolutely without evidence, and absolutely unknowable. An increase of understanding, or of the capacity of discerning, has no tendency, and makes no advance, inwards discerning any signs or evidences of it, let it be increased never so much; yea, if it be increased infinitely. The increase of the strength of sight may have a tendency to enable to discern the evidence which is far off, and very much hid, and deeply involved in clouds and darkness; but it has no tendency to enable to discern evidence where there is none. If the sight be infinitely strong, and the capacity of discerning infinitely great, it will enable to see all that there is, and to see it perfectly, and with ease; yet it has no tendency at all to enable a being to discern that evidence which is not; but on the contrary, it has a tendency to enable to discern with great certainty that there is none.

III. To suppose the future volitions of moral agents not to be necessary events; or, which is the same thing, events which it is not impossible but that they may not come to pass; and yet to suppose that God certainly foreknows them, and knows all things; is to suppose God's knowledge to be inconsistent with itself. For to say, that God certainly, and without all conjecture, knows that a thing will infallibly be, which at the same time he knows to be so contingent, that it may possibly not be, is to suppose his knowledge inconsistent with itself; or that one thing he knows, is utterly inconsistent with another thing he knows. It is the same as to say, he now knows a proposition to be of certain infallible truth, which he knows to be of contingent uncertain truth. If a future volition is so without all Necessity, that nothing hinders but it may not be, then the proposition which asserts its future existence, is so uncertain, that nothing hinders, but that the truth of it may entirely fail. And if God knows all things, he knows this proposition to be thus uncertain. And that is inconsistent with his knowing that it is infallibly true; and so inconsistent with his infallibly knowing that it is true. If the thing be indeed contingent, God views it so, and judges it to be contingent, if he views things as they are. If the event be not necessary, then it is possible it may never be: and if it be possible it may never be, God knows it may possibly never be; and that is to know that the proposition, which affirms its existence, may possibly not be true; and that is to know that the truth of it is uncertain; which surely is inconsistent with his knowing it as a certain truth. If volitions are in themselves contingent events, without all Necessity, then it is no argument of perfection of knowledge in any being to determine peremptorily that they will be; but on the contrary, an argument of ignorance and mistake; because it would argue, that he supposes that proposition to be certain, which in its own nature, and all things considered, is uncertain and contingent. To say, in such a case, that God may have ways of knowing contingent events which we cannot conceive of, is ridiculous; as much so, as to say, that God may know contradictions to be true, for ought we know; or that he may know a thing to be certain, and at the same time know it not to be certain, though we cannot conceive how; because he has ways of knowing which we cannot comprehend.

Corol. 1. From what has been observed it is evident, that the absolute decrees of God are no more inconsistent with human liberty, on account of any Necessity of the event, which follows from such decrees, than the absolute Foreknowledge of God. Because the connexion between the event and certain Foreknowledge, is as infallible and indissoluble, as between the event and an absolute decree. That is, it is no more impossible, that the event and decree should not agree together, than that the event and absolute Knowledge should disagree. The connexion between the event and Foreknowledge is absolutely perfect, by the supposition: because it is supposed, that the certainty and infallibility of the knowledge is absolutely perfect. And it being so, the certainty cannot be increased; and therefore the connexion, between the Knowledge and thing known, cannot be increased; so that if a decree be added to the Foreknowledge, it does not at all increase the connexion, or make it more infallible and indissoluble. If it were not so, the certainty of Knowledge might be increased by the addition of a decree; which is contrary to the supposition, which is, that the Knowledge is absolutely perfect, or perfect to the highest possible degree.

There is as much impossibility but that the things which are infallibly foreknown, should be, or, which is the same thing, as great a Necessity of their future existence, as if the event were already written down, and was known and read by all mankind, through all preceding ages, and there was the most indissoluble and perfect connexion possible between the writing and the thing written. In such a case, it would be as impossible the event should fail of existence, as if it had existed already; and a decree cannot make an event surer or more necessary than this.

And therefore, if there be any such Foreknowledge, as it has been proved there is, then Necessity of connexion and consequence is not at all inconsistent with any liberty which man, or any other creature, enjoys. And from hence it may be inferred, that absolute decrees, which do not at all increase the necessity, are not inconsistent with the liberty which man enjoys, on any such account, as that they make the event decreed necessary, and render it utterly impossible but that it should come to pass. Therefore, if absolute decrees are inconsistent with man's liberty as a moral agent, or his liberty in a state of probation, or any liberty whatsoever that he enjoys, it is not on account of any Necessity which absolute decrees infer.

Dr. Whitby supposes, there is a great difference between God's foreknowledge, and his decrees, with regard to necessity of future events. In his Discourse on the five points, (p. 474, &c.) he says, God's Prescience has no influence at all on our actions.—Should God, says he, by immediate revelation, give me the knowledge of the event of any man's state or actions, would my knowledge of them have any influence upon his actions? Surely none at all.—Our knowledge doth not affect the things we know, to make them more certain, or more fixture, than they could be without it. Now, Foreknowledge in God is knowledge. As therefore Knowledge has no influence on things that are, so neither has Foreknowledge on things that shall be. And consequently, the Foreknowledge of any action that would be otherwise free, cannot alter or diminish that freedom. Whereas God's decree of election is powerful and active, and comprehends the preparation and exhibition of such means, as shall unfrustrably produce the end.—Hence God's Prescience renders no actions necessary." And to this purpose, (p. 473.) he cites Origen, where he says, "God's Prescience is not the cause of things future, but their being future is the cause of God's Prescience that they will be:" and Le Blanic, where he says, "This is the truest resolution of this difficulty, that Prescience is not the cause that things are future; but their being future is the cause they are foreseen." In like manner, Dr. Clark, in his Demonstration of the Being and Attributes of God, (p. 95–99.) And the Author of The Freedom of the Will, in God and Creation, speaking to the like purpose with Dr. Whitby, represents "Foreknowledge as having no more influence on things known, to make them necessary, than afterknowledge, or to that purpose.

To all which I would say; that what is said about knowledge, its not having influence on the thing known to make it necessary, is nothing to the purpose, nor does it in the least affect the foregoing reasoning. Whether Prescience be the thing that makes event necessary or no, it alters not the case. Infallible Foreknowledge may prove the Necessity of the event foreknown, and yet not be the thing which causes the Necessity. If the foreknowledge be absolute, this proves the event known to be necessary, or proves that it is impossible but that the event should be, by some means or other, either by a decree, or some other way, if there be any other way: because, as was said before, it is absurd to say, that a proposition is known to be certainly and infallibly true, which yet may possibly prove not true.

The whole of the seeming force of this evasion lies in this; that, inasmuch as certain Foreknowledge does not cause an event to be necessary, as a decree does; therefore it does not prove it to be necessary, as a decree does. But there is no force in this arguing: for it is built wholly on this supposition, that nothing can prove or be an evidence of a thing being necessary, but that which has a causal influence to make it so. But this can never be maintained. If certain Foreknowledge of the future existence of an event be not the thing which first makes it impossible that it should fail of existence; yet it may, and certainly does demonstrate, that it is impossible it should fail of it, however that impossibility comes. If Foreknowledge be not the cause, but the effect of this impossibility, it may prove that there is such an impossibility, as much as if it were the cause. It is as strong arguing from the effect to the cause, as from the cause to the effect. It is enough, that an existence, which is infallibly foreknown, cannot fail, whether that impossibility arises from the Foreknowledge, or is prior to it. It is as evident as any thing can be, that it is impossible a thing, which is infallibly known to be true, should prove not to be true; therefore there is a Necessity that it should be otherwise; whether the Knowledge be the cause of this Necessity, or the Necessity the cause of the Knowledge.

All certain knowledge, whether it be Foreknowledge or Afterknowledge, or concomitant knowledge, proves the thing known now to be necessary, by some means or other; or proves that it is impossible it should now be otherwise than true.—I freely allow, that Foreknowledge does not prove a thing to be necessary any more than Afterknowledge: but then After-knowledge, which is certain and infallible, proves that it is now become impossible but that the proposition known should be true. Certain After-knowledge proves that it is now, by some means or other, become impossible but that the proposition, which predicates past existence on the event, should be true. And so does certain Foreknowledge prove, that now in the time of the knowledge, it is, by some means or other, become impossible but that the proposition, which predicates future existence on the event, should be true. The necessity of the truth of the propositions, consisting in the present impossibility of the non-existence of the event affirmed, in both cases, is the immediate ground of the certainty of the Knowledge; there can be no certainty of knowledge without it.

There must be a certainty in things themselves, before they are certainly known, or which is the same thing, known to be certain. For certainty of knowledge is nothing else but knowing or discerning the certainty there is in the things themselves, which are known. Therefore there must be a certainty in things to be a ground of certainty of knowledge, and to render things capable of being known to be certain. And there is nothing but the necessity of truth known, or its being impossible but that it should be true; or, in other words, the firm and infallible connexion between the subject and predicate of the proposition that contains that truth. All certainty of Knowledge consists in the view of the firmness of that connexion. So God's certain foreknowledge of the future existence of any event, is his view of the firm and indissoluble connexion of the subject and predicate of the proposition that affirms its future existence. The subject is that possible event; the predicate is its future existence, but if future existence be firmly and indissolubly connected with that event, then the future existence of that event is necessary. If God certainly knows the future existence of an event which is wholly contingent, and may possibly never be, then, he sees a firm connexion between a subject and predicate that are not firmly connected; which is a contradiction.

I allow what Dr. Whitby says to be true, that mere Knowledge does not affect the thing known, to make it more certain or more future. But yet, I say, it supposes and proves the thing to be already, both future and certain; i.e. necessarily future. Knowledge of futurity, supposes futurity; and a certain knowledge of futurity, supposes certain futurity, antecedent to that certain Knowledge. But there is no other certain futurity of a thing, antecedent to certainty of Knowledge, than a prior impossibility but that the thing should prove true; or, which is the same thing, the necessity of the event.

I would observe one thing further; that if it be as those forementioned writers suppose, that God's Foreknowledge is not the cause, but the effect of the existence of the event foreknown; this is so far from showing that this Foreknowledge doth not infer the Necessity of the existence of that event, that it rather shows the contrary the more plainly. Because it shows the existence of the event to be so settled and firm, that it is as if it had already been; inasmuch as in effect it actually exists already; its future existence has already had actual influence and efficiency, and has produced an effect, viz. Prescience: the effect exists already; and as the effect supposes the cause, and depends entirely upon it, therefore it is as if the future event, which is the cause, had existed already. The effect is firm as possible, it having already the possession of existence, and has made sure of it. But the effect cannot be more firm and stable than its cause, ground, and reason. The building cannot be firmer than the foundation.

To illustrate this matter; let us suppose the appearances and images of things in a glass, for instance, a reflecting telescope, to be the real effects of heavenly bodies (at a distance, and out of sight) which they resemble: if it be so, then, as these images in the telescope have had a past actual existence, and it is become utterly impossible now that it should be otherwise than that they have existed; so they being the true effects of the heavenly bodies they resemble, this proves the existence of those heavenly bodies to be as real, infallible, firm, and necessary, as the existence of these effects; the one being connected with, and wholly depending on the other.—Now let us suppose future existences, some way or other, to have influence back, to produce effects beforehand, and cause exact and perfect images of themselves in a glass, a thousand years before they exist, yea, in all preceding ages; but yet that these images are real effects of these future existences, perfectly dependent on, and connected with their cause. These effects and images having already had actual existence, render that matter of their existence perfectly firm and stable, and utterly impossible to be otherwise; and this proves, as in the other instance, that the existence of the things, which are their causes, is also equally sure, firm, and necessary; and that it is alike impossible but that they should be, as if they had been already, as their effects have. And if instead of images in a glass, we suppose the antecedent effects to be perfect ideas of them in the Divine Mind, which have existed there from all eternity, which are as properly effects, as truly and properly connected with their cause, the case is not altered.

Another thing which has been said by some Arminians, to take off the force of what is urged from God's Prescience, against the continuance of the volitions of moral agents, is to this purpose; " That when we talk of Foreknowledge in God, there is no strict propriety in our so speaking; and that although it be true, that there is in God the most perfect Knowledge of all events from eternity to eternity, yet there is no such thing as before and after in God, but he sees all things by one perfect unchangeable view, without any succession."—To this I answer, 1. It has been already shown, that all certain Knowledge proves the Necessity of the truth known; whether it be before, after, or at the same time.—Though it be true, that there is no succession in God's Knowledge, and the manner of his Knowledge is to us inconceivable, yet thus much we know concerning it, that there is no event, past, present, or to come, that God is ever uncertain of. He never is, never was, and never will be without infallible Knowledge of it; he always sees the existence of it to be certain and infallible. And as he always sees things just as they are in truth; hence there never is in reality any thing contingent in such a sense, as that possibly it may happen never to exist. If, strictly speaking, there is no Foreknowledge in God, it is because those things, which are future to us, are as present to God, as if they already had existence: and that is as much as to say, that future events are always in God's view as evident, clear, sure, and necessary, as if they already were. If there never is a time wherein the existence of the event is not present with God, then there never is a time wherein it is not as much impossible for it to fail of existence, as if its existence were present, and were already come to pass.

God viewing things so perfectly and unchangeably, as that there is no succession in his ideas or judgment, does not hinder but that there is properly now, in the mind of God, a certain and perfect Knowledge of the moral actions of men, which to us are an hundred years hence: yea the objection supposes this; and therefore it certainly does not hinder but that, by the foregoing arguments, it is now impossible these moral actions should not come to pass.

We know, that God foreknows the future voluntary actions of men, in such a sense, as that he is able particularly to foretell them, and cause them to be recorded, as he often has done; and therefore that necessary connexion which there is between God's Knowledge and the event known, as much proves the event to be necessary beforehand, as if the Divine Knowledge were in the same sense before the event, as the prediction or writing is. If the Knowledge be infallible, then the expression of it in the written prediction is infallible; that is, there is an infallible connexion between that written prediction and the event. And if so, then it is impossible it should ever be otherwise, than that the prediction and the event should agree: and this is the same thing as to say, it is impossible but that the event should come to pass: and this is the same as to say that its coming to pass is necessary.—So that it is manifest, that there being no proper succession in God's mind, makes no alteration as to the Necessity of the existence of the events known. Yea,

2. This is so far from weakening the proof, given of the impossibility of future events known, not coming to pass, as that it establishes the foregoing arguments, and shows the clearness of the evidence. For,

(1.) The very reason, why God's Knowledge is without succession, is, because it is absolutely perfect, to the highest possible degree of clearness and certainty. All things, whether past, present, or to come, being viewed with equal evidence and fulness; future things being seen with as much clearness, as if they were present; the view is always in absolute perfection; and absolute constant perfection admits of no alteration, and so no succession; the actual existence of the thing known, does not at all increase or add to the clearness or certainty of the thing known: God calls the things that are not, as though they were; they are all one to him as if they had already existed. But herein consists the strength of the demonstration before given; that it is as impossible they should fail of existence, as if they existed already. This objection, instead of weakening the argument, sets it in the strongest light; for it supposes it to be so indeed, that the existence of future events is in God's view so much as if it already had been, that when they come actually to exist, it makes not the least alteration or variation in his knowledge of them.

(2.) The objection is founded on the immutability of God's knowledge: for it is the immutability of Knowledge that makes it to be without succession. But this most directly and plainly demonstrates the thing I insist on, viz. that it is utterly impossible the known events should fail of existence. For if that were possible, then a change in God's Knowledge and view of things, were possible. For if the known event should not come into being, as God expected, then he would see it, and so would change his mind, and see his former mistake; and thus there would be change and succession in his knowledge. But as God is immutable, and it is infinitely impossible that His view should be changed; so it is, for the same reason, just so impossible that the foreknown event should not exist; and that is to be impossible in the highest degree; and therefore the contrary is necessary. Nothing is more impossible than that the immutable God should be changed, by the succession of time; who comprehends all things, from eternity to eternity, in one, most perfect, and unalterable view; so that his whole eternal duration is *vitae interminabilis, tota, simul et perfecta possessio.*

On the whole, I need not fear to say, that there is no geometrical theorem or proposition whatsoever, more capable of strict demonstration, than that God's certain Prescience of the volitions of moral agents is inconsistent with such a Contingence of these events, as is without all Necessity; and so is inconsistent with the Arminian notion of liberty.

Corol. 2. Hence the doctrine of the Calvinists, concerning the absolute decrees of God, does not all infer any more fatality in things, than will demonstrably follow from the doctrine of the most Arminian divines, who acknowledge God's omniscience, and universal Prescience. Therefore all objections they make against the doctrine of the Calvinists, as implying Hobbes's doctrine of Necessity, or the stoical doctrine of fate, lie no more against the doctrine of Calvinists, than their own doctrine: and therefore it doth not become those divines, to raise such an outcry against the Calvinists, on this account.

Corol. 3. Hence all arguments of Arminians, who own God's omniscience, against the doctrine of the inability of unregenerate men to perform the conditions of salvation, and the commands of God requiring spiritual duties, and against the Calvinistic doctrine of efficacious grace; on this ground, that those doctrines, though they do not suppose men to be under any constraint or coaction, yet suppose them under Necessity, must fall to the ground. And their arguments against the necessity of men's volitions, taken from the reasonableness of God's commands, promises, and threatenings, and the sincerity of his counsels and invitations; and all objections against any doctrines of the Calvinists as being inconsistent with human liberty, because they infer Necessity; I say, all these arguments and objections must be justly esteemed vain and frivolous, as coming from them; being leveled against their own doctrine, as well as against that of the Calvinists.

PART II. SECTION XIII. WHETHER WE SUPPOSE THE VOLITIONS OF MORAL AGENTS TO BE CONNECTED WITH ANY THING ANTECEDENT, OR NOT, YET THEY MUST BE NECESSARY IN SUCH A SENSE AS TO OVERTHROW ARMINIAN LIBERTY.

Every act of the Will has a cause, or it has not. If it has a cause, then, according to what has already been demonstrated, it is not contingent, but necessary; the effect being necessarily dependent and consequent on its cause, let that cause be what it will. If the cause is the Will itself, by antecedent acts choosing and determining; still the determined caused act must be a necessary effect. The act, that is the determined effect of the foregoing act which is its cause, cannot prevent the efficiency of its cause; but must be wholly subject to its determination and command, as much as the motions of the hands and feet. The consequent commanded acts of the Will are as passive and as necessary, with respect to the antecedent determining acts, as the parts of the body are to the volitions which determine and command them. And therefore, if all the free acts of the will are all determined effects determined by the will itself, that is by antecedent choice, then they are all necessary; they are all subject to, and decisively fixed by, the foregoing act, which is their cause: yea, even the determining act itself; for that must be determined and fixed by another act preceding, if it be a free and voluntary act; and so must be necessary. So that by this, all the free acts of the will are necessary, and cannot be free unless they are necessary: because they cannot be free, according to the Arminian notion of freedom, unless they are determined by the Will; and this is to be determined by antecedent choice, which being their cause, proves them necessary. And yet they say, Necessity is utterly inconsistent with Liberty. So that, by their scheme, the acts of the will cannot be free unless they are necessary, and yet cannot be free if they be necessary!

But if the other part of the dilemma be taken, that the free acts of the Will have no cause, and are connected with nothing whatsoever that goes before and determines them, in order to maintain their proper and absolute Contingence, and this should be allowed to be possible; still it will not serve their turn. For if the volition come to pass by perfect Contingence, and without any cause at all, then it is certain, no act of the Will, no prior act of the soul, was the cause, no determination or choice of the soul had any hand in it. The will, or the soul, was indeed the subject of what happened to it accidentally, but was not the cause. The Will is not active in causing or determining, but purely the passive subject; at least, according to their notion of action and passion. In this case, Contingence as much prevents the determination of the Will, as a proper cause; and as to the Will, it was necessary, and could be no otherwise. For to suppose that it could have been otherwise, if the Will or soul had pleased, is to suppose that the act is dependent on some prior act of choice or pleasure, contrary to what is now supposed; it is to suppose that it might have been otherwise, if its cause had ordered it otherwise. But this does not agree to it having no cause or orderer at all. That must be necessary as to the soul, which is dependent on no free act of the soul: but that which is without a cause, is dependent on no free act of the soul; because, by the supposition, it is dependent on nothing, and is connected with nothing. In such a case, the soul is necessarily subjected to what accident brings to pass, from time to time, as much as the earth that is inactive, is necessarily subjected to what falls upon it. But this does not consist with the Arminian notion of Liberty, which is the Will's power of determining itself in its own acts, and being wholly active in it, without passiveness, and without being subject to necessity.—Thus, Contingence belongs to the Arminian notion of Liberty, and yet is inconsistent with it.

I would here observe, that the author of the Essay on the Freedom of the Will, in God and the Creature, (p. 76, 77.) says as follows. "The word chance always means something done without design. Chance and design stand in direct opposition to each other: and Chance can never be properly applied to acts of the will, which is the spring of all design, and which designs to choose whatsoever it doth choose, whether there be any superior fitness in the thing which it chooses, or no; and it designs to determine itself to one thing, where two things, perfectly equal, are proposed, merely because it will." But herein appears a very great inadvertence. For if the will be the spring of all design, as he says, then certainly it is not always the effect of design; and the acts of the will themselves must sometimes come to pass, when they do not spring from design; and consequently come to pass by chance, according to his own definition of Chance. And if the will designs to choose whatever it does choose, and designs to determine itself, as he says, then it designs to determine all its designs. Which carries us back from one design to a foregoing design determining that, and to another determining that; and so on in infinitum. The very first design must be the effect of foregoing design, or else it must be by Chance, in his notion of it.

Here another alternative may be proposed, relating to the connexion of the acts of the Will with something foregoing that is their cause, not much unlike to the other; which is this: either human liberty may well stand with volitions being necessarily connected with the views of the understanding, and so is consistent with Necessity; or it is inconsistent with and contrary to such a connexion and Necessity. The former is directly subversive of the Arminian notion of Liberty, consisting in freedom from all Necessity. And if the latter be chosen, and it be said, that liberty is inconsistent with any such necessary connexion of volition with foregoing views of the understanding, it consisting in freedom from any such Necessity of the Will as that would imply; then the

Liberty of the soul consists, partly at least, in freedom from restraint, limitation, and government, in its actings, by the understanding, and in Liberty and liableness to act contrary to the views and dictates of the understanding: and consequently the more the soul has of this disengagedness in its acting, the more Liberty. Now let it be considered to what this brings the noble principle of human Liberty, particularly when it is possessed and enjoyed in its perfection, viz. a full and perfect freedom and liableness to act altogether at random, without the least connexion with, or restraint or government by, any dictate of reason, or any thing whatsoever apprehended, considered, or viewed by the understanding; as being inconsistent with the full and perfect sovereignty of the Will over its own determinations.—The notion mankind have conceived of Liberty, is some dignity or privilege, something worth claiming. But what dignity or privilege is there, in being given up to such a wild Contingence as this, to be perfectly and constantly liable to act unreasonably, and as much without the guidance of understanding, as if we had none, or were as destitute of perception, as the smoke that is driven by the wind!

PART III. WHEREIN IT IS CONSIDERED WHETHER THERE IS OR CAN BE ANY SORT OF FREEDOM OF WILL, AS THAT WHEREIN ARMINIANS PLACE THE ESSENCE OF THE LIBERTY OF ALL MORAL AGENTS; AND WHETHER ANY SUCH THING EVER WAS OR CAN BE CONCEIVED OF.

1. God's moral Excellency necessary, yet virtuous and praiseworthy.

2. The Acts of the Will of the human soul of Jesus Christ, necessarily holy, yet truly virtuous, praise-worthy, rewardable, &c.

3. The case of such as are given up of God to sin, and of fallen man in general, proves moral Necessity and Inability to be consistent with Blameworthiness.

4. Command and Obligation to Obedience, consistent with moral Inability to obey.

5. That Sincerity of Desires and Endeavours, which is supposed to excuse in the non-performance of things in themselves good, particularly considered.

6. Liberty of indifference, not only not necessary to Virtue, but

utterly inconsistent with it; and all, either virtuous or vicious habits or inclinations, inconsistent with Arminian notions of Liberty and moral Agency.

7. Arminian notions of moral Agency inconsistent with all Influence of Motive and Inducement, in either virtuous or vicious actions.

PART III. SECTION I. GOD'S MORAL EXCELLENCY NECESSARY, YET VIRTUOUS AND PRAISEWORTHY.

Having considered the first thing proposed, relating to that freedom of Will which Arminians maintain; namely, Whether any such thing does, ever did, or ever can exist, I come now to the second thing proposed to be the subject of inquiry, viz. Whether any such kind of liberty be requisite to moral agency, virtue and vice, praise and blame, reward and punishment, &c.

I shall begin with some consideration of the virtue and agency of the Supreme moral Agent, and Fountain of all Agency and Virtue.

Dr. Whitby in his Discourse on the five Points, (p. 14.) says, " If all human actions are necessary, virtue and vice must be empty names; we being capable of nothing that is blameworthy, or deserveth praise; for who can blame a person for doing only what he could not help, or judge that he deserveth praise only for what he could not avoid?" To the like purpose he speaks in places innumerable; especially in his Discourse on the Freedom of the Will; constantly maintaining, that a freedom not only from coaction, but necessity, is absolutely requisite, in order to actions being either worthy of blame, or deserving of praise. And to this agrees, as is well known, the current doctrine of Arminian writers, who, in general, hold, that there is no virtue or vice, reward or punishment, nothing to be commended or blamed, without this freedom. And yet Dr. Whitby (p. 300.) allows, that God is without this freedom; and, Arminians, so far as I have had opportunity to observe, generally acknowledge, that God is necessarily holy, and his will necessarily determined to that which is good.

So that, putting these things together, the infinitely holy God—who always used to be esteemed by God's people not only virtuous, but a Being in whom is all possible virtue, in the most absolute purity and perfection, brightness and amiableness; the most perfect pattern of virtue, and from whom all the virtue of others is but as beams from the sun; and who has been supposed to be, (being thus every where represented in Scripture,) on the account of his virtue and holiness, infinitely more worthy to be esteemed, loved, honoured, admired, commended, extolled, and praised, than any creature—this Being, according to this notion of Dr. Whitby, and other Arminians, has no virtue at all; virtue, when ascribed to him, is but on empty name; and he is deserving of no commendation or praise; because he is under necessity, he cannot avoid being holy and good as he is; therefore no thanks to him for it. It seems, the holiness, justice, faithfulness, &c. of the Most High, must not be accounted to be of the nature of that which is virtuous and praiseworthy. They will not deny, that these things in God are good; but then we must understand them, that they are no more virtuous, or of the nature of any thing commendable, than the good that is in any other being that is not a moral agent as the brightness of the sun, and the fertility of the earth, are good, but not virtuous, because these properties are necessary to these bodies, and not the fruit of self-determining power.

There needs no other confutation of this notion, to Christians acquainted with the Bible, but only stating and particularly representing it. To bring texts of Scripture, wherein God is represented, as in every respect, in the highest manner virtuous, and supremely praiseworthy, would be endless, and is altogether needless to such as have been brought up in the light of the gospel.

It were to be wished, that Dr. Whitby and other divines of the same sort, had explained themselves, when they have asserted, that that which is necessary, is not deserving of praise; at the same time that they have owned God's perfection to be necessary, and so in effect representing God as not deserving praise. Certainly, if their words have any meaning at all, by praise, they must mean the exercise or testimony of esteem, respect, or honourable regard. And will they then say, that men are worthy of that esteem, respect, and honour for their virtue, small and imperfect as it is, which yet God is not worthy of, for his infinite righteousness, holiness, and goodness? If so, it must be, because of some sort of peculiar excellency in the virtuous man, which is his prerogative, wherein he really has the preference; some dignity, that is entirely distinguished from any Excellency or amiableness in God; not in dependence, but in pre-eminence; which therefore he does not receive from God, nor is God the fountain or pattern of it; nor can God, in that respect, stand in competition with him, as the object of honour and regard; but man may claim a peculiar esteem, commendation, and glory, to which God can have no pretension. Yea, God has no right, by virtue of his necessary holiness, to intermeddle with that grateful respect and praise, due to the virtuous man, who chooses virtue, in the exercise of a freedom *ad utrumque;* any more than a precious stone, which. cannot avoid being hard and beautiful.

And if it be so, let it be explained what that peculiar respect is, that is due to the virtuous man, which differs in nature and kind, in some way of pre-eminence, from all that is due to God. What is the name or description of that peculiar affection? Is it esteem, love, admiration, honour, praise, or gratitude? The Scripture every where represents God as the highest object of all these: there we read of the soul magnifying the Lord, of "loving him with all the heart, with all the soul, with all the mind, and with all the strength;" admiring him, and his righteous acts, or greatly regarding them, as marvelous and wonderful; honouring, glorifying, exalting, extolling, blessing, thanking, and praising him; giving unto him all the glory of the good which is done or received, rather than unto men; "that no flesh should glory in his presence;" but that he should be regarded as the Being to whom all glory is due. What then is that respect? What passion, affection, or exercise is it, that Arminians call praise, diverse from all these things, which men are worthy of for their virtue, and which God is not worthy of, in any degree?

If that necessity which attends God's moral perfections and actions, be as inconsistent with being worthy of praise, as a necessity of co-action; as is plainly implied in, or inferred from, Dr. Whitby's discourse; then why should we thank God for his goodness, any more than if he were forced to be good, or any more than we should thank one of our fellow-creatures who did us good, not freely, and of good will, or from any kindness of heart, but from mere compulsion, or extrinsical necessity? Arminians suppose, that God is necessarily a good and gracious being; for this they make the ground of some of their main arguments against many doctrines maintained by Calvinists; they say, these are certainly false, and it is impossible they should be true, because they are not consistent with the goodness of God. This supposes, that it is impossible but that God should be good: for if it be possible that he should be otherwise, then that impossibility of the truth of these doctrines ceases according to their own argument.

That virtue in God is not, in the most proper sense, rewardable, is not for want of merit in his moral perfections and actions, sufficient to deserve rewards from his creatures; but because he is infinitely above all capacity of receiving any reward. He is already infinitely and unchangeably happy, and we cannot be profitable unto him. But still he is worthy of our supreme benevolence for his virtue: and would be worthy of our beneficence, which is the fruit and expression of benevolence, if our goodness could extend to him. If God deserves to be thanked and praised for his goodness, he would, for the same reason, deserve that we should also requite his kindness, if that were possible. "What shall I render unto the Lord for all his benefits?" is the natural language of thankfulness: and so far as in us lies, it is our duty to render again according to benefits received. And that we might have opportunity for so natural an expression of our gratitude to God, as beneficence, notwithstanding his being infinitely above our reach, he has appointed others to be his receivers, and to stand in his stead, as the objects of our beneficence; such are especially our indigent brethren.

PART III. SECTION II. THE ACTS OF THE WILL OF THE HUMAN SOUL OF JESUS CHRIST, NECESSARILY HOLY, YET TRULY VIRTUOUS, PRAISE-WORTHY, REWARDABLE, &C.

I have already considered how Dr. Whitby insists upon it, that a freedom, not only from coaction, but necessity, is requisite either to virtue or vice, praise or dispraise, reward or punishment. He also insists on the same freedom as absolutely requisite to a person being the subject of a law, of precepts, or prohibitions; in the book before mentioned, (p. 301, 314, 328, 339, 340, 341, 342, 347, 361, 373, 410.) Areal of promises and threatenings, (p. 298, 301, 305, 311, 339, 340, 363.) And as requisite to a state of trial, p. 297, &c.

Now, therefore, with an eye to these things, I would inquire into the moral conduct and practices of our Lord Jesus Christ, which he exhibited in his human nature, in his state of humiliation. And first, I would show, that His holy behaviour was necessary; or that it was impossible it should be otherwise, than that he should behave Himself holy, and that he should be perfectly holy in each individual act of his life. And secondly, that his holy behaviour was properly of the nature of virtue, and was worthy of praise; and that he was the subject of law, precept, or commands, promises and rewards; and that he was in a state of trial.

I. It was impossible, that the Acts of the will of Christ's human soul should, in any instance, degree, or circumstance, be otherwise than holy, and agreeable to God's nature and Will. The following things make this evident.

1. God had promised so effectually to preserve and up hold him by his Spirit, under all his temptations, that he could not fail of the end for which he came into the world; but he would have failed, had he fallen into sin. We have such a promise, (Isa. xliii. 1–4.) " Behold my Servant, whom I uphold; mine Elect, in whom my soul delighteth: I have put my Spirit upon him: he shall bring forth judgment to the Gentiles: he shall not cry, nor lift up, nor cause his voice to be heard in the street.— He shall bring forth judgment unto truth. He shall not fail, nor be discouraged, till he have set judgment in the earth; and the isles shall wait his law." This promise of God's Spirit put upon him, and his not crying and lifting up his voice, &c. relates to the time of Christ's appearance on earth; as is manifest from the nature of the promise, and also the application of it in the New Testament, (Matt. xii. 18.) And the words imply a promise of his being so upheld by God's Spirit, that he should be preserved from sin; particularly from pride and vain-glory; and from being overcome by any temptations he should be under to affect the glory of this world, the pomp of an earthly prince, or the applause and praise of men: and that he should be so upheld, that he should by no means fail of obtaining the end of his earning into the world, of bringing forth judgment unto victory, and establishing his kingdom of grace in the earth. And in the following verses, this promise is confirmed, with the greatest imaginable solemnity. "Thus saith the Lord, he that created the heavens, and stretched them out; he that spread forth the earth, and that which cometh out of it; he that giveth breath unto the people upon it, and spirit to them that walk therein: I the Lord have called thee in righteousness, and will hold thine hand; and will keep thee, and give thee for a Covenant of the people, for a Light of the Gentiles, to open the blind eyes, to bring out the prisoners from the prison, and them that sit in darkness out of the prison-house. I am JEHOVAH, that is my name," &c.

Very parallel with these promises is another, (Isa. xlix. 7, 8, 9.) which also has an apparent respect to the time of Christ's humiliation on earth.—"Thus saith the Lord, the Redeemer of Israel, and his Holy One, to him whom man despiseth, to him whom the nation abhorreth, to a servant of rulers; kings shall see and arise, princes also shall worship;

because of the Lord that is faithful, and the Holy One of Israel, and he shall choose thee. Thus saith the Lord, in an acceptable time have I heard thee; in a day of salvation have I helped thee; and I will preserve thee, and give thee for a covenant of the people, to establish the earth," &.c.

And in Isa. 50:5, 6. we have the Messiah expressing his assurance, that God would help him, by so opening his ear, or inclining his heart to God's commandments, that he should not be rebellious, but should persevere, and not apostatize, or turn his back: that through God's help, he should be immovable in obedience, under great trials of reproach and suffering; setting his face like a flint: so that he knew he should not be ashamed, or frustrated in his design; and finally should be approved and justified, as having done his work faithfully. "The Lord hath opened mine ear; so that I was not rebellious, neither turned away my back: I gave my back to the smiters, and my cheeks to them that plucked off the hair; I hid not my face from shame and spitting. For the Lord God will help me; therefore shall I not be confounded: therefore have I set my face as a flint, and I know that I shall not be ashamed. He is near that justifieth me: who will contend with me? Let us stand together. Who is mine adversary? Let him come near to me. Behold the Lord God will help me: who is he that shall condemn me? Lo, they shall all wax old as a garment, the moth shall eat them up."

2. The same thing is evident from all the promises which God made to the Messiah, of his future glory, kingdom, and success, in his office and character of a Mediator: which glory could not have been obtained, if his holiness had failed, and he had been guilty of sin. God's absolute promise makes the things promised necessary, and their failing to take place absolutely impossible: and, in like manner, it makes those things necessary, on which the thing promised depends, and without which it cannot take effect. Therefore it appears, that it was utterly impossible that Christ's holiness should fail, from such absolute promises as these, (Psal. cx. 4.) "The Lord hath sworn, and will not repent, thou art a priest for ever, after the order of Melchizedek." And from every other promise in that psalm, contained in each verse of it. (And Psal. ii. 6, 7.) "I will declare the decree: The Lord hath said unto me, Thou art my Son, this day have I begotten thee: Ask of me, and I will give thee the heathen for thine inheritance," &c. (Psal. xlv. 3, 4, &c.) " Gird thy sword on thy thigh, O most mighty, with thy glory and thy majesty; and in thy majesty ride prosperously." And so every thing that is said from thence to the end of the psalm. (See Isa. iii. 13–15. and liii. 10–12.)

And all those promises which God makes to the Messiah, of success, dominion, and glory in the character of a Redeemer, (Isa. chap. xlix.)

3. It was often promised to the church of God of old, for their comfort, that God would give them a righteous, sinless Saviour. (Jer. xxiii. 5, 6.) "Behold, the days come, saith the Lord, that I will rise up unto David a righteous branch; and a king shall reign and prosper, and shall execute judgment and justice in the earth. In his days shall Judah be saved, and Israel shall dwell safely. And this is the name whereby he shall be called, The Lord our righteousness." (So, Jer. xxxiii. 15.) "I will cause the branch of righteousness to grow up unto David, and he shall execute judgment and righteousness in the land." (Isa. xi. 6, 7.) "For unto us a child is born;—upon the throne of David and of his kingdom, to order it and to establish it with judgment and justice, from henceforth, even for ever: the zeal of the Lord of hosts will do this." (Chap. xi. 1, &c.) "There shall come forth a rod out of the stem of Jesse, and a branch shall grow out of his roots; and the Spirit of the Lord shall rest upon him,—the spirit of knowledge, and the fear of the Lord:—with righteousness shall he judge the poor, and reprove with equity:—Righteousness shall be the girdle of his loins, and faithfulness the girdle of his reins." (Chap. lii. 13.) "My servant shall deal prudently." (Chap. liii. 9.) "Because he had done no violence, neither was guile found in his mouth." If it be impossible, that these promises should fail, and it be easier for heaven and earth to pass away, than for one jot or tittle of them to pass away, then it was impossible that Christ should commit any sin.—Christ himself signified, that it was impossible but that the things which were spoken concerning him, should be fulfilled. (Luke xxiv. 44.) "That all things must be fulfilled, which were written in the law of Moses, and in the prophets, and in the psalms concerning Me." (Matt. xxvi. 53, 54.) "But how then shall the scripture be fulfilled, that thus it must be?" (Mark xiv. 49.) "But the scriptures must be fulfilled." And so the apostle, (Acts I. 16, 17.) "This scripture must needs have been fulfilled."

4. All the promises, which were made to the church of old, of the Messiah as a future Saviour, from that made to our first parents in paradise, to that which was delivered by the prophet Malachi show it to be impossible that Christ should not have persevered in perfect holiness. The ancient predictions given to God's church, of the Messiah as a Saviour, were of the nature of promises; as is evident by the predictions themselves, and the manner of delivering them. But they are expressly

and very often called promises in the New Testament; (as in Luke I. 54, 55, 72, 73. Acts xiii. 32, 33. Rom. I. 1–3. and chap. xv. 8. Heb. vi. 13, &c.) These promises were often made with great solemnity, and confirmed with an oath; as, (Gen. xxii. 16, 17.), "By myself have I sworn, saith the Lord, that in blessing I will bless thee, and in multiplying I will multiply thy seed, as the stars of heaven, and as the sand which is upon the sea-shore:—And in thy seed shall all the nations of the earth be blessed." (Compare Luke I. 72, 73. and Gal. iii. 8, 1,5, 16.) The apostle in Heb. vi. 17, 18. speaking of this promise to Abraham, says, "Wherein God willing more abundantly to show to the heirs of promise the immutability of his counsel, confirmed it by an oath; that by two IMMUTABLE things, in which it was IMPOSSIBLE for God to lie, we might have strong consolation." In which words, the necessity of the accomplishment, or (which is the same thing) the impossibility of the contrary, is fully declared. So God confirmed the promise of the Messiah's great salvation, made to David, by an oath; (Psal. lxxxix. 3, 4.) "I have made a covenant with my chosen, I have sworn unto David my servant; thy seed will I establish for ever, and build up thy throne to all generations." There is nothing so abundantly set forth in Scripture, as sure and irrefragable, as this promise and oath to David. (See Psalm. lxxxix. 34–36. 2 Sam. xxiii. 5. Isa. lv. 4. Acts ii. 29, 30. and xiii. 34.) The Scripture expressly speaks of it as utterly impossible that this promise and oath to David, concerning the everlasting dominion of the Messiah, should fail. (Jer. xxxiii. 15, &c.) "In those days, and at that time, I will cause the Branch of righteousness to grow up unto David.—For thus saith the Lord, David shall never want a man to sit upon the throne of the house of Israel." (Ver. 20, 21.) "If you can break my covenant of the day, and my covenant of the night, and that there should not be day and night in their season; then may also my covenant be broken with David my servant, that he should not have a son to reign upon his throne." (So in ver. 25, 26.) Thus abundant is the Scripture in representing how impossible it was, that the promises made of old concerning the great salvation and kingdom of the Messiah should fail: which implies, that it was impossible that this Messiah, the second Adam, the promised seed of Abraham, and of David, should fall from his integrity, as the first Adam did.

5. All the promises that were made to the church of God under the Old Testament, of the great enlargement of the church, and advancement of her glory, in the days of the gospel, after the coming of the Messiah;

the increase of her light, liberty, holiness, joy, triumph over her enemies, &c. of which so great a part of the Old Testament consists; which are repeated so often, are so variously exhibited, so frequently introduced with great pomp and solemnity, and are so abundantly sealed with typical and symbolical representations; I say, all these promises imply, that the Messiah should perfect the work of redemption: and this implies, that he should persevere in the work, which the Father had appointed him, beings in all things conformed to his Will. These promises were often confirmed by an oath. (See Isa. liv. 9. with the context; chap. lxii. 18.) And it is represented as utterly impossible that these promises should fail. (Isa. xlix. 15. with the context, chap. liv. 10. with the context; chap. li. 4–8. chap. xl. 8. with the context.) And therefore it was impossible that the Messiah should fail, or commit sin.

6. It was impossible that the Messiah should fail of persevering in integrity and holiness, as the first Adam did, because this would have been inconsistent with the promises, which God made to the blessed Virgin, his mother, and to her husband; implying, that he should "save his people from their sins," that God would "give him the throne of his father David," that he should "reign over the house of Jacob for ever;" and that "of his kingdom there shall be no end." These promises were sure, and it was impossible they should fail, and therefore the Virgin Mary, in trusting fully to them, acted reasonably, having an immovable foundation of her faith; as Elizabeth observes, (ver. 45.) "And blessed is she that believeth; for there shall be a performance of those things which were told her from the Lord."

7. That it should have been possible that Christ should sin, and so fail in the work of our redemption, does not consist with the eternal purpose and decree of God, revealed in the Scriptures, that he would provide salvation for fallen man in and by Jesus Christ, and that salvation should be offered to sinners through the preaching of the gospel. Thus much is implied in many scriptures, (as 1 Cor. ii. 7.—Eph. I. 4, 5. and chap. iii. 9–11.—1 Pet. I. 19, 20.) Such an absolute decree as this, Arminians allow to be signified in many texts; their election of nations and societies, and general election of the Christian church, and conditional election of particular persons, imply this. God could not decree before the foundation of the world, to save all that should believe in and obey Christ, unless, he had absolutely decreed, that salvation should be provided, and effectually wrought out by Christ. And since (as the Arminians themselves strenuously maintain) a decree of God infers necessity;

hence it became necessary, that Christ should persevere and actually work out salvation for us, and that he should not fail by the commission of sin.

8. That it should have been possible for Christ's holiness to fail, is not consistent with what God promised to his Son, before all ages. For that salvation should be offered to men, through Christ, and bestowed on all his faithful followers, is at least implied in that certain and infallible promise spoken of by the apostle, (Tit. I. 2.) "In hope of eternal life; which God, that cannot lie, promised before the world began." This does not seem to be controverted by Arminians.

9. That it should be possible for Christ to fail of doing his Father's Will, is inconsistent with the promise made to the Father by the Son, the Logos that was with the Father from the beginning, before he took the human nature: as may be seen in Ps. xl. 6–8. (compared with the apostle's interpretation, Heb. x. 5–9.) "Sacrifice and offering thou didst not desire: mine ears hast thou opened, (or bored;) burnt-offering and sin-offering thou hast not required. Then said I, Lo, I come; in the volume of the book it is written of me, I delight to do thy will, O my God, yea, thy law is within my heart." Where is a manifest allusion to the covenant, which the willing servant, who loved his master's service, made with his master, to be his servant for ever, on the day wherein he had his ear bored; which covenant was probably inserted in the public records, called the VOLUME OF THE BOOK, by the judges, who were called to take cognizance of the transaction; (Exod. xxi.) If the Logos, who was with the Father before the world, and who made the world, thus engaged in covenant to do the Will of the Father in the human nature, and the promise was as it were recorded, that it, might be made sure, doubtless it was impossible that it should fail; and so it was impossible that Christ should fail of doing the Will of the Father in the human nature.

10. If it was possible for Christ to have failed of doing the Will of his Father, and so to have failed of effectually working out redemption for sinners, then the salvation of all the saints, who were saved from the beginning of the world, to the death of Christ, was not built on a firm foundation. The Messiah, and the redemption which he was to work out by his obedience unto death, was the saving foundation of all that ever were saved. Therefore, if when the Old-Testament saints had the pardon of their sins and the favour of God promised them, and salvation bestowed upon them, still it was possible that the Messiah, when he

came, might commit sin, then all this was on a foundation that was not firm and stable, but liable to Evil; something which it was possible might never be. God did as it were trust to what his Son had engaged and promised to do in future time, and depended so much upon it, that he proceeded actually to save men on the account of it, though it had been already done. But this trust and dependence of God, on the supposition of Christ's being liable to fail of doing his Will, was leaning on a staff that was weak, and might possibly break. The saints of old trusted on the promises of a future redemption to be wrought out and completed by the Messiah, and built their comfort upon it: Abraham saw Christ's day, and rejoiced; and he and the other Patriarchs died in the faith of the promise of it, (Heb. xi. 13.) But on this supposition, their faith, their comfort, and their salvation, was built on a fallible foundation; Christ was not to them "a tried stone, a sure foundation;" (Isa. xxviii. 16.) David entirely rested on the covenant of God with him, concerning the future glorious dominion and salvation of the Messiah; and said it was all his salvation, and all his desire; and comforts himself that this covenant was an "everlasting covenant, ordered in all things and sure," (2 Sam. xxiii.5.) But if Christ's virtue might fail, he was mistaken: his great comfort was not built so "sure" as he thought it was, being founded entirely on the determinations of the Free Will of Christ's human soul; which was subject to no necessity, and might be determined either one way or the other. Also the dependence of those, who "looked for redemption in Jerusalem, and wailed for the consolation of Israel," (Luke ii. 25, and 38.) and the confidence of the disciples of Jesus, who forsook all and followed him, that they might enjoy the benefits of his future kingdom, were built on a sandy foundation.

11. The man Christ Jesus, before he had finished his course of obedience, and while in the midst of temptations and trials, was abundant in positively predicting his own future glory in his kingdom, and the enlargement of his church, the salvation of the Gentiles through him, &c. and in promises of blessings he would bestow on his true disciples in his future kingdom; on which promises he required the full dependence of his disciples, (John xiv.) But the disciples would have no ground for such dependence, if Christ had been liable to fail in his work: and Christ himself would have been guilty of presumption, in so abounding in peremptory promises of great things, which depended on a mere contingence; viz. the determinations of his Free Will, consisting in a freedom *ad ulrumque,* to either sin or holiness, standing in indifference,

and incident, in thousands of future instances, to go either one way or the other.

Thus it is evident, that it was impossible that the Acts of the will of the human soul of Christ should be otherwise than holy, and conformed to the Will of the Father; or, in other words, they were necessarily so conformed.

I have been the longer in the proof of this matter, it being a thing denied by some of the greatest Arminians, by Episcopius in particular; and because I look upon it as a point clearly and absolutely determining the controversy between Calvinists and Arminians, concerning the necessity of such a freedom of Will as is insisted on by the latter, in order to moral agency, virtue, command or prohibition, promise or threatening, reward or punishment, praise or dispraise, merit or demerit. I now therefore proceed, II. To consider whether CHRIST, in his holy behaviour on earth, was not thus a moral agent, subject to commands, promises, &c.

Dr. Whitby very often speaks of what he calls a freedom *ad utrumlibet*, without necessity, as requisite to law and commands: and speaks of necessity as entirely inconsistent with injunctions and prohibitions. But yet we read of Christ being the subject of His Father's commands, (John x. 18. and xv. 10.) And Christ tells us, that every thing that he said, or did, was in compliance with "commandments he had received of the Father;" (John xii. 49, 50. and xiv. 31.) And we often read of Christ's obedience to his Father's commands, (Rom. v. 19. Phil. ii. 18. Heb. v. 8.)

The forementioned writer represents promises offered as motives to persons to do their duty, or a being moved and induced by promises, as utterly inconsistent with a state wherein persons have not a liberty *ad utrumlibet*, but are necessarily determined to one. (See particularly, p. 298, and 311.) But the thing which this writer asserts, is demonstrably false, if the Christian religion be true. If there be any truth in Christianity or the Holy Scriptures, the man Christ Jesus had his Will infallibly and unalterably determined to good, and that alone; but yet he had promises of glorious rewards made to him, on condition of his persevering in and perfecting the work which God had appointed him; (Isa. liii. 10, 11, 12. Psal. ii. and cx. Isa. xlix. 7, 8, 9.) In Luke xxii. 28, 20 Christ says to his disciples, "Ye are they which have continued with me in my temptations; and I appoint unto you a kingdom, as my Father hath appointed unto me." The word most properly signifies to appoint by covenant, or promise. The plain meaning of Christ's words is this: "As you have partaken of my temptations and trials, and have been steadfast, and have overcome;

I promise to make you partakers of my reward, and to give you a kingdom; as the Father has promised me a kingdom for continuing steadfast and overcoming in those trials." And the words are well explained by those in Rev. iii. 21. "To him that overcometh, will I grant to sit with me on my throne; even as I also overcame, and am set down with my Father in his throne." And Christ had not only promises of glorious success and rewards made to his obedience and sufferings, but the Scriptures plainly represent him as using these promises for motives and inducements to obey and suffer; and particularly that promise of a kingdom which the Father had appointed him, or sitting with the Father on his throne; (as in Heb. xii. 1, 2.) "Let us lay aside every weight, and the sin which doth easily beset us, and let us run with patience the race that is set before us, looking unto Jesus the author and finisher of our faith; who for the joy that was set before him, endured the cross, despising the shame, and is set down on the right hand of the throne of God."

And how strange would it be to hear any Christian assert, that the holy and excellent temper and behaviour of Jesus Christ, and that obedience which he performed under such great trials, was not virtuous or praiseworthy; because his Will was not free *ad utrumque*, to either holiness or sin, but was unalterably determined to one; that upon this account, there is no virtue at all in all Christ's humility, meekness, patience, charity, forgiveness of enemies, contempt of the world, heavenly-mindedness, submission to the Will of God, perfect obedience to his commands unto death, even the death of the cross, his great compassion to the afflicted, his unparalleled love to mankind, his faithfulness to God and man, under such great trials; his praying for his enemies, even when nailing him to the cross; that virtue, when applied to these things, is but an empty name; that there was no merit in any of these things; that is, that Christ was worthy of nothing at all on account of them, worthy of no reward, no praise, no honour or respect from God or man; because his will was not indifferent, and free either to these things, or the contrary; but under such a strong inclination or bias to the things that were excellent, as made it impossible that he should choose the contrary; that upon this account, to use Dr. Whitby's language, it would be sensibly unreasonable that the human nature should be rewarded for any of these things.

According to this doctrine, that creature who is evidently set forth in Scripture as the first-born of every creature, as having in all things the pre-eminence, and as the highest of all creatures in virtue, honour, and worthiness of esteem, praise, and glory, on account of his virtue, is less worthy of reward or praise, than the very least of saints; yea, no more worthy than a clock or mere machine, that is purely passive, and moved by natural necessity.

If we judge by scriptural representations of things, we have reason to suppose, that Christ took on him our nature, and dwelt with us in this world, in a suffering state, not only to satisfy for our sins; but that he, being in our nature and circumstances, and under our trials, might be our most fit and proper example, leader, and captain, in the exercise of glorious and victorious virtue, and might be a visible instance of the glorious end and reward of it; that we might see in Him the beauty, amiableness, and true honour and glory, and exceeding benefit, of that virtue, which it is proper for us human beings to practice; and might thereby learn, and be animated, to seek the like glory and honour, and to obtain the like glorious reward. (See Heb. ii. 9–14. with v. 8, 9. and xii. 1, 2, 3. John xv. 10. Rom. viii. 17. 2 Tim. ii. 11, 12. 1 Pet. ii. 19, 20. and iv. 1:3.) But if there was nothing of any virtue or merit, or worthiness of any reward, glory, praise, or commendation at all, in all that he did, because it was all necessary, and he could not help it; then how is here any thing so proper to animate and incite us, free creatures, by patient continuance in well-doing, to seek for honour, glory, and virtue?

God speaks of himself as peculiarly well pleased with the righteousness of this distinguished servant. (Isa. xlii. 21.) "The Lord is well pleased for his righteousness' sake." The sacrifices of old are spoken of as a sweet savor to God, but the obedience of Christ as far more acceptable than they. (Psal. xl. 6, 7.) "Sacrifice and offering thou didst not desire: mine ear hast thou opened [as thy servant performing willing obedience;] burnt-offering and sin-offering hast thou not required. Then said I, Lo, I come, [as a servant that cheerfully answers the calls of his master:] I delight to do thy will, O my God, and thy law is within mine heart." (Matt. xvii. 5.) "This is my beloved Son, in whom I am well-pleased." And Christ tells us expressly, that the Father loves Him for that wonderful instance of his obedience, his voluntary yielding himself to death, in compliance with the Father's command, (John x. 17, 18.) "Therefore doth my Father love me, because I lay down my life:—No man taketh it from me; but I lay it down of myself—This commandment received I of my Father."

And if there was no merit in Christ's obedience unto death, if it was not worthy of praise, and of the most glorious rewards, the heavenly hosts were exceedingly mistaken, by the account that is given of them, (Rev. v. 8–12.) "The four beasts, and the four and twenty elders, fell down before the Lamb, having every one of them harps, and golden vials full of odours;—and they sung a new song, saying, Thou art worthy to take the book, and to open the seals thereof; for thou wast slain.— And I beheld, and I heard the voice of many angels round about the throne, and the beasts, and the elders, and the number of them was ten thousand times ten thousand, and thousands of thousands, saying with a loud voice, Worthy is the Lamb that was slain, to receive power, and riches, and wisdom, and strength, and honour, and glory, and blessing."

Christ speaks of the eternal life which he was to receive, as the reward of his obedience to the Father's commandments. (John xii. 49, 50.) "I have not spoken of myself; but the Father which sent me, he gave me a commandment what I should say, and what I should speak; and I know that his commandment is life everlasting: whatsoever I speak therefore, even as the Father said unto me, so I speak."—God promises to divide him a portion with the great, &c. for his being his righteous servant, for his glorious virtue under such great trials and afflictions. (Isa. liii. 11, 12.) "He shall see the travail of his soul and be satisfied; by his knowledge shall my righteous servant justify many; for he shall bear their iniquities. Therefore will I divide him a portion with the great, and he shall divide the spoil with the strong, because he hath poured out his soul unto death." The Scriptures represent God as rewarding him far above all his other servants. (Phil. ii. 7–9.) "He took on him the form of a servant, and was made in the likeness of men; and being found in fashion as a man, he humbled himself, and became obedient unto death, even the death of the cross; wherefore God also hath highly exalted him, and given him a name above every name." (Psal. xlv. 7.) "Thou lovest righteousness, and hatest wickedness; therefore God, thy God, hath anointed thee with the oil of gladness above thy fellows."

There is no room to pretend, that the glorious benefits bestowed in consequence of Christ's obedience, are not properly of the nature of a reward. What is a reward, in the most proper sense, but a benefit be-stowed in consequence of something morally excellent in quality or behaviour, in testimony of well-blessedness in that moral excellency, and of respect and favour on that account? If we consider the nature of a reward most strictly, and make the utmost of it, and add to the things contained in this description proper merit or worthiness, and the bestowment of the benefit in consequence of a promise; still it will be found, there is nothing belonging to it, but what the Scripture most expressly ascribes to the glory bestowed on Christ, after his sufferings; as appears from what has been already observed; there was a glorious benefit bestowed in consequence of something morally excellent, being called Righteousness and Obedience; there was great favour, love, and well-pleasedness, for this righteousness and obedience, in the bestower; there was proper merit, or worthiness of the benefit, in the obedience; it was bestowed in fulfilment of promises, made to that obedience; and was bestowed therefore, or because he had performed that obedience.

I may add to all these things, that Jesus Christ, while here in the flesh, was manifestly in a state of trial. The last Adam, as Christ is called, (1 Cor. xv. 45. Rom. v. 14.) taking on him the human nature, and so the form of a servant, and being under the law, to stand and act for us, was put into a state of trial, as the first Adam was.—Dr. Whitby mentions these three things as evidences of persons being in a state of trial, (on the five Points, p. 298, 299.) namely, their afflictions being spoken of as their trials or temptations, their being the subjects of promises, and their being exposed to Satan's temptations. But Christ was apparently the subject of each of these. Concerning promises made to him, I have spoken already. The difficulties and afflictions he met with in the course of his obedience, are called his temptations or trials, (Luke xxii. 28.) "Ye are they which have continued with me in my temptations and trials." (Heb. ii. 18.) "For in that he himself hath suffered, being tempted [or tried,] he is able to succor them that are tempted." And, (chap. iv. 15.) "We have not an high-priest, which cannot be touched with the feeling of our infirmities; but was in all points tempted like as we are, yet without sin." And as to his being tempted by Satan it is what none will dispute.

PART III. SECTION III. THE CASE OF SUCH AS ARE GIVEN UP OF GOD TO SIN, AND OF FALLEN MAN IN GENERAL, PROVES MORAL NECESSITY AND INABILITY TO BE CONSISTENT WITH BLAMEWORTHINESS.

Dr. Whitby asserts freedom, not only from coaction, but Necessity, to be essential to any thing deserving the name of sin, and to an action being culpable; in these words, (Discourse on Five Points, edit. 3. p. 348.)

"If they be thus necessitated, then neither their sins of omission or commission could deserve that name: it being essential to the nature of sin, according to St. Austin's definition, that it be an action *a duo liberum est abstinere*. Three things seem plainly necessary to make an action or omission culpable; 1. That it be in our power to perform or forbear it: for, as Origen, and all the fathers, say, no man is blameworthy for not doing what he could not do." And elsewhere the Doctor insists, that "when any do evil of Necessity, what they do is no vice, that they are guilty of no fault, are worthy of no blame, dispraise, or dishonour, but are unblamable."

If these things are true, in Dr. Whitby's sense of Necessity, they will prove all such to be blameless, who are given up of God to sin, in what they commit after they are thus given up.—That there is such a thing as men being judicially given up to sin, is certain, if the Scripture rightly informs us; such a thing being often there spoken of: as in Psal. lxxxi. 12. "So I gave them up to their own hearts' lust, and they walked in their own counsels." (Acts vii. 42.) "Then God turned, and gave them up to worship the host of heaven." (Rom. 1. 24.) " Wherefore, God also gave them up to uncleanness, through the lusts of their own hearts, to dishonour their own bodies between themselves." (Ver. 26.) "For this cause God gave them up to vile affections." (Ver. 28.) "And even as they did not like to retain God in their knowledge, God gave them over to a reprobate mind, to do those things that are not convenient."

It is needless to stand particularly to inquire, what God's "giving men up to their own hearts' lusts" signifies: it is sufficient to observe, that hereby is certainly meant God so ordering or disposing things, in some respect or other, either by doing or forbearing to do, as that the consequence should be men continuing in their sins. So much as men are given up to, so much is the consequence of their being given up, whether that be less or more. If God does not order things so, by action or permission, that sin will be the consequence, then the event proves that they are not given up to that consequence. If good be the consequence, instead of evil, then God's mercy is to be acknowledged in that good; which mercy must be contrary to God's judgment in giving up to evil. If the event must prove, that they are given up to evil as the consequence, then the persons, who are the subjects of this judgment, must be the subjects of such an event, and so the event is necessary.

If not only coaction, but all Necessity, will prove men blameless, then Judas was blameless, after Christ had given him over, and had already declared his certain damnation, and that he should verily betray him. He was guilty of no sin in betraying his Master, on this supposition; though his so doing is spoken of by Christ as the most aggravated sin, more heinous than the sin of Pilate in crucifying him. And the Jews in Egypt, in Jeremiah's time, were guilty of no sin, in their not worshiping the true God, after God had "sworn by his great name, that his name should be no more named in the mouth of any man of Judah, in all the land of Egypt," (Jer. xliv. 26.)

Dr. Whitby (Disc. on five Points, p. 302, 303.) denies, that men, in this world, are ever so given up by God to sin, that their Wills should be necessarily determined to evil; though he owns, that hereby it may become exceeding difficult for men to do good, having a strong bent and powerful inclination to what is evil. But if we should allow the case to be just as he represents, the judgment of giving up to sin will no better agree with his notions of that liberty, which is essential to praise or blame, than if we should suppose it to render the avoiding of sin impossible. For if an impossibility of avoiding sin wholly excuses a man; then for the same reason, its being difficult to avoid it, excuses him in part; and this just in proportion to the degree of difficulty.—If the influence of moral impossibility or inability be the same, to excuse persons in not doing or not avoiding any thing, as that of natural inability, (which is supposed,) then undoubtedly, in like manner, mortal difficulty has the same influence to excuse with natural difficulty. But all allow, that natural impossibility wholly excuses, and also that natural difficulty excuses in part, and makes the act or omission less blamable in proportion to the difficulty. All natural difficulty, according to the plainest dictates of the light of nature, excuses in some degree, so that the neglect is not so blamable, as if there had been no difficulty in the case: and so the greater the difficulty is, still the more excusable, in proportion to the increase of the difficulty. And as natural impossibility wholly excuses, and excludes all blame, so the nearer the difficulty approaches to impossibility, still the nearer a person is to blamelessness in proportion to that approach. And if the case of moral impossibility or Necessity, be just the same with natural Necessity or coaction, as to its influence to excuse a neglect, then also, for the same reason, the case of natural difficulty does not differ in influence, to excuse a neglect, from moral difficulty, arising from a strong bias or bent to evil, such as Dr. Whitby owns in the case of those that are given up to their own hearts' lusts. So that the fault of such persons must be lessened, in proportion to the difficulty, and approach to impossibility. If ten degrees of moral difficulty make the action quite impossible, and so wholly excuse, then if there be nine degrees of difficulty, the person is in great part excused, and is nine degrees in ten less blameworthy, than if there had been no difficulty at all; and he has but one degree of blameworthiness. The reason is plain, on Arminian principles; viz. because as difficulty, by antecedent bent and bias on the Will, is increased, liberty of indifference, and self-determination in the Will, is diminished; so much hindrance, impediment is there, in the way of the will acting freely, by mere self-determination. And if ten degrees of such hindrance take away all such liberty, then nine degree,—take away nine parts in ten, and leave but one degree of liberty. And therefore there is but one degree of blameableness in the neglect; the man being no further blamable in what he does, or neglects, than he has liberty in that affair: for blame or praise (say they) arises wholly from a good use or abuse of liberty.

From all which it follows, that a strong bent and bias one way, and difficulty of going the contrary, never causes a person to be at all more exposed to sin, or any thing blamable: because, as the difficulty is increased, so much the less is required and expected. Though in one respect, exposedness to sin is increased, viz. by an increase of exposedness to the evil action or omission; yet it is diminished in another respect, to balance it; namely, as the sinfulness or blamableness of the action or omission is diminished in the same proportion. So that, on the whole, the affair, as to exposedness to guilt or blame, is left just as it was.

To illustrate this, let us suppose a scale of a balance to be intelligent, and a free agent, and indued with a self-moving power, by virtue of which it could act and produce effects to a certain degree, ex. gr. to move itself up or down with a force equal to a weight of ten pounds; and that it might therefore be required of it, in ordinary circumstances, to move itself down with that force; for which it has power and full liberty, and therefore would be blameworthy if it failed of it. But then let us suppose a weight of ten pounds to be put in the opposite scale, which in force entirely counterbalances its self-moving power, and so renders it impossible for it to move down at all; and therefore wholly excuses it from any such motion. But if we suppose there to be only nine pounds in the opposite scale, this renders its motion not impossible, but yet more difficult; so that it can now only move down with the force of one pound; but however, this is all that is required of it under these circumstances; it is wholly excused from nine parts of its motion;

and if the scale, under these circumstances, neglect to move, and remain at rest, all that it will be blamed for, will be its neglect of that one tenth part of its motion; for which it had as much liberty and advantage, as in usual circumstances it has for the greater motion, which in such a case would be required. So that this new difficulty does not at all increase its exposedness to any thing blameworthy.

And thus the very supposition of difficulty in the way of a man's duty, or proclivity to sin, through a being given up to hardness of heart, or indeed by any other means whatsoever, is an inconsistence, according to Dr. Whitby's notions of liberty, virtue and vice, blame and praise. The avoiding of sin and blame, and the doing of what is virtuous and praiseworthy, must be always equally easy.

Dr. Whitby's notions of liberty, obligation, virtue. sin, &c. lead him into another great inconsistence. He abundantly insists, that necessity is inconsistent with the nature of sin or fault. He says, in the forementioned treatise, (p. 14.) Who can blame a person for doing what he could not help? And, (p. 15.) It being sensibly unjust, to punish any man for doing that which was never in his power to avoid. And, (p. 341.) to confirm his opinion, he quotes one of the fathers, saying, Why doth God command, if man hath not free will and power to obey? And again, in the same and the next page, Who will not cry out, that it is folly to command him, that hath not liberty to do what is commanded; and that it is unjust to condemn him, that has it not in his power to do what is required? And, (p. 373.) he cites another saying, A law is given to him that can turn to both parts; i.e. obey or transgress it; but no Law can be against him who is bound by nature.

And yet the same Dr. Whitby asserts, that fallen man is not able to perform perfect obedience. In p. 165, he has these words: "The nature of Adam had power to continue innocent, and without sin; whereas, it is certain our nature never had." But if we have not power to continue innocent and without sin, then sin is not inconsistent with Necessity, and we may be sinful in that which we have not power to avoid; and those things cannot be true, which he asserts elsewhere, namely,"That if we be necessitated, neither sins of omission nor commission, would deserve that name," (p. 348.) If we have it not in our power to be innocent, then we have it not in our power to be blameless; and if so, we are under a Necessity of being blameworthy. And how does this consist with what he so often asserts, that Necessity is inconsistent with blame or praise? If we have it not in our power to perform perfect obedience to all the commands of God, then we are under a Necessity of breaking some commands, in some degree; having no power to perform so much as is commanded. And if so, why does he cry out of the unreasonableness and folly of commanding beyond what men have power to do?

Arminians in general are very inconsistent with themselves, in what they say of the Inability of fallen man in this respect. They strenuously maintain, that it would be unjust in God, to require any thing of us beyond our present power and ability to perform; and also hold that we are now unable to perform perfect obedience, and that Christ died to satisfy for the imperfections of our obedience and has made way, that our imperfect obedience might be accepted instead of perfect; wherein they seem insensibly to run themselves into the grossest inconsistence. For (as I have observed elsewhere) "they hold that God, in mercy to mankind, has abolished that rigorous constitution or law, that they were under originally, and instead of it, has introduced a more mild constitution, and put us under a new law, which requires no more than imperfect sincere obedience, in compliance with our poor infirm impotent circumstances since the fall." Now how can these things be made consistent? I would ask, of what law are these imperfections of our obedience a breach? If they are a breach of no law that we were ever under, then they are not sins. And if they be not sins, what need of Christ dying to satisfy for them? But if they are sins, and the breach of some law, what law is it? They cannot be a breach of their new law, for that requires no other than imperfect obedience, or obedience with imperfections: and therefore to have obedience attended with imperfections, is no breach of it; for it is as much as it requires. And they cannot be a breach of their old law: for that, they say, is entirely abolished; and we never were under it.— They say, it would not be just in God to require of us perfect obedience, because it would not be just to require more than we can perform, or to punish us for failing of it. And, therefore, by their own scheme, the imperfections of our obedience do not deserve to be punished. What need therefore of Christ dying, to satisfy for them? What need of his suffering, to satisfy for that which is no fault, and in its own nature deserves no suffering? What need of Christ dying, to purchase, that our imperfect obedience should be accepted, when, according to their scheme, it would be unjust in itself, that any other obedience than imperfect should be required? What need of Christ dying to make way for God's accepting of such obedience, as it would be unjust in him not to accept? Is there any need of Christ dying to prevail with God not to do unrighteously?—If it be said, that Christ died to satisfy that old law for us, that so we might not be under it, but that there might be room for our being under a more mild law; still I would inquire, what need of Christ dying, that we might not be under a law, which (by their principles) it would be in itself unjust that we should be under, whether Christ had died or no, because, in our present state, we are not able to keep it? So the Arminians are inconsistent with themselves, not only in what they say of the need of Christ's satisfaction to atone for those imperfections, which we cannot avoid, but also in what they say of the grace of God, granted to enable men to perform the sincere obedience of the new law. "I grant indeed, (says Dr. Stebbing,) that by original sin, we are utterly disabled for the performance of the condition, without new grace from God. But I say then, that he gives such a grace to all of us, by which the performance of the condition, is truly possible; and upon this ground he may and doth most righteously require it." If Dr. Stebbing intends to speak properly, by grace he must mean, that assistance which is of grace, or of free favour and kindness. But yet in the same place he speaks of it as very unreasonableness, unjust, and cruel, for God to require that, as the condition of pardon, that is become impossible by original sin. If it be so, what grace is there in giving assistance and ability to perform the condition of pardon? Or why is that called by the name of grace, that is an absolute debt, which God is bound to bestow, and which it would be unjust and cruel in him to withhold, seeing he requires that, as the condition of pardon, which he cannot perform without it?

PART III. SECTION IV. COMMAND AND OBLIGATION TO OBEDIENCE, CONSISTENT WITH MORAL INABILITY TO OBEY.

It being so much insisted on by Arminian writers, that necessity is inconsistent with law or command, and particularly, that it is absurd to suppose God by his command should require that of men which they are unable to do; not allowing in this case for any difference between natural and moral Inability; I would therefore now particularly consider this matter.—And for greater clearness I would distinctly lay down the following things.

I. The Will itself, and not only those actions which are the effects of the will, is the proper object of Precept or Command. That is, such a state or acts of men's Wills, are in many cases properly required of them by Commands; and not only those alterations in the state of their bodies or minds that are the consequences of volition. This is most manifest; for it is the soul only that is properly and directly the subject of Precepts or Commands; that only being capable of receiving or perceiving Commands. The motions or state of the body are matter of Command, only as they are subject to the soul, and connected with its acts. But now the soul has no other faculty whereby it can, in the most direct and proper sense, consent, yield to, or comply with any Command, but the faculty of the Will; and it is by this faculty only, that the soul can directly disobey, or refuse compliance: for the very notions of consenting, yielding, accepting, complying, refusing, rejecting, &c. are, according to the meaning of the terms, nothing but certain acts of the will. Obedience, in the primary nature of it, is the submitting and yielding of the Will of one, to the will of another. Disobedience is the not consenting, not complying of the Will of the commanded, to the manifested Will of the commander. Other acts that are not the acts of the Will, as certain motions of the body and alterations in the soul, are Obedience or Disobedience only indirectly, as they are connected with the state or actions of the will, according to an established law of nature. So that it is manifest, the Will itself may be required: and the being of a good Will is the most proper, direct, and immediate subject of Command; and if this cannot be prescribed or required by Command or Precept, nothing can; for other things can be required no otherwise than as they depend upon, and are the fruits of a good Will.

Corol. 1. If there be several acts of the Will, or a series of acts, one following another, and one the effect of another, the first and determining act is properly the subject of Command, and not only the consequent acts, which are dependent upon it. Yea, this more especially is that to which Command or Precept has a proper respect; because it is this act that determines the whole affair: in this act the Obedience or Disobedience lies, in a peculiar manner; the consequent acts being all governed and determined by it. This governing act must be the proper object of Precept, or none.

Corol. 2. It also follows, from what has been observed, that if there be any act, or exertion of the soul, prior to all free acts of choice in the case, directing and determining what the acts of the Will shall be; that act of the soul cannot properly be subject to any Command or Precept, in any respect whatsoever, either directly or indirectly, immediately or remotely. Such acts cannot be subject to Commands directly, because they are no acts of the Will; being by the supposition prior to all acts of the Will, determining and giving rise to all its acts: they not being acts of the Will, there can be in them no consent to or compliance with any Command. Neither can they be subject to Command or Precept indirectly or remotely; for they are not so much as the sects or consequences of the Will, being prior to all its acts. So that if there be any Obedience in that original act of the soul, determining all volitions, it is an act of Obedience wherein the Will has no concern at all; it preceding every act of Will. And therefore, if the soul either obeys or disobeys in this act, it is wholly involuntarily; there is no willing Obedience or rebellion, no compliance or opposition of the Will in the affair: and what sort of Obedience or rebellion is this?

And thus the Arminian notion of the freedom of the will consisting in the soul's determining its own acts of Will, instead of being essential to moral agency, and to men being the subjects of moral government, is utterly inconsistent with it. For if the soul determines all its acts of Will, it is therein subject to no Command or moral government, as has been now observed; because its original determining act is no act of Will or choice, it being prior, by the supposition, to every act of Will. And the soul cannot be the subject of Command in the act of the Will itself, which depends on the foregoing determining act, and is determined by it; in as much as this is necessary, being the necessary consequence and effect of that prior determining act, which is not voluntary. Nor can the man be the subject of Command or government in his external actions; because these are all necessary, being the necessary effects of the acts of the Will themselves. So that mankind, according to this scheme, are subjects of Command or moral government in nothing at all; and all their moral agency is entirely excluded, and no room is left for virtue or vice in the world.

So that the Arminian scheme, and not that of the Calvinists, is utterly inconsistent with moral government, and with all use of laws, precepts, prohibitions, promises, or threatenings. Neither is there any way whatsoever to make their principles consist with these things. For if it be said, that there is no prior determining act of the soul, preceding the acts of the Will, but that volitions are events that come to pass by pure accident, without any determining cause, this is most palpably inconsistent with all use of laws and precepts; for nothing is more plain than that laws can be of no use to direct and regulate perfect accident: which, by the supposition of its being pure accident, is in no case regulated by any thing preceding; but happens, this way or that, perfectly by chance, without any cause or rule. The perfect uselessness of laws and precepts also follows from the Arminian notion of indifference, as essential to that liberty, which is requisite to virtue or vice. For the end of laws is to bind to one side; and the end of Commands is to turn the Will one way: and therefore they are of no use, unless they turn or bias the Will that way. But if liberty consists in indifference, then their biassing the Will one way only, destroys liberty; as it puts the Will out of equilibrium. So that the will, having a bias, through the influence of binding law, laid upon it, is not wholly left to itself, to determine itself which way it will, without influence from without.

II. Having shown that the Will itself, especially in those acts which are original, leading and determining in any case, is the proper subject of Precept and Command—and not only those alterations in the body, &c. which are the effects of the Will—I now proceed, in the second place, to observe, that the very opposition or defect of the Will itself, in its original and determining act in the case, to a thing proposed or commanded, or its failing of compliance, implies a moral inability to that thing: or, in other words, whenever a Command requires a certain state or act of the Will, and the person commanded, notwithstanding the Command and the circumstances under which it is exhibited, still finds his will opposite or wanting, in that, belonging to its state or acts, which is original and determining in the affair, that man is morally unable to obey that Command.

This is manifest from what was observed in the first part concerning the nature of moral Inability, as distinguished from natural: where it was observed, that a man may then be said to be morally unable to do a thing, when he is under the influence or prevalence of a contrary inclination, or has a want of inclination, under such circumstances and views. It is also evident, from what has been before proved, that the Will is always, and in every individual act, necessarily determined by the strongest motive; and so is always unable to go against the motive, which, all things considered, has now the greatest strength and advantage to move the Will.—But not further to insist on these things, the truth of the position now laid down, viz. that when the Will is opposite to, or failing of a compliance with, a thing, in its original determination or act, it is not able to comply, appears by the consideration of these two things.

1. The Will in the time of that diverse or opposite leading act or inclination, and when actually under its influence, is not able to exert itself to the contrary, to make an alteration, in order to a compliance. The inclination is unable to change itself; and that for this plain reason, that it is unable to incline to change itself. Present choice cannot at present choose to be otherwise: for that would be at present to choose something diverse from what is at present chosen. If the will, all things now considered, inclines or chooses to go that way, then it cannot choose, all things now considered, to go the other way, and so cannot choose to be made to go the other way. To suppose that the mind is now sincerely inclined to change itself to a different inclination, is to suppose the mind is now truly inclined otherwise than it is now inclined. The Will may oppose some future remote act that it is exposed to, but not its own present act.

2. As it is impossible that the Will should comply with the thing commanded, with respect to its leading act, by any act of its own, in the time of that diverse or opposite leading and original act, or after it has actually come under the influence of that determining choice or inclination; so it is impossible it should be determined to a compliance by any foregoing act; for, by the very supposition, there is no foregoing act; the opposite or noncomplying act being that act which is original and determining in the case. Therefore it must be so, that if this first determining act be found non-complying, on the proposal of the command, the mind is morally unable to obey. For to suppose it to be able to obey, is to suppose it to be able to determine and cause its first determining act to be otherwise, and that it has power better to govern and regulate its first governing and regulating act, which is absurd; for it is to suppose a prior act of the Will, determining its first determining act; that is, an act prior to the first, and leading and governing the original and governing act of all; which is a contradiction.

Here if it should be said, that although the mind has not any ability to will contrary to what it does will, in the original and leading act of the Will, because there is supposed to be no prior act to determine and order it otherwise, and the will cannot immediately change itself, because it cannot at present incline to a change; yet the mind has an ability for the present to forbear to proceed to action, and taking time for deliberation; which may be an occasion of the change of the inclination.

I answer, (1.) In this objection, that seems to be forgotten which was observed before, viz. that the determining to take the matter into consideration, is itself an act of the Will: and if this be all the act wherein the mind exercises ability and freedom, then this, by the supposition, must be all that can be commanded or required by precept. And if this act be the commanding act, then all that has been observed concerning the commanding act of the Will remains true, that the very want of it is a moral Inability to exert it, &c. (2.) We are speaking concerning the first and leading act of the will about the affair; and if determining to deliberate, or, on the contrary, to proceed immediately without deliberating, be the first and leading act; or whether it be or no, if there be another act before it, which determines that; or whatever be the original and leading act; still the foregoing proof stands good, that the non-compliance of the leading act implies moral Inability to comply.

If it should be objected, that these things make all moral Inability equal, and suppose men morally unable to will otherwise than they actually do will, in all cases, and equally so in every instance.—In answer to this objection, I desire two things may be observed.

First, That if by being equally unable, be meant, as really unable; then, so far as the Inability is merely moral, it is true; the will, in every instance, acts by moral necessity, and is morally unable to act otherwise, as truly and properly in one case as another; as, I humbly conceive, has been perfectly and abundantly demonstrated by what has been said in the preceding part of this essay. But yet, in some respect, the Inability may be said to be greater in some instances than others: though the man may be truly unable, (if moral inability can truly be called Inability.) yet he may be further from being able to do Some things than others. As it is in things, which men are naturally unable to do. A person, whose strength is no more than sufficient to lift the weight of one hundred pounds, is as truly and really unable to lift one hundred and one pounds, as ten thousand pounds; but yet he is further from being able to lift the latter weight than the former; and so, according to the common use of speech, has a greater Inability for it. So it is in moral Inability. A man is truly morally unable to choose contrary to a present inclination, which in the least degree prevails; or, contrary to that motive, which, all things considered, has strength and advantage now to move the Will, in the least degree, superior to all other motives in view: but yet he is further from ability to insist a very strong habit, and a violent and deeply rooted inclination, or a motive vastly exceeding all others in strength. And again, the Inability may, in some respects, be called greater in some instances than others, as it may be more general and extensive to all acts of that kind. So men may be said to be unable in a different sense, and to be further from moral ability, who have that moral Inability which is general and habitual, than they who have only that Inability which is occasional and particular. Thus in cases of natural inability; he that is born blind may be said to be unable to see, in a different manner, and is, in some respects, further from being able to see, than he whose sight is hindered by a transient cloud or mist.

And besides, that which was observed in the first part of this discourse, concerning the Inability which attends a strong and settled habit, should be there remembered; viz. that a fixed habit is attended with this peculiar moral inability, by which it is distinguished from occasional volition, namely, that endeavours to avoid future volitions of that kind, which are agreeable to such a habit, much more frequently and commonly prove vain and insufficient. For though it is impossible there should be any sincere endeavours against a present choice, yet there may be against volitions of that kind, when viewed at a distance. A person may desire and use means to prevent future exercises of a certain inclination; and, in order to it, may wish the habit might be removed; but his desires and endeavours may be ineffectual. The man may be said in some sense to be unable; yea, even as the word unable is a relative term, and has relation to ineffectual endeavours; yet not with regard to present, but remote endeavours.

Secondly, it must be borne in mind, according to what was observed before, that indeed no Inability whatsoever, which is merely moral, is properly called by the name of Inability; and that in the strictest propriety of speech, a man may be said to have a thing in his power, if he has it at his election, and he cannot be said to be unable to do a thing, when he can, if he now pleases, or whenever he has a proper, direct, and immediate desire for it. As to those desires and endeavours, that may be against the exercises of a strong habit, with regard to which men may be said to be unable to avoid those exercises, they are remote desires and endeavours in two respects. first, as to time; they are never against present volitions, but only against volitions of such a kind, when viewed at a distance. Secondly, as to their nature; these opposite desires are not directly and properly against the habit and inclination itself, or the volitions in which it is exercised; for these, in themselves considered, are agreeable: but against something else that attends them, or is their consequence; the opposition of the mind is leveled entirely against this; the volitions themselves are not at all opposed directly, and for their own sake; but only indirectly and remotely, on the account of something foreign.

III. Though the opposition of the Will itself, or the very want of Will to a thing commanded, implies a moral inability to that thing; yet, if it be, as has been already shown, that the being of a good state or act of will, is a thing most properly required by Command; then, in some cases, such a state or act of Will may properly be required, which at present is not, and which may also be wanting after it is commanded. And therefore those things may properly be commanded, for which men have a moral Inability.

Such a state or act of the Will, may be required by Command, as does not already exist. For if that volition only may be commanded to be, which already is, there could be no use of precept: Commands in all cases would be perfectly vain and impertinent. And not only may such a Will be required, as is wanting before the Command is given, but also such as may possibly be wanting afterwards; such as the exhibition of the Command may not be effectual to produce or excite. Otherwise, no such thing as disobedience to a proper and rightful Command is possible in any case; and there is no case possible, wherein there can be a faulty disobedience. Which Arminians cannot affirm, consistently with their principle: for this makes obedience to just and proper Commands always necessary, and disobedience impossible. And so the Arminian would overthrow himself, yielding the very point we are upon, which he so strenuously denies, viz. that Law and Command are consistent with necessity.

If merely that Inability will excuse disobedience, which is implied in the opposition or defect of inclination, remaining after the Command is exhibited, then wickedness always carries that in it which excuses it. By how much the more wickedness there is in a man's heart, by so much is his inclination to evil the stronger, and by so much the more, therefore, has he of moral Inability to the good required. His moral Inability consisting in the strength of his evil inclination, is the very thing wherein his wickedness consists; and yet, according to Arminian principles, it must be a thing inconsistent with wickedness; and by how much the more he has of it, by so much is he the further from wickedness.

Therefore, on the whole, it is manifest, that moral Inability alone (which consists in disinclination) never renders any thing improperly the subject matter of Precept or Command, and never can excuse any person in disobedience, or want of conformity to a command.

Natural Inability, arising from the want of natural capacity, or external hindrance, (which alone is properly called Inability,) without doubt wholly excuses, or makes a thing improperly the matter of Command. If men are excused from doing or acting any good thing, supposed to be commanded, it must be through some defect or obstacle that is not in the Will itself, but either in the capacity of understanding, or body, or outward circumstances.—Here two or three things may be observed,

1. As to spiritual acts, or any good thing in the state or imminent acts of the will itself, or of the affections, (which are only certain modes of the exercise of the Will,) if persons are justly excused, it must be through want of capacity in the natural faculty of understanding. Thus the same spiritual duties, or holy affections and exercises of heart, cannot be required of men, as may be of angels; the capacity of understanding being so much inferior. So men cannot be required to love those amiable persons, whom they have had no opportunity to see, or hear of, or know in any way agreeable to the natural state and capacity of the human understanding. But the insufficiency of motives will not excuse; unless their being insufficient arises not from the moral state of the Will or inclination itself, but from the state of the natural understanding. The great kindness and generosity of another may be a motive insufficient to excite gratitude in the person that receives the kindness, through his vile and ungrateful temper: in this case, the insufficiency of the motive arises from the state of the Will or inclination of heart, and does not at all excuse. But if this generosity is not sufficient to excite gratitude, being unknown, there being no means of information adequate to the state and measure of the person's faculties, this insufficiency is attended with a natural Inability, which entirely excuses it.

2. As to such motions of body, or exercises and alterations of mind, which do not consist in the iminent acts or state of the Will itself— but are supposed to be required as effects of the will, in cases wherein there is no want of a capacity of understanding that inability, and that only, excuses, which consists in want of connexion between them and the Will. If the will fully complies, and the proposed effect does not prove, according to the laws of nature, to be connected with his volition, the man is perfectly excused; he has a natural Inability to the thing required. For the Will itself, as has been observed, is all that can be directly and immediately required by Command; and other things only indirectly, as connected with the Will. If therefore, there be a full compliance of Will, the person has done his duty; and if other things do not

prove to be connected with his volition, that is not criminally owing to him.

3. Both these kinds of natural Inability, and all Inability that excuses, may be resolved into one thing; namely, want of natural capacity or strength; either capacity of understanding, or external strength. For when there are external defects and obstacles, they would be no obstacles, were it not for the imperfection and limitations of understanding and strength.

Corol. If things for which men have a moral Inability may properly be the matter of Precept or Command, then they may also of invitation and counsel. Commands and invitations come very much to the same thing; the difference is only circumstantial: Commands are as much a manifestation of the will of him that speaks, as invitations, and as much testimonies of expectation of compliance. The difference between them lies in nothing that touches the affair in hand. The main difference between Command and invitation consists in the enforcement of the Will of him who commands or invites. In the latter it is his kindness, the goodness from which his Will arises: in the former it is his authority. But whatever be the ground of Will in him that speaks, or the enforcement of what he says, yet, seeing neither his Will, nor his expectation, is any more testified in the one case than the other; therefore, a person being directed by invitation, is no more an evidence of insincerity in him that directs—in manifesting either a Will or expectation which he has not—than a person being known to be morally unable to do what he is directed by command is an evidence of insincerity. So that all this grand objection of Arminians against the Inability of fallen men to exert faith in Christ, or to perform other spiritual duties, from the sincerity of God's counsels and invitations, must be without force.

PART III. SECTION V. THAT SINCERITY OF DESIRES AND ENDEAVOURS, WHICH, IS SUPPOSED TO EXCUSE IN THE NON-PERFORMANCE OF THINGS IN THEMSELVES GOOD, PARTICULARLY CONSIDERED.

It is much insisted on by many, that some men, though they are not able to perform spiritual duties, such as repentance of sin, love to God, a cordial acceptance of Christ as exhibited and offered in the gospel, &c.

yet may sincerely desire and endeavor after these things; and therefore must be excused; it being unreasonable to blame them for the omission of those things, which they sincerely desire and endeavour to do, but cannot. Concerning this matter, the following things may be observed.

1. What is here supposed, is a great mistake, and gross absurdity; even that men may sincerely choose and desire those spiritual duties of love, acceptance, choice, rejection, &c. consisting in the exercise of the Will itself, or in the disposition and inclination of the heart; and yet not able to perform or exert them. This is absurd, because it is absurd to suppose that a man should directly, properly, and sincerely incline to have an inclination, which at the same time is contrary to his inclination: for that is to suppose him not to be inclined to that which he is inclined to. If a man, in the state and acts of his will and inclination, properly and directly falls in with those duties, he therein performs them: for the duties themselves consist in that very thing; they consist in the state and acts of the Will being so formed and directed. If the soul properly and sincerely falls in with a certain proposed act of Will or choice, the soul therein makes that choice its own. Even as when a moving body falls in with a proposed direction of its motion, that is the same thing as to move in that direction.

2. That which is called a Desire and Willingness for those inward duties, in such as do not perform them, has respect to these duties only indirectly and remotely, and is improperly so called; not only because (as was observed before) it respects those good volitions only in a distant view, and with respect to future time; but also because evermore, not these things themselves, but something else that is foreign, is the object that terminates these volitions and Desires.

A drunkard, who continues in his drunkenness, being under the power of a violent appetite to strong drink, and without any love to virtue; but being also extremely covetous and close, and very much exercised and grieved at the diminution of his estate, and prospect of poverty, may in a sort desire the virtue of temperance; and though his present Will is to gratify his extravagant appetite, yet he may wish he had a heart to forbear future acts of intemperance, and forsake his excesses, through an unwillingness to part with his money: but still he goes on with his drunkenness; his wishes and endeavours are insufficient and ineffectual: such a man has no proper, direct, sincere Willingness to forsake this vice, and the vicious deeds which belong to it; for he acts voluntarily in continuing to drink to excess: his Desire is very improperly called a willingness to be temperate; it is no true Desire of that virtue; for it is not that virtue, that terminates his wishes; nor have they any direct respect at all to it. It is only the saving of his money, or the avoiding of poverty, that terminates and exhausts the whole strength of his Desire. The virtue of temperance is regarded only very indirectly and improperly, even as a necessary means of gratifying the vice of covetousness.

So, a man of an exceedingly corrupt and wicked heart, who has no love to God and Jesus Christ, but, on the contrary, being very profanely and carnally inclined, has the greatest distaste of the things of religion, and enmity against them; yet being of a family, that, from one generation to another, have most of them died, in youth, of an hereditary consumption; and so having little hope of living long; and having been instructed in the necessity of a supreme love to Christ, and latitude for his death and sufferings, in order to his salvation from eternal misery; if under these circumstances he should, through fear of eternal torments, wish he had such a disposition; but his profane and carnal heart remaining, he continues still in his habitual distaste of; and enmity to God and religion, and wholly without any exercise of that love and gratitude, (as doubtless the very devils themselves, notwithstanding all the devilishness of their temper, would wish for a holy heart, if by that means they could get out of hell:) in this case, there is no sincere Willingness to love Christ and choose him as his chief good: these holy dispositions and exercises are not at all the direct object of the Will: they truly share no part of the inclination or desire of the soul; but all is terminated on deliverance from torment: and these graces and pious volitions, notwithstanding this forced consent, are looked upon as in themselves undesirable; as when a sick man desires a dose he greatly abhors, in order to save his life. From these things it appears, 3. That this indirect Willingness is not that exercise of the Will which the command requires; but is entirely a different one; being a volition of a different nature, and terminated altogether on different objects; wholly falling short of that virtue of Will, to which the command has respect, 4. This other volition, which has only some indirect concern with the duty required, cannot excuse for the want of that good will itself, which is commanded; being not the thing which answers and fulfils the command, and being wholly destitute of the virtue which the command seeks.

Further to illustrate this matter: If a child has a most excellent father that has ever treated him with fatherly kindness and tenderness, and has every way, in the highest degree, merited his love and dutiful regard, and is withal very wealthy; but the son is of so vile a disposition, that he inveterately hates his father; and yet, apprehending that his hatred of him is like to prove his ruin, by bringing him finally to those abject circumstances, which are exceedingly adverse to his avarice and ambition; he, therefore, wishes it were otherwise: but yet remaining under the invincible power of his vile and malignant disposition, he continues still in his settled hatred of his father. Now, if such a son's indirect willingness to love and honour his father, at all acquits or excuses before God, for his failing of actually exercising these dispositions towards him, which God requires, it must be on one of these accounts. (1.) Either, that it answers and fulfils the command. But this it does not by the supposition; because the thing commanded is love and honour to his worthy parent. If the command be proper and just, as is supposed, then it obliges to the thing commanded; and so nothing else but that can answer the obligation. Or, (2.) it must be at least, because there is that virtue or goodness in his indirect willingness, that is equivalent to the virtue required; and so balances or countervails it, and makes up for the want of it. But that also is contrary to the supposition. The willingness the son has merely from a regard to money and honour, has no goodness in it, to countervail the want of the pious filial respect required.

Sincerity and reality, in that indirect Willingness, which has been spoken of, does not make it the better. That which is real and hearty is often called sincere; whether it be in virtue or vice. Some persons are sincerely bad; others are sincerely good; and others may be sincere and hearty in things, which are in their own nature indifferent; as a man may be sincerely desirous of eating when he is hungry. But being sincere, hearty, and in good earnest, is no virtue, unless it be in a thing that is virtuous. A man may be sincere and hearty in joining a crew of pirates, or a gang of robbers. When the devils cried out, and besought Christ not to torment them, it was no mere pretense; they were very hearty in their desires not to be tormented: but this did not make their Will or Desire virtuous. And if men have sincere Desires, which are in their kind and nature no better, it can be no excuse for the want of any required virtue.

And as a man's Sincerity in such an indirect Desire or willingness to do his duty, as has been mentioned, cannot excuse for the want of performance; so it is with Endeavours arising from such a Willingness. The Endeavours can have no more goodness in them, than the Will of which they are the effect and expression. And, therefore, however sincere and real, and however great a person's Endeavours are; yea, though they should be to the utmost of his ability; unless the Will from which they proceed be truly good and virtuous, they can be of no avail or weight whatsoever in a moral respect. That which is not truly virtuous is, in God's sight, good for nothing: and so can be of no value, or influence, in his account, to make up for any moral defect. For nothing can counterbalance evil, but good. If evil be in one scale, and we put a great deal into the other of sincere and earnest Desires, and many and great endeavours; yet, if there be no real goodness in all, there is no weight in it; and so it does nothing towards balancing the real weight, which is in the opposite scale. It is only like subtracting a thousand noughts from before a real number, which leaves the sum just as it was.

Indeed such Endeavours may have a negatively good influence. Those things, which have no positive virtue, have no positive moral influence; yet they may be an occasion of persons avoiding some positive evils. As if a man were in the water with a neighbor to whom he had ill will, and who could not swim, holding him by his hand; this neighbor was much in debt to him,—the man is tempted to let him sink and drown—but refuses to comply with the temptation; not from love to his neighbor, bet from the love of money, and because by his drowning he should lose his debt; that which he does in preserving his neighbor from drowning, is nothing good in the sight of God: yet hereby he avoids the greater guilt that would have been contracted, if he had designedly let his neighbor sink and perish. But when Arminians, in their disputes with Calvinists, insist so much on sincere Desires and Endeavours, as what must excuse men, must be accepted of God, &c., it is manifest they have respect to some positive moral weight or influence of those Desires and Endeavours. Accepting, justifying, or excusing on the account of sincere Endeavours, (as they are called,) and men doing what they can, &c. has relation to some moral value, something that is accepted as good, and as such, countervailing some defect.

But there is a great and unknown deceit, arising from the ambiguity of the phrase, sincere Endeavours. Indeed there is a vast indistinctness and unfixedness in most, or at least very many of the terms used to express things pertaining to moral and spiritual matters, whence arise innumerable mistakes, strong prejudices, inextricable confusion, and endless controversy.—The word sincere is most commonly used to signify something that is good: men are habituated to understand by it the same as honest and upright; which terms excite an idea of something good in the strictest and highest sense; good in the sight of him, who sees not only the outward appearance, but the heart. And, therefore, men think that if a person be sincere, he will certainly be accepted. If it be said that any one is sincere in his endeavours, this suggests, that his heart is good, that there is no defect of duty, as to virtuous inclination; he honestly and uprightly desires and endeavours to do as he is required; and this leads them to suppose, that it would be very hard and unreasonable to punish him, only because he is unsuccessful in his endeavours, the thing endeavored after being beyond his power.—Whereas it ought to be observed, that the word sincere has these different significations.

1. Sincerity, as the word is sometimes used, signifies no more than reality of will and Endeavour, with respect to any thing that is professed or pretended; without any consideration of the nature of the principle or aim, whence this real Will and true endeavour arises. If a man has some real Desire either direct or indirect to obtain a thing, or does really endeavour after it, he is said sincerely to desire or endeavour, without any consideration of the goodness of the principle from which he acts, or any excellency or worthiness of the end for which he acts. Thus a man who is kind to his neighbour's wife, who is sick and languishing, and very helpful in her case, makes a show of desiring and endeavouring her restoration to health and vigor; and not only makes such a show, but there is a reality in his pretense, he does heartily and earnestly desire to have her health restored, and uses his true and utmost Endeavours for it: he is said sincerely to desire and endeavour after it, because he does so truly or really; though perhaps the principle he acts from, is no other than a vile and scandalous passion; having lived in adultery with her, he earnestly desires to have her health and vigor restored, that he may return to his criminal pleasures. Or,

2. By Sincerity is meant, not merely a reality of will and Endeavour of some sort, and from some consideration or other, but a virtuous Sincerity. That is, that in the performance of those particular acts, that are the matter of virtue or duty, there be not only the matter, but the form and essence of virtue, consisting in the aim that governs the act, and the principle exercised in it. There is not only the reality of the act, that is as it were the body of the duty; but also the soul, which should properly belong to such a body. In this sense, a man is said to be sincere, when he acts with a pure intention; not from sinister views: he not only in reality desires and seeks the thing to be done, or qualification to be

obtained, for some end or other; but he wills the thing directly and properly, as neither forced nor bribed; the virtue of the thing is properly the object of the Will.

In the former sense, a man is said to be sincere, in opposition to a mere pretense, and show of the particular thing to be done or exhibited, without any real Desire or Endeavour at all. In the latter sense, a man is said to be sincere, in opposition to that show of virtue there is in merely doing the matter of duty, without the reality of the virtue itself in the soul. A man may be sincere in the former sense, and yet in the latter be in the sight of God, who searches the heart, a vile hypocrite.

In the latter kind of sincerity, only, is there any thing truly valuable or acceptable in the sight of God. And this is what in Scripture is called Sincerity, uprightness, integrity, "truth in the inward parts," and "heirs of a perfect heart." And if there be such a Sincerity, and such a degree of it as there ought to be, and there be any thing further that the man is not able to perform, or which does not prove to be connected with his sincere Desires and Endeavours, the man is wholly excused and acquitted in the sight of God; his Will shall surely be accepted for his deed: and such a sincere Will and Endeavour is all that in strictness is required of him, by any command of God, but as to the other kind of Sincerity of Desires and Endeavours, having no virtue in it, (as was observed before,) it can be of no avail before God, in any case, to recommend, satisfy, or excuse, and has no positive moral weight or influence whatsoever.

Corol. 1. Hence it may be inferred, that nothing in the reason and nature of things appears from the consideration of any moral weight in the former kind of Sincerity, leading us to suppose, that God has made any positive promises of salvation, or grace, or any saving assistance, or any spiritual benefit whatsoever, to any Desires, prayers, Endeavours, striving, or obedience of those, who hitherto have no true virtue or holiness in their hearts; though we should suppose all the Sincerity, and the utmost degree of Endeavour, that is possible to be in persons without holiness.

Some object against God requiring, as the condition of salvation, those holy exercises, which are the result of a supernatural renovation; such as a supreme respect to Christ, love to God, loving holiness for its own sake, &c. that these inward dispositions and exercises are above men's power, as they are by nature; and therefore that we may conclude, that when men are brought to be sincere in their Endeavours, and do as well as they can, they are accepted; and that this must be all that God requires, in order to their being received as the objects of his favour, and must be what God has appointed as the condition of salvation. Concerning this, I would observe, that in such manner of speaking as "men being accepted because they are sincere, and do as well as they can," there is evidently a supposition of some virtue, some degree of that which is truly good; though it does not go so far as were to be wished. For if men do what they can, unless their so doing be from some good principle, disposition, or exercise of heart, some virtuous inclination or act of the will; their so doing what they can, is in some respect not a whit better than if they did nothing at all. In such a case, there is no more positive moral goodness in a man doing what he can, than in a windmill doing what it can; because the action does no more proceed from virtue: and there is nothing in such Sincerity of Endeavour, or doing what we can, that should render it any more a fit recommendation to positive favour and acceptance, or the condition of any reward or actual benefit, than doing nothing; for both the one and the other are alike nothing, as to any true moral weight or value.

Corol. 2. Hence also it follows, there is nothing that appears in the reason and nature of things, which can justly lead us to determine, that God will certainly give the necessary means of salvation, or some way or other bestow true holiness and eternal life on those heathens, who are sincere (in the sense above explained) in their Endeavours to find out the Will of the Deity, and to please him, according to their light, that they may escape his future displeasure and wrath, and obtain happiness in the future state, through his favour.

PART III. SECTION VI. LIBERTY OF INDIFFERENCE, NOT ONLY NOT NECESSARY TO VIRTUE, BUT UTTERLY INCONSISTENT WITH IT; AND ALL, EITHER VIRTUOUS OR VICIOUS HABITS OR INCLINATIONS, INCONSISTENT WITH ARMINIAN NOTIONS OF LIBERTY AND MORAL AGENCY.

To suppose such a freedom of will, as Arminians talk of, to be requisite to Virtue and Vice, is many ways contrary to common sense.

If Indifference belong to Liberty of Will, as Arminians suppose, and it be essential to a virtuous action, that it be performed in a state of

Liberty, as they also suppose; it will follow, that it is essential to a virtuous action, that it be performed in a state of Indifference: and if it be performed in a state of indifference, then doubtless it must be performed in the time of Indifference. And so it will follow, that in order to the Virtue of an act, the heart must be indifferent in the time of the performance of that act and the more indifferent and cold the heart is with relation to the act performed, so much the better; because the act is performed with so much the greater Liberty. But is this agreeable to the light of nature? Is it agreeable to the notions which mankind in all ages have of Virtue, that it lies in what is contrary to Indifference, even in the tendency and inclination of the heart to virtuous action; and that the stronger the inclination, and so the further from Indifference, the more virtuous the heart, and so much the more praiseworthy the act which proceeds from it?

If we should suppose (contrary to what has been before demonstrated) that there may be an act of will in a state of Indifference; for instance, this act, viz. The will determining to put itself out of a state of Indifference, and to give itself a preponderation one way; then it would follow, on Arminian principles, that this act or determination of the will is that alone wherein Virtue consists, because this only is performed, while the mind remains in a state of Indifference, and so in a state of Liberty: for when once the mind is put out of its equilibrium, it is no longer in such a state; and therefore all the acts, which follow afterwards, proceeding from bias, can have the nature neither of Virtue nor Vice. Or if the thing which the will can do, while yet in a state of Indifference, and so of Liberty, be only to suspend acting, and determine to take the matter into consideration; then this determination is that alone wherein Virtue consists, and not proceeding to action after the scale is turned by consideration. So that it will follow, from these principles, that whatever is done after the mind, by any means, is once out of its equilibrium, and arises from an inclination, has nothing of the nature of Virtue or Vice, and is worthy of neither blame or praise. But how plainly contrary is this to the universal sense of mankind, and to the notion they have of sincerely virtuous actions! Which is, that they proceed from a heart well disposed and well inclined; and the stronger, the more fixed and determined, the good disposition of the heart, the greater the sincerity of Virtue, and so the more of its truth and reality. But if there be any acts, which are done in a state of equilibrium, or spring immediately from perfect Indifference and coldness of heart, they cannot arise from any good principle or disposition in the heart; and, consequently, according to common sense, have no sincere goodness in them, having no Virtue of heart in them. To have a virtuous heart, is to have a heart that favours Virtue, and is friendly to it, and not one perfectly cold and indifferent about it.

And besides, the actions that are done in a state of Indifference, or that arise immediately out of such a state, cannot be virtuous, because, by the supposition, they are not determined by any preceding choice. For if there be preceding choice, then choice intervenes between the act and the state of Indifference; which is contrary to the supposition of the act arising immediately out of Indifference. But those acts which are not determined by preceding choice, cannot be virtuous or vicious, by Arminian principles, because they are not determined by the Will. So that neither one way, nor the other, can any actions be virtuous or vicious, according to those principles. If the action be determined by a preceding act of choice, it cannot be virtuous; because the action is not done in a state of Indifference, nor does immediately arise from such a state; and so is not done in a state of Liberty. If the action be not determined by a preceding act of choice, then it cannot be virtuous; because then the Will is not self-determined in it. So that it is made certain, that neither Virtue nor Vice can ever find any place in the universe!

Moreover, that it is necessary to a virtuous action that it be performed in a state of Indifference, under a notion of that being a state of Liberty, is contrary to common sense; as it is a dictate of common sense, that indifference itself, in many cases, is vicious, and so to a high degree. As if when I see my neighbour or near friend, and one who has in the highest degree merited of me, in extreme distress, and ready to perish, I find an Indifference in my heart with respect to any thing proposed to be done, which I can easily do, for his relief. So if it should be proposed to me to blaspheme God, or kill my father, or do numberless other things, which might be mentioned; the being indifferent, for a moment, would be highly vicious and vile.

And it may be further observed, that to suppose this Liberty of Indifference is essential to Virtue and Vice, destroys the great difference of degrees of the guilt of different crimes, and takes away the heinousness of the most flagitious, horrid iniquities; such as adultery, bestiality, murder, perjury, blasphemy, &c. For, according to these principles, there is no harm at all in having the mind in a state of perfect Indifference with respect to these crimes; nay, it is absolutely necessary in order to any Virtue in avoiding them, or Vice in doing them. But for the mind to be in a state of Indifference with respect to them, is to be next door to doing them: it is then infinitely near to choosing, and so committing the fact: for equilibrium is the next step to a degree of preponderation; and one, even the least degree of preponderation (all things considered) is choice. And not only so, but for the Will to be in a state of perfect equilibrium with respect to such crimes, is for the mind to be in such a state, as to be full as likely to choose them as to refuse them, to do them as to omit them. And if our minds must be in such a state, wherein it is as near to choosing as refusing, and wherein it must of necessity, according to the nature of things, be as likely to commit them, as to refrain from them; where is the exceeding heinousness of choosing and committing them? If there be no harm in often being in such a state, where in the probability of doing and forbearing are exactly equal, there being an equilibrium, and no more tendency to one than the other; then, according to the nature and laws of such a contingence, it may be expected, as an inevitable consequence of such a disposition of things, that we should choose them as often as reject them: that it should generally so fall out is necessary, as equality in the effect is the natural consequence of the equal tendency of the cause, or of the antecedent state of things from which the effect arises. Why then should we be so exceedingly to blame, if it does so fall out?

It is many ways apparent, that the Arminian scheme of Liberty is utterly inconsistent with the being of any such things as either virtuous or vicious habits or dispositions. If Liberty of Indifference be essential to moral Agency, then there can be no Virtue in any habitual inclinations of the heart; which are contrary to Indifference, and imply in their nature the very destruction and exclusion of it. They suppose nothing can be virtuous in which no Liberty is exercised; but how absurd is it to talk of exercising Indifference under bias and preponderation!

And if self-determining power in the will be necessary to moral Agency, praise, blame, &c. then nothing done by the will can be any further praiseworthy or blameworthy, than so far as the will is moved, swayed, and determined by itself, and the scales turned by the sovereign power the Will has over itself. And therefore the Will must not be out of its balance, preponderation must not be determined and effected before-hand; and so the self-determining act anticipated. Thus it appears another way, that habitual bias is inconsistent with that Liberty, which

Arminians suppose to be necessary to Virtue or Vice; and so it follows, that habitual bias itself cannot be either virtuous or vicious.

The same thing follows from their doctrine concerning the Inconsistence of Necessity with Liberty, praise, dispraise, &c. None will deny, that bias and inclination may be so strong as to be invincible, and leave no possibility of the Will determining contrary to it; and so be attended with Necessity. This Dr. Whitby allows concerning the Will of God, angels, and glorified saints, with respect to good; and the Will of devils, with respect to evil. Therefore, if Necessity be inconsistent with Liberty, then, when fixed inclination is to such a degree of strength, it utterly excludes all Virtue, Vice, praise, or blame. And, if so, then the nearer habits are to this strength, the more do they impede Liberty, and so diminish praise and blame. If very strong habits destroy Liberty, the lesser ones proportionably hinder it, according to their degree of strength. And therefore it will follow, that then is the act most virtuous or vicious, when performed without any inclination or habitual bias at all; because it is then performed with most Liberty.

Every prepossessing fixed bias on the mind brings a degree of moral inability for the contrary; because so far as the mind is biased and prepossessed, so much hindrance is there of the contrary. And therefore if moral inability be inconsistent with moral Agency, or the nature of Virtue and Vice, then, so far as there is any such thing as evil disposition of heart, or habitual depravity of inclination; whether covetousness, pride, malice, cruelty, or whatever else; so much the more excusable persons are; so much the less have their evil acts of this kind the nature of Vice. And on the contrary, whatever excellent dispositions and inclinations they have so much are they the less virtuous.

It is evident, that no habitual disposition of heart can be in any degree virtuous or vicious, or the actions which proceed from them at all praiseworthy or blameworthy. Because, though we should suppose the habit not to be of such strength, as wholly to take away all moral ability and self-determining power; or may be partly from bias, and in part from self-determination; yet in this case, all that is from antecedent bias must be set aside, as of no consideration; and in estimating the degree of Virtue or Vice, no more must be considered than what arises from self-determining power, without any influence of that bias, because Liberty is exercised in no more: so that all that is the exercise of habitual inclination is thrown away, as not belonging to the morality of the action.

By which it appears, that no exercise of these habits, let them be stronger or weaker, can ever have any thing of the nature of either virtue or Vice.

Here if any one should say, that notwithstanding all these things, there may be the nature of Virtue and Vice in the habits of the mind; because these habits may be the effects of those acts, wherein the mind exercised Liberty; that however the forementioned reasons will prove that no habits, which are natural, or that are born or created with us, can be either virtuous or vicious; yet they will not prove this of habits, which have been acquired and established by repeated free acts.

To such an objector I would say, that this evasion will not at all help the matter. For if freedom of Will be essential to the very nature of Virtue and Vice, then there is no Virtue or Vice but only in that very thing, wherein this Liberty is exercised. If a man in one or more things that he does, exercises Liberty, and then by those acts is brought into such circumstances, that his Liberty ceases, and there follows a long series of acts or events that come to pass necessarily; those consequent acts are not virtuous or vicious, rewardable or punishable; but only the free acts that established this necessity; for in them alone was the man free. The following effects, that are necessary, have no more of the nature of Virtue or Vice, than health or sickness of body have properly the nature of Virtue or Vice, being the effects of a course of free acts of temperance or intemperance; or than the good qualities of a clock are of the nature of Virtue, which are the effects of free acts of the artificer; or the goodness and sweetness of the fruits of a garden are moral Virtues, being the effects of the free and faithful acts of the gardener. If Liberty be absolutely requisite to the morality of actions, and necessity wholly inconsistent with it, as Arminians greatly insist; then no necessary effects whatsoever, let the cause be never so good or bad, can be virtuous or vicious; but the Virtue or Vice must be only in the free cause. Agreeably to this, Dr. Whitby supposes, the necessity that attends the good and evil habits of the saints in heaven, and damned in hell, which are the consequence of their free acts in their state of probation, are not rewardable or punishable.

On the whole, it appears, that if the notions of Arminians concerning Liberty and moral Agency be true, it will follow, that there is no virtue in any such habits or qualities as humility, meekness, patience, mercy, gratitude, generosity, heavenly-mindedness; nothing at all praiseworthy in loving Christ above father and mother, wife and children, or our own lives; or in delight in holiness, hungering and thirsting after righteousness, love to enemies, universal benevolence to mankind: and, on the other hand, there is nothing at all vicious, or worthy of dispraise, in the most sordid, beastly, malignant, devilish dispositions; in being ungrateful, profane, habitually hating God, and things sacred and holy; or in being most treacherous, envious, and cruel towards men. For all these things are dispositions and inclinations of the heart. And in short, there is no such thing as any virtuous or vicious quality of mind; no such thing as inherent virtue and holiness, or vice and sin: and the stronger those habits or dispositions are, which used to be called virtuous and vicious, the further they are from being so indeed; the more violent men's lusts are, the more fixed their pride, envy, ingratitude, and maliciousness, still the further are they from being blameworthy. If there be a man that by his own repeated acts, or by any other means, is come to be of the most hellish disposition, desperately inclined to treat his neighbours with injuriousness, contempt, and malignity; the further they should be from any disposition to be angry with him, or in the least to blame him. So, on the other hand, if there be a person, who is of a most excellent spirit, strongly inclining him to the most amiable actions, admirably meek, benevolent, &c. so much is he further from any thing rewardable or commendable. On which principles, the man Jesus Christ was very far from being praiseworthy for those acts of holiness and kindness which he performed, these propensities being strong in his heart. And above all, the infinitely holy and gracious God is infinitely remote from any thing commendable, his good inclinations being infinitely strong, and he, therefore, at the utmost possible distance from being at Liberty. And in all cases, the stronger the inclinations of any are to Virtue, and the more they love it, the less virtuous, and the more they love wickedness, the less vicious they are.—Whether these things are agreeable to Scripture, let every Christian, and every man who has read the Bible, judge: and whether they are agreeable to common sense, let every one judge, that has human understanding in exercise.

And, if we pursue these principles, we shall find that Virtue and Vice are wholly excluded out of the world; and that there never was, nor ever can be, any such thing as one or the other; either in God, angels, or men. No propensity, disposition, or habit can be virtuous or vicious, as has been shown; because they, so far as they take place, destroy the freedom of the will, the foundation of all moral Agency, and exclude all capacity of either Virtue or Vice.—And if habits and dispositions themselves be not virtuous nor vicious, neither can the exercise of these dispositions be so: for the exercise of bias is not the exercise of free self-determining will, and so there is no exercise of Liberty in it. Consequently, no man is virtuous or vicious, either in being well or ill disposed, nor in acting from a good or bad disposition. And whether this bias or disposition be habitual or not, if it exists but a moment before the act of Will which is the effect of it, it alters not the case, as to the necessity of the effect. Or if there be no previous disposition at all, either habitual or occasional, that determines the act, then it is not choice that determines it: it is therefore a contingence, that happens to the man, arising from nothing in him; and is necessary, as to any inclination or choice of his; and, therefore, cannot make him either the better or worse; any more than a tree is better than other trees, because it oftener happens to be lighted upon by a nightingale; or a rock more vicious than other rocks, because rattle-snakes have happened oftener to crawl over it. So, that there is no Virtue nor Vice in good or bad dispositions, either fixed or transient; nor any Virtue or Vice in acting from any good or bad previous inclination; nor yet any Virtue or Vice in acting wholly without any previous inclination. Where then shall we find room for Virtue or Vice?

PART III. SECTION VII. ARMINIAN NOTIONS OF MORAL AGENCY INCONSISTENT WITH ALL INFLUENCE OF MOTIVE AND INDUCEMENT, IN EITHER VIRTUOUS OR VICIOUS ACTIONS.

As Arminian notions of that liberty which is essential to virtue or vice, are inconsistent with common sense, in their being inconsistent with all virtuous or vicious habits and dispositions; so they are no less inconsistent with all influence of motives in moral actions.—Such influence equally against those notions of liberty, whether there be, previous to the act of choice, a preponderancy of the inclination, or a preponderancy of those circumstances, which have a tendency to move the inclination. And, indeed, it comes to just the same thing: to say, the circumstances of the mind are such as tend to sway and turn its inclination one way, is the same thing, as to say, the inclination of the mind, as under such circumstances, tends that way.

Or if any think it most proper to say, that Motives do alter the inclination, and give a net bias to the mind, it will not alter the case, as to the present argument. For if Motives operate by giving the mind an inclination, then they operate by destroying the mind's indifference, and laying it under a bias. But to do this, is to destroy the Arminian freedom: it is not to leave the will to its own self-determination, but to bring it into subjection to the power of something extrinsic, which operates upon it, sways and determines it, previous to its own determination. So that what is done from Motive, cannot be either virtuous or vicious. Besides, if the acts of the will are excited by Motives, those Motives are the causes of those acts of the Will; which makes the acts of the will necessary; as effects necessarily follow the efficiency of the cause. And if the influence and power of the Motive causes the volition, then the influence of the motive determines volition, and volition does not determine itself; and so is not free, in the sense of Arminians, (as has been largely shown already,) and consequently can be neither virtuous nor vicious.

The supposition which has already been taken notice of as an insufficient evasion in other cases, would be, in like manner, impertinently alleged in this case; namely, the supposition that liberty consists in a power of suspending action for the present, in order to deliberation. If it should be said, Though it be true, that the Will is under a necessity of finally following the strongest Motive; yet it may, for the present, forbear to act upon the Motive presented, till there has been opportunity thoroughly to consider it, and compare its real weight with the merit of other Motives. I answer as follows:

Here again, it must be remembered, that if determining thus to suspend and consider, be that act of the will, wherein alone liberty is exercised, then in this all virtue and vice must consist; and the acts that follow this consideration, and are the effects of it, being necessary, are no more virtuous or vicious than some good or bad events, which happen when they are fast asleep, and are the consequences of what they did when they were awake. Therefore, I would here observe two things:

1. To suppose, that all virtue and vice, in every case, consists in determining whether to take time for consideration or not, is not agreeable to common sense. For, according to such a supposition, the most horrid crimes, adultery, murder, sodomy, blasphemy, &c. do not at all consist in the horrid nature of the things themselves, but only in the neglect of thorough consideration before they were perpetrated, which brings their viciousness to a small matter, and makes all crimes equal. If it be said, that neglect of consideration, when such heinous evils are

proposed to choice, is worse than in other cases: I answer, this is inconsistent, as it supposes the very thing to be, which, at the same time, is supposed not to be; it supposes all moral evil, all viciousness and heinousness, does not consist merely in the want of consideration. It supposes some crimes in themselves, in their own nature, to be more heinous than others, antecedent to consideration, or inconsideration, which lays the person under a previous obligation to consider in some cases more than others.

2. If it were so, that all virtue and vice, in every case, consisted only in the act of the will, whereby it determines whether to consider or no, it would not alter the case in the least, as to the present argument. For still in this act of the Will on this determination, it is induced by some Motive, and necessarily follows the strongest Motive; and so is necessarily, even in that act wherein alone it is either virtuous or vicious.

One thing more I would observe, concerning the inconsistence of Arminian notions of moral Agency with the Influence of Motives.—I suppose none will deny, that it is possible for such powerful Motives to be set before the mind, exhibited in so strong a light, and under such advantageous circumstances, as to be invincible; and such as the mind cannot but yield to. In this case, Arminians will doubtless say, liberty is destroyed. And if so, then if Motives are exhibited with half so much power, they hinder liberty in proportion to their strength, and go halfway towards destroying it. If a thousand degrees of Motive abolish all liberty, then five hundred take it half away. If one degree of the influence of motive does not at all infringe or diminish liberty, then no more do two degrees; for nothing doubled, is still nothing. And if two degrees do not diminish the Will's liberty, no more do four, eight, sixteen, or six thousand. For nothing however multiplied comes to but nothing. If there be nothing in the nature of Motive or moral suasion, that is at all opposite to liberty, then the greatest degree of it cannot hurt liberty. But if there be somewhat, in the nature of the thing, against liberty, then the least degree of it hurts in some degree; and consequently diminishes virtue. If invincible Motives to that action which is good, take away all the freedom of the act, and so all the virtue of it; then the more forcible the Motives are, so much the worse, so much the less virtue; and the weaker the Motives are, the better for the cause of virtue; and none is best of all.

Now let it be considered, whether these things are agreeable to common sense. If it should be allowed, that there are some instances wherein the soul chooses without any motive, what virtue can there be in such a choice? I am sure there is no prudence or wisdom in it. Such a choice is made for no good end; being made for no end at all. If it were for any end, the view of the end would be the motive exciting to the act; and if the act be for no good end, and so from no good aim, then there is no good intention in it: and, therefore, according to all our natural notions of virtue, no more virtue in it than in the motion of the smoke, which is driven to and fro by the wind, without any aim or end in the thing moved, and which knows not whither, nor wherefore, it is moved.

Corol. 1. By these things it appears, that the argument against the Calvinists, taken from the use of counsels, exhortations, invitations, expostulations, &c. so much insisted on by Arminians, is truly against themselves. For these things can operate no other way to any good effect, than as in them is exhibited Motive and Inducement, tending to excite and determine the acts of the will. But it follows, on their principles, that the acts of will excited by such causes, cannot be virtuous; because, so far as they are from these, they are not from the Will's self-determining power. Hence it will follow, that it is not worth while to offer any arguments to persuade men to any virtuous volition or voluntary action; it is in vain to set before them the wisdom and amiableness of ways of virtue, or the odiousness and folly of way of vice. This notion of liberty and moral Agency frustrates all endeavours to draw men to virtue by instruction or persuasion, precept or example: for though these things may induce them to what is materially virtuous, yet at the same time they take away the form of virtue, because they destroy liberty; as they, by their own power, put the Will out of its equilibrium, determine and turn the scale, and take the work of self-determining power out of its hands. And the clearer the instructions given, the more powerful the arguments used, and the more moving the persuasions or examples, the more likely they are to frustrate their own design; because they have so much the greater tendency to put the Will out of its balance, to hinder its freedom of self-determination; and so to exclude the very form of virtue, and the essence of whatsoever is praiseworthy.

So it clearly follows, from these principles, that God has no hand in any man's virtue, nor does at all promote it, either by a physical or moral influence; that none of the moral methods he uses with men to promote virtue in the world, have any tendency to the attainment of that end; that all the instructions he has given men, from the beginning of the world to this day, by prophets or apostles, or by his Son Jesus Christ; that all his counsels, invitations, promises, threatenings, warnings, and expostulations; that all means he has used with men, in ordinances, or providences; yea, all influences of his Spirit, ordinary and extraordinary, have had no tendency at all to excite any one virtuous act of the mind, or to promote any thing morally good and commendable, in any re-spect.—For there is no way that these or any other means can promote virtue, but one of these three. Either, (1.) By a physical operation on the heart. But all effects that are wrought in men in this way, have no virtue in them, by the concurring voice of all Arminians. Or, (2.) Morally, by exhibiting Motives to the understandings, to excite good acts in the Will. But it has been demonstrated, that volitions excited by Motives, are necessary, and not excited by a self-moving power; and therefore, by their principles, there is no virtue in them. Or, (3.) By merely giving the Will an opportunity to determine itself concerning the objects proposed, either to choose or reject, by its own uncaused, unmoved, uninfluenced self-determination. And if this be all, then all those means do no more to promote virtue than vice: for they do nothing but give the Will opportunity to determine itself either way, either to good or bad, without laying it under any bias to either: and so there is really as much of an opportunity given to determine in favour of evil, as of good.

Thus that horrid blasphemous consequence will certainly follow from the Arminian doctrine, which they charge on others; namely, that God acts an inconsistent part in using so many counsels, warnings, invitations, entreaties, &c. with sinners, to induce them to forsake sin, and turn to the ways of virtue; and that all are insincere and fallacious. It will follow, from their doctrine, that God does these things when he knows, at the same time, that they have no manner of tendency to promote the effect he seems to aim at; yea, knows that if they have any influence, this very influence will be inconsistent with such an effect, and will prevent it. But what an imputation of insincerity would this fix on him, who is infinitely holy and true!—So that theirs is the doctrine which, if pursued in its consequences, does horribly reflect on the Most High, and fix on him the charge of hypocrisy; and not the doctrine of the Calvinist, according to their frequent and vehement exclamations and invectives.

Corol 2. From what has been observed in this section, it again appears, that Arminian principles and notions, when fairly examined and pursued in their demonstrable consequences, do evidently shut all virtue out of the world, and make it impossible that there should ever be any such thing, in any case; or that any such thing should ever be conceived of. For, by these principles, the very notion of virtue or vice implies absurdity and contradiction. For it is absurd in itself, and contrary to common sense, to suppose a virtuous act of mind without any good intention or aim; and, by their principles, it is absurd to suppose a virtuous act with a good intention or aim; for to act for an end, is to act from a Motive. So that if we rely on these principles, there can be no virtuous act with a good design and end; and it is self-evident, there can be none without: consequently there can be no virtuous act at all.

Corol. 3. It is manifest, that Arminian notions of moral Agency, and the being of a faculty of Will, cannot consist together; and that if there can be any such thing as either a virtuous or vicious act, it cannot be an act of the Will; no Will can be at all concerned in it. For that act which is performed without inclination, without Motive, without end, must be performed without any concern of the Will. To suppose an act of the Will without these, implies a contradiction. If the soul in its act has no motive or end; then, in that act (as was observed before) it seeks nothing, goes after nothing, exerts no inclination to any thing; and this implies, that in that act it desires nothing, and chooses nothing; so that there is no act of choice in the case: and that is as much as to say, there is no act of Will in the case. Which very effectually shuts all vicious and virtuous acts out of the universe; inasmuch as, according to this, there can be no vicious or virtuous act wherein the Will is concerned: and according to the plainest dictates of reason, and the light of nature, and also the principles of Arminians themselves, there can be no virtuous or vicious act wherein the Will is not concerned. And therefore there is no room for any virtuous or vicious acts at all.

Corol. 4. If none of the moral actions of intelligent beings are influenced by either previous inclination or motives, another strange thing will follow; and this is, that God not only cannot foreknow any of the future moral actions of his creatures, but he can make no conjecture, can give no probable guess concerning them. For all conjecture in things of this nature must depend on some discerning or apprehension of these two things, previous Disposition and Motive, which, as has been observed, Arminian notions of moral Agency, in their real consequence, altogether exclude.

Part IV. WHEREIN THE CHIEF GROUNDS OF THE REASONINGS OF ARMINIANS, IN SUPPORT AND DEFENCE OF THE FOREMENTIONED NOTIONS OF LIBERTY, MORAL AGENCY, &c. AND AGAINST THE OPPOSITE DOCTRINE, ARE CONSIDERED.

1. The essence of the virtue and vice of dispositions of the heart, and acts of the will, lies not in their cause, but their nature.

2. The Falseness and Inconsistence of that Metaphysical Notion of Action and Agency Which Seems to be Generally Entertained by the Defenders of the Arminian Doctrine concerning Liberty, Moral Agency, &c

3. The Reasons Why Some Think It Contrary To Common Sense, To Suppose Those Things Which Are Necessary, To Be Worthy of Either Praise Or Blame.

4. It Is Agreeable To Common sense, And The Natural Notions of Mankind, To Suppose Moral Necessity To Be Consistent With Praise And Blame, Reward And Punishment.

5. Concerning Those Objections, That This Scheme Of Necessity Renders All Means and Endeavours For The Avoiding Of Sin, Or The Obtaining Virtue And Holiness, Vain And To No Purpose; And That It makes Men No More Than Mere Machines In Affairs Of Morality And Religion.

6. Concerning That Objection Against The Doctrine Which Has Been Maintained, That It Agrees With The Stoical Doctrine Of Faith, And The Opinions of Mr. Hobbes.

7. Concerning The Necessity Of The Divine Will.

PART IV. SECTION I. THE ESSENCE OF THE VIRTUE AND VICE OF DISPOSITIONS OF THE HEART AND ACTS OF THE WILL, LIES NOT IN THEIR CAUSE, BUT THEIR NATURE.

One main foundation of the reasons which are brought to establish the fore-mentioned notions of liberty, virtue, vice, &c. is a supposition, that the virtuousness of the dispositions, or acts of the will, consists not in the nature of these dispositions or acts, but wholly in the origin or cause of them: so that if the disposition of the mind, or acts of the will, be ever so good, yet if the cause of the disposition or act be not our virtue, there is nothing virtuous or praiseworthy in it; and, on the contrary, if the will, in its inclination or acts, be never so bad, yet unless it arises from something that is our vice or fault, there is nothing vicious or blameworthy in it. Hence their grand objection and pretended demonstration, or self-evidence, against any virtue and commendableness, or vice and blameworthiness, of those habits or acts of the Will, which are not from some virtuous or vicious determination of the will itself. Now, if this matter be well considered, it will appear to be altogether a mistake, yea, a gross absurdity; and that it is most certain, that if there be any such things as a virtuous or vicious disposition, or volition of mind, the virtuousness or viciousness of them consists not in the origin or cause of these things, but in the nature of them. If the essence of virtuousness or commendableness, and of viciousness or fault, does not lie in the nature of the dispositions or acts of mind, which are said to be our virtue or our fault, but in their cause, then it is certain it lies no where at all. Thus, for instance, if the vice of a vicious act of will lies not in the nature of the act, but the cause; so that its being of a bad nature will not make it at all our fault, unless it arises from some faulty determination of ours, as its cause, or something in us that is our fault; then, for the same reason, neither can the viciousness of that cause lie in the nature of the thing itself, but in its cause: that evil determination of ours is not our fault, merely because it is of a bad nature, unless it arises from some cause in us that is our fault. And when we are come to this higher cause, still the reason of the thing holds good; though this cause be of a bad nature, yet we are not at all to blame on that account, unless it arises from something faulty in us. Nor yet can blameworthiness lie in the nature of this cause but in the cause of that. And thus we must drive faultiness back from step to step, from a lower cause to a higher, in infinitum; and that is thoroughly to banish it from the world, and to allow it no possibility of existence any where in the universality of things. On these principles, vice, or moral evil cannot exist in any thing that is an effect; because fault does not consist in the nature of things, but in their cause; as well as because effects are necessary, being unavoidably connected with their cause: therefore the cause only is to blame. And so it follows, that faultiness can lie only in that cause, which is a cause only, and no effect of anything. Nor yet can it lie in this; for then it must lie in the nature of the thing itself; not in its being from any determination of ours, nor anything faulty in us, which is the cause, nor indeed from any cause at all; for, by the supposition, it is no effect, and has no cause. And thus he that will maintain it is not the nature of habits or acts of will that makes them virtuous or faulty, but the cause, must immediately run himself out of his own assertion; and, in maintaining it, will insensibly contradict and deny it. This is certain, that if effects are vicious and faulty, not from their nature, or from any thing inherent in them, but because they are from a bad cause, it must be on account of the badness of the cause: a bad effect in the will must be bad, because the cause is bad, or of an evil nature, or has badness as a quality inherent in it: and a good effect in the will must be good, by reason of the goodness of the cause, or its being of a good kind and nature. And if this be what is meant, the very supposition of fault and praise lying not in the nature of the thing, but the cause, contradicts itself, and does at least resolve the essence of virtue and vice into the nature of things, and supposes it originally to consist in that.—And if a caviler has a mind to run from the absurdity, by saying, "No, the fault of the thing, which is the cause, lies not in this, that the cause itself is of an evil nature, but that the cause is evil in that sense, that it is from another bad cause,"—still the absurdity will follow him; for if so, then the cause before charged is at once acquitted, and all the blame must be laid to the higher cause, and must consist in that's being evil, or of an evil nature. So now we are come again to lay the blame of the thing blameworthy, to the nature of the thing, and not to the cause. And if any is so foolish as to go higher still, and ascend from step to step, till he is come to that which is the first cause concerned in the whole affair, and will say, all the blame lies in that; then, at last, he must be forced to own, that the faultiness of the thing which he supposes alone blamewor- thy, lies wholly in the nature of the thing, and not in the original or cause of it; for the supposition is, that it has no original, it is determined by no act of ours, is caused by nothing faulty in us, being absolutely without any cause. And so the race is at an end, but the evader is taken in his flight! It is agreeable to the natural notions of mankind, that moral evil, with its desert of dislike and abhorrence, and all its other ill-deservings, consists in a certain deformity in the nature of certain dispositions of the heart and acts of the will; and not in the deformity of something else, diverse from the very thing itself; which deserves abhorrence, supposed to be the cause of it;—which would be absurd, because that would be to suppose a thing that is innocent and not evil, is truly evil and faulty, because another thing is evil. It implies a contra- diction; for it would be to suppose, the very thing which is morally evil and blameworthy, is innocent and not blameworthy; but that something else, which is its cause, is only to blame. To say, that vice does not consist in the thing which is vicious, but in its cause, is the same as to say, that vice does not consist in vice, but in that which produces it. It is true a cause may be to blame for being the cause of vice: it may be wickedness in the cause that it produces wickedness. But it would imply a contradiction, to suppose that these two are the same individual wickedness. The wicked act of the cause in producing wickedness, is one wickedness; and the wickedness produced, if there be any produced, is another. And therefore the wickedness of the latter does not lie in the former, but is distinct from it; and the wickedness of both lies in the evil nature of the things which are wicked. The thing which makes sin hateful, is that by which it deserves punishment; which is but the expression of hatred. And that which renders virtue lovely, is the same with that on the account, of which, it is fit to receive praise and reward; which are but the expressions of esteem and love. But that which makes vice hateful, is its hateful nature; and that which renders virtue lovely, is its amiable nature. It is a certain beauty or deformity that are inherent in that good or evil will, which is the soul of virtue and vice (and not in the occasion of it), which is their worthiness of esteem or disesteem, praise, or dispraise, according to the common sense of mankind. If the cause or occasion of the rise of a hateful disposition or act of will, be also hateful, suppose another antecedent evil will; that is entirely another sin, and, deserves punishment by itself, under a distinct consideration. There is worthiness of dispraise in the nature of an evil volition, and not wholly in some foregoing act, which is its cause; otherwise the evil volition, which is the effect, is no moral evil, any more than sickness, or some other natural calamity, which arises from a cause morally evil. Thus, for instance, ingratitude is hateful and worthy of dispraise, according to common sense; not because something as bad, or worse than ingratitude, was the cause that produced it; but because it is hateful in itself, inherent deformity. So, the love of virtue is amiable and worthy of praise, not merely because something else went before this love of virtue in our minds, which caused it to take place there;—for instance, our own choice; we choose to love virtue, and, by some method or other, wrought ourselves into the love of it;—but because of the amiableness and condescendency of such a disposition and inclination of heart. If that was the case, that we did choose to love virtue, and so produced that love in ourselves, this choice itself could be no otherwise amiable or praiseworthy, than as love to virtue, or some other amiable inclination, was exercised and implied in it. If that choice was amiable at all, it must be so on account of some amiable quality in the nature of the choice. If we chose to love virtue, not in love to virtue, or any thing that was good and exercised no sort of good disposition to the choice, the choice itself was not virtuous nor worthy of any praise, according to common sense, because the choice was not of a good nature. It may not be improper here to take notice of something said by an author, that has lately made a mighty noise in America. "A necessary holiness (says he) is no holiness. Adam could not be originally created in righteousness and true holiness, because he must choose to be righteous, before he could be righteous. And therefore he must exist, he must be created; yea, he must exercise thought and reflection, before he was righteous." There is much more to the same effect in that place, and also in pp. 437, 438, 439, 440. If these things are so, it will certainly follow, that the first choosing to be righteous is no righteous choice; there is no righteousness or holiness in it, because no choosing to be righteous goes before it. For he plainly speaks of choosing to be righteous, as what must go before righteousness; and that which follows the choice, being the effect of the choice, cannot be righteousness or holiness; for an effect is a thing necessary, and cannot prevent the influence or efficacy of its cause; and therefore is unavoidably dependent upon the cause; and he says a necessary holiness is no holiness. So that neither can a choice of righteousness be righteousness or holiness, nor can any thing that is consequent on that choice, and the effect of it, be righteousness or holiness; nor can any thing that is without choice, be righteousness or holiness. So that by this scheme, all righteousness and holiness is at once shut out of the world, and no door left open by which it can ever possibly enter into the world.

I suppose the way that men came to entertain this absurd inconsistent notion, with respect to internal inclinations and volitions themselves (or notions that imply it,) viz. that the essence of their moral good or evil lies not in their nature, but their cause, was, that it is indeed a very plain dictate of common sense, that it is so with respect to all outward actions and sensible motions of the body; that the moral good or evil of them does not lie at all in the motions themselves, which, taken by themselves, are nothing of a moral nature; and the essence of all the moral good or evil that concerns them, lies in those internal dispositions and volitions which are the cause of them. Now, being always used to determine this, without hesitation or dispute, concerning external actions, which are the things that, in the common use of language, are signified by such phrases as men's actions, or their doings; hence, when they came to speak of volitions, and internal exercises of their inclinations, under the same denomination of their actions, or what they do, they unwarily determined the case must also he the same with these as with external actions; not considering the vast difference in the nature of the case.

If any shall still object and say, why is it not necessary that the cause should be considered, in order to determine whether any thing be worthy of blame or praise? is it agreeable to reason and common sense, that a man is to be praised or blamed for that which he is not the cause or author of, and has no hand in?

I answer: Such phrases as being the cause, being the author, having a hand, and the like, are ambiguous. They are most vulgarly understood for being the designing voluntary cause, or cause by antecedent choice; and it is most certain, that men are not, in this sense, the causes or authors of the first act of their wills, in any case, as certain as any thing is or ever can be; for nothing can be more certain than that a thing is not before it is, nor a thing of the same kind before the first thing of that kind, and so no choice before the first choice.—As the phrase, being the author, may be understood, not of being the producer by an antecedent act of will, but as a person may be said to be the author of the act of will itself, by his being the immediate agent, or the being that is acting, or in exercise in that act; if the phrase of being the author is used to signify this, then doubtless common sense requires men's being the authors of their own acts of will, in order to their being esteemed worthy of praise or dispraise, on account of them. And common sense teaches, that they must be the authors of external actions, in the former sense, namely, their being the causes of them by an act of will or choice, in order to their being justly blamed or praised: but it teaches no such thing with respect to the acts of the will themselves. But this may appear more manifest by the things which will be observed in the following section.

PART IV. SECTION II. THE FALSENESS AND INCONSISTENCE OF THAT METAPHYSICAL NOTION OF ACTION AND AGENCY WHICH SEEMS TO BE GENERALLY ENTERTAINED BY THE DEFENDERS OF THE ARMINIAN DOCTRINE CONCERNING LIBERTY, MORAL AGENCY, &c.

One thing, that is made very much a ground of argument and supposed demonstration by Arminians, in defense of the fore-mentioned principles concerning moral agency, virtue, vice, &c., is their metaphysical notion of agency and action. They say, unless the soul has a self-determining power, it has no power of action; if its volitions be not caused by itself, but are excited and determined by some extrinsic cause, they cannot be the soul's own acts; and that the soul cannot be active, but must be wholly passive, in those effects which it is the subject of necessarily, and not from its own free determination.

Mr. Chubb lays the foundation of his scheme of liberty, and of his arguments to support it, very much in this position, that man is an agent, and capable of action,—which doubtless is true: but self-determination belongs to his notion of action, and is the very essence of it; whence he infers, that it is impossible for a man to act and be acted upon, in the same thing, at the same time; and that nothing that is an action, can be the effect of the action of another: and he insists, that a necessary agent, or an agent that is necessarily determined to act, is a plain contradiction.

But those are a precarious sort of demonstrations, which men build on the meaning that they arbitrarily affix to a word; especially when that meaning is abstruse, inconsistent, and entirely diverse from the original sense of the word in common speech.

That the meaning of the word action, as Mr. Chubb and many others use it, is utterly unintelligible and inconsistent, is manifest, because it belongs to their notion of an action, that it is something wherein is no passion or passiveness; that is, (according to their sense of passiveness,) it is under the power, influence, or action of no cause. And this implies, that action has no cause, and is no effect; for to be an effect implies passiveness, or the being subject to the power and action of its cause. And yet they hold, that the mind's action is the effect of its own determination; yea, the mind's free and voluntary determination, which is the same with free choice. So that action is the effect of something preceding, even a preceding act of choice: and consequently, in this effect, the mind is passive, subject to the power and action of the preceding cause, which is the foregoing choice, and therefore cannot be active. So that here we have this contradiction, that action is always the effect of foregoing choice, and therefore cannot be action; because it is passive to the power of that preceding causal choice; and the mind cannot be active and passive in the same thing, at the same time. Again, they say, necessity is utterly inconsistent with action, and a necessary action is a contradiction; and so their notion of action implies contingence, and excludes all necessity. And, therefore, their notion of action implies, that it has no necessary dependence or connection with any thing foregoing; for such a dependence or connection excludes contingence, and implies necessity. And yet their notion of action implies necessity, and supposes that it is necessary, and cannot he contingent. For they suppose that whatever is properly called action, must be determined by the will and free choice; and this is as much as to say, that it must be necessary, being dependent upon, and determined by, something foregoing, namely, a foregoing act of choice. Again, it belongs to their notion of action, of that which is a proper and mere act, that it is the beginning of motion, or of exertion of power, but yet it is implied in their notion of action, that it is not the beginning of motion or exertion of power, but is consequent and dependent on a preceding exertion of power, viz. the power of will and choice; for they say there is no proper action but what is freely chosen, or, which is the same thing, determined by a foregoing act of free choice. But if any of them shall see cause to deny this, and say they hold no such thing, as that every action is chosen or determined by a foregoing choice, but that the very first exertion of will only, undetermined by any preceding act, is properly called action; then I say, such a man's notion of action implies necessity; for what the mind is the subject of, without the determination of its own previous choice, it is the subject of necessarily, as to any hand that free choice has in the affair, and without any ability the mind has to prevent it by any will or election of its own; because, by the supposition, it precludes all previous acts of will or choice in the case, which might prevent it. So that it is again, in this other way, implied in their notion of act, that it is both necessary and not necessary, Again, it belongs to their notion of an act, that it is no effect of a predetermining bias or preponderation, but springs immediately out of indifference; and this implies, that it cannot be from foregoing choice, which is foregoing preponderation: if it be not habitual, but occasional, yet if it cause the act, it is truly previous, efficacious, and determining. And yet, at the same time, it is essential to their notion of the act, that it is what the agent is the author of, freely and voluntarily, and that is by previous choice and design.

So that, according to their notion of the act, considered with regard to its consequences, these following things are all essential to it; viz. that it should be necessary, and not necessary; that it should be from a cause, and no cause; that it should be the fruit of choice and design, and not the fruit of choice and design; that it should be the beginning of motion or exertion, and yet consequent on previous exertion; that it should be before it is; that it should spring immediately out of indifference and equilibrium, and yet be the effect of preponderation; that it should be self-originated, and also have its original from something else; that it is what the mind causes itself, of its own will, and can produce or prevent, according to its choice or pleasure, and yet what the mind has no power to prevent, precluding all previous choice in the affair.

So that an act, according to their metaphysical notion of it, is something of which there is no idea; it is nothing but a confusion of the mind, excited by words, without any distinct meaning, and is an absolute nonentity; and that in two respects.

(1.) There is nothing in the world that ever was, is, or can be, to answer the things which must belong to its description, according to what they suppose to be essential to it. And

(2) There neither is, nor ever was, nor can be, any notion or idea to answer the word, as they use and explain it. For, if we should suppose any such notion, it would many ways destroy itself. But it is impossible any idea or notion should subsist in the mind, whose very nature and essence which constitutes it, destroys it. If some learned philosopher, who had been abroad, in giving an account of the curious observations he had made in his travels, should say, he had been in Terra del Fuego, and there had seen an animal, which he calls by a certain name, that begat and brought forth itself, and yet had a sire and dam distinct from itself; that it had an appetite, and was hungry before it had a being; that his master, who led him, and governed him at his pleasure, was always governed by him, and driven by him where he pleased; that when he moved, he always took a step before the first step; that he went with his head first, and yet always went tail foremost; and this, though he had neither tail nor head: it would be no impudence at all to tell such a traveler, though a learned man, that he himself had no notion or idea of such an animal as he gave an account of, and never had, nor ever should have.

As the fore-mentioned notion of action is very inconsistent, so it is wholly diverse from the original meaning of the word. The more usual signification of it, in vulgar speech, seems to be some motion or exertion of power, that is voluntary, or that is the effect of the will, and is used in the same sense as doing; and most commonly it is used to signify outward actions. So thinking is often distinguished from acting, and desiring and willing from doing.

Besides this more usual and proper signification of the word action, there are other ways in which the word is used that are less proper, which yet have place in common speech. Oftentimes it is used to signify some motion or alteration in inanimate things, with relation to some object and effect. So, the spring of a watch is said to act upon the chain and wheels; the sunbeams, to act upon plants and trees; and the fire, to act upon wood. Sometimes the word is useful to signify motions, alterations, and exertions of power, which are seen in corporeal things, considered absolutely; especially when these motions seem to arise from some internal cause which is hidden; so that they have a greater resemblance of those motions of our bodies which are the effects of natural volition, or invisible exertions of will. So, the fermentation of liquor, the operations of the loadstone, and of electrical bodies, are called the action of these things. And sometimes, the word action is used to signify the exercise of thought, or of will and inclination: so meditating, loving, hating, inclining, disinclining, choosing, and refusing, may be sometimes called acting; though more rarely (unless it be by philosophers and metaphysicians) than in any of the other senses.

But the word is never used in vulgar speech in that sense which Arminian divines use it in, namely, for the self-determinate exercise of the will, or an exertion of the soul, that arises without any necessary connection with any thing foregoing. If a man does something voluntarily, or as the effect of his choice, then, in the most proper sense, and as the word is most originally and commonly used, he is said to act; But whether that choice or volition be self-determined, or no; whether it be connected with foregoing, habitual bias; whether it be the certain effect of the strongest motive, or some intrinsic cause, never comes into consideration in the meaning of the word. And if the word action is arbitrarily used by some men otherwise, to suit some scheme of metaphysics or morality, no argument can reasonably be founded on such a use of this term, to prove any thing but their own pleasure. For divines and philosophers strenuously to urge such arguments, as though they were sufficient to support and demonstrate a whole scheme of moral philosophy and divinity, is certainly to erect a mighty edifice on the sand, or rather on a shadow. And though it may now perhaps, through custom, have become natural for them to use the word in this sense, (if that may be called a sense or meaning, which is inconsistent with itself,) yet this does not prove that it is agreeable to the natural notions men have of things, or that there can be any thing in the creation that should answer such a meaning. And though they appeal to experience, yet the truth is, that men are so far from experiencing any such thing, that it is impossible for them to have any conception of it.

If it should be objected, that action and passion are doubtless words of a contrary sanification; but to suppose that the agent, in its action, is under the power and influence of something intrinsic, is to confound action and passion, and make them the same thing:

I answer, that action and passion are doubtless, as they are sometimes used, words of opposite signification; but not as signifying opposite existences, but only opposite relations. The words cause and effect are terms of opposite signification; but, nevertheless, if I assert that, the same thing may, at the same time, in different respects and relations, be both cause and effect, this will not prove that I confound the terms. The soul may be both active and passive in the same thing in different respects; active with relation to one thing, and passive with relation to another. The word passion, when set in opposition to action, or rather activeness, is merely a relative: it signifies no effect or cause, nor any proper existence; but is the same with passiveness, or a being passive, or a being acted upon by something. Which is a mere relation of a thing to some power or force exerted by some cause, producing some effect in it or upon it. And action, when set properly in opposition to passion, or passiveness, is no real existence; it is not the same with an action, but is a mere relation: it is the activeness of something on another thing, being the opposite relation to the other, viz. a relation of power, or force, exerted by some cause towards another thing, which is the subject of the effect of that power. Indeed, the word action is frequently used to signify something not merely relative, but more absolute, and a real existence; as when we say an action; when the word is not used transitively, but absolutely, for some motion or exercise of body or mind, without any relation to any object or effect: and as used thus, it is not properly the opposite of passion, which ordinarily signifies nothing absolute, but merely the relation of being acted upon. And therefore, if the word action be useful in the like relative sense, then action and passion are only two contrary relations. And it is no absurdity to suppose, that contrary relations may belong to the same thing, at the same time, with respect to different things. So, to suppose that there are acts of the soul by which a man voluntarily moves, and acts upon objects, and produces effects which yet themselves are effects of something else, and wherein the soul itself is the object of something acting upon, and influencing that, does not at all confound action and passion. The words may nevertheless be properly of opposite signification: there may be as true and real a difference between acting and being caused to act, though we should suppose the soul to be both in the same volition, as there is between living and being quickened, or made to live. It is no more a contradiction, to suppose that action may be the effect of some other cause besides the agent or being that acts, than to suppose, that life may be the effect of some other cause, besides the liver, or the being that lives, in whom life is caused to be.

The thing which has led men into this inconsistent notion of action, when applied to volition, as though it were essential to this internal action, that the agent should be self-determined in it, and that the will should be the cause of it, is probably this,—that, according to the sense of mankind, and the common use of language, it is so, with respect to men's external actions, which are what originally, and according to the vulgar use and most proper sense of the word, are called actions. Men in these are self-directed, self-determined, and their wills are the cause of the motions of their bodies, and the external things that are done; so that unless men do them voluntarily, and of choice, and the action be determined by their antecedent volition, it is no action or doing of theirs. Hence some metaphysicians have been led unwarily, but exceeding absurdly, to suppose the same concerning volition itself, that that also must be determined by the will; which is to be determined by antecedent volition, as the motion of the body is; not considering the contradiction it implies.

But it is very evident, that in the metaphysical distinction between action and passion, (though long since become common and the general vogue,) due care has not been taken to conform language to the nature of things, or to any distinct, clear ideas;—as it is in innumerable other philosophical, metaphysical terms, used in these disputes; which has occasioned inexpressible difficulty, contention, error, and confusion.

And thus probably it came to be thought that necessity was inconsistent with action, as these terms are applied to volition. First, these terms, action and necessity, are changed from their original meaning, as signifying external voluntary action and constraint, (in which meaning they are evidently inconsistent,) to signify quite other things, viz. volition itself, and certainty of existence. And when the change of signification is made, care is not taken to make proper allowances and abatements for the difference of sense; but still the same things are unwarily attributed to action and necessity, in the new meaning of the words, which plainly belonged to them in their first sense; and on this ground, maxims are established without any real foundation, as though they were the most certain truths, and the most evident dictates of reason.

But, however strenuously it is maintained, that what is necessary cannot be properly called action, and that a necessary action is a contradiction, yet it is probable there are few Arminian divines, who, if thoroughly tried, would stand to these principles. They will allow, that God is, in the highest sense, an active being, and the highest fountain of life and action; and they would not probably deny, that those that are called God's acts of righteousness, holiness, and faithfulness, are truly and properly God's acts, and God is really a holy agent in them; and yet, I trust, they will not deny, that God necessarily acts justly and faithfully, and that it is impossible for Him to act unrighteously and unholy.

PART IV. SECTION III. THE REASONS WHY SOME THINK IT CONTRARY TO COMMON SENSE, TO SUPPOSE THOSE THINGS WHICH ARE NECESSARY, TO BE WORTHY OF EITHER PRAISE OR BLAME.

It is abundantly affirmed and urged by Arminian writers, that it is contrary to common sense, and the natural notions and apprehensions of mankind, to suppose otherwise than that necessity (making no distinction between natural and moral necessity) is inconsistent, with virtue and vice, praise and blame, reward and punishment. And their arguments from hence have been greatly triumphed in; and have been not a little perplexing to many, who have been friendly to the truth, as clearly revealed in the holy Scriptures: it has seemed to them indeed difficult, to reconcile Calvinistic doctrines with the notions men commonly have of justice and equity. And the true reasons of it seem to be these that follow.

I. It is indeed a very plain dictate of common sense, that natural necessity is wholly inconsistent with just praise or blame. If men do things which in themselves are very good, fit to be brought to pass, and very happy effects, properly against their wills, and cannot help it; or do them from a necessity that is without their wills, or with which their wills have no concern or connection; then it is a plain dictate of common sense, that it is none of their virtue, nor any moral good in them; and that they are not worthy to be rewarded or praised, or at all esteemed, honoured, or loved on that account. And, on the other hand, that if, from like necessity, they do those things which in themselves are very unhappy and pernicious, and do them because they cannot help it; the necessity is such, that it is all one whether they will them or no; and the reason why they are done, is from necessity only, and not from their wills: it is a very plain dictate of common sense, that they are not at all to blame; there is no vice, fault, or moral evil at all in the effect done; nor are they who are thus necessitated, in any wise worthy to be punished, hated, or in the least disrespected, on that account.

In like manner, if things, in them selves good and desirable, are absolutely impossible, with a natural impossibility, the universal reason of mankind teaches, that this wholly and perfectly excuses persons in their not doing them.

And it is also a plain dictate of common sense, that if the doing things in themselves good, or avoiding things in themselves evil, is not absolutely impossible, with such a natural impossibility, but very difficult, with a natural difficulty, that is, a difficulty prior to, and not at all consisting in, will and inclination itself, and which would remain the same, let the inclination be what it will; then a person's neglect or omission is excused in some measure, though not wholly; his sin is less aggravated than if the thing to be done were easy. And if instead of difficulty and hindrance, there be a contrary natural propensity in the state of things to the thing to be done, or effect to be brought to pass, abstracted from any consideration of the inclination of the heart; though the propensity be not so great as to amount to a natural necessity, yet being some approach to it, so that the doing the good thing be very much from this natural tendency in the state of things, and but little from a good inclination; then it is a dictate of common sense, that there is so much the less virtue in what is done; and so it is less praiseworthy and rewardable. The reason is easy, viz. because such a natural propensity or tendency is an approach to natural necessity; and the greater the propensity, still so much the nearer is the approach to necessity. And, therefore, as natural necessity takes away or shuts out all virtue, so this propensity approaches to an abolition of virtue; that is, it diminishes it. And, on the other hand, natural difficulty, in the state of things, is an approach to natural impossibility. And as the latter, when it is complete and absolute, wholly takes away blame, so such difficulty takes away some blame, or diminishes blame; and makes the thing done to be less worthy of punishment.

II. Men, in their first use of such phrases as these,—must, cannot, cannot help it, cannot avoid it, necessary, unable, impossible, unavoidable, irresistible, &c.,—use them to signify a necessity of constraint or restraint, a natural necessity or impossibility; or some necessity that the will has nothing to do in; which may be, whether men will or no; and which may be supposed to be just the same, let men's inclinations and desires be what they will. Such kind of terms, in their original use, I suppose, among all nations, are relative; carrying in their signification (as was before observed) a reference or respect to some contrary will, desire, or endeavour, which, it is supposed, is, or may be, in the case. All men find, and begin to find in early childhood, that there are innumerable things that cannot be done, which they desire to do; and innumerable things, which they are averse to, that must be,—they cannot avoid them, they will be, whether they choose them or no. It is to express this necessity, which men so soon and so often find, and which so greatly and early affects them in innumerable cases, that such terms and phrases are first formed; and it is to signify such a necessity, that they are first used, and that they are most constantly used, in the common affairs of life; and not to signify any such metaphysical, speculative, and abstract notion, as that connection in the nature or course of things, which is between the subject and predicate of a proposition, and which is the foundation of the certain truth of that proposition; to signify which, they who employ themselves in philosophical inquiries into the first origin and metaphysical relations and dependencies of things, have borrowed these terms, for want of others. But we grow up from our cradles in a use of such terms and phrases entirely different from this, and carrying a sense exceeding diverse from that in which they are commonly used in the controversy between Arminians and Calvinists. And it being, as was said before, a dictate of the universal sense of mankind, evident to us as soon as we begin to think, that the necessity signified by these terms, in the sense in which we first learn them, does excuse persons and free them from all fault or blame; hence our idea of excusableness or faultlessness is tied to these terms and phrases by a strong habit, which is begun in childhood, as soon as we begin to speak, and grows up with us, and is strengthened by constant use and custom, the connection growing stronger and stronger.

The habitual connection which is in men's minds between blamelessness and those forementioned terms, must,—cannot, unable, necessary, impossible, unavoidable, &c.—becomes very strong; because as soon as ever men begin to use reason and speech, they have occasion to excuse themselves, from the natural necessity signified by these terms, in numerous instances—I cannot do it; I could not help it. And all mankind have constant and daily occasion to use such phrases in this sense, to excuse themselves aud others, in almost all the concerns of life, with respect to disappointments and things that happen, which concern and affect ourselves and others, that are hurtful, or disagreeable to us or them, or things desirable, that we or others fail of.

That a being accustomed to an union of different ideas, from early childhood, makes the habitual connection exceeding strong, as though such connection were owing to nature, is manifest in innumerable instances. It is altogether by such an habitual connection of ideas, that men judge of the bigness or distance of the objects of sight, from their appearance. Thus, it is owing to such a connection early established, and growing up with a person, that he judges a mountain, which he sees at ten miles distance, to be bigger than his nose, or further off than the end of it. Having been used so long to join a considerable distance and magnitude with such an appearance, men imagine it is by a dictate of natural sense: whereas, it would be quite otherwise with one that had his eyes newly opened, who had been born blind: he would have the same visible appearance, but natural sense would dictate no such thing, concerning the magnitude or distance of what appeared.

III. When men, after they had been so habituated to connect ideas of innocency or blamelessness with such terms, that the union seems to be the effect of mere nature, come to hear the same terms used, and learn to use them themselves, in the fore-mentioned new and metaphysical sense, to signify quite another sort of necessity, which has no such kind of relation to a contrary supposable will and endeavour; the notation of plain and manifest blamelessness, by this means, is, by a strong prejudice, insensibly and unwarily transferred to a case to which it by no means belongs: the change of the use of the terms, to a signification which is very diverse, not being taken notice of, or adverted to. And there are several reasons why it is not.

1. The terms, as used by philosophers, are not very distinct and clear in their meaning: few use them in a fixed, determined sense. On the contrary, their meaning is very vague and confused,—which is what commonly happens to the words used to signify things intellectual and moral, and to express what Mr. Locke calls mixed modes. If men had a clear and distinct understanding of what is intended by these metaphysi-

cal terms, they would be able more easily to compare them with their original and common sense; and so would not be so easily led into delusion by any sort of terms in the world, as by words of this sort.

2. The change of the signification of the terms, is the more insensible, because the things signified, though indeed very different, yet do in some generals agree. In necessity (that which is vulgarly so called) there is a strong connection between the thing said to be necessary, and some thing antecedent to it in the order of nature; so there is also in philosophical necessity. And though in both kinds of necessity the connection cannot be called by that name, with relation to an opposite will or endeavour, to which it is superior; which is the case in vulgar necessity; yet, in both the connection is prior to will and endeavour, and so, in some respect, superior. In both kinds of necessity, there is a foundation for some certainty of the proposition that affirms the event.—The terms used being the same, and the things signified agreeing in these and some other general circumstances; and the expressions, as used by philosophers, being not well defined, and so of obscure and loose signification; hence persons are not aware of the great difference and the notions of innocence or faultiness, which were so strongly associated with them, and were strictly united in their minds, ever since they can remember, remain united with them still, as if the union were altogether natural and necessary; and they that go about to make a separation, seem to them to do great violence, even to nature itself.

IV. Another reason why it appears difficult to reconcile it with reason, that men should be blamed for that which is necessary with a moral necessity, which, as was observed before, is a species of philosophical necessity, is, that for want of due consideration, men inwardly entertain that apprehension, that this necessity may be against men's wills and sincere endeavors. They go away with that notion, that men may truly will, and wish, and strive, that it may be otherwise, but that invincible necessity stands in the way. And many think thus concerning themselves: some, that are wicked men, think they wish that they were good, that they love God and holiness; but yet do not find that their wishes produce the effect.—The reasons why men think so, are as follow:

(1.) They find what may be called an indirect willingness to have a better will, in the manner before observed. For it is impossible, and a contradiction, to suppose the will to be directly and properly against itself. And they do not consider, that this indirect willingness is entirely a different thing from properly willing the thing that is the duty and virtue required; and that there is no virtue in that sort of willingness which they have. They do not consider, that the volitions which a wicked man may have that he loved God, are no acts of the will at all against the moral evil of not loving God; but only some disagreeable consequences. But the making the requisite distinction requires more care of reflection and thought than most men are used to. And men, through a prejudice in their own favour, are disposed to think well of their own desires and dispositions, and to account them good and virtuous, though their respect to virtue be only indirect and remote, and it is nothing at all that is virtuous that truly excites or terminates their inclinations.

(2.) Another thing that insensibly lends and beguiles men into a supposition that this moral necessity or impossibility is, or may be, against men's wills and true endeavors, is the derivation and formation of the terms themselves, that are often used to express it, which is such as seems directly to point to, and holds this forth. Such words, for instance, as unable, unavoidable, impossible, irresistible, which carry a plain reference to a supposable posable exerted, endeavors used, resistance made, in opposition to the necessity; and the persons that hear them, not considering nor suspecting but that they are used in their proper sense; that sense being therefore understood, there does naturally, and as it inhere necessarily, arise in their minds a supposition, that it may be so indeed, that true desires and endeavors may take place, but that invincible necessity stands in the way, and renders them vain and to no effect.

V. Another thing, which makes persons more ready to suppose it to be contrary to reason, that men should be exposed to the punishments threatened to sin, for doing those things which are morally necessary, or not doing those things morally impossible, is, that imagination strengthens the argument, and adds greatly to the power and influence of the seeming reasons against it, from the greatness of that punishment. To allow that they may be justly exposed to a small punishment, would not be so difficult. Whereas, if there were any good reason in the case, if it were truly a dictate of reason, that such necessity was inconsistent with faultiness, or just punishment, the demonstration would be equally certain with respect to a small punishment, or any punishment at all, as a very great one; but it is not equally easy to the imagination. They that argue against the justice of damning men for those things that are thus necessary, seem to make their argument the stronger, by setting forth the greatness of the punishment in strong expressions:—"That a man should be cast into eternal burnings, that he should be made to fry in hell to all eternity, for those things which he had no power to avoid, and was under a fatal, unfrustrable, invincible necessity of doing."

PART IV. SECTION IV. IT IS AGREEABLE TO COMMON SENSE, AND THE NATURAL NOTIONS OF MANKIND, TO SUPPOSE MORAL NECESSITY TO BE CONSISTENT WITH PRAISE AND BLAME, REWARD AND PUNISHMENT.

Whether the reasons that have been given, why it appears difficult to some persons to reconcile with common sense the praising or blaming, rewarding or punishing those things which are morally necessary, are thought satisfactory, or not; yet it most evidently appears, by the following things, that if this matter be rightly understood, setting aside all delusion arising from the impropriety and ambiguity of terms, this is not at all inconsistent with the natural apprehensions of mankind, and that sense of things which is found every where in the common people, who are furthest from having their thoughts perverted from their natural channel, by metaphysical and philosophical subtleties; but, on the contrary, altogether agreeable to, and the very voice and dictate of, this natural and vulgar sense.

I. This will appear, if we consider what the vulgar notion of blameworthiness is. The idea which the common people, through all ages and nations, have of faultiness, I suppose to be plainly this; a person's being or doing wrong, with his own will and pleasure; containing these two things:

1. His doing wrong when he does as he pleases.

2. His pleasures being wrong.

Or, in other words, perhaps more intelligibly expressing their notion, a person's having his heart wrong; and doing wrong from his heart. And this is the sum total of the matter.

The common people do not ascend up in their reflections and abstractions to the metaphysical sources, relations, and dependencies of things, in order to form their notion of faultiness or blameworthiness. They do not wait till they have decided by their refinings, what first determines the will; whether it be determined by something extrinsic or intrinsic; whether volition determines volition, or whether the understanding determines the will; whether there be any such thing as metaphysicians mean by contingence (if they have any meaning); whether there be a sort of a strange, unaccountable sovereignty in the will, in the exercise of which, by its own sovereign acts, it brings to pass all its own sovereign acts. They do not take any part of their notion of fault or blame from the resolution of any such question. If this were the case, there are multitudes, yea, the far greater part of mankind, nine hundred and ninety-nine out of a thousand, would live and die without having any such notion as that of fault ever entering into their heads, or without so much as one having any conception that any body was to be either blamed or commended for any thing. To be sure it would be a long time before men came to have such notions. Whereas it is manifest, they are some of the first notions that appear in children; who discover, as soon as they can think, or speak, or act at all as rational creatures, a sense of desert. And certainly, in forming their notion of it, they make no use of metaphysics. All the ground they go upon consists in these two things: experience, and a natural sensation of a certain fitness or agreeableness which there is in uniting such moral evil as is above described, viz, a being or doing wrong with the will, and resentment in others, and pain inflicted on the person in whom this moral evil is. Which natural sense is what we call by the name of conscience.

It is true, the common people and children, in their notion of any faulty act or deed, of any person, do suppose that it is the person's own act and deed. But this is all that belongs to what they understand by a thing's being a person's own deed or action; even that it is something done by him of choice. That some exercise or motion should begin of itself, does not belong to their notion of an action or doing. If so, it would belong to their notion of it, that it is something which is the cause of its own beginning; and that is as much as to say, that it is before it begins to be. Nor is their notion of an action, some motion or exercise that begins accidentally, without any cause or reason; for that is contrary to one of the prime dictates of common sense, namely, that every thing that begins to be, has some cause or reason why it is.

The common people, in their notion of a faulty or praiseworthy deed or work done by any one, do suppose that the man does it in the exercise of liberty. But then their notion of liberty is only a person's having opportunity of doing as he pleases. They have no notion of liberty consisting in the will's first acting, and so causing its own acts; and determining, and so causing its own determinations; or choosing, and so causing its own choice. Such a notion of liberty is what none have, but those that have darkened their own minds with confused meta-physical speculation, and abstruse and ambiguous terms. If a man is not restrained from acting as his will determines, or constrained to act otherwise, then he has liberty, according to common notions of liberty, without taking into the idea that grand contradiction of all, the determinations of a man's free will being the effects of the determinations of his free will.—Nor have men commonly any notion of freedom consisting in indifference. For if so, then it would be agreeable to their notion, that the greater indifference men act with, the more freedom they act with; whereas the reverse is true. He that, in acting, proceeds with the fullest inclination, does what he does with the greatest freedom, according to common sense. And so far is it from being agreeable to common sense, that such liberty as consists in indifference is requisite to praise or blame, that, on the contrary, the dictate of every man's natural sense through the world is, that the further he is from being indifferent in his acting good or evil, and the more he does either with full and strong inclination, the more is he esteemed or abhorred, commended or condemned.

II. If it were inconsistent with the common sense of mankind, that men should be either to be blamed or commended in any volitions they have or fail of, in case of moral necessity or impossibility; then it would surely also be agreeable to the same sense and reason of mankind, that the nearer the case approaches to such a moral necessity or impossibility, either through a strong antecedent moral propensity, on the one hand or a great antecedent opposition and difficulty on the other, the nearer does it approach to a being neither blameable nor commendable; so that acts exerted with such preceding propensity, would be worthy of proportionably less praise; and when omitted, the act being attended with such difficulty, the omission would be worthy of less blame. It is so, as was observed before, with natural necessity and impossibility, propensity and difficulty: as it is a plain dictate of the sense of all mankind, that natural necessity and impossibility take away all blame and praise; and therefore, that the nearer the approach is to these, through previous propensity or difficulty, so praise and blame are proportionably diminished. And if it were as much a dictate of common sense, that moral necessity of doing or impossibility of avoiding takes away all praise and blame, as that natural necessity or impossibility does this; then, by a perfect parity of reason, it would be as much the dictate of common sense, that an approach to moral necessity of doing, or impossibility of avoiding, diminishes praise and blame, as that an approach to natural necessity and impossibility does so. It is equally the voice of common sense, that persons are excusable in part in neglecting things difficult against their wills, as that they are excusable wholly in neglecting things impossible against their wills. And if it made no difference, whether the impossibility were natural and against the will, or moral lying in the will, with regard to excusableness; so neither would it make any difference, whether the difficulty, or approach to necessity, be natural against the will, or moral, lying in the propensity of the will.

But it is apparent, that the reverse of these things is true. If there be an approach to a moral necessity in a man's exertion of good acts of will, they being the exercise of a strong propensity to good, and a very powerful love to virtue; it is so far from being the dictate of common sense, that he is less virtuous, and the less to be esteemed, loved, and praised; that it is agreeable to the natural notions of all mankind, that he is so much the better man, worthy of greater respect, and higher commendation. And the stronger the inclination is, and the nearer it approaches to necessity in that respect; or to impossibility of neglecting the virtuous act, or of doing a vicious one; still the more virtuous, and worthy of higher commendation. And, on the other hand, if a man exerts evil acts of mind; as for instance, acts of pride or malice, from a rooted and strong habit or principle of haughtiness and maliciousness, and a violent propensity of heart to such acts; according to the natural sense of men, he is so far from being the less hateful and blameable on that account, that he is so much the more worthy to be detested and condemned by all that observe him.

Moreover, it is manifest that it is no part of the notion, which mankind commonly have of a blameable or praiseworthy act of the will, that it is an act which is not determined by an antecedent bias or motive, but by the sovereign power of the will itself; because, if so, the greater hand such causes have in determining any acts of the will, so much the less virtuous or vicious would they be accounted; and the less hand, the more virtuous or vicious. Whereas the reverse is true: men do not think a good act to be the less praiseworthy for the agent's being much determined in it by a good inclination or a good motive, but the more. And if good inclination or motive has but little influence in determining the agent, they do not think his act so much the more virtuous, but the less. And so concerning evil acts, which are determined by evil motives or inclinations.

Yea, if it be supposed, that good or evil dispositions are implanted in the hearts of men by nature itself; (which, it is certain, is vulgarly supposed in innumerable cases,) yet it is not commonly supposed, that men are worthy of no praise or dispraise for such dispositions; although what is natural is undoubtedly necessary, nature being prior to all acts of the will whatsoever. Thus, for instance, if a man appears to be of a very haughty or malicious disposition, and is supposed to be so by his natural temper, it is no vulgar notion, no dictate of the common sense and apprehension of men, that such dispositions are no vices or moral evils, or that such persons are not worthy of disesteem, or odium and dishonour; or that the proud or malicious acts which flow from such natural dispositions, are worthy of no resentment. Yea, such vile natural dispositions, and the strength of them, will commonly be mentioned rather as an aggravation of the wicked acts that come from such a fountain, than an extenuation of them. Its being natural for men to act thus, is often observed by men in the height of their indignation: they will say, "It is his very nature; he is of a vile natural temper; it is as natural to him to act so, as it is to breathe; he cannot help serving the devil," &c. But it is not thus with regard to hurtful, mischievous things, that any are the subjects or occasions of, by natural necessity, against their inclinations. In such a case, the necessity, by the common voice of mankind, will be spoken of as a full excuse.—Thus, it is very plain, that common sense makes a vast difference between these two kinds of necessity, as to the judgment it makes of their influence on the moral quality and desert of men's actions.

And these dictates of men's minds are so natural and necessary, that it may be very much doubted whether, the Arminians themselves have ever got rid of them; yea, their greatest doctors, that have gone furthest in defense of their metaphysical notions of liberty, and have brought their arguments to their greatest strength, and, as they suppose, to a demonstration, against the consistence of virtue and vice with any necessity; it is to be questioned, whether there is so much as one of them, but that, if he suffered very much from the injurious acts of a man under the power of an invincible haughtiness and malignancy of temper, would not, from the fore-mentioned natural sense of mind, resent it far otherwise, than if as great sufferings came upon him from the wind that blows, and fire that burns, by natural necessity; and otherwise than he would, if he suffered as much from the conduct of a man perfectly delirious; yea, though he first brought his distraction upon him some way by his own fault.

Some seem to disdain the distinction that we make between natural and moral necessity, as though it were altogether impertinent in this controversy: "that which is necessary (say they) is necessary; it is that which must be, and cannot be prevented. And that which is impossible, is impossible, and cannot be done: and therefore none can be to blame for not doing it." And such comparisons are made use of, as the commanding of a man to walk who has lost his legs, and condemning and punishing him for not obeying; inviting and calling upon a man who is shut up in a strong prison, to come forth, &c. But, in these things, Arminians are very unreasonable. Let common sense determine whether there be not a great difference between these two cases; the one, that of a man who has offended his prince, and is cast into prison; and after he has laid there a while, the king comes to him, calls him to come forth to him; and tells him, that if he will do so, and will fall down before him, and humbly beg his pardon, he shall be forgiven and set at liberty, and also be greatly enriched, and advanced to honour; the prisoner heartily repents of the folly and wickedness of his offence against his prince, is thoroughly disposed to abase himself, and accept of the king's offer; but is confined by strong walls, with gates of brass, and bars of iron. The other case is, that of a man who is of a very unreasonable spirit, of a haughty, ungrateful, wilful disposition; and, moreover, has been brought up in traitorous principles, and has his heart possessed with an extreme and inveterate enmity to his lawful sovereign; and for his rebellion is cast into prison, and lies long there, loaded with heavy chains, and in miserable circumstances. At length the compassionate prince comes to the prison, orders his chains to be knocked off, and his prison-doors to be set wide open; calls to him, and tells him, if he will come forth to him, and fall down before him, acknowledge that he has treated him unworthily, and ask his forgiveness, he shall be forgiven, set at liberty, and set in a place of great dignity and profit in his court. But he is stout and stomachful, and full of haughty malignity, that he cannot be willing to accept the offer: his rooted strong pride and malice have perfect power over him, and as it were bind him, by binding his heart: the opposition of his heart has the mastery over him, having an influence on his mind far superior to the king's grace and condescension, and to all his kind offers and promises. Now, is it agreeable to common sense to assert, and stand to it, that there is no difference between these two cases, as to any worthiness of blame in the prisoners; because, forsooth, there is a necessity in both, and the required act in each case is impossible?

It is true, a man's evil dispositions may be as strong and immoveable as the bars of a castle. But who cannot see, that when a man, in the latter case, is said to be unable to obey the command, the expression is used improperly, and not in the sense it has originally, and in common speech; and that it may properly be said to be in the rebel's power to come out of prison, seeing he can easily do it if he pleases; though by reason of his vile temper of heart, which is fixed and rooted, it is impossible that it should please him?

Upon the whole, I presume there is no person of good understanding, who impartially considers the things which have been observed, but will allow, that it is not evident, from the dictates of the common sense, or natural notions of mankind, that moral necessity is inconsistent with praise and blame. And, therefore, if the Arminians would prove any such inconsistency, it must be by some philosophical and metaphysical arguments, and not common sense.

There is a grand illusion in the pretended demonstration of Arminians from common sense. The main strength of all these demonstrations lies in that prejudice, that arises through the insensible change of the use and meaning of such terms as liberty, able, unable, necessary, impossible, unavoidable, invincible, action, &c. from their original and vulgar sense, to a metaphysical sense, entirely diverse; and the strong connection of the ideas of blamelessness, &c. with some of these terms, by a habit contracted and established while these terms were used in their first meaning. This prejudice and delusion is the foundation of all those positions they lay down as maxims, by which most of the Scriptures, which they allege in this controversy, are interpreted, and on which all their pompous demonstrations from Scripture and reason depend. From this secret delusion and prejudice they have almost all their advantages; it is the strength of their bulwarks, and the edge of their weapons. And this is the main ground of all the right they have to treat their neighbours in so assuming a manner, and to insult others, perhaps as wise and good as themselves, as weak bigots, men that dwell in the dark caves of superstition, perversely set, obstinately shutting their eyes against the noon-day light, enemies to common sense, maintaining the first-born of absurdities, &c. &c. But perhaps an impartial consideration of the things which have been observed in the preceding parts of this Inquiry, may enable the lovers of truth better to judge, whose doctrine is indeed absurd, abstruse, self-contradictory, and inconsistent with common sense, and many ways repugnant to the universal dictates of the reason of mankind.

Corol. From things which have been observed, it will follow, that it is agreeable to common sense to suppose that the glorified saints have not their freedom at all diminished in any respect: and that God himself has the highest possible freedom according to the true and proper meaning of the term; and that he is, in the highest possible respect, an agent and active in the exercise of his infinite holiness; though he acts therein, in the highest degree necessarily: and his actions of this kind, are in the highest, most absolutely perfect manner, virtuous and praiseworthy; and are so, for that very reason, because they are most perfectly necessary.

PART IV. SECTION V. CONCERNING THOSE OBJECTIONS, THAT THIS SCHEME OF NECESSITY RENDERS ALL MEANS AND ENDEAVOURS FOR THE AVOIDING OF SIN, OR THE OBTAINING VIRTUE AND HOLINESS, VAIN AND TO NO PURPUSE; AND THAT IT MAKES MEN NO MORE THAN MERE MACHINES IN AFFAIRS OF MORALITY AND RELIGION

Arminians say, if it be so, that sin and virtue come to pass by a necessity consisting in a sure connection of causes and effects, antecedents and consequents, it can never be worth the while to use any means or endeavours to obtain the one, and avoid the other; seeing no endeavours can alter the futurity of the event, which is become necessary by a connection already established.

But I desire that this matter may be fully considered; and that it may be examined with a thorough strictness, whether it will follow, that endeavours and means, in order to avoid or obtain any future thing, must be more in vain, on the supposition of such a connection of antecedents and consequents than if the contrary be supposed. For endeavours to be in vain, is for them not to be successful; that is to say, for them not eventually to be the means of the thing aimed at, which cannot be but in one of these two ways; either, first, That although the means are used, yet the event aimed at does not follow; or, secondly, If the event does follow, it is not because of the means, or from any connection or dependence of the event on the means: the event would have come to pass as well without the means as with them. If either of these two things is the case, then the means are not properly successful, and are truly in vain. The successfulness or unsuccessfulness of means, in order to an effect, or their being in vain or not in vain, consists in those means being connected or not connected with the effect, in such a manner as this, viz. that the effect is with the means, and not without them; or, that the being of the effect is, on the one hand, connected with means, and the want of the effect, on the other hand, is connected with the want of the means. If there be such a connection, as this between means and end, the means are not in vain; the more there is of such a connection, the further they are from being in vain; and the less of such a connection, the more they are in vain.

Now, therefore, the question to be answered, (in order to determine, whether it follows from this doctrine of the necessary connection between foregoing things and consequent ones, that means used in order to any effect are more in vain than they would be otherwise), is, whether it follows from it that there is less of the forementioned connection between means and effect; that is, whether, on the supposition of there being a real and true connection between means and effect, than on the supposition of there being no fixed connection between antecedent things and consequent ones; and the very stating of this question is sufficient to answer it. It must appear to every one that will open his eyes, that this question cannot be affirmed without the grossest absurdity and inconsistence. Means are foregoing things, and effects are following things. And if there were no connection between foregoing things and following ones, there could be no connection between means and end; and so all means would be wholly vain and fruitless. For it is by virtue of some connection only, that they become successful. It is some connection observed or revealed, or otherwise known, between antecedent things and following ones, that is what directs in the choice of means. And if there were no such thing as an established connection, there could be no choice as to means; one thing would have no more tendency to an effect than another; there would be no such thing as tendency in the case. All those things which are successful means of other things, do therein prove connected antecedents of them; and therefore, to assert that a fixed connection between antecedents and consequents makes means vain and useless, or stands in the way to hinder the connection between means and end, is just as ridiculous as to say, that a connection between antecedents and consequents stands in the way to hinder a connection between antecedents and consequents.

Nor can any supposed connection of the succession or train of antecedents and consequents, from the very beginning of all things, the
connection being made already sure and necessary, either by established
laws of nature, or by these together with a decree of sovereign immediate
interpositions of Divine power, on such and such occasions, or any other
way (if any other there be); I say, no such necessary connection of a
series of antecedents and consequents can in the least tend to hinder, but
that the means we use may belong to the series; and so may be some of
those antecedents which are connected with the consequents we aim at
in the established course of things. Endeavours which we use, are things
that exist; and therefore they belong to the general chain of events; all
the parts of which chain are supposed to be connected; and so endeavours
are supposed to be connected with some effects, or some consequent
things or other. And certainly this does not hinder but that the events
they are connected with, may be those which we aim at, and which we
choose, because we judge them most likely to have a connection with
those events from the established order and course of things which we
observe, or from something in Divine revelation.

Let us suppose a real and true connection between a man's having
his eyes open in the clear day-light, with good organs of sight, and
seeing; so that seeing is connected with his opening his eyes, and not
seeing with his not opening his eyes; and also the like connection between such a man's attempting to open his eyes, and his actually doing
it: the supposed established connection between these antecedents and
consequents, let the connection be never so sure and necessary, certainly
does not prove that it is in vain for a man in such circumstances to
attempt to open his eyes, in order to seeing: his aiming at that event,
and the use of the means, being the effect of his will, does not break the
connection, or hinder the success.

So that the objection we are upon does not lie against the doctrine
of the necessity of events by a certainty of connection and consequence;
on the contrary, it is truly forcible against the Arminian doctrine of
contingence and self-determination; which is inconsistent with such a
connection. If there be no connection between those events wherein
virtue and vice consist, and any thing antecedent; then there is no connection between these events and any means or endeavours used in order
to them; and if so, then those means must be in vain. The less there is
of connection between foregoing things and following ones, so much

the less there is between means and end, endeavours and success; and in the same proportion are means and endeavours ineffectual and in vain.

It will follow from Arminian principles that there is no degree of connection between virtue or vice, and any foregoing event or thing; or, in other words, that the determination of the existence of virtue or vice does not in the least depend on the influence of any thing that comes to pass antecedently, from which the determination of its existence is, as its cause, means, or ground; because so far as it is so, it is not from self-determination; and, therefore, so far there is nothing of the nature of virtue or vice. And so it follows, that virtue and vice are not at all, in any degree, dependent upon, or connected with, any foregoing event or existence, as its cause, ground, or means. And if so, then all foregoing means must be totally in vain.

Hence it follows, that there cannot, in any consistence with the Arminian scheme, be any reasonable ground of so much as a conjecture concerning the consequence of any means and endeavours, in order to escaping vice, or obtaining virtue, or any choice or preference of means, as having a greater probability of success by some than others; either from any natural connection or dependence of the end on the means, or through any divine constitution, or revealed way of God's bestowing or bringing to pass these things, in consequence of any means, endeavours, prayers, or deeds. Conjectures in this latter ease, depend on a supposition, that God himself is the giver, or determining cause, of the events sought; but if they depend on self-determination, then God is not the determining or disposing author of them; and if these things are not of his disposal, then no conjecture can be made, from any revelation he has given, concerning any way or method of his disposal of them.

Yea, on these principles, it will not only follow, that men cannot have any reasonable ground of judgment or conjecture that their means and endeavours to obtain virtue, or avoid vice, will be successful, but they may be sure they will not; they may be certain that they will be in vain; and that if ever the thing, which they seek, comes to pass, it will not be at all owing to the means they use. For means and endeavours can have no effect at all, in order to obtain the end, but in one of those two ways; either (1.) Through a natural tendency and influence to prepare and dispose the mind more to virtuous acts, either by causing the disposition of the heart to be more in favour of such acts, or by bringing the mind more into the view of powerful motives and inducements; or, (2) By putting persons more in the way of God's bestowment of the benefit. But neither of these can be the case. Not the latter; for, as has been just observed, it does not consist with the Arminian notion of self-determination, which they suppose essential to virtue, that God should be the bestower, or (which is the same thing) the determining disposing author of virtue. Not the form; for natural influence aud tendency supposes causality and connection, and supposes necessity of event, which is inconsistent with Arminian liberty. A tendency of means, by biasing the heart in favour of virtue, or by bringing the will under the influence and power of motives in its determinations, are both inconsistent with Arminian liberty of will, consisting in indifference, and sovereign self-determination, as has been largely demonstrated.

But for the more full removal of this prejudice against the doctrine of necessity, which has been maintained, as though it tended to encourage a total neglect of all endeavours as vain; the following things may be considered:—The question is not, Whether men may not thus improve this doctrine,—we know that many true and wholesome doctrines are abused; but, whether the doctrine gives any just occasion for such an improvement; or whether, on the supposition of the truth of the doctrine, such a use of it would be unreasonable? If any shall affirm, that it would not, but that the very nature of the doctrine is such as gives just occasion for it, it must be on this supposition; namely, that such an invariable necessity of all things already settled, must render the interposition of all means, endeavours, conclusions, or actions of ours, in order to the obtaining any future end whatsoever, perfectly insignificant; because they cannot in the least alter or vary the course and series of things, in any event or circumstance; all being already fixed unutterably by necessity; and that therefore it is folly for men to use any means for any end; but their wisdom to save themselves the trouble of endeavours, and take their ease. No person can draw such an inference from this doctrine, and come to such a conclusion, without contradicting himself, and going counter to the very principles he pretends to act upon; for he comes to a conclusion and takes a course, in order to an end, even his ease, or the saving himself from trouble; he seeks something future, and uses means in order to a future thing, even in his drawing up that conclusion, that he will seek nothing, and use no means in order to any thing in future; he seeks his future ease, and the benefit and comfort of indolence. If prior necessity, that determines all things, makes vain, all actions or conclusions of ours, in order to any thing future; then it makes vain all conclusions and conduct of ours, in order to our future ease. The measure of our ease, with the time, manner, and every circumstance of it, is already fixed, by all-determining necessity, as much as any thing else. If he says within himself, "What future happiness or misery I shall have, is already, in effect, determined by the necessary course and connection of things; therefore, I will save myself the trouble of labor and diligence which cannot add to my determined degree of happiness, or diminish my misery; but will take my ease, and will enjoy the comfort of sloth and negligence,"—such a man contradicts himself; he says, the measure of his future happiness and misery is already fixed, and he will not try to diminish the one, nor add to the other; but yet, in his very conclusion, he contradicts this; for, he takes up this conclusion, to add to his future happiness, by the ease and comfort of his negligence, and to diminish his future trouble and misery by saving himself the trouble of using means and taking pains.

Therefore, persons cannot reasonably make this improvement of the doctrine of necessity, that they will go into a voluntary negligence of means for their own happiness. For the principles they must go upon, in order to this, are inconsistent with their making any improvement at all of the doctrine; for to make some improvement of it, is to be influenced by it, to come to some voluntary conclusion, in regard to their own conduct, with some view or aim; but this, as has been shown, is inconsistent with the principles they pretend to act upon. In short, the principles are such as cannot be acted upon at all, or, in any respect, consistently. And therefore, in every pretense of acting upon them, or making any improvement at all of them, there is a self-contradiction.

As to that objection against the doctrine, which I have endeavoured to prove, that it makes men no more than mere machines; I would say, that notwithstanding this doctrine, man is entirely, perfectly, and unspeakably different from a mere machine, in that he has reason and understanding, and has a faculty of will, and is so capable of volition and choice; and in that his will is guided by the dictates or views of his understanding; and in that his external actions and behavior, and in many respects also his thoughts, and the exercises of his mind, are subject to his will; so that he has liberty to act according to his choice, and do what he pleases; and, by means of these things, is capable of moral habits and moral acts, such inclinations and actions, as, according to the common sense of mankind, are worthy of praise, esteem, love, and reward; or, on the contrary, of disesteem, detestation, indignation, and punishment.

In these things is all the difference from mere machines, as to liberty and agency, that would be any perfection, dignity, or privilege, in any respect; all the difference that can be desired, and all that can be conceived of; and indeed all that the pretensions of the Arminians themselves come to, as they are forced often to explain themselves. (Though their explications overthrow and abolish the things asserted, and pretended to be explained,) For they are forced to explain a self-determining power of will, by a power in the soul to determine as it chooses or wills; which comes to no more than this, that a man has a power of choosing, and in many instances, can do as he chooses,—which is quite a different thing from that contradiction, his having power of choosing his first act of choice in the case.

Or, if their scheme makes any other difference than this between men and machines, it is for the worse; it is so far from supposing men to have a dignity and privilege above machines, that it makes the manner of their being determined still more unhappy. Whereas machines are guided by an understanding cause, by the skillful hand of the workman or owner; the will of man is left to the guidance of nothing but absolute blind contingence.

PART IV. SECTION VI. CONCERNING THAT OBJECTION AGAINST THE DOCTRINE WHICH HAS BEEN MAINTAINED, THAT IT AGREES WITH THE STOICAL DOCTRINE OF FAITH, AND THE OPINIONS OF MR. HOBBES.

When Calvinists oppose the Arminian notion of the freedom of will, and contingence of volition, and insist that there are no acts of the will, nor any other event whatsoever, but what are attended with some kind of necessity; their opposers cry out of them, as agreeing with the ancient Stoics in their doctrine of fate, and with Mr. Hobbes in his opinion of necessity.

It would not be worth while to take notice of so impertinent an objection, had it not been urged by some of the chief Arminian writers. There were many important truths maintained by the ancient Greek and Roman philosophers, and especially the Stoics, that are never the worse for being held by them. The Stoic philosophers, by the general agreement of Christian divines, and even Arminian divines, were the greatest, wisest, and most virtuous of all the heathen philosophers; and in their doctrine and practice came the nearest to Christianity of any of their sects. How frequently are the sayings of these philosophers, in many of the writings and sermons, even of Arminian divines, produced, not as arguments of the falseness of the doctrines which they delivered, but as a confirmation of some of the greatest truths of the Christian religion, relating to the unity and perfections of the Godhead, a future state, the duty and happiness of mankind, &c., as observing how the light of nature, and reason, in the wisest and best of the heathen, harmonized with and confirms the gospel of Jesus Christ.

And it is very remarkable, concerning Dr. Whitby, that although he alleges the agreement of the Stoics with us, wherein he supposes they maintained the like doctrine with us, as an argument against the truth of our doctrine; yet this very Dr. Whitby alleges the agreement of the Stoics with the Arminians, wherein he supposes they taught the same doctrine with them, as an argument for the truth of their doctrine. So that, when the Stoics agree with them, this (it seems) is a confirmation of their doctrine, and a confutation of ours, as showing that our opinions are contrary to the natural sense and common reason of mankind: nevertheless, when the Stoics agree with us, it argues no such thing in our favour; but, on the contrary, is a great argument against, us, and shows our doctrine to be heathenish.

It is observed by some Calvinistic writers, that the Arminians symbolise with the Stoics in some of those doctrines wherein they are opposed by the Calvinists; particularly in their denying an original, innate, total corruption and depravity of heart; and in what they held of man's ability to make himself truly virtuous and conformed to God; and in some other doctrines.

It may be further observed, it is certainly no better objection against our doctrine, that it agrees, in some respects, with the doctrine of the ancient Stoic philosophers, than it is against theirs, wherein they differ from us, that it agrees, in some respects, with the opinion of the very worst of the heathen philosophers, the followers of Epicurus, that father of atheism and licentiousness, and with the doctrine of the Sadducees and Jesuits.

I am not much concerned to know precisely what the ancient Stoic philosophers held concerning fate, in order to determine what is truth; as though it were a sure way to be in the right, to take good heed to differ from them. It seems that they differed among themselves; and probably the doctrine of fate, as maintained by most of them, was, in some respects, erroneous. But whatever their doctrine was, if any of them held such a fate as is repugnant to any liberty, consisting in our doing as we please, I utterly deny such a fate. If they held any such fate as is not consistent with the common and universal notions that mankind have of liberty, activity, moral agency, virtue and vice; I disclaim any such thing, and think I have demonstrated that the scheme I maintain is no such scheme. If the Stoics, by fate, meant any thing of such a nature as can be supposed to stand in the way of the advantage and benefit of the use of means and endeavours, or make it less worth the while for men to desire and seek after any thing wherein their virtue and happiness consists; I hold no doctrine that is clogged with any such inconvenience, any more than any other scheme whatsoever; and by no means so much as the Arminian scheme of contingence; as has been shown. If they held any such doctrine of universal fatality as is inconsistent with any kind of liberty, that is or can be any perfection, dignity, privilege or benefit, or any thing desirable, in any respect, for any intelligent creature, or indeed with any liberty that is possible or conceivable; I embrace no such doctrine. If they held any such doctrine of fate as is inconsistent with the world's being in all things subject to the disposal of an intelligent wise Agent, that presides, not as the soul of the world, but as the sovereign Lord of the universe, governing all things by proper will, choice, and design, in the exercise of the most perfect liberty conceivable, without subjection to any constraint, or being properly under the power or influence of any thing before, above, or without himself; I wholly renounce any such doctrine.

As to Mr. Hobbes's maintaining the same doctrine concerning necessity; I confess it happens I never read Mr. Hobbes. Let his opinion be what it will, we need not reject all truth which is demonstrated by clear evidence, merely because it was once held by some mad man. This great truth, that Jesus is the Son of God, was not spoiled because it was once and again proclaimed with a loud voice by the devil. If truth is so defiled, because it is spoken by the mouth, or written by the pen, of some ill-minded mischievous man, that it must never be received, we shall never know when we hold any of the most precious and evident truths by a sure tenure. And if Mr. Hobbes has made a bad use of this truth, that is to be lamented; but the truth is not to be thought worthy of rejection on that account. It is common for the corruptions of the hearts of evil men to abuse the best things to vile purposes. I might also take notice of its having been observed, that the Arminians agree with Mr.

Hobbes in many more things than the Calvinists;—as, in what he is said to hold concerning original sin, in denying the necessity of supernatural illumination, in denying infused grace, in denying the doctrine of justification by faith alone; and other things.

PART IV. SECTION VII. CONCERNING THE NECESSITY OF THE DIVINE WILL

Some may possibly object against what has been supposed of the absurdity and inconsistence of a self-determining power in the will, and the impossibility of its being otherwise than that the will should be determined in every case by some motive, and by a motive which (as it stands in the view of the understanding) is of superior strength to any appearing on the other side; that if these things are true, it will follow, that not only the will of created minds, but the will of God himself, is necessary in all its determinations. Concerning which, says the author of the Essay on the Freedom of Will in God and in the Creature, (pp. 85, 86) "What strange doctrine is this, contrary to all our ideas of the dominion of God? does it not destroy the glory of his liberty of choice, and take away from the Creator and Governor and Benefactor of the world, that most free and sovereign agent, all the glory of this sort of freedom? does it not seem to make him a kind of mechanical medium of fate, and introduce Mr. Hobbe's doctrine of fatality and necessity into all things that God hath to do with? Does it not seem to represent the blessed God as a being of vast understanding, as well as power and efficiency, but still to leave him without a will to choose among all the objects within his view? In short, it seems to make the blessed God a sort of almighty minister of fate, under its universal and supreme influence; as it was the professed sentiment of some of the ancients, that fate was above the gods."

This is declaiming, rather than arguing; and an application to men's imaginations and prejudices, rather than to mere reason. But I would calmly endeavour to consider, whether there be any reason in this frightful representation.—But before I enter upon a particular consideration of the matter, I should observe this: that it is reasonable to suppose, it should be much more difficult to express or conceive things according to exact metaphysical truth, relating to the nature and manner of the existence of things in the Divine understanding and will, and the operation of these faculties (if I may so call them) of the Divine mind, than in the human mind; which is infinitely more within our view, and nearer to a proportion to the measure of our comprehension, and more commensurate to the use and import of human speech. Language is indeed very deficient in regard of terms to express precise truth concerning our own minds, and their faculties and operations. Words were first formed to express external things; and those that are applied to express things internal and spiritual, are almost all borrowed, and used in a sort of figurative sense. Whence they are, most of them, attended with a great deal of ambiguity and unfixedness in their signification, occasioning innumerable doubts, difficulties, and confusions, in inquiries and controversies about things of this nature. But language is much less adapted to express things in the mind of the incomprehensible Deity precisely as they are.

We find a great deal of difficulty in conceiving exactly of the nature of our own souls. And notwithstanding all the progress which has been made, in past and present ages, in this kind of knowledge, whereby our metaphysics, as it relates to these things, is brought to greater perfection than once it was; yet, here is still work enough left for future inquiries and researches, and room for progress still to be made, for many ages and generations. But we had need to be infinitely able metaphysicians, to conceive with clearness, according to strict, proper, and perfect truth, concerning the nature of the Divine Essence, and the modes of the action and operation of the powers of the Divine Mind.

And it may be noted particularly, that though we are obliged to conceive of some things in God as consequent and dependent on others, and of some things pertaining to the Divine nature and will as the foundation of others, and so before others in the order of nature; as, we must conceive of the knowledge and holiness of God as prior, in the order of nature, to his happiness; the perfection of his understanding, as the foundation of his wise purposes and decrees; the holiness of his nature, as the cause and reason of his holy determinations. And yet, when we speak of cause and effect, antecedent and consequent, fundamental and dependent, determining and determined, in the first Being, who is self-existent, independent, of perfect and absolute simplicity and immutability, and the first cause of all things; doubtless there must be less propriety in such representations, than when we speak of derived dependent beings, who are compounded, and liable to perpetual mutation and succession.

Having premised this, I proceed to observe concerning the fore-mentioned author's exclamation about the necessary determination of God's will, in all things, by what he sees to be fittest and best.

That all the seeming force of such objections and exclamations must arise from an imagination that there is some sort of privilege or dignity in being without such a moral necessity as will make it impossible to do any other than always choose what is wisest and best; as though there were some disadvantage, meanness, and subjection, in such a necessity; a thing by which the will was confined, kept under, and held in servitude by something, which, as it were, maintained a strong and invincible power and dominion over it, by bonds that held him fast, and that he could, by no means, deliver himself from. Whereas, this must be all mere imagination and delusion. It is no disadvantage or dishonour to a being, necessarily to act in the most excellent and happy manner, from the necessary perfection of his own nature. This argues no imperfection, inferiority, or dependence, nor any avant of dignity, privilege, or ascendancy. It is not inconsistent with the absolute and most perfect sovereignty of God. The sovereignty of God is his ability and authority to do whatever pleases him; whereby "he doth according to his will in the armies of heaven, and amongst the inhabitants of the earth; and none can stay his hand, or say unto him, What dost thou?"—The following things belong to the sovereignty of God: viz.

(1.) Supreme, universal, and infinite power: whereby he is able to do what he pleases, without control, without any confinement of that power, without any subjection, in the least measure, to any other power; and so without any hindrance or restraint, that it should be either impossible, or at all difficult, for him to accomplish his will; and without any dependance of his power on any other power, from whence it should be derived, or which it should stand in any need of; so far from this, that all other power is derived from him, and is absolutely dependent on him.

(2.) That he has supreme authority; absolute and most perfect right to do what he wills, without subjection to any superior authority, or any derivation of authority from any other, or limitation by any distinct independent authority, either superior, equal, or inferior; he being the head of all dominion, and fountain of all authority; and also without restraint by any obligation, implying either subjection, derivation, or dependence, or proper limitation.

(3.) That his will is supreme, underived, and independent on any thing without himself; being in every thing determined by his own counsel, having no other rule but his own wisdom; his will not being subject to, or restrained by, the will of any other, and other wills being perfectly subject to his.

(4.) That his wisdom, which determines his will, is supreme, perfect, underived, self-sufficient, and independent; so that it may be said, as in Isaiah 40:14, 'With whom took he counsel, and who instructed him, and taught him in the path of judgment, and taught him knowledge, and showed to him the way of understanding?'—There is no other Divine sovereignty but this; and this is properly absolute sovereignty: no other is desirable; nor would any other be honourable or happy and, indeed, there is no other conceivable or possible: It is the glory and greatness of the Divine Sovereign, that Goal's will is determined by his own infinite, all-sufficient wisdom in every thing; and in nothing at all is either directed by any inferior wisdom, or by no wisdom; whereby it would become senseless arbitrariness, determining and acting without reason, design, or end.

If God's will is steadily and surely determined in every thing by supreme wisdom, then it is in every thing necessarily determined to that which is most wise. And, certainly, it would be a disadvantage and indignity to be otherwise. For if the Divine will was not necessarily determined to that which, in every case, is wisest and best, it must be subject, to some degree of undesigning contingence; and so in the same degree liable to evil. To suppose the Divine will liable to be carried hither and thither at random, by the uncertain wind of blind contingence, which is guided by no wisdom, no motive, no intelligent dictate whatsoever, (if any such thing were possible,) would certainly argue a great degree of imperfection and meanness, infinitely unworthy of the Deity. If it be a disadvantage for the Divine will to be attended with this moral necessity, then the more free from it, and the more left at random, the greater dignity and advantage. And, consequently, to be perfectly free from the direction of understanding, and universally and entirely left to senseless, unmeaning contingence, to act absolutely at random, would be the supreme glory.

It no more argues any dependence of God's will, that his supremely wise volition is necessary, than it argues a dependence of his being, that his existence is necessary. If it be something too low for the Supreme Being to have his will determined by moral necessity, so as necessarily, in every case, to will in the highest degree holy and happily; then why is it not also something too low for him to have his existence, and the infinite perfection of his nature, and his infinite happiness, determined by necessity? It is no more to God's dishonour to be necessarily wise, than to be necessarily holy. And if neither of them be to his dishonour, then it is not to his dishonour necessarily to act holily and wisely. And if it be not dishonorable to be necessarily holy and wise, in the highest possible degree, no more is it mean and dishonorable, necessarily to act holily and wisely in the highest possible degree; or, which is the same thing, to do that, in every case, which, above all other things, is wisest and best.

The reason why it is not dishonorable to be necessarily most holy, is, because holiness in itself is an excellent and honourable thing. For the same reason, it is no dishonour to be necessarily most wise, and, in every case, to act most wisely, or do the thing which is the wisest of all; for wisdom is also in itself excellent and honourable.

The fore-mentioned author of the "Essay on the Freedom of Will," &c. as has been observed, represents that doctrine of the Divine will's being in every thing necessarily determined by a superior fitness, as making the blessed God a kind of almighty minister and mechanical medium of fate; and he insists, (pp. 93, 94,) that this moral necessity and impossibility is, in effect, the same thing with physical and natural necessity and impossibility; and in pp. 54, 55, he says, "The scheme which determines the will always and certainly by the understanding, and understanding by the appearance of things, seems to take away the true nature of vice and virtue. For the sublimest of virtues, and the vilest of vices, seem rather to be matters of fate and necessity, flowing naturally and necessarily from the existence, the circumstances, and present situation of persons and things; for this existence and situation necessarily makes such an appearance to the mind; from this appearance flows a necessary perception and judgment concerning these things: this judgment necessarily determines the will; and thus, by this chain of necessary causes, virtue and vice would lose their nature, and become natural ideas, and necessary things, instead of moral and free actions."

And yet this same author allows, (pp. 30, 31,) that a perfectly wise being will constantly and certainly choose what is most fit; and says, pp. 102, 103, "I grant, and always have granted, that wheresoever there is such antecedent superior fitness of things, God acts according to it, so as never to contradict it; and, particularly, in all his judicial proceedings as a governor, and distributor of rewards and punishments." Yea, he says expressly, (p. 42,) "That it is not possible for God to act otherwise than according to this fitness and goodness in things."

So that, according to this author, putting these several passages of this essay together, there is no virtue, nor any thing of a moral nature, in the most sublime and glorious acts and exercises of God's holiness, justice, and faithfulness; and he never does any thing which is in itself supremely worthy, and, above all other things, fit and excellent, but only as a king of mechanical medium of fate; and in what he does as the judge and moral governor of the world, he exercises no moral excellency, exercising no freedom in these things, because he acts by moral necessity, which is, in effect, the same with physical or natural necessity; and therefore he only acts by an Hobbistical fatality; "as a being indeed of vast understanding, as well as power and efficiency, (as he said before,) but without a will to choose, being a kind of almighty administer of fate, acting under its supreme influence." For he allows, that in all these things, God's will is determined constantly and certainly by a superior fitness, and that it is not possible for him to act otherwise. And if these things are so, what glory or praise belongs to God for doing holily and justly; or taking the most fit, holy, wise, and excellent course, in any one instance? Whereas, according to the Scriptures, and also the common sense of mankind, it does not, in the least, derogate from the honour of any being, that through the moral perfection of his nature he necessarily acts with supreme wisdom and holiness; but on the contrary, his praise is the greater; herein consists the height of his glory.

The same author (p. 56) supposes that herein appears the excellent "character of a wise and good man, that though he can choose contrary to the fitness of things, yet he does not; but suffers himself to be directed by fitness;" and that, in this conduct, "he imitates the blessed God." And yet he supposes it is contrariwise with the blessed God; not that he suffers himself to be directed by fitness, when he can choose, contrary to the fitness of things, but that he cannot choose contrary to the fitness of things; as he says, (p. 42,) "that it is not possible for God to act otherwise than according to this fitness, where there is any fitness or goodness in things." Yea, he supposes, (p. 31,) that if a man "were perfectly wise and good, he could not do otherwise than be constantly and certainly determined by the fitness of things."

One thing more I would observe, before I conclude this section; and that is, that if it derogates nothing from the glory of God to be necessarily determined by superior fitness in some things, then neither does it to be thus determined in all things; from any thing in the nature of such necessity, as at all detracting from God's freedom, independence, absolute supremacy, or any dignity or glory of his nature, state, or manner of acting; or as implying any infirmity, restraint, or subjection. And if the thing be such as well consists with God's glory, and has nothing tending at all to detract from it; then we need not be afraid of ascribing it to God in too many things, lest thereby we should detract from God's glory too much.

The End

DEC 2 2 2000

DATE DUE

GAYLORD			PRINTED IN U.S.A.